VITAL RECORDS OF RYE NEW HAMPSHIRE

A TRANSCRIPT OF THE BIRTHS, BAPTISMS, MARRIAGES, AND DEATHS IN THIS TOWN TO THE YEAR 1890

BY

KATHLEEN E HOSIER

HERITAGE BOOKS INC.

Copyright 1992 By

Kathleen E. Hosier

Published 1992 By:

HERITAGE BOOKS INC.
1540E Pointer Ridge Place, Bowie, Maryland 20716
(301) 390-7709

ISBN 1-55613-621-8

A Complete Catalog Listing Hundreds of Titles on
History, Genealogy & Americana
Free on Request

DEDICATION

****

To the memory of Kenneth Long (1902-1974) whose ancestors were among the first to settle in Rye, NH.

****

PREFACE

Settlements in the territory now known as Rye, NH were made as early as 1635. Rye was originally part of Portsmouth, New Castle, and Hampton, NH and became separated by an act passed by the provincial legislature on 30 April 1726.

The vital records in this book have been extracted from three sources: microfilmed copies of the original town records; genealogical records of Thomas J. Parsons and his son Langdon B. Parsons, who both, at different periods, served as town clerks; and from the records of the Congregational church which was organized 20 July 1726.

Those entries which were difficult to read because of torn or faded pages have been omitted. All other entries have been indexed by surnames followed alphabetically by given names.

The last section of this book contains the families living in Rye at the time of the first census of the United States in 1790.

The first census act was passed by Congress on 1 March 1790 and signed by President Washington. By the terms of this law, nine months were allowed to complete the enumeration. The schedules were lists of names containing only the heads of families. The details of each family were given by the number of male and female persons living in the household. Using the vital records of Rye as well as other references, members of each household have been added.

TABLE OF CONTENTS

	Page
Births	1
Baptisms	34
Marriages	87
Deaths	172
1790 Census	233
References for Census	318
Index to Census	319

RYE BIRTHS

ALLEN (ALIN), Samuel, son of Elizabeth, b. 17 Oct 1796
BERRY, Abigail, dau of Ebenezer & Keziah, b. 21 Jun 1719
  Abigail, dau of Merifield & Huldey, b. 26 Dec 1769
  Abigail, dau of Samuel Brackett & Abigail, b. 18 Dec 1810
  Abigail M., child of Nathaniel & Esther, b. 18 Nov 1814
  Alfred, child of Jeremiah & Sally, b. 29 Oct 1808
  Betsey M., child of Nathaniel & Esther, b. 4 Oct 1809
  Brackett, son of Samuel Brackett & Abigail, b. 14 May 1798
  Brackett M., child of Jeremiah & Sally, b. 3 Sep 1816
  Charity, dau of Ebenezer & Keziah, b. 4 Apr 1726
  Charlotte, dau of Samuel Brackett & Abigail, b. 20 Jan 1806
  Clarissa L., child of Nathaniel & Esther, b. 14 Sep 1819
  Ebenezer, son of Merifield & Huldah, b. 15 Mar 1766
  Ebenezer, son of James & Hannah, b. 23 Jun 1781
  Eliner, dau of Ebenezer & Keziah, b. 9 Apr 1722
  Elizabeth, dau of William & Judith, b. 16 Mar 1680
  Elizabeth M., dau of Nathaniel & Betsey, b. 9 Jan 1800
  Elly, dau of William & Lovey, b. 25 Apr 1786
  Ephrem, son of Steven & Ann, b. 11 Oct 1727
  Gilman Chase, son of Samuel Brackett & Abigail, b. 26 Dec 1816
  Hannah, dau of Nehemiah & Sarah, b. 23 Sep 1740
  Hannah, dau of Jeremiah & Hannah, b. 27 Jun 1747
  Hannah, dau of Jeremiah & Elener, b. 21 Aug 1773
  Hannah, dau of William & Lovey, b. 25 Mar 1781
  Hannah Lock, dau of Levi & Sary, b. 19 Jun 1791
  Huldah, dau of Merifield & Huldah, b. 26 Oct 1760
  Huldah, dau of James & Hannah, b. 4 Feb 1785
  Ira, child of Jeremiah & Sally, b. 19 Jun 1810
  Isaac, son of Jacob & Rachel, b. 20 Apr 1767
  Jacob, son of Nehemiah & Sarah, b. 7 Jul 1738

RYE BIRTHS

BERRY, James, son of Steven & Ann, b. 25 Mar 1731
James, son of James & Hannah, b. 28 Feb 1779
James Towle, son of Merifield & Hulday, b. 15 Mar 1758
Jeremiah, son of Jeremiah & Hannah, b. 2 Apr 1755
Jeremiah, son of William & Love, b. 16 Dec 1783
John, son of Nathaniel & Ester, b. 22 Mar 1725
John, son of Nehemiah & Sarah, b. 10 Mar 1736
John Wilkes Parsons, child of Nathaniel & Esther, b. 22 Nov 1823
Joseph H., child of Nathaniel & Esther, b. 13 Apr 1811
Joseph Jenness, b. 17 May 1789
Jotham S., child of Nathaniel & Esther, b. 22 Dec 1821
Levi, son of Jeremiah & Hannah, b. 29 Feb 1760
Lovey, dau of William & Lovey, b. 17 May 1788
Lydia, dau of Jeremiah & Elener, b. 27 Nov 1776
Martha M., child of Nathaniel & Esther, b. 7 May 1816
Mary, dau of Jeremiah & Hannah, b. 24 Mar 1751
Mary Ann, dau of Samuel Brackett & Abigail, b. (no date)
Merifield, son of Ebenezer & Mary, b. 15 Aug 1733
Moley, dau of Levi & Sary, b. 17 Apr 1785
Molly, dau of Nathaniel & Betsey, b. 16 Feb 1798
Nathaniel, son of Nathaniel & Ester, b. 10 Jul 1727
Nathaniel, son of Samuel & Molly, b. 7 Aug 1775
Nathaniel F., child of Nathaniel & Esther, b. 8 Jun 1807
Oliver, son of Samuel Brackett & Abigail, b. 29 Oct 1813
Olle, dau of Merifield, b. 19 Sep 1763
Olley, dau of Levi & Sarah, b. 24 Jun 1793
Pashene, dau of Jeremiah & Hannah, b. 13 Feb 1762
Patey, dau of William & Love, b. 21 Jul 1792
Rachel, dau of Ebenezer & Keziah, b. 13 Nov 1721
Robinson F., child of Jeremiah & Sally, b. 5 Sep 1813
Ruth, dau of Ebenezer & Mary, b. 4 Jun 1727
Sally, b. 8 Feb 1787
Sally, dau of Nathaniel & Betsey, b. 30 Mar 1802
Samuel, child of Nathaniel & Esther, b. 10 Aug 1804

RYE BIRTHS

BERRY, Samuel Brackett, son of William & Lovey, b. 14 Apr 1777
  Samuel Chapman, son of Samuel Brackett & Abigail, b. 23 Feb 1807
  Samuel F., child of Nathaniel & Esther, b. 10 Mar 1806
  Sarah, dau of Jeremiah & Hannah, b. 6 Jul 1749
  Sarah Ann, child of Jeremiah & Sally, b. 30 Sep 1818
  Simon, son of Ebenezer & Mary, b. 4 Jun 1735
  Solomon, son of Jeremiah & Hannah, b. 11 Nov 1765
  Susanah, dau of Ebenezer & Mary, b. 13 Dec 1730
  Susanna, dau of Nehemiah & Sarah, b. 23 Aug 1725
  William, son of Jeremiah & Hannah, b. 1 Apr Old Stile or twelf New 1753
  William, son of William & Love, b. 10 Nov 1790
  William, son of Samuel Brackett & Abigail, b. 19 Aug 1803
BLAKE, Hannah, dau of Elisha & Mary, b. 3 Nov 1770 (probably an error in the year)
  Mary, dau of Elisha & Mary, b. 5 Aug 1770
BOND, Mary, dau of John & Easter, b. 26 Jul 1753
BRACKETT, Lovey, dau of Samuel & Elener, b. 9 Aug 1758
BROWN, Abigail, dau of Joseph & Abigail, b. 19 Apr 1752
  Abigail, dau of Jonathan & Mary, b. 29 Jul 1769
  Elizabeth, dau of Joseph & Abigail, b. May 1750
  Elizabeth, dau of Jonathan & Mary, b. 21 Jun 1755
  John, son of Jonathan & Mary, b. 13 Nov 1759
  John Sam Jenness, son of John & Comfort, b. 10 May 1798
  Jonathan, b. 22 Dec 1725
  Jonathan, son of Samuel & Susanna, b. 15 Sep 1747
  Jonathan, son of Jonathan & Mary, b. 13 Apr 1762
  Joseph, son of Joseph & Abigail, b. 5 Apr 1754
  Joseph, son of Jonathan & Mary, b. 27 Apr New Stiel 1757
  Mary (Mrs.), b. 27 Apr 1729
  Mary, dau of Samuel & Susanna, b. 21 Apr 1746
  Mary, dau of Jonathan & Mary, b. 24 Aug 1766
  Richard, son of Joseph & Abigail, b. 16 Apr 1748
CASWELL, Albert M., child of Michael & Dorcas, b. 25 Jan 1837
  Alfred S., son of Richard G. & Anna, b. 19 Apr 1833

RYE BIRTHS

CASWELL, Almira, child of Michael & Dorcas, b. 23 Dec 1827
  Asa, son of Michael & Dorcas, b. 21 Nov 1821
  Charles Green, son of Michael & Dorcas, b. 5 Oct 1819
  Charles R., son of Richard G. & Anna, b. 21 Feb 1831
  Elizabeth A., dau of Richard G. & Anna, b. 12 Nov 1835
  Elizabeth Jane, child of William & Polly, b. 21 Jul 1824
  Emily, child of Michael & Dorcas, b. 25 Jun 1825
  John, son of Samuel & Polly, b. 15 Jul 1811
  Joseph, son of Michael & Dorcas, b. 2 Mar 1817
  Maria Salter, child of William & Polly, b. 9 Aug 1835
  Mary, dau of William & Polly, b. 5 Feb 1822
  Mary E., dau of Samuel & Polly, b. 3 Dec 1813
  Mary H., dau of Richard G. & Anna, b. 20 Dec 1828
  Richard, son of Samuel & Polly, b. 5 Dec 1808
  Sally Ann, child of William & Polly, b. 12 Nov 1828
  Samuel, son of Samuel & Polly, b. 4 Jan 1815
  Sarah Angelette, dau of Richard G. & Anna, b. 9 Oct 1838
  Warren, child of William & Polly, b. 10 May 1832
  William, son of William & Polly, b. 14 Nov 1819
  William, son of Michael & Dorcas, b. 16 Dec 1833
CHAMBERLAIN, John, son of Wm & Mary, b. 14 Jul 1749
  Lydia, dau of William & Mary, b. 3 Apr 1737
  Mary, dau of Wm & Mary, b. 20 Jul 1746
  Samuel, son of Wm & Mary, b. 18 Aug 1740
  William, son of Wm & Mary, b. 17 May 1743
CLIFFORD (CLEFFORD), Peter, son of Peter & Hannah, b. 12 Sep 1753
CONNER, Samuel, son of Joseph & Mary, b. 8 Sep 1739
  Sarah, dau of Joseph & Mary, b. 28 Apr 1744
DOLBEE (DOLBER, DOLBEER), Abigail, dau of Jonathan & Hannah, b. 5 Jan 1751
  Abigail, dau of Jonathan & Hannah, b. 24 Dec 1756
  Daniel, son of Nickles & Sarah, b. 17 Mar 1724
  Hannah, dau of Isral & Sarah, b. 12 Mar 1741/2
  Hannah, dau of Jonathan & Hannah, b. 22 Jul 1761
  Isral, son of Isral & Sarah, b. 6 Jan 1737/8

RYE BIRTHS

DOLBEE, Jonathan, son of Nickols & Sarah, b. 17 Apr 1725
  Jonathan, son of Jonathan & Hannah, b. 7 Aug 1750
  Mary, dau of Nickles & Sarah, b. 18 Apr 1726
  Nicholas, son of Jonathan & Hannah, b. 8 May 1748
  Ruth, dau of Jonathan & Hannah, b. 2 Dec 1745
  Stephen, son of Jonathan & Hannah, b. 12 Jul 1753
DOW (DOWE), Hannah, dau of Henry & Marthey, b. 15 Oct 1752
  Isaac, son of Henry & Marthey, b. 13 Dec 1754
  James, son of Henry & Marthey, b. 18 Jan 1765
  Marthey, dau of Henry & Marthey, b. 6 Oct 1758
  Mary, dau of Henry & Marthey, b. 23 Dec 1761
  Moley, dau of John & Susanah, b. 27 Nov 1756
DOWNS, Anna Thomas, dau of Samuel & Betsy, b. 25 Jun 1822
  Betsy, dau of Samuel & Betsy, b. 13 Oct 1818
  Samuel Washington, son of Samuel & Betsy, b. 30 Nov 1823
DOWRST (DOUST), Abial, dau of Solomon & Elizabeth, b. 24 Sep 1728
  Abial, dau of Ozem & Elizabeth, b. 12 Dec 1739
  Comfort, dau of Ozem & Elizabeth, b. 21 Aug 1731
  Elizabeth, dau of Solomon & Elizabeth, b. 11 Jan 1732
  John, son of Ozem & Elizabeth, b. 22 Feb 1762
  Jonathan, son of Ozem & Elizabeth, b. 5 Dec 1764
  Mary, dau of Samuel & Rachel, b. 8 May 1723
  Mary, dau of Ozem & Elizabeth, b. 20 Oct 1734
  Ozem, son of Ozem & Elizabeth, b. 3 Mar 1737
  Rachel, dau of Solomon & Elizabeth, b. 1 Aug 1735
  Samuel, son of Solomon & Elizabeth, b. 26 Mar 1726
  Sarah, dau of Solomon & Elizabeth, b. 19 Jan 1729
  Sary, dau of Ozem & Elizabeth, b. 23 Sep 1725
  Simeon, son of Samuel & Rachel, b. 27 Sep 1730
  Solomon, son of Solomon & Elizabeth, b. 23 May 1728
  Thomas, son of Solomon & Elizabeth, b. 28 Aug 1724
DRAKE, Abraham, b. Mar 1786
  Abraham, child of Abraham & Mary, b. 23 Feb 1821
  Abram Joseph, child of Joseph J. & Clarissa, b.

RYE BIRTHS

DRAKE, Adams Elisha, child of Joseph J. & Clarissa, b. 4 Nov 1849
Anna, child of Abraham & Mary, b. 28 Feb 1812
Anna Dwight, child of Joseph J. & Clarissa, b. 26 Sep 1840
Clara Josephine, child of Joseph J. & Clarissa, b. 3 Jan 1854
James Buchanan, child of Joseph J. & Clarissa, b. 16 May 1856
John Haven, child of Joseph J. & Clarissa, b. 18 Jul 1847
John Orin, child of Joseph J. & Clarissa, b. 14 Nov 1851
Joseph J., child of Abraham & Mary, b. 22 Dec 1816
Leonie Sarah, child of Joseph J. & Clarissa, b. 3 Nov 1862
Mary Jenness, child of Joseph J. & Clarissa, b. 2 May 1843
Nathan Dwight, child of Joseph J. & Clarissa, b. 16 Feb 1839
Orin, child of Abraham & Mary, b. 30 Jan 1830
Sarah W., child of Abraham & Mary, b. Feb 1819
_____, son of Abraham & Mary, b. 13 Jan 1816
ELKINS, Abigail, dau of Samuel & Olive, b. 18 Apr 1786
Catherine, dau of Henry & Catherine, b. 20 Jun 1741
Elizebeth, dau of Henry & Catherine, b. 11 Mar 1733
Hannah, dau of Henry & Catherine, b. Jun 1734 ?
Henry, son of Henry & Catherine, b. 21 Sep 1739
Henry, son of Samuel & Olive, b. 23 Apr 1775
James, son of Samuel & Olive, b. 3 May 1777
Joanna, dau of Henry & Catherine, b. 14 May 1743
Mary, dau of Henry & Catherine, b. 16 Feb 1731
Mary, dau of Henry & Catherine, b. 12 Nov 1734
Mary, dau of Samuel & Olive, b. 25 Jun 1781
Olive, dau of Samuel & Olive, b. 3 Oct 1783
Samuel, son of Henry & Catherine, b. 30 Jan 1744
Samuel, son of Samuel & Olive, b. 14 May 1779
William, son of Samuel & Olive, b. 21 Dec 1788
FOSS, Benjamin, child of William & Abaiel, b. 28 Apr 1794
Chalcedony, child of Richard & Eliza, b. (no date)
Charlotte D., dau of Robinson & Charlotte, b. 22 Oct 1835

14 Sep 1845

RYE BIRTHS

FOSS, Daniel M., son of Robinson & Charlotte, b. 10 Mar 1834
Dorothy, dau of Job & Sarah, b. 14 Aug 1758
Eliza E., dau of Richard & Eliza, b. 7 Jul 1832
Elizabeth, dau of Elizabeth, b. 6 Jun 1784
Harderson, son of Robinson & Patty, b. 23 Jan 1821
Henry D., son of Robinson & Charlotte, b. 18 Sep 1832
Joel, child of Benjamin & Dorcas, b. 7 Dec 1821
John, son of Willes & Mary, b. 7 Jul 1746
John H., son of Robinson & Charlotte, b. 9 Dec 1831
John Henry, son of Richard & Eliza, b. 27 Mar 1820
John O., son of Richard & Eliza, b. 17 Aug 1830
Joshua, child of William & Abaiel, b. 21 Jun 1790
Joshua, child of Benjamin & Dorcas, b. 7 Sep 1816
Mary, child of Benjamin & Dorcas, b. 5 Dec 1819
Mehitable J., dau of Robinson & Patty, b. 5 Feb 1819
Orin, son of Richard & Eliza, b. 4 Dec 1822
Rachel, child of William & Abaiel, b. 3 Aug 1795
Robert S., son of Richard & Eliza, b. 7 Apr 1827
Robinson T., son of Robinson & Charlotte, b. 22 Sep 1837
Sally, child of William & Abaiel, b. 3 Dec 1791
Sally, child of Benjamin & Dorcas, b. 13 May 1818
Samuel, son of Wallis & Mary, b. 25 Oct 1739
Sarah, dau of John & Abigail, b. 18 Sep 1731
Sarah, dau of Job & Sarah, b. 1 Aug 1754
William, child of Joshua & Rachel, b. 12 Jul 1769
William, child of Benjamin & Dorcas, b. 20 Jul 1814
FULLER (FULER), Elizabeth, dau of James & Mary, b. 28 Jun 1715
Elizabeth, dau of Joseph & Joanna, b. 14 Sep 1733
Elizabeth, dau of Joseph & Joanna, b. 25 Sep 1740
George, son of Jermi & Mary, b. 16 May 1746
Jeremiah, son of James & Mary, b. 25 Sep 1717
Joanna, dau of Joseph & Joanna, b. 6 Dec 1734
Joseph, son of Joseph & Joanah, b. 4 Nov 1735
Love, dau of James & Mary, b. 14 May 1721

RYE BIRTHS

FULLER, Mary, dau of Joseph & Joanna, b. 5 Aug 1736
  Richard, son of Jeremiah & Mary, b. 21 Jul 1747
GARLAND, Abigail, child of John & Abigail, b. 14 Aug 1782
  Abigail P., dau of Reuel L. & Patty, b. 12 Feb 1833
  Benjamin, child of John & Abigail, b. 30 Jul 1791
  Charles, son of Moses L. & Lucretia, b. 11 Sep 1822
  Elvira L., dau of Reuel L. & Patty, b. 23 Oct 1827
  Gilman, son of Moses L. & Lucretia, b. 27 Nov 1825
  James, child of John & Abigail, b. 15 Nov 1784
  John, son of Abigail, b. 23 Nov 1776 (according to statement made by Abigail Garland 12 Apr 1831 she was not married until nearly two years after his birth, in 1778)
  Joseph William, son of Reuel L. & Patty, b. 4 Sep 1836
  Malvina G., dau of Moses L. & Lucretia, b. 1 Dec 1844
  Mary Abba, dau of Moses L. & Lucretia, b. 3 Jun 1841
  Mary Leavitt, dau of Peter & Mehitable, b. 12 Dec 1799
  Moses Leavitt, son of Peter & Mehitable, b. 21 Mar 1801
  Reuel, child of John & Abigail, b. 31 Dec 1798
  Sally, dau of Peter & Mehitable, b. 24 Mar 1798
  Thomas, child of John & Abigail, b. 3 Mar 1779
  Thomas R., son of Reuel L. & Patty, b. 7 Feb 1839
  William, son of Peter & Mehitable, b. 9 Sep 1795
GOSS, Abby Francett, child of James M. & Lucinda, b. 10 Jan 1842
  Abigail, dau of Richard & Rachel, b. 2 Oct 1724
  Betsy, dau of Elizabeth, b. 7 Apr 1794
  Esther, dau of Jethro & Esther, b. 5 Feb 1734
  James, b. 28 Mar 1805
  James Granvill, child of James M. & Lucinda, b. 28 Dec 1836
  James M., b. 5 Sep 1809
  John Sheridan, son of Thomas & Abigail, b. 26 Oct 1817
  Jose, son of Jose & Hannah Berry, b. 24 Jun 1795
  Josiah Snow, child of James M. & Lucinda, b. 14

RYE BIRTHS

Mar 1846
GOSS, Levi, son of Jethro & Esther, b. 3 Feb 1735
  Margret, dau of Richard & Rachel, b. 18 Feb 1731
  Mary, dau of Jethro & Ester, b. 16 Aug 1738
  Mary Ann, dau of Daniel & Hannah, b. 24 Jan 1823
  Michael D., son of Betsy, b. 20 Mar 1777
  Richard, son of Jonathan & Salome, b. 3 Nov 1738
  Salome, dau of Jonathan & Salome, b. 22 Feb 1741
  Samuel, son of Jethro & Esther, b. 21 Aug 1728
  Sarah, dau of Jethro & Esther, b. 12 Jun 1736
  Sarah Ann, dau of Thomas & Sarah, b. 10 Apr 1815
  Sarah Jane, dau of Daniel & Hannah, b. 15 Mar 1821
  Sheridan, son of Thomas & Sarah, b. 11 May 1809
  Tobias T., son of M. D. & Sally, b. 26 Feb 1801
  William, son of Thomas & Sarah, b. 21 Jan 1803
GREEN (GREENE), Charles, child of Richard & Mary, b. 3 Mar 1795
  Charles A., son of Charles & Mary, b. 15 Nov 1829
  Cyrus Fayette, son of Charles & Mary, b. 23 Jun 1834
  Cyrus W., son of Charles & Mary, b. 9 Oct 1836
  Dolly, child of Richard & Mary, b. 5 Aug 1791
  Dorcas M., child of Richard & Mary, b. 19 Nov 1793
  Ephraim, child of Richard & Mary, b. 2 Jun 1786
  John, child of Richard & Mary, b. 2 Apr 1784
  Joseph, child of Richard & Mary, b. 5 Aug 1798
  Maria Elizabeth, child of Thomas & Elizabeth, b. 9 Dec 1835
  Martha O., dau of Charles & Mary, b. 4 Oct 1839
  Mary Jane, dau of Charles & Mary, b. 20 Feb 1832
  Orin Smith, son of Charles & Mary, b. 23 Oct 1845
  Richard, child of Richard & Mary, b. 13 Mar 1779
  Rosillah, child of Thomas & Elizabeth, b. 23 Nov 1837
  Samuel Marden, child of Richard & Mary, b. 31 May 1799
  Thomas, child of Richard & Mary, b. 15 May 1788
  Thomas L., son of Dorcas, b. 9 Apr 1811
  Thomas Otis, child of Thomas & Elizabeth, b. 23 Feb 1834
  Vercilda M., dau of Charles & Mary, b. 9 Mar 1827
HALL, Esther, dau of Joseph & Mary, b. 18 Sep 1781
HOBBS, Betsy Jenness, b. 4 Sep 1780
  Jonathan, b. 8 Nov 1778

RYE BIRTHS

HOBBS, Lucy, dau of James & Mary, b. 8 Nov 1774
  Lucy, b. 2 Sep 1782
  Nathaniel, b. 12 Jun 1786
  Poley, b. 4 Sep 1776
HOLMES (HOLMS), Anna, dau of Eperham & Bety, b. 31 Jul 1746
  Deborah, dau of Eperham & Bety, b. 2 Jun 1735
  Elizabeth, dau of Eperham & Bety, b. 1 Oct 1744
  Eperham, son of Eperham & Bety, b. 22 Dec 1739
  Samuel, son of Eperham & Bety, b. 1 Sep 1748
JENNESS (JANNES, JENNES), Abraham, child of David & Mary, b. 1828
  Adaline S., dau of Simon Jr. & Nancy, b. 27 Oct 1820
  Albert Jewell, child of Lowell & Ann, b. Nov 1846
  Albion Jewell, child of Lowell & Ann, b. Nov 1846
  Anna, dau of Joshua & Hannah, b. 8 Aug 1733
  Anna Y., dau of Joseph, b. 14 Jul 1813
  Benjamin, son of Joseph, b. 19 Jun 1791
  Betsy, child of Noah & Elizabeth, b. 24 Jun 1794
  David, child of David & Mary, b. 1833
  David A., son of Simon Jr. & Nancy, b. 26 Aug 1814
  Deliverance, dau of Joshua & Hannah, b. 14 Jan 1741
  Elizabeth, dau of John & Elizabeth, b. 4 Apr 1734
  Elizabeth, dau of Frances & Sarah, b. 9 Sep 1741
  Elizabeth, wife of Noah, b. 27 Feb 1755
  Elizabeth, dau of Joseph, b. 7 Sep 1820
  Elizabeth H., child of Richard Jr. & Betsey, b. 6 Jul 1820
  Frances, son of John & Mary, b. 7 Jun 1721
  Hannah, dau of John & Hannah, b. 1 Nov 1712
  Hannah, dau of Jobe & Mary, b. 10 Oct 1738
  Hannah, dau of Joshua & Hannah, b. 30 Jan 1736
  Hannah, dau of John & Elizabeth, b. 29 Mar 1741
  Hezekiah, son of Jobe & Mary, b. 26 Aug 1736
  Isaac, son of Francis & Sarah, b. 30 Dec 1744
  Isaac, son of Joseph & Mary, b. 9 Oct 1755
  Job, son of Benjamin & Hannah, b. 17 Mar 1757
  Job, son of John & Hannah, b. 15 Oct 1708
  Jonathan, son of Frances & Sarah, b. 25 Jan 1743
  Jonathan, son of Joseph & Mary, b. 25 Jul 1760
  Joseph, son of Richard & Mary, b. 28 Feb 1727
  Joseph, son of Joseph & Mary, b. 12 Feb 1771
  Joseph, son of Richard & Mary, b. 18 Jun 1786

RYE BIRTHS

JENNESS, Joseph D., son of Joseph, b. 30 Sep 1818
Joses, child of Noah & Elizabeth, b. 10 Jan 1787
Joshua, son of Joshua & Hannah, b. 7 Apr 1739
Langdon S., child of Richard Jr. & Betsey, b. 24 Nov 1815
Levi W., son of Simon Jr. & Nancy, b. 24 Apr 1824
Lowell, child of Richard Jr. & Betsey, b. 11 Mar 1813
Luce, dau of John & Luce, b. 28 Feb 1728
Mark, son of John & Hannah, b. 12 Oct 1710
Mary, dau of Hezekiah & Ann, b. 25 Jan 1718
Mary, dau of John & Elizabeth, b. 5 Aug 1738
Mary, dau of Frances & Sarah, b. 22 Feb 1746/7
Mary, dau of Joseph, b. 19 Jun 1793
Minerva S., dau of Oliver & Sidney L. Seavey, b. 9 May 1844
Nathaniel, son of John & Mary, b. 22 Aug 1725
Noah, son of Nathaniel & Hannah, b. 2 Mar 1762
Oliver, child of Richard Jr. & Betsey, b. 30 Mar 1818
Polly, child of Noah & Elizabeth, b. 27 Mar 1797
Reuben P., son of Joseph, b. 2 Dec 1807
Richard, son of John & Hannah, b. 25 Sep 1719
Richard, son of Job & Mary, b. 8 Dec 1751
Richard, son of Joseph & Mary, b. 24 Dec 1757
Richard, child of Richard Jr. & Betsey, b. 13 Jul 1825
Rufus K., child of Richard Jr. & Betsey, b. 27 Oct 1822
Samuel, son of Richard & Mary, b. 19 May 1724
Sarah, dau of John & Elizabeth, b. 28 Apr 1736
Sarah, dau of Frances & Sarah, b. 7 Apr 1749
Sarah, dau of Benjamin & Hannah, b. 1 Jan 1755
Sarah, dau of Joseph & Mary, b. 11 May 1764
Sarah, dau of Richard Jr. & Mary, b. 24 Aug 1782
Semira P., dau of Simon Jr. & Nancy, b. 6 Aug 1826
Sheridan, son of Joseph, b. 12 May 1824
Simon, child of Noah & Elizabeth, b. 19 May 1785
Sophia P., dau of Simon Jr. & Nancy, b. 6 Aug 1826
Thomas, son of John & Mary, b. 16 Dec 1722
William, son of John & Hanah, b. 28 Mar 1706
JOHNSON, Peter, son of Peter & Mary, b. 6 Aug 1778
JONES, Abiah, dau of John & Anne, b. 5 May 1758
Anne, dau of John & Anne, b. 9 Nov 1741
Catherine, dau of John & Anne, b. 15 Apr 1740
John, son of John & Anne, b. 17 Mar 1748

RYE BIRTHS

JONES, Mary, dau of John & Ann, b. Nov 1740
  Sarah, dau of John & Ann, b. 23 Apr 1737
  Susannah, dau of John & Anne, b. 17 Oct 1745
  William, son of John & Ann, b. Jun 1735
KINGMAN (KINGMEN), Elijah, son of William & Mary, b. 5 Aug 1743
  Ruth, dau of William & Mary, b. 11 Oct 1745
KNOWLES (KNOWLS), Amos, son of Ezekiel & Mary, b. 4 Nov 1722
  David, son of Ezekiel & Mary, b. 1 Sep 1725
  Deliverance, dau of Joseph & Love, b. 26 Oct 1751
  Hannah, dau of Ezekiel & Mary, b. 1 Mar 1713
  John, son of Joseph & Sarah, b. 8 Apr 1760
  Joseph, son of Simon & Deliverance, b. 13 Dec 1727
  Joseph, son of Joseph & Sarah, b. 15 Jun 1758
  Love, dau of Joseph & Sarah, b. 26 Aug 1754
  Mary, dau of Ezekiel & Mary, b. 2 Nov 1718
  Rachel, dau of Joseph & Sarah, b. 8 Jan 1756
  Samuel, son of Joseph & Love, b. 27 Oct 1749
  Simon, son of Joseph & Love, b. 16 May 1748
LAMPREY (LAMPERIL), Deborah, dau of Benjamin & Sarah, b. 19 Nov 1727
LANE, Daniel, son of John & Hannah, b. 8 Jul 1735
  David, son of John & Mary, b. 21 Feb 1740/1
  Ezekiel, son of John & Mary, b. 4 Jul 1739
  Hannah, dau of John & Mary, b. 25 Dec 1744
  John, son of John & Hannah, b. 11 Oct 1733
  Mary, dau of John & Mary, b. 24 Feb 1742/3
  Nathan, son of John & Mary, b. 12 Jun 1747
  Olive, dau of Nathaniel & Abial, b. 9 Jul 1739
LANG, Benjamin, son of Benjamin & Eleanor, b. 28 Jul 1765
  Betey, dau of Benjamin & Eleanor, b. 25 Aug 1771
  Eleanor, dau of Benjamin & Eleanor, b. 11 Apr 1759
  Elizabeth Ann, dau of Leonard & Data, b. 9 Feb 1832
  Emeline E., dau of Leonard & Data, b. 28 Sep 1829
  Hannah, dau of Benjamin & Eleanor, b. 5 Jan 1761
  William B., son of Leonard & Data, b. 18 Feb 1835
LANGMAID (LANGMADE), John, son of William & Deborah, b. 23 Apr 1745
LEAR, Elizabeth, dau of Alexander & Sarah, b. 18 Jul 1771
LEAVITT, Eben True, son of Carr & Eliza Jane

RYE BIRTHS

Foster, b. 15 Aug 1839
LIBBY (LEBBE, LEEBE, LIBEY), Aaron Seavey, child of Samuel & Mehitable, b. 10 Aug 1781
Abigail, dau of Abraham, b. 13 Nov 1763
Abraham, son of Jacob & Sarah, b. 29 Dec 1739
Abraham, son of Abraham & Mary, b. 10 Feb 1777
Arter, son of Isaac & Mary, b. 5 Apr 1728
Benjamin, son of Jacob & Sarah, b. 25 Feb 1737
Benjamin, son of Abraham & Mary, b. 20 Jun 1782
Daniel Rand, child of Samuel & Mehitable, b. 28 Feb 1800
Elizabeth, dau of Isaac & Mary, b. 31 Feb 1725 (perhaps intended for 13 Feb 1725)
Hannah, dau of Jacob & Sarah, b. 18 Jun 1731
Isaac, son of Isaac & Mary, b. 31 Feb 1725 (see note on Elizabeth)
Jacob, son of Jacob & Sarah, b. 25 Jul 1729
Jacob, son of Abraham & Mary, b. 19 Dec 1770
Jane, dau of Isaac & Mary, b. 11 Sep 1733
Job, son of Jacob & Sarah, b. 15 Feb 1734
Job, son of Abraham, b. 18 Jun 1767
Johammah, dau of Isaac & Mary, b. 16 Oct 1737
John, son of Isaac & Mary, b. 1 Aug 1720
Joseph, son of Jacob & Sarah, b. 25 Feb 1737
Joseph, son of Abraham & Mary, b. 10 Nov 1765
Mary, dau of Isaac & Mary, b. 4 Mar 1722
Mary, dau of Abraham & Mary, b. 28 Aug 1768
Mehitable, child of Samuel & Mehitable, b. 1 Feb 1795
Nancy Griffith, child of Samuel & Mehitable, b. 13 Jul 1789
Ruben, son of Isaac & Mary, b. 11 Aug 1734
Ruth, dau of Jacob & Sarah, b. 21 Jan 1727
Ruth, dau of Isaac & Mary, b. 5 Sep 1730
Samuel, child of Samuel & Mehitable, b. 14 Mar 1783
Samuel, son of Jacob & Sarah, b. 9 Feb 1720
Sarah, dau of Jacob & Sarah, b. 2 Feb 1724
Sarah, b. 20 Jun 1779
Sarah, child of Samuel & Mehitable, b. 15 May 1785
William, child of Samuel & Mehitable, b. 26 Feb 1787
LOCKE (LOCK), Aba M., dau of Richard R. & Sarah A. Leavitt, b. 18 Jun 1829
Abigail, dau of Jonathan & Sarah, b. 5 Sep 1736
Abigail, dau of James & Sarah, b. 25 Mar 1742
Abigail, dau of William & Elizabeth, b. 4 Mar 1743

RYE BIRTHS

LOCKE, Abigail, dau of Jonathan, b. 21 Jul 1764
  Abigail, dau of David & Annah, b. 20 Nov 1778
  Abigail, child of John & Abigail, b. 21 Nov 1792
  Abigail T., child of Joseph Jr. & Abigail, b. 8 Feb 1797
  Abner, son of Jonathan & Sarah, b. 31 Jul 1742
  Abner, son of Jonathan & Abigail, b. 30 Oct 1760
  Albert C., son of Richard R. & Sarah A. Leavitt, b. 22 Jan 1837
  Anna, dau of James & Sarah, b. 10 Oct 1726
  Anna, dau of David & Annah, b. 27 Mar 1774
  Asa, b. 14 Aug 1775
  Asa Jr., son of Asa & Betsey, b. 18 Oct 1801
  Asa D., son of Lemuel & Esther Y., b. 18 Jun 1834
  Benjamin, son of David & Hannah, b. 28 Dec 1780
  Betsey J., wife of Asa, b. 4 Sep 1780
  Daniel, son of Jonathan & Abigail, b. 26 Oct 1772
  David, son of Jonathan & Sarah, b. 24 Aug 1735
  David, son of David & Annah, b. 24 Nov 1765
  Deliverence, dau of Frances & Deliverance, b. 16 Aug 1726
  Elizabeth, dau of James & Sarah, b. 12 Oct 1730
  Elizabeth, dau of William & Elizabeth, b. 3 Mar 1739/40
  Elizabeth, dau of Francis & Sarah, b. 2 May 1755
  Elizabeth, child of John & Abigail, b. 21 Jan 1788
  Elizabeth G., dau of Lemuel & Esther Y., b. 14 Sep 1832
  Elizabeth M., dau of Joseph & Hannah Knowles, b. 18 Mar 1844
  Ellener, dau of Frances & Deliverance, b. 16 Mar 1728
  Elvin, child of John & Abigail, b. 3_ Mar 1809
  Epheram, son of Frances & Deliverance, b. 4 Feb 1730
  Frances, son of Frances & Deliverance, b. 27 Jun 1724
  Frances, son of Frances & Sarah, b. 12 Oct 1757
  Gardner T., son of Asa & Betsey, b. 8 Feb 1816
  Hannah, dau of Frances & Deliverance, b. 8 Jan 1719
  Hannah, dau of William & Elizabeth, b. 18 Feb 1737/8
  Hannah, dau of Joseph & Hannah, b. 3 Jun 1740
  Hannah, dau of Jonath & Sarah, b. 14 Dec 1746
  Hannah W., child of Joseph Jr. & Abigail, b. 7

RYE BIRTHS

LOCKE, Harriet J., dau of Richard R. & Sarah A. Leavitt, b. 15 Jan 1835
Feb 1795
Horace W., son of Joseph & Hannah Knowles, b. 2 Jun 1837
Hulde, dau of Elijah & Hulde, b. 2 Oct 1739
Isaac M., son of Lemuel & Esther Y., b. 18 Jun 1834
Jacob, son of John & Sarah, b. 12 Nov 1727
James, son of James & Sarah, b. 30 Jun 1729
James H., son of Asa & Betsey, b. 27 Nov 1804
James W., child of Joseph Jr. & Abigail, b. Oct 1818
Jemima, dau of William & Hannah, b. 20 Jan 1720
Jethro, son of Jonathan & Abigail, b. 29 Jun 1775
Jethro, child of John & Abigail, b. 19 Nov 1797
John, son of James & Sarah, b. 3 Oct 1737
John, son of Jonathan & Sarah, b. 9 Dec 1748
John, son of Jonathan & Abigail, b. 15 Jul 1767
John, son of David & Annah, b. 22 May 1772
John O., son of Asa & Betsey, b. 3 Dec 1821
Jonathan, son of Jonathan & Sarah, b. 29 Jan 1732
Jonathan, son of Jonathan Jr. & Abigail, b. 1 Jan 1759
Jonathan, son of David & Annah, b. 19 Feb 1768
Jonathan, child of John & Abigail, b. 9 Apr 1800
Jonathan, child of Joseph Jr. & Abigail, b. 17 Aug 1813
Jonathan D., son of Asa & Betsey, b. 1 Apr 1811
Joseph, son of Jonathan & Abigail, b. 21 Mar 1770
Joseph, child of Joseph Jr. & Abigail, b. 30 Nov 1806
Judith, dau of Nathaniel & Judith, b. 16 May 1656
Ledy, dau of James & Sarah, b. 3 Jun 1735
Lemuel, son of Asa & Betsey, b. 19 Nov 1806
Levi, son of David & Annah, b. 7 Feb 1770
Lucretia, child of Joseph Jr. & Abigail, b. 8 Jun 1803
Margeret, dau of Jonathan & Sarah, b. 20 Jul 1740
Mary, dau of John & Sarah, b. 13 Nov 1722
Mary, dau of James & Sarah, b. 21 Jan 1732
Mary, dau of Jonathan & Sarah, b. 20 Sep 1733
Mary, dau of William & Elizabeth, b. 6 Apr 1751
Mary, dau of David & Annah, b. 7 May 1764

RYE BIRTHS

LOCKE, Mary, child of John & Abigail, b. 11 Feb 1803
Mary, child of Joseph Jr. & Abigail, b. 25 Sep 1809
Mary E., dau of Asa & Betsey, b. 2 Mar 1824
Merebeth, dau of James & Sarah, b. 13 Oct 1733
Merebeth, dau of William & Elizabeth, b. 5 Aug 1735
Nancy, dau of David & Annah, b. 9 Mar 1785
Olive Shapley, child of John & Abigail, b. 11 May 1795
Pamela Ann, child of William & Elizabeth, b. 14 Oct 1827
Pashence, dau of Jonathan & Sarah, b. 10 Feb 1730
Patty, child of Joseph Jr. & Abigail, b. 14 May 1801
Perna T., dau of Asa & Betsey, b. 27 Dec 1808
Perna T., dau of Asa & Betsey, b. 16 Jun 1813
Prudence, dau of Frances & Deliverance, b. 20 Mar 1732
Richard, son of John & Sarah, b. 28 Jul 1720
Richard, son of Joseph & Hannah, b. 4 Sep 1744
Richard L., son of Richard R. & Sarah A. Leavitt, b. 26 Oct 1831
Richard R., b. 16 Jul 1794
Ruben, son of David & Annah, b. 26 Apr 1758
Salley H., dau of Asa & Betsey, b. 15 Feb 1800
Salley H., dau of Asa & Betsey, b. 11 Aug 1825
Samuel Jenness, child of John & Abigail, b. 1 Mar 1790
Sarah, dau of Frances & Deliverance, b. 17 Feb 1722
Sarah, dau of James & Sarah, b. 27 Jul 1725
Sarah, dau of Jonathan & Sarah, b. 3 Jan 1728
Sarah, dau of Jonathan & Sarah, b. 28 Aug 1744
Sarah, dau of Frances & Sarah, b. 13 Oct 1751
Sarah, dau of David & Annah, b. 21 Nov 1761
Sarah A., dau of Joseph & Hannah Knowles, b. 2 Mar 1840
Sarah A. Leavitt, wife of Richard R., b. at No. Hampton, 20 Jan 1800
Sarah Ann, child of Joseph Jr. & Abigail, b. 1 Apr 1799
Sarah E., dau of Richard R. & Sarah A. Leavitt, b. 16 Oct 1826
Simon, son of David & Annah, b. 31 Mar 1760
Sula A., dau of Richard R. & Sarah A. Leavitt, b. 11 Oct 1824

RYE BIRTHS

LOCKE, William, son of Jonathan & Sarah, b. 26 Jul 1738
  William, son of William & Elizabeth, b. 9 Sep 1745
  William, son of David & Hannah, b. 9 Apr 1776
  William, child of Joseph Jr. & Abigail, b. 17 Aug 1812
  William Harvey, son of William & Elizabeth, b. 9 Aug 1830
MACE, Ithamer, son of John & Rachel, b. 30 May 1795
  John, son of John & Rachel, b. 12 Jan 1798
MARDEN, Abbie A., dau of Nathaniel & Elizabeth, b. 10 Jun 1866
  Abial, dau of Benjamin & Rachel, b. 27 Feb 1767
  Abial, dau of Benjamin & Rachel, b. 27 Feb 1768
  Abigail, dau of James & Judah, b. 21 Mar 1731
  Abigail, dau of James & Judeth, b. 11 Sep 1738
  Abigail, dau of Stephen & Charity, b. 22 Jul 1739
  Abigail, dau of Eben & Ester, b. 12 Aug 1740 (note in original record: "this birth is a mistake")
  Abigail, child of William & Hannah, b. 31 Mar 1776
  Ahipzabah, dau of Samuel & Margaret, b. 7 Jun 1774
  Anna Brown, dau of Reuben & Hannah, b. 25 Jun 1810
  Benjamin, son of William & Dorcis, b. 22 Jun 1727
  Benjamin, son of Stephen & Charity, b. 9 Aug 1729
  Benjamin, son of Benjamin & Rebecer, b. 4 Feb 1751
  Benjamin, son of Benjamin & Rachel, b. 14 Jun 1769
  Benjamin W., son of Samuel & Nancy, b. 27 Jul 1800
  Betey, dau of Nathanel & Anna, b. 6 Jan 1777
  Charity, dau of Benjamin & Rachel, b. 9 Mar 1760
  Charles H., son of Reuben & Charlotte, b. 3 May 1842
  Clara, dau of Nathaniel & Elizabeth, b. 27 Jan 1850
  Daniel, son of Joseph & Mary, b. 14 Aug 1782
  Daniel, son of Samuel & Sally, b. 14 Jun 1812
  Darkes, dau of Samuel & Sarah, b. 14 Apr 1735
  David Ward, son of Reuben & Charlotte, b. 23 Dec

RYE BIRTHS

1837
MARDEN, Eben W., son of Ebenezer & Lovey, b. 22 Jun 1818
Ebenezer, b. 22 Jan 1779
Eliza A., dau of Reuben & Charlotte, b. 3 May 1842
Elizabeth, dau of Stephen & Charity, b. 12 Apr 1734
Elizabeth, dau of Ebenr & Ester, b. 18 Dec 1743
Elizabeth, dau of William & Rachel, b. 6 Jan 1746
Elizabeth, dau of Benjamin & Rebecer, b. 30 Jun 1754
Elizabeth, dau of Benjamin & Rachel, b. 9 Feb 1762
Elizabeth, b. 17 Dec 1787
Elizabeth M., dau of Ebenezer & Lovey, b. 26 Apr 1810
Elizabeth Moulton, dau of Nathaniel & Elizabeth, b. 6 Nov 1793
Elvira G., dau of Nathaniel & Elizabeth, b. 8 Nov 1857
Emeritt E., dau of Nathaniel & Elizabeth, b. 6 Oct 1863
Emery Boardman, son of William & Lucy Ann, b. 4 Oct 184_
Ervin W., son of Nathaniel & Elizabeth, b. 21 Nov 1851
Esther, b. 20 Jul 1785
Esther R., dau of Ebenezer & Lovey, b. 3 Mar 1816
Francis I., son of Ebenezer & Lovey, b. 22 Mar 1824
Fred H., son of Nathaniel & Elizabeth, b. 20 Dec 1859
George, son of Ebenr & Ester, b. 29 Jun 1741
Hannah, dau of Stephen & Charity, b. 13 Mar 1723
Hannah, dau of James & Judah, b. 14 May 1736
Hannah, b. 5 Jan 1772
Hannah, dau of Nathaniel & Anna, b. 12 Jul 1780
Hannah, child of William & Hannah, b. 4 Apr 1781
Hannah, dau of Samuel & Sally, b. 27 Jul 1806
Hepsebeth, dau of Samuel & Sarah, b. 2 Apr 1729
Hepsebeth, dau of Samuel & Sarah, b. 28 Sep 1738
Hepsebeth, dau of Jonathan & Hepsebeth, b. 1 Nov 1742
Hollis N., son of Nathaniel & Elizabeth, b. 23 May 1856
James, son of James & Judah, b. 6 Sep 1729

RYE BIRTHS

MARDEN, James, son of Ebenr & Ester, b. 5 Apr 1748
James, b. 6 May 1781
James, child of William & Hannah, b. 21 Apr 1784
James L., son of William & Lucy Ann, b. 1 Dec 1832
James William, son of William & Lucy Ann, b. 2 Oct 183_
Jennes, son of William & Lucy Ann, b. 9 Jul 1837
John, son of James & Judah, b. 29 Feb 1725
John, son of John & Sarah, b. 30 Nov 1747
John, son of Benjamin & Rebecer, b. 6 May 1762
John S., son of Ebenezer & Lovey, b. 8 Apr 1825
John Towle, son of Reuben & Charlotte, b. 26 Feb 1836
Jonathan, son of Jonathan & Hepzebeth, b. 9 Oct 1732
Jonathan, son of Nathaniel & Elizabeth, b. 24 Apr 1770
Jonathan, son of Samuel & Margaret, b. 25 Oct 1772
Jonathan, son of Joseph & Mary, b. 22 Feb 1780
Jonathan Towle, son of Nathaniel & Anna, b 29 Jan 1796
Joseph, son of Jonathan & Hepzebeth, b. 22 Mar 1738
Joseph, son of Joseph & Mary, b. 3 Apr 1774
Judith, dau of James & Judith, b. 10 Jun 1741
Kezia, dau of Nathaniel & Hannah, b. 22 Feb 1770
Levi Wattson, son of William & Lucy Ann, b. 27 Mar 184_
Lovey B., dau of Ebenezer & Lovey, b. 31 Oct 1807
Lovina, dau of James & Sarah, b. 8 Jan 1810
Lucy, b. 28 Sep 1776
Lucy, wife of Ebenezer, b. 17 May 1788
Mary, dau of James & Judah, b. 20 Sep 1727
Mary, dau of Samuel & Sarah, b. 1 Nov 1733
Mary, b. 1 Feb 1749
Mary, dau of Ebenr & Ester, b. 1 Feb 1749/50
Mary, dau of Benjamin & Rebecer, b. (no date)
Mary B., dau of Ebenezer & Lovey, b. 10 Aug 1813
Mary E., dau of Reuben & Charlotte, b. 16 Jan 1840
Mehetebel, dau of Samuel & Margaret, b. 5 Mar 1770
Molly, dau of Benjamin & Hannah, b. 24 Mar 1779
Nancy Tredwel, dau of Benjamin & Hannah, b. 20 Mar 1777
Nathan, son of James & Judah, b. 15 Nov 1721

RYE BIRTHS

MARDEN, Nathaniel, son of Jonathan & Hepzebeth, b. 11 Mar 1730
Nathaniel, son of Jonathan & Hepsebeth, b. 25 Jul 1745
Nathaniel, son of Ebenr & Ester, b. 22 Mar 1745/6
Nathaniel, son of Nathaniel & Anna, b. 26 Apr 1792
Nathaniel, son of Reuben & Hannah, b. 20 Feb 1817
Oley, dau of Nathanl & Elizabeth, b. 27 Aug 1774
Oli, dau of James & Judith, b. 6 Jan 1747
Phebe, dau of Samuel & Sarah, b. 3 May 1731
Polly A.W., dau of Nathaniel & Elizabeth, b. 7 Jul 1848
Prudence Perry, dau of Nathaniel & Hannah, b. 1 Jan 1769
Rachel, dau of Benjamin & Rachel, b. 9 Jan 1766
Rebecca, dau of Benjamin & Hanah, b. 10 Jan 1773
Reuben, b. 21 Apr 1783
Rhoda, dau of James & Sarah, b. 2 Apr 1803
Ruth, dau of Stephen & Charity, b. 8 Dec 1731
Sally, dau of Samuel & Sally, b. 5 Jan 1811
Samuel, son of Benjamin & Rebecer, b. 30 Apr 1748
Samuel, son of Jonathan & Hepsebeth, b. 11 Sep 1750/1
Samuel, son of Samuel & Margaret, b. 1 Oct 1772
Samuel, son of Benjamin & Rebeca, b. 25 Jan 1773
Samuel, son of Samuel & Sally, b. 19 Feb 1821
Samuel A., son of Nathaniel & Elizabeth, b. 3 Mar 1854
Samuel Hunt, son of Joseph & Mary, b. 14 Jan 1777
Sarah, dau of Samuel & Sarah, b. 27 Jun 1727
Sarah, child of William & Hannah, b. 29 Oct 1778
Solomon Dowst, son of Benjamin & Rachel, b. 25 Sep 1757
Stephen, son of Stephen & Charity, b. 27 Sep 1736
Stephen, son of Benjamin & Rachel, b. 3 Nov 1764
Timothy, son of Jonathan & Hepzebeth, b. 28 Aug 1735
William, son of James & Judah, b. 13 Oct 1733
William, son of James & Judith, b. 13 May 1744
William, son of James & Judith, b. 30 May 1744
William, son of Benjamin & Rebecer, b. 9 Sep 1759
William, son of James & Polly, b. 24 Dec 1810

RYE BIRTHS

MARDEN, Willie P., son of Nathaniel & Elizabeth, b. 14 Dec 1861
MARSTON (MASTON), Hannah, dau of Joseph & Hannah, b. 25 Sep 1726
MOORE (MORE), Anne, dau of Wm & Anne, b. 22 May 1750
MORRILL (MOREL, MORIEL), Amelia, dau of Rev. Nathaniel & Sarah, b. 6 May 1731
  Benjamin, son of Joseph & Tabitha, b. 17 Feb 1728
  Levi, son of Rev. Nathaniel & Sarah, b. 28 Feb 1728/9
  Nathaniel, son of Rev. Nathaniel & Sarah, b. 26 Apr 1727
  Sarah, dau of Nathll & Sarah, b. 8 Feb 1724/5
  Theofelus, son of Joseph & Tabitha, b. 20 Dec 1730
MORRISON, Mary, dau of Alexander & Sarah Coats, b. 22 May 1770
MOULTON, Anne, dau of Nehemiah & Sarah, b. 14 Jun 1762
  Bethiah, dau of Joseph & Bethiah, b. 26 Nov 1683
  Daniel, son of Jonathan & Elisabeth, b. 9 May 1731
  Elizabeth, dau of Ruben & Hannah, b. 8 Feb 1751
  Febe, dau of Daniel & Febe, b. 3 Apr 1735
  Jonathan, son of Jonathan & Elizabeth, b. 1 Apr 1730
  Jonathan, son of Ruben & Hannah, b. 27 Oct 1749
  Lidde, dau of Daniel & Febe, b. 28 Aug 1740
  Luce, dau of Jonathan & Elizabeth, b. 20 Mar 1735
  Luce, dau of Ruben & Hannah, b. 4 Aug 1757
  Mary, dau of Daniel & Phebe, b. 13 May 1729
  Nathan, son of Daniel & Febe, b. 2 Mar 1738
  Robert, son of Jonathan & Elizabeth, b. 20 May 1733
  Rubin, son of Jonathan & Elizabeth, b. 4 Jan 1729
MOW (MOWE, MOEW), Hannah, dau of Epehrem & Dorckes b. 10 ___ 1760 (no month in original)
  Mary, dau of Epehrem & Dorckes, b. 16 Dec 1757
  Sarah, dau of Epehrem & Dorckes, b. 6 Dec 1755
MURRAY (MOREY), Elizabeth, dau of Samuel & Hannah, b. 29 Jul 1770
  Samuel, son of Samuel & Elizabeth, b. 19 Jan 1757
  Susanah, dau of Samuel & Elizabeth, b. 6 Apr 1759

RYE BIRTHS

PAIN (PANE), Christien, dau of John & Sarah, b. 13 May 1740
 Mary, dau of John & Sary, b. 1 Jul 1736
 Moses, son of William & Hana, b. 10 Apr 1736
 William, son of William & Susannah, b. 8 Sep 1744
PALMER, James, son of Jona & Abigail, b. 10 Jan 1753
 Jona, son of Christopher & Elizabeth, b. 16 May 1707
 Joseph, son of William & Jane, b. 8 May 1740
 Samuel, son of Jonathan & Ann, b. 28 Jan 1736/7
PARSONS (PERSONS), Abby S., child of John W. & Abigail, b. 3 Mar 1820
 Abigail, wife of John W., b. 14 Aug 1782
 Abigail, child of John W. & Abigail, b. 4 Jan 1811
 Albion Dalton, child of Thomas J. & Eliza B., b. 17 Feb 1829
 Charles G., child of John W. & Abigail, b. 29 Feb 1808
 Charles Henry, child of Thomas J. & Eliza B., b. 23 Dec 1835
 Charles William, child of Thomas J. & Eliza B., b. 4 Jan 1831
 Daniel Dearborn, child of Thomas J. & Eliza B., b. 5 May 1833
 Eliza Esther, child of Thomas J. & Eliza B., b. 10 Jun 1838
 Emily, dau of John W. & Abigail, b. 2 May 1806
 John, child of John W. & Abigail, b. 4 Jan 1816
 John W., b. 12 Dec 1778
 John William, child of Thomas J. & Eliza B., b. 1 Aug 1841
 Langdon Brown, child of Thomas J. & Eliza B., b. 24 Dec 1844
 Mary, dau of Rev. Samuel & Mary, b. 15 Jul 1740
 Samuel, son of Rev. Samuel & Mary, b. 31 Aug 1742
 Semira, child of John W. & Abigail, b. 27 Feb 1828
 Thomas Henry, child of Thomas J. & Eliza B., b. 26 Sep 1824
 Thomas J., son of John W. & Abigail, b. 4 Jan 1804
 Warren, child of John W. & Abigail, b. 28 May 1818
 William H., child of John W. & Abigail, b. 21 Jul 1813

RYE BIRTHS

PHILBRICK, Abigail, dau of Joseph & Anna, b. 28 Sep 1768
Adaline, dau of Joseph Jr. & Patty, b. 23 Dec 1825
Anna, dau of Joseph & Anna, b. 23 Jan 1764
Benjamin, son of Joses & Susannah, b. 27 Sep 1785
Benjamin Pitman, child of Benjamin & Mary, b. 18 Dec 1819
Bethiah, dau of Ebenezer & Bethiah, b. 28 Jun 1718
Betsy Brown, dau of Jonathan & Sarah, b. 7 Feb 1796
Charles Pinckney, son of Joses & Susannah, b. 7 Oct 1799
Christiane Robinson, child of Ephraim & Sally, b. 27 Aug 1822
Clinton, son of Joses & Susannah, b. 29 May 1805
Daniel, son of Joseph & Anna, b. 19 Jan 1776
Daniel, son of Jonathan & Sarah, b. 10 Jun 1805
Ebenezer, son of James & Hannah, b. 29 Oct 1683
Ebenezer, son of Ebenezer & Bethiah, b. 27 May 1721
Elizabeth, dau of James & Elizabeth, b. 22 May 1739
Emeline, child of Benjamin & Mary, b. 30 Jun 1807
Hannah, dau of Joseph & Anna, b. 12 Dec 1770
Hannah, dau of Reuben & Mary, b. 7 Jan 1776
Hannah, dau of Joses & Susannah, b. 7 Apr 1795
Ira, son of Jonathan & Sarah, b. 24 Sep 1807
Irene, child of Benjamin & Mary, b. 28 Oct 1815
James, son of Ebenezer & Bethiah, b. 21 Jun 1714
James, son of James & Elizabeth, b. 30 Aug 1737
James, son of Joseph & Anna, b. 8 Jul 1780
John Ira, son of Joseph Jr. & Patty, b. 4 Apr 1835
John Colby, child of Ephraim & Sally, b. 9 Apr 1818
John Walbach, son of Joses & Susannah, b. 22 Aug 1808
Jonathan, son of James & Elizabeth, b. 6 Apr 1741
Jonathan, son of Joseph & Anna, b. 17 Sep 1773
Jonathan, son of Jonathan & Sarah, b. 5 May 1802
Joseph, son of Joseph & Anne, b. 14 Jun 1783
Joseph, son of Joses & Susannah, b. 19 Sep 1788
Joseph, son of Jonathan & Sarah, b. 12 Nov 1797
Joseph N., son of Joseph Jr. & Patty, b. 2 Mar

RYE BIRTHS

1830
PHILBRICK, Joses, son of Joseph & Anna, b. 12 Sep 1761
  Joses, son of Daniel & Abigail, b. 22 Jul 1766
  Joses, son of Reuben & Mary, b. 19 May 1781
  Josiah Webster, child of Ephraim & Sally, b. 2 Oct 1807
  Juliann, child of Benjamin & Mary, b. 6 Sep 1809
  Levi, son of Joseph & Anna, b. 6 May 1778
  Lyman, son of Joses & Susannah, b. 3 Oct 1802
  Martha Ann, dau of Joseph Jr. & Patty, b. 18 Oct 1820
  Mary Sherburne, child of Benjamin & Mary, b. 8 May 1811
  Mercy, dau of Daniel & Abigail, b. 8 Jan 1763
  Moses Cheney, child of Ephraim & Sally, b. 6 Apr 1813
  Nancey, dau of Joses & Susannah, b. 8 Apr 1792
  Newell, son of Jonathan & Sarah, b. 28 Jan 1810
  Oliver Blunt, child of Benjamin & Mary, b. 28 Feb 1813
  Poley, dau of Joses & Susanah, b. 5 Dec 1782
  Reuben, son of Reuben & Mary, b. 9 Sep 1773
  Reuben, son of Joses & Susannah, b. 1 Sep 1798
  Ruth, dau of Ebenezer & Bethiah, b. 15 May 1711
  Sally, dau of Joseph & Aney, b. 30 Aug 178_
  Sally, dau of Jonathan & Sarah, b. 7 Apr 1800
  Sarah, dau of Daniel & Abigail, b. 30 Jul 1764
  Sarah, dau of Reuben & Mary, b. 13 Apr 1778
  Sarah Ann, child of Ephraim & Sally, b. 7 Nov 1811
  Sarah E., dau of Joseph Jr. & Patty, b. 18 Feb 1823
  Sheridan, b. 20 May 1813
  Titus, son of James & Elizabeth, b. 4 Apr 1743
PORTER, Caroline, dau of Rev. Huntington & Susannah, b. 23 Oct 1793
  John, son of Rev. Huntington & Susannah, b. 29 Sep 1791
  Maria, dau of Rev. Huntington & Sally, b. 12 Feb 1798
  Nathaniel Sargeant, son of Rev. Huntington & Susannah, b. 29 May 1789
  Samuel Huntington, son of Rev. Huntington & Susannah, b. 11 Jul 1787
RAND, Abigail, dau of Samuel & Sarah, b. 6 Oct 1759
  Amos, son of Nathaniel & Bethier, b. 29 Jan 1767
  Anne, dau of Amos & Esther, b. 13 Aug 1727

RYE BIRTHS

RAND, Apphiah, dau of Nathaniel & Mary, b. 5 Feb 1784
Bethiah, dau of Joshua & Ruth, b. 8 Jun 1742
Betsy, dau of George & Amey, b. 14 Feb 1774
Billy, son of Samuel & Sarah, b. 30 Oct 1766
Billy, son of Samuel & Sarah, b. 31 Oct 1766
David, son of Epheram & Mary, b. 17 Oct 1772
David L., son of John & Sydney, b. 27 Feb 1815
Deborah, dau of Joseph & Deborah, b. 3 Sep 1765
Dowst, son of Samuel & Sarah, b. 24 Jun 1764
Ebenezer, son of George & Amey, b. 15 Feb 1784
Eliza, dau of John & Sydney, b. 25 May 1812
Elizabeth, dau of Nathaniel & Elizabeth, b. 2 Aug 1716
Elizabeth, dau of Thomas & Hannah, b. 22 Apr 1730
Elizabeth, dau of Amos & Esther, b. 12 Apr 1736
Elizabeth, dau of Joshua & Ruth, b. 16 Feb 1754
Elizabeth, dau of Samuel & Sarah, b. 8 Jan 1757
Elizabeth, child of Joseph & Olly, b. 14 Nov 1804
Enoch, son of George & Amey, b. 20 Sep 1780
Epheram, son of Thomas & Hannah, b. 23 Mar 1737
Epheram, son of Epheram & Mary, b. 2 Nov 1769
Esther, dau of Amos & Esther, b. 13 May 1732
George, son of Joshua & Ruth, b. 4 Apr 1744
George, son of George & Amey, b. 9 Apr 1777
Gilman, b. 27 Apr 1847
Hannah, dau of Thomas & Hannah, b. 12 May 1728
Hannah B., dau of Joseph Jr. & Eleanor, b. 13 Apr 1829
Harriet Jane, dau of John & Sydney, b. 4 Sep 1809
Hepsibeth, dau of Joshua & Ruth, b. 28 Mar 1746
Ira, child of Joseph & Olly, b. 28 Sep 1814
Isarel, son of Epehrem & Mary, b. 12 Jul 1757
James B., son of Billy & Charlotte, b. 5 Sep 1811
John, son of William & Sarah, b. 20 Jan 1756
John, son of George & Amey, b. 5 Mar 1772
John J., son of Billy & Charlotte, b. 20 May 1823
John Oris, son of John & Sydney, b. 13 Mar 1820
John Tuck, son of Thomas & Mary, b. 7 Jul 1791
Jonathan, son of Ephraim & Mary, b. 5 Sep 1767
Joseph, son of Amos & Esther, b. 1 Mar 1734
Joseph, son of Joseph & Deborah, b. 11 Jan 1763
Joseph, child of Joseph & Olly, b. 21 Jan 1796
Joshua, son of Nathaniel & Elizabeth, b. 25 Dec

RYE BIRTHS

1703
RAND, Joshua, son of Joshua & Ruth, b. 23 Aug 1735
  Joshua, son of Nathaniel & Bethier, b. 22 Apr 1769
  Julia Ann, dau of Joseph Jr. & Eleanor, b. 10 Feb 1833
  Levi, son of Billy & Patty, b. 24 Oct 1810
  Levi, child of Joseph & Olly, b. 23 Apr 1811
  Martha, dau of George & Amey, b. 20 Jan 1769
  Mary, dau of Thomas & Hannah, b. 18 Aug 1726
  Mary, dau of Richard & Abiall, b. 8 Feb 1726
  Mary, dau of Nathaniel & Mary, b. 21 Mar 1764
  Mary, dau of Joseph & Deborah, b. 15 Mar 1759
  Mary, child of Joseph & Olly, b. 29 Jan 1808
  Mary A., dau of Billy & Charlotte, b. 23 Jun 1818
  Mary Emerit, dau of Joseph Jr. & Eleanor, b. 4 Jan 1838
  Mary Jones Wallis, b. 12 Mar 1793
  Mehitabel, dau of Nathaniel & Mary, b. 10 Dec 1770
  Merebe, dau of Thomas & Hannah, b. 26 Apr 1735
  Micah, son of Joshua & Ruth, b. 28 Nov 1748
  Nathaniel, son of Richard & Abiall, b. 12 Mar 1737
  Nathaniel, son of Amos & Ester, b. 21 May 1740
  Nathaniel, son of Nathaniel, b. 8 Sep 1766
  Nathaniel M., child of Joseph & Olly, b. 16 Sep 1806
  Oley, b. 5 Apr 1762
  Olive W., dau of Joseph Jr. & Eleanor, b. 14 Oct 1826
  Philbrick, son of Amos & Esther, b. 11 Dec 1729
  Philbrick, son of Joseph & Deborah, b. 25 Mar 1761
  Philimon, son of Joshua & Ruth, b. 18 Jan 1732
  Rachel, dau of Samuel & Sarah, b. 20 Apr 1762
  Richard, son of Nathaniel & Mary, b. 18 Mar 1758
  Richard, son of George & Amey, b. 29 Oct 1778
  Ruben, son of Ruben & Elizabeth, b. 22 Aug 1759
  Rubin, son of Thomas & Hannah, b. 7 Mar 1739
  Ruth, dau of Joshua & Ruth, b. 12 Jul 1733
  Ruth, b. 1 Aug 1776
  Saley, dau of Nathaniel, b. 25 Dec 1772
  Samuel, son of Samuel & Abigail, b. 6 Aug 1724
  Samuel, son of Epheram & Mary, b. 18 Nov 1751
  Samuel, son of Samuel & Sarah, b. 10 Dec 1753
  Samuel, b. 28 Jan 1760
  Samuel 2d, b. 11 Jan 1780

RYE BIRTHS

RAND, Samuel, son of Thomas & Mary, b. 16 Feb 1796
  Samuel, son of Billy & Patty, b. 20 Jul 1803
  Samuel H., child of Joseph & Olly, b. 28 Apr 1803
  Sarah, dau of Amos & Esther, b. 12 Feb 1738
  Sarah, dau of Joshua & Ruth, b. 30 Mar 1740
  Sarah, dau of Samuel & Sarah, b. 16 Nov 1751
  Sarah, dau of Epheram & Mary, b. 2 Nov 1764
  Sarah, b. 31 Jul 1774
  Sarah, dau of Billy & Patty, b. 12 Apr 1801
  Sarah Jane G., dau of Joseph Jr. & Eleanor, b. 6 Feb 1835
  Susan, child of Joseph & Olly, b. 28 Jul 1809
  Susanah, dau of Nathaniel, b. 31 Aug 1768
  Sylvanis, son of Ira & Sarah Ann, b. 31 May 1843
  Sylvia, dau of Joseph Jr. & Eleanor, b. 11 Apr 1831
  Temperance, dau of Joshua & Ruth, b. 13 Jun 1735
  Thomas, son of Thomas & Hannah, b. 9 Mar 1732
  Thomas, son of Ruben & E., b. 31 Dec 17__
  Thomas, son of Samuel & Sarah, b. 27 Mar 1749
  Thomas, son of Samuel & Sarah, b. 6 Jun 1760
  Thomas Jefferson, son of John & Sydney, b. 11 Jun 1813
  William J., son of Billy & Charlotte, b. 2 Mar 1815
RANDALL (RENDEL), Abigail, wife of Mark, b. 11 Nov 1730
  Abigail, child of Mark & Abigail, b. 5 Dec 1749
  Daniel, child of Mark & Abigail, b. 26 Oct 1769
  Deborah, child of Mark & Abigail, b. 11 Jun 1764
  Elizabeth, child of Mark & Abigail, b. 10 Apr 1755
  Elizabeth W., dau of Levi D. & Abigail, b. 15 Aug 1809
  George, son of Edward & Hannah, b. 15 Sep 1733
  Hannah, child of Mark & Abigail, b. 30 Aug 1778
  James Maston, son of William & Hannah, b. 7 Mar 1746
  John, son of John & Hannah, b. 14 Apr 1746
  John, child of Mark & Abigail, b. 18 Jun 1762
  Jonathan, son of William & Hannah, b. 27 Mar 1759
  Joseph, son of William & Hannah, b. 17 Apr 1756
  Joses, child of Mark & Abigail, b. 11 Apr 1751
  Lucey, dau of William & Hannah, b. 29 Dec 1767
  Mark, b. 25 Oct 1726
  Mark, child of Mark & Abigail, b. 18 Jun 1757
  Mary, dau of William & Hannah, b. 20 Sep 1750

RYE BIRTHS

RANDALL, Mary, dau of Levi & Abigail, b. 18 Dec 1810
  Olive, child of Mark & Abigail, b. 21 Oct 1772
  Reuben, child of Mark & Abigail, b. 9 Feb 1760
  Reuben, son of Levi & Abigail, b. 7 Dec 1812
  Samuel, son of William & Hannah, b. 2 May 1762
  Samuel, child of Mark & Abigail, b. 3 Jul 1767
  Sarah, child of Mark & Abigail, b. 28 Oct 1752
  Stephen, son of William & Hannah, b. 2 Jul 1753
  Thomas, son of William Jr., b. 4 Sep 1770
  William, son of William & Hannah, b. May 1748
REID, Betsy, dau of John G. of Portsmouth, b. 1 Jan 1788
REMICK, George William, child of William & Caroline, b. 1 Aug 1834
  Joseph, child of William & Caroline, b. 4 Oct 1836
SALTER, Alexander, son of Alexander & Elizabeth, b. 3 Oct 1744
  John, son of Alexander & Elizabeth, b. 19 Sep 1748
SAUNDERS (SANDERS), Abigail, dau of John & Trifaney, b. 7 Oct 1760
  Betsy, dau of William & Sarah, b. 15 Sep 1785
  George, b. 18 Apr 1732 Old Stile
  George, son of George & Sarah, b. 3 Jun 1769
  Elizabeth, dau of George & Sarah, b. 29 Jun 1755
  Hannah, dau of George & Sarah, b. 4 Jun 1779
  John, son of William & Sarah, b. 2 Mar 1789
  Martha, dau of George & Sarah, b. 29 May 1766
  Mary, dau of George & Sarah, b. 13 Aug 1776
  Mercy, dau of George & Sarah, b. 24 Aug 1767
  Samuel, son of George & Sarah, b. 21 Nov 1771
  Sarah, wife of George, b. 13 Jan 1736 Old Stile
  Sarah, dau of John & Trifaney, b. 28 Jul 1763
  Sarah, dau of George & Sarah, b. 20 Aug 1773
  William, son of George & Sarah, b. 19 Oct 1759
  William, son of William & Sarah, b. 7 Nov 1783
SCHEDEL (SHEGEL, SKEGEL, SCEGGELL), Benjamin, son of Christopher & Deborah, b. 27 Nov 1727
  Jacob, son of Christopher & Deborah, b. 25 Oct 1736
  Mary, dau of Christopher & Deborah, b. 1 May 1720
SEAVEY (SEAVE), Abigail, dau of Samuel & Abigail, b. 25 Feb 1723
  Betsy, dau of Joshua & Betty, b. 31 Jul 1797
  Cataran, dau of Henery & Mary, b. 21 Oct 1741
  Charles, child of Theodore & Betsey, b. (no

RYE BIRTHS

date)
SEAVEY, Deborah, dau of Samuel & Hannah, b. 4 Nov 1737
  Elijah, son of Henry & Mary, b. 5 Aug 1743
  Eliza Jane, child of Theodore & Betsey, b. (no date)
  Elizabeth, dau of Ithamer & Mary, b. 10 Jun 1737
  Hannah, dau of Joseph & Hannah, b. 7 Jun 1741
  Hannah, dau of Joshua & Betty, b. 16 May 1812
  Henry, son of Samuel & Abigail, b. 23 Apr 1719
  Ithamar, son of Samuel & Abigail, b. 27 Jan 1712
  James, son of James & Abigail, b. 1 Mar 1743
  Johannah, dau of Joseph & Hannah, b. 21 Aug 1712
  Jonathan, son of Samuel & Abigail, b. 2 Feb 1732
  Mary, dau of Ithamar & Mary, b. 23 Dec 1734
  Mary, dau of Samuel & Abigail, b. 25 Apr 1721
  Mary Moses, dau of Joshua & Betsy, b. 24 Jan 1808
  Mehitable, dau of Samuel & Abigail, b. 21 Oct 1729
  Mehitable, dau of Paul & Sarah, b. 19 Feb 1775
  Moses, son of Samuel & Abigail, b. 30 Jan 1735
  Nathaniel, b. 29 Jan 1805
  Oliver, child of Theodore & Betsey, b. (no date)
  Olly, dau of Joshua & Betty, b. 15 May 1800
  Ruth, dau of Henry & Mary, b. 11 Oct 1745
  Sally, dau of Joshua & Betsy, b. 2 Nov 1798
  Samuel, child of Theodore & Betsey, b. (no date)
  Samuel, son of Samuel & Abigail, b. 18 May 1714
  Samuel, son of Samuel & Abigail, b. 18 May 1715
  Samuel, son of Samuel & Hannah, b. 17 Sep 1739
  Sarah, dau of Samuel & Abigail, b. 20 Nov 1716
  Solomon, son of Samuel & Hannah, b. 26 Feb 1736
  Sophrona, child of Theodore & Betsey, b. 6 Jan 1823
  William Garland, child of Theodore & Betsey, b. 24 Apr 1821
  Wintrup, son of Joshua & Betsy, b. 26 Jan 1802
  _____, b. 11 Aug 1810
SHANNON (SHANEN, SHANIN), Elizabeth, dau of Thomas & Anne, b. 18 Sep 1753
  John, son of Thomas & Anne, b. 16 Aug 1757
  William, son of Thomas & Anna, b. 26 Aug 1755
SHAPLEY, Dorcas P., dau of Henry & Molly, b. 17 Nov 1792
  Samuel B., son of Samuel & Rachel, b. 24 Oct 1821
SHERBURNE (SHERBORN, SHURBORN), Andrew, b. 22 May 1738

RYE BIRTHS

SHERBURNE, Andrew, son of Andrew & Susanah, b. 30 Sep 1765
  Elizabeth, dau of Andrew & Susanah, b. 20 Nov 1768
  Marthy, dau of Andrew & Susanah, b. 7 Jul 1762
  Marthy, dau of Andrew & Susanah, b. 7 Mar 1764
  Samuel, son of Andrew & Susannah, b. 16 May 1767
  Susanah, b. 6 Mar 1741
  Thomas, son of Andrew & Susannah, b. 15 Jun 1761
SMITH, David, son of David & Sarah, b. 18 Jan 1741
  Deborah, dau of David & Sarah, b. 18 Jun 1730
  Isreal, son of David & Sarah, b. 6 Oct 1728
  Mary, dau of David & Sarah, b. 25 Sep 1736
  Merebeth, dau of David & Sarah, b. 13 Jul 1734
  Sarah, dau of David & Sarah, b. 26 Nov 1726
STIVERS, Andrew, son of Sarah Hall, b. 16 Jun 1765
TOWLE (TOLE), Anne, dau of Jonathan & Anne, b. 28 Mar 1741
  James, son of Jonathan & Anne, b. 28 Oct 1737
  Jonathan, son of Jonathan & Anne, b. 4 Jul 1729
  Joseph, son of Jonathan & Anne, b. 21 Mar 1733
  Levi, son of Jonathan & Anne, b. 22 Sep 1731
  Nathan, son of Jonathan & Anne, b. 29 May 1745
  Samuel, son of Jonathan & Anne, b. 5 Nov 1735
TREFETHERN (TREFERRIN), Abigail, wife of Robinson, b. 7 Nov 1726 Old Stile
  Abigail, dau of Robinson & Abigail, b. 6 Apr 1755 New Stile
  Dennis Hill, son of John & Mary, b. 21 Oct 1837
  Edwin J., son of John & Mary, b. 16 Dec 1843
  Hannah J., dau of William & Hannah, b. 3 Dec 1844
  Henry, son of Robinson & Abigail, b. 16 Aug 1769 New Stile
  Isette Morris, dau of John & Mary, b. 31 May 1835
  Joseph, son of Robinson & Abigail, b. 14 Aug 1757 New Stile
  Joseph Jr., son of Robinson & Abigail, b. 5 Mar 1759 New Stile
  Lucretia, dau of Robinson & Abigail, b. 24 May 1763 New Stile
  Lydia Mary, dau of William & Hannah, b. 14 Jan 1839
  Margaret, dau of Robinson & Abigail, b. 28 May 1767 New Stile
  Martha Semira, dau of John & Mary, b. 6 Jul 1841
  Mary, dau of Robinson & Abigail, b. 12 Apr 1748 Old Stile

RYE BIRTHS

TREFETHERN, Nathaniel, son of Wm & Elizabeth, b. (no date)
  Robinson, son of Henery & Mary Locke, b. Newcastle, Apr 1721
  Robinson, son of Robinson & Abigail, b. 3 Mar 1753 Old Stile and died at sea
  Salome, dau of Robinson & Abigail, b. 1 May 1765 New Stile
  William, son of Robinson & Abigail, b. 5 Jun 1751 Old Stile
  William, son of William & Elizabeth, b. 24 Apr 1775
  William, son of William & Elizabeth, b. (no date)
TRUNDY, Sally, dau of Abigail Rand, b. 4 Feb 1778
TUCKER, Elizabeth, wife of Nathaniel, b. 31 Dec 1732
  Elizabeth, dau of Nathaniel & Elizabeth, b. 19 Nov 1753
  Elizabeth Hall, dau of Joseph & Elizabeth, b. 13 Nov 1802
  Ester, dau of William & Mary, b. 28 Dec 1734
  James, son of Joseph & Betsey, b. 17 Aug 1810
  John, son of Joseph & Elizabeth, b. 11 Jan 1799
  John W., son of Joseph & Betsy, b. 11 Jun 1808
  Joseph, son of Nathaniel & Elizabeth, b. 19 Sep 1773
  Joseph Parsons, son of Joseph & Elizabeth, b. 30 Sep 1797
  Mary, dau of William & Mary, b. 11 Feb 1725
  Mary, dau of William & Mary, b. 25 Oct 1740
  Nathaniel, son of William & Mary, b. 18 Sep 1732
  Nathaniel, son of William & Mary, b. 19 Sep 1733
  Nathaniel, son of Nathaniel & Elizabeth, b. 23 Sep 1758
  Nathaniel, son of Joseph & Elizabeth, b. 24 Jan 1792 ?
  Richard, son of Nathaniel & Elizabeth, b. 27 Nov 1764
  Sarah, dau of William & Mary, b. 18 May 1737
  Sarah, dau of Nathaniel & Elizabeth, b. 31 May 1756
  Susannah, dau of William & Mary, b. 25 Aug 1730
  William, son of William & Mary, b. 19 Jun 1727
  William, son of Nathaniel & Elizabeth, b. 31 Jan 1763
VARRELL (VERRIL), Abigail Lock, dau of Joseph & Sarah, b. 25 Aug 1803
  Elizabeth Mary, dau of Samuel & Elizabeth, b. 31

RYE BIRTHS

Aug 1813
VARRELL, Jonathan Waldron, son of Samuel & Elizabeth, b. 30 Oct 1814
  Joseph, son of Joseph & Sarah, b. 8 Dec 1794
  Joseph, son of Joseph & Sarah, b. 21 Jun 1796
  Joses, son of Joseph & Sarah, b. 8 Dec 1794
  Maria, dau of Richard Tucker & Mary, b. 6 Feb 1803
  Martha Lang, dau of Samuel & Elizabeth, b. 12 Apr 1822
  Phina Philbrick, dau of Joseph & Sarah, b. 23 Mar 1801
  Sally, dau of Joseph & Sarah, b. 18 Apr 1799
WALDRON (WALDON), Elizabeth Sanders, dau of Jonathan Belcher & Elizabeth, b. 16 Dec 1790
  George, son of Jonathan B. & Elizabeth, b. 21 Feb 1802
  Joshua Foss, son of Jonathan B. & Elizabeth, b. 11 Dec 1796
  Polly Westbrook, dau of Jonathan B. & Elizabeth, b. 17 Aug 1792
  Richard Harvey, son of Jonathan B. & Elizabeth, b. 30 Sep 1798
  Robert Sanders, son of Jonathan B. & Elizabeth, b. 9 Jun 1794
WALKER, Jonathan, b. 26 Sep 1804
  Levi Henry, child of Jonathan & Mary Esther, b. 9 Feb 1840
  Lewis Everett, child of Jonathan & Mary Esther, b. 8 Aug 1842
  William Chauncey, child of Jonathan & Mary Esther, b. 15 Feb 1833
WALLIS, Hannah, dau of Samuel & Sarah, b. 2 Aug 1745
WEBSTER, Abiah, dau of Josiah & Martha, b. 3 Sep 1742
  Abigail, child of Richard & Elizabeth, b. 24 Aug 1780
  Betsy, child of Richard & Elizabeth, b. 3 Mar 1779
  David, son of Josiah & Sarah, b. 23 Sep 1785
  Elizabeth, dau of Josiah & Martha, b. 29 Feb 1740
  Fanny, dau of Josiah & Sarah, b. 26 Mar 1790
  Hannah, child of Richard & Elizabeth, b. 16 Dec 1784
  John, son of Josiah & Martha, b. 18 Jan 1751
  John, son of Josiah & Sarah, b. 23 Jun 1788
  Josiah, son of John & Abiah, b. at Hampton, Apr

RYE BIRTHS

WEBSTER, Josiah, son of Josiah & Martha, b. 9 Jul 1706
  Josiah, son of Josiah & Martha, b. 11 May 1748
  Josiah, son of Josiah & Sarah, b. 6 Jan 1751
  Levi L., son of Josiah & Sarah, b. 2 Mar 1783
  Mark R., child of Richard & Elizabeth, b. 20 Apr 1797
  Martha, wife of Josiah, b. 3 Sep 1714
  Martha, dau of Josiah & Martha, b. 11 Feb 1755
  Martha, child of Richard & Elizabeth, b. 25 Nov 1781
  Martha, dau of Josiah & Sarah, b. 10 Apr 1795
  Mary, dau of Josiah & Sarah, b. 17 Apr 1781
  Nathaniel, son of Josiah & Sarah, b. 4 Mar 1793
  Olly R., child of Richard & Elizabeth, b. 19 Nov 1786
  Richard, son of Josiah & Martha, b. 1 Jan 1754
  Richard, child of Richard & Elizabeth, b. 6 Oct 1788
  Sarah, dau of Josiah & Martha, b. 19 Apr 1745
  Sarah, child of Richard & Elizabeth, b. 12 Jul 1783
  Sarah, dau of Josiah & Sarah, b. 18 Mar 1787
WELLS (WILLS), Anne, dau of Samuel & Pursila, b. 10 Oct 1747
  Debora, dau of Samuel & Pursila, b. 5 Oct 1740
  Isaiah, son of Samuel & Pursila, b. 29 Apr 1743
  John, son of Samuel & Pursila, b. 4 Oct 1745
  John, son of Samuel & Pursila, b. 12 Aug 1750
  (Note: there are lines drawn through the name John; perhaps there was a mistake in the first name)
  Samuel, son of Samuel & Pursila, b. 2 Dec 1735
  Sarah, dau of Samuel & Elizabath, b. 21 Nov 1765
  Simeon, son of Samuel & Pursila, b. 11 May 1738

RYE BAPTISMS

ACKERMAN, John, son of Peter, bpt. 20 Nov 1785
  Joseph, son of Peter, bpt. Aug 1782
  Peter, son of Peter, bpt. Aug 1782
  Phineas, son of Peter, bpt. 22 Jun 1783
AIMEY, Joel, son of Joel, bpt. 15 Jun 1777
ALLEN, Elizabeth Locke, dau of Jude, bpt. 19 Apr 1778
  Joseph, son of Betty, bpt. 9 Jan 1801
  Joshua, son of Jude, bpt. 9 Aug 1761
  Jude, son of Jude, bpt. 18 Sep 1743
  Nathaniel, son of Jude, bpt. 12 Jul 1746/7
  Salome, dau of Jude, bpt. 9 Aug 1761
BACHELDER (BATCHELDER), Jonathan Cotton, son of Josiah, bpt. 29 Jun 1800
BECK, John, son of James, bpt. 18 Sep 1796
BELL, Frederick Morgan, son of Shadrach, bpt. Nov 1749
  Margaret, dau of Shadrach, bpt. 22 Feb 1741
  Meshech, son of _____, bpt. 4 Sep 1748
BERERLAND, Margaret, dau of David, bpt. Feb 1740
BERRY, Abigail, dau of John, bpt. 13 Sep 1746/7
  Abigail, dau of Nathaniel Jr., bpt. 12 Jan 1752
  Abigail, dau of Samuel B., bpt. 17 Jun 1810
  Alfred, son of Jeremiah, bpt. 10 Sep 1809
  Anna Jenness, dau of Levi, bpt. 8 May 1803
  Benjamin, son of Nathaniel Jr., bpt. 4 Apr 1762
  Betsey, dau of Levi, bpt. 7 Oct 1798
  Betsey Garland, dau of Ebenezer, bpt. 15 Aug 1790
  Brackett, son of Samuel Brackett, bpt. 28 Oct 1798
  Brackett Monroe, son of Jeremiah, bpt. 30 Mar 1817
  Caleb, son of Zachariah, bpt. 9 Jan 1736/7
  Charlotte, dau of Samuel B., bpt. 26 Jan 1806
  Ebenezer, son of Merrifield, bpt. 23 Mar 1766
  Ebenezer, son of Ebenezer, bpt. 11 Oct 1789
  Eli, son of Hannah, bpt. 22 Aug 1800 by his grandfather Jeremiah Berry
  Elizabeth, dau of Nathaniel Jr., bpt. 8 Aug 1756
  Elizabeth, dau of Samuel, bpt. 4 Mar 1764
  Elizabeth Marden, dau of Nathaniel, bpt. 7 Sep 1800
  Ellenor, dau of William, bpt. 20 May 1787
  Esther, dau of Nathaniel, bpt. 29 Nov 1746/7
  George, son of John, bpt. 28 Apr 1751
  George, son of Nathaniel Jr., bpt. 9 Jun 1765

RYE BAPTISMS

BERRY, Gilman Chase, son of Samuel B., bpt. 30 Mar 1817
Hannah, dau of Nehemiah, bpt. 28 Sep 1740
Hannah, dau of Jeremiah, bpt. 28 Jun 1747
Hannah, dau of Jeremiah, bpt. 22 Aug 1773
Hannah, dau of William Jr., bpt. Jun 1781
Hannah Locke, dau of Levi, bpt. 4 Sep 1791
Huldah, dau of Merrifield, bpt. Nov 1760
Huldah, dau of James, bpt. 29 May 1785
Ira, son of Jeremiah, bpt. 27 Aug 1811
Isaac, son of Jacob, bpt. Dec 1768
Isaac, son of Richard, bpt. 22 Dec 1804
James, son of James Towle, bpt. 22 Aug 1779
James Towle, son of Merrifield, bpt. 6 May 1759
James Towle, son of Hannah, bpt. 20 Jun 1816
Jeremiah, son of Jeremiah, bpt. 13 Apr 1755
Jeremiah, son of William, bpt. 30 May 1784
John, son of Zachariah, bpt. 3 May 1747
John, son of John, bpt. 4 Aug 1754
John, son of John Jr., bpt. Feb 1759
John, bpt. 5 Oct 1794
Joseph, son of Timothy, bpt. 21 Sep 1777
Joseph Hall, son of Nathaniel, bpt. 1 Sep 1811
Joseph Jenness, son of Levi, bpt. 11 Jul 1789
Joseph William, son of Joseph J., bpt. 29 Oct 1820
Joses, son of Jeremiah, bpt. 9 Oct 1757
Joses, son of Hannah, bpt. 22 Jul 1796
Josiah, son of Jeremiah, bpt. 16 Jun 1764
Jotham, son of Timothy, bpt. 24 Jul 1767
Jotham, son of Samuel, bpt. 5 Oct 1769
Judith, dau of Jotham, bpt. Jun 1745
Levi, son of Jeremiah, bpt. 4 Mar 1760
Lydia, dau of William Jr., bpt. 24 Sep 1775
Lydia, dau of Jeremiah, bpt. 1 Dec 1776
Louisa, dau of Joseph J., bpt. 10 Oct 1813
Lovey, dau of William, bpt. 26 Jul 1789
Mary, dau of Jeremiah, bpt. 24 Mar 1751
Mary, dau of Nathaniel Jr., bpt. 14 Apr 1754
Mary, dau of Timothy, bpt. 12 May 1765
Mehitable, dau of Timothy, bpt. 6 Sep 1772
Mehitable, dau of Timothy, bpt. 9 Sep 1775
Merrifield, child of Ebenezer, bpt. May 1747/8
Molly, dau of Samuel, bpt. 24 Nov 1765
Molly, dau of Samuel, bpt. 13 Sep 1767
Molly, dau of Levi, bpt. 21 May 1786
Molly, dau of Nathaniel, bpt. 22 Apr 1798
Molly, bpt. 5 Oct 1794
Nathaniel, son of Nehemiah, bpt. 1 Jun 1746

RYE BAPTISMS

BERRY, Nathaniel, son of John, bpt. 19 Feb 1758
  Nathaniel, son of Nathaniel Jr., bpt. 23 Apr 1758
  Nathaniel, son of Samuel, bpt. 13 Aug 1775
  Olly, dau of Merrifield, bpt. 25 Sep 1763
  Olly, dau of Levi, bpt. 16 Mar 1794
  Oliver, son of Samuel B., bpt. 11 Jul 1813
  Patience, dau of Jeremiah, bpt. 14 Feb 1762
  Patty, dau of William, bpt. 28 Oct 1792
  Rachel, dau of Jotham, bpt. 3 Jul 1743
  Richard, son of Jacob, bpt. 26 Apr 1772
  Robinson Foss, son of Jeremiah, bpt. 3 Jul 1814
  Sally, dau of Levi, bpt. 20 May 1787
  Sally, dau of Nathaniel Jr., bpt. 6 Jun 1802
  Samuel, son of Jotham, bpt. 20 Apr 1741
  Samuel, son of Nathaniel Jr., bpt. 4 May 1760
  Samuel, son of Timothy, bpt. Sep 1769
  Samuel, son of Nathaniel Jr., bpt. 16 Sep 1804
  Samuel Brackett, son of William Jr., bpt. 20 Apr 1777
  Samuel Chapman, son of Samuel B., bpt. 1807
  Samuel Foss, son of Nathaniel Jr., bpt. 29 Jun 1806
  Samuel Symes, son of John, bpt. 29 Jan 1749
  Sarah, dau of Zachariah, bpt. 30 Aug 1741
  Sarah, dau of Jeremiah, bpt. 20 Apr 1746
  Sarah, dau of Jeremiah, bpt. 16 Jul 1749
  Sarah, dau of John, bpt. 24 Dec 1752
  Sarah, dau of Timothy, bpt. 3 May 1761
  Sarah, dau of Jacob, bpt. 30 Nov 1777
  Sarah Ann, dau of Jeremiah, bpt. 23 Mar 1820
  Sarah March, dau of Nathaniel, bpt. 22 Apr 1810
  Sarah Wedgewood, dau of Joseph J., bpt. 29 Oct 1815
  Sarah Wentworth, dau of William, bpt. 2 Jan 1797
  Simeon, child of Ebenezer, bpt. May 1737/8
  Solomon, son of Jeremiah, bpt. 17 Nov 1765
  Stephen, son of Nathaniel Jr., bpt. 6 Nov 1749
  Susanna, child of Ebenezer, bpt. 1737/8
  Susanna, dau of Timothy, bpt. 10 Apr 1763
  Thedoria, dau of Zachariah, bpt. 10 Jun 1744
  Thomas, son of Jno, bpt. Mar 1756
  Thomas, son of Ebenezer, bpt. 11 Oct 1789
  Timothy, son of Samuel, bpt. 13 Mar 1773
  William, son of Jeremiah, bpt. 15 Apr 1753
  William, son of Nathaniel Jr., bpt. 9 Jun 1754
  William, son of Nathaniel Jr., bpt. 25 Dec 1763
  William, son of William, bpt. 26 Nov 1790
  William, son of Samuel B., bpt. 14 Jun 1801

RYE BAPTISMS

BERRY, William, son of Samuel B., bpt. 27 Nov 1803
BICKFORD, Joshua, son of Joseph, bpt. 21 Nov 1762
BLAKE, Elisha, son of John, bpt. 3 Jul 1743
   Hannah, dau of Elisha, bpt. 8 Nov 1770
   Hepsibah, dau of Samuel, bpt. 19 Jan 1746
   James, son of Samuel, bpt. Aug 1757
   John, son of John, bpt. 3 Nov 1745
   Mary, dau of Samuel, bpt. 20 Jul 1746
   Mary, dau of John, bpt. 13 Dec 1746/7
   Samuel, son of Samuel, bpt. 15 Sep 1751
   Sarah, dau of Samuel, bpt. 16 Oct 1748
   _____, dau of Elisha, bpt. 6 Dec 1767
BLUE, Jonathan, son of Edward, bpt. Jan 1755
   Samuel, son of Edward, bpt. 1 May 1757
BOND, Mary, dau of John, bpt. 2 Sep 1753
BRACKETT, Love, dau of Widow Eleanor, bpt. Aug 1758
BRAGG, Edward Varrel, son of John, bpt. 30 Jul 1811
   Hannah, dau of John, bpt. 2 May 1802
   Henry, son of John, bpt. 30 Jul 1811
   Polly, dau of John, bpt. 22 Apr 1798
BROWN, Abigail, dau of Joseph Jr,., bpt. 26 Apr 1752
   Abigail, dau of Joseph Jr., bpt. 11 Mar 1758
   Abigail, dau of Richard, bpt. 20 Oct 1776
   Alexander, son of John, bpt. 4 May 1760
   Anna, dau of Richard, bpt. 26 Jun 1774
   Catherine, dau of _____ & Catherine, bpt. 30 Oct 1763
   Daniel, son of John 3rd, bpt. 21 Dec 1804
   Data, dau of Jonathan, bpt. 1 Jun 1823
   Eliza, dau of Simon, bpt. 3 Mar 1805
   Eliza, dau of John 3rd, bpt. 21 Dec 1805
   Elizabeth, dau of Joseph Jr., bpt. 20 May 1750
   Emily, dau of Ira, bpt. 20 May 1821
   Hannah, dau of Jonathan, bpt. 6 Aug 1815
   Hannah Rundlet, dau of John Jr., bpt. 16 Sep 1821
   Henry, son of Simon, bpt. 25 Sep 1803
   Ira (twin), son of John Jr., bpt. 20 Jun 1811
   James, son of Joseph, bpt. 8 May 1763
   Job, son of Joseph Jr., bpt. Mar 1756
   Job Jenness, son of John, bpt. 28 Aug 1791
   John, son of John Jr., bpt. 17 Jan 1807
   John, son of John Jr., bpt. 19 Jun 1814
   John Henry, son of Simon, bpt. 7 Sep 1817
   Jonathan, son of Samuel, bpt. 20 Sep 1747
   Jonathan, son of Joseph, bpt. 3 Aug 1760

RYE BAPTISMS

BROWN, Jonathan, son of Jonathan, bpt. 15 Apr 1762
  Jonathan, son of Jonathan, bpt. 1807
  Joseph, son of Joseph Jr., bpt. 7 Apr 1754
  Joseph, son of Jonathan, bpt. 26 Aug 1804
  Langdon, son of Simon, bpt. 27 Aug 1815
  Martha, dau of Jonathan, bpt. 2 Dec 1819
  Martha Adaline, dau of Simon, bpt. 6 Oct 1822
  Mary, dau of Samuel, bpt. 27 Apr 1746
  Mary, dau of Jonathan, bpt. 25 Aug 1765
  Mary, dau of John 3rd, bpt. 25 Apr 1802
  Mary Esther, dau of Simon, bpt. 1807
  Mercy, dau of Richard, bpt. 23 Jan 1785
  Oliver (twin), son of John Jr., bpt. 20 Jun 1811
  Richard, son of Joseph, bpt. 17 Apr 1748
  Samuel, son of Joseph, bpt. 5 Oct 1766
  Sarah, dau of John of Newbury, bpt. 27 Oct 1770
  Sarah Ann, dau of Simon, bpt. 12 Nov 1809
  Sarah Ann, dau of Jonathan, bpt. 1 Jul 1810
  Sarah Hook, dau of Joseph, bpt. Jan 1779
  Simon, son of Simon, bpt. 5 Jul 1812
BUNKER, Lemuel James Hobbs, son of James L., bpt. 28 Dec 1825
  Mary Ann Elizabeth, dau of James L., bpt. 16 Jun 1822
  Sarah Balinda, dau of James L., bpt. 2 Jun 1828
BURNHAM, Orpa, bpt. 23 Jul 1809
CARROLL, Polly, dau of John, bpt. Sep 1802
  Richard, son of John A., bpt. 25 Nov 1795
CASWELL, John, son of Samuel, bpt. 27 Oct 1811
  Mary Elizabeth, dau of Samuel, bpt. 25 Jan 1814
  Richard Green, son of Samuel, bpt. 22 Oct 1809
  Samuel, son of Samuel, bpt. 23 Sep 1816
CATE (KATE), Francis, son of Daniel, bpt. 14 Oct 1792
CHAMBERLAIN, Lydia, dau of William, bpt. 25 Apr 1736/7
  Samuel, son of William, bpt. 14 Aug 1740
  William, son of William, bpt. 29 May 1743
CHAPMAN, Lubina, dau of John, bpt. 11 Mar 1750
  Phebe, dau of Jonathan, bpt. 12 Apr 1752
CLARK (CLARKE), Andrew, son of John, bpt. 4 Apr 1773
  Betsey, dau of Andrew, bpt. 3 Apr 1803
  Daniel, son of Andrew, bpt. 1807
  Emily, dau of Andrew, bpt. 21 Nov 1813
  Hannah, dau of Andrew, bpt. 24 Nov 1811
  Judith, dau of Samuel of Epping, bpt. 9 Jul 1769
  Mary Ann, dau of Andrew, bpt. 16 Oct 1808
  Molly, dau of John, bpt. 1 Jul 1770

RYE BAPTISMS

CLARK, Olly, dau of Samuel of Epping, bpt. 9 Jul 1769
  Susanna, dau of Thomas, bpt. 22 Jul 1764
  Thomas Remick, son of Andrew, bpt. 11 Aug 1799
  William, son of Thomas, bpt. 11 May 1766
CLERK, Jenny, dau of William, bpt. 22 Oct 1752
  John, son of Samuel, bpt. 23 Mar 1760
  Joseph, son of John, bpt. Jul 1768
CLIFFORD, Peter, son of _____, bpt. 23 Sep 1753
COLEMAN, Nathaniel, son of Nathaniel, bpt. 5 May 1799
  Robert Hodgkins, son of Nathaniel, bpt. 17 Sep 1797
  William Jenness, son of Mrs. Mary, bpt. 20 Aug 1804
CONNER, Benjamin, son of Joseph, bpt. 13 Sep 1746/7
  Samuel, son of Joseph, bpt. 24 May 1741
  Sarah, dau of Joseph, bpt. 10 Jun 1744
COTTON, Adam, son of Thomas, bpt. 30 Apr 1738
  Abigail, dau of Thomas, bpt. 28 Aug 1748
  Hannah, dau of Thomas, bpt. 24 Jul 1791
  Nathaniel, son of Thomas, bpt. 3 Aug 1740
DALTON, Abigail, dau of Michael, bpt. 16 Jun 1782
  Anna Leavitt, dau of Benjamin, bpt. 1 Nov 1818
  Daniel Philbrick, son of Michael, bpt. 10 Jul 1785
  Elizabeth, dau of Benjamin, bpt. 26 Jun 1814
  Mercy Philbrick, dau of Benjamin, bpt. 13 May 1810
  Molly, dau of Michael, bpt. 15 Jul 1792
  Moses, son of Benjamin, bpt. 1 Nov 1818
  _____, son of Michael, bpt. 12 Aug 1781
DAVIDSON (DAVISON), Abigail Taylor, dau of Josiah, bpt. 11 Jun 1797
  Billy, son of Josiah, bpt. 16 May 1801
  Benjamin Shaw, son of Josiah, bpt. 3 Dec 1815
  Elias, son of Josiah, bpt. 4 Jun 1809
  Elizabeth R., dau of Josiah, bpt. 27 Sep 1818
  John Brown, son of Josiah, bpt. 6 Oct 1811
  Josiah Martin, son of Josiah, bpt. 10 Feb 1799
  Nancy, dau of Josiah, bpt. 11 Nov 1804
  Newhall, son of Josiah, bpt. 5 Apr 1796
  Newhall, son of Josiah, bpt. 1807
  Patty Plummer, dau of Josiah, bpt. 14 Nov 1802
  Patty Plummer, dau of Josiah, bpt. 15 Aug 1813
DAVIS, Betsey, dau of Samuel, bpt. 1784
  Billy, son of Samuel, bpt. 2 Oct 1785
  David, son of John, bpt. 21 Oct 1759

RYE BAPTISMS

DAVIS, Ephraim, son of Ephraim, bpt. 8 Aug 1779
  Hannah, dau of Eunice, bpt. 1 May 1763
  Samuel, son of John, bpt. Oct 1761
  Samuel, son of Ephraim, bpt. 15 Dec 1776
  William, son of John, bpt. 22 May 1757
DEARBORN, Abigail, dau of Reuben, bpt. 15 Sep 1776
  Annah, dau of Reuben, bpt. 23 May 1774
  Anne, dau of Reuben, bpt. 14 Nov 1772
  Josiah, son of Reuben, bpt. 23 May 1774
  Mary Ann Adaline, dau of Levi, bpt. 21 Oct 1796
DOCKUM, Ephraim, son of _____, bpt. 30 Aug 1767
DOE, Molly, dau of Susanna, bpt. 21 Oct 1759
DOLBEAR (DOLBEE), Abigail, dau of Jonathan, bpt. 22 Jan 1757
  Billy, son of Nicholas, bpt. 13 Dec 1789
  Daniel, son of Israel, bpt. 10 Feb 1745
  Eli, son of John, bpt. 9 Sep 1744
  Hannah, dau of Israel, bpt. 23 May 1742
  Hannah, dau of Widow Dolbear, bpt. 30 Aug 1761
  Isabella, dau of John, bpt. 4 Mar 1750
  Israel, son of Israel, bpt. 20 Apr 1740
  Jesse, son of John, bpt. 11 Oct 1747
  John, son of Nicholas, bpt. 23 Aug 1778
  Jonathan, son of Jonathan, bpt. 12 Aug 1750
  Jonathan, son of Nicholas, bpt. 13 Mar 1774
  Judith, dau of John, bpt. 8 May 1743
  Molly, dau of Nicholas, bpt. 13 Aug 1786
  Nicholas, son of Jonathan, bpt. 15 May 1748
  Patty, dau of Nicholas, bpt. 15 Apr 1781
  Ruth, dau of Jonathan, bpt. 15 Dec 1745
  Sarah, dau of Israel, bpt. 6 Nov 1748
  Stephen, son of Jonathan, bpt. 15 Jul 1753
  _____, child of Nicholas, bpt. 1783
DOW, Albert, son of James Jr., bpt. 27 Jun 1819
  Amos, son of Isaac, bpt. 9 Jun 1781
  Betsey, dau of Isaac, bpt. 17 Jul 1791
  Daniel, son of Noah, bpt. 20 May 1764
  Eli Sawtell, son of James Jr., bpt. 29 Jun 1828
  Elizabeth Seavey, dau of James Jr., bpt. 19 Jul 1817
  Hannah, dau of Henry, bpt. 17 Dec 1752
  Henry, son of Isaac, bpt. 1783
  Isaac, son of Henry, bpt 15 Dec 1754
  Isaac, son of Isaac, bpt. 21 Sep 1788
  James, son of Isaac, bpt. 13 Nov 1785
  Jonathan, son of Noah, bpt. 21 Feb 1773
  Jonathan Drake, son of James Jr., bpt. 23 Jul 1815
  Martha, dau of Henry, bpt. 8 Oct 1758

RYE BAPTISMS

DOW, Martha Ann, dau of James Jr., bpt. 20 Dec 1823
  Mary, dau of Henry, bpt. 27 Dec 1761
  Nathan, son of Noah, bpt. 26 Jun 1768
  Patty, dau of Isaac, bpt. 23 May 1779
  Patty Locke, dau of James, bpt. 8 Sep 1799
  Sarah Angeline, dau of James Jr., bpt. 1 Jul 1821
  Simon, son of Noah, bpt. 12 Sep 1762
  Simon, son of Widow Patty S., bpt. 5 May 1816
DOWRST (DOWST), Eliza, dau of Ozem Jr., bpt. 13 Jun 1773
  Elizabeth, dau of Ozem, bpt. 12 Feb 1744
  John, son of Ozem Jr., bpt. 21 Aug 1763
  Jonathan, son of Ozem Jr., bpt. 10 Dec 1764
  Lydia, dau of Ozem, bpt. 9 Jun 1781
  Molly, dau of Ozem Jr., bpt. 3 Jun 1770
  Samuel, son of Ozem, bpt. 6 Nov 1749
  Sarah, dau of Ozem, bpt. 29 Nov 1767
  Sarah Morrill, dau of Jonathan, bpt. 4 Sep 1790
DRAKE, Amos Garland, son of Jonathan Jr., bpt. 22 Nov 1818
  Anna, dau of Abraham, bpt. 2 Aug 1812
  Cotton Ward, son of Jonathan Jr., bpt. 5 Jul 1801
  Eliza Ann, dau of Jonathan Jr., bpt. 17 Oct 1824
  John, son of Jonathan, bpt. 18 Mar 1804
  Joseph Jenness, son of Abraham, bpt. 22 Jun 1817
  Orren, son of Abraham, bpt. 1 Aug 1824
  Oliver, son of Jonathan Jr., bpt. 23 Jul 1820
  William Garland, son of Jonathan Jr., bpt. 22 Sep 1822
DRISCO, John, son of John, bpt. Sep 1756
  Robert, son of Thomas, bpt. 29 Sep 1754
EDMONDS, Edward, son of Edward, bpt. 17 Jun 1764
  Else, dau of Edward, bpt. 27 May 1770
  Erie, son of Jonathan, bpt. 15 Aug 1802
  Hannah, dau of Edward, bpt. 21 Jun 1746/7
  James (twin), son of Jonathan, bpt. 7 Aug 1808
  Jonathan, son of Edward, bpt. Oct 1756
  Mary, dau of Edward, bpt. 4 May 1760
  Mehitable, dau of Edward, bpt. 30 Jun 1751
  Nathaniel, son of Edward, bpt. 9 Oct 1768
  Polly Jenness, dau of Jonathan, bpt. 16 Jun 1805
  Samuel, son of Jonathan, bpt. 13 Apr 1818
  Sarah Rand, dau of Edward, bpt. 25 Aug 1754
  Susanna, dau of Edward of Hawke, bpt. 4 Oct 1772
  Thomas, son of Edward, bpt. 5 Mar 1749
  William, son of Edward, bpt. 3 Jul 1762

RYE BAPTISMS

EDMONDS, William (twin), son of Jonathan, bpt. 7 Aug 1808
ELKINS, Abigail, dau of Samuel, bpt. 25 Jun 1786
  David, son of James, bpt. 5 Sep 1813
  Henry, son of Samuel, bpt. 18 Jun 1775
  James, son of Samuel, bpt. 1 Jun 1777
  James Seavey, son of James, bpt. 5 Aug 1810
  Olly, dau of Samuel, bpt. Dec 1783
  Samuel, son of Samuel, bpt. 17 Jun 1779
  William, son of Samuel, bpt. 21 Jun 1789
FIELDS, Sarah Fogg, dau of Stephen, bpt. 22 May 1803
FITZGERALD, Molly, bpt. 21 Sep 1794
  Nancy, bpt. 21 Sep 1794
FOSS, Abigail, dau of George, bpt. 14 Oct 1750
  Abigail, dau of Wallis, bpt. 24 May 1752
  Abigail, dau of Mark, bpt. 5 Jul 1752
  Abigail, dau of Wallis, bpt. 30 Jan 1757
  Alexander, son of Job, bpt. 5 Apr 1822
  Almira Pitman, dau of Benjamin, bpt. 8 May 1825
  Anna Partridge, dau of John, bpt. 8 Oct 1797
  Benjamin, son of ____ Foss of Greenland, bpt. Mar 1756
  Benjamin Marden, son of William, bpt. 29 Jul 1794
  Betsey (twin), dau of John, bpt. 14 Jul 1793
  Betty, granddau of Nathaniel, bpt. 10 Apr 1774
  Comfort, dau of Job, bpt. 17 May 1772
  Dorothy, dau of Job, bpt. 19 Aug 1753
  Ebenezer, son of Job, bpt. 20 Sep 1767
  Eliza, bpt. 3 Apr 1785
  Eliza, dau of Eliza, bpt. 29 Sep 1793
  Elizabeth, dau of Wallis, bpt. 26 Jun 1748
  Elizabeth Parsons, dau of Solomon, bpt. 1 Jul 1810
  Elizabeth Wendall, dau of Job, bpt. 27 Aug 1811
  Esther Yeaton, dau of Solomon, bpt. 10 Jul 1808
  George, son of Mark, bpt 27 Jul 1755
  Hannah, dau of Job, bpt 17 Aug 1755
  Hannah, dau of Samuel Dowrst, bpt. 15 Jul 1779
  Hannah, dau of Ebenezer, bpt. 3 Jun 1792
  Isaac Remick, son of Solomon, bpt. 16 Mar 1804
  James Seavey, son of Samuel Dowrst, bpt. 22 Jun 1788
  Jane, dau of Nathaniel, bpt. 9 Dec 1753
  Janny, dau of Nathaniel Jr., bpt. 18 Nov 1792
  Jeremiah, son of Job, bpt. 5 Apr 1822
  Jeremiah Berry, son of Samuel Dowrst, bpt. 23 Jul 1780

RYE BAPTISMS

FOSS, Job, son of Nathaniel, bpt. 13 May 1759
  Job, son of Job, bpt. 8 Jul 1759
  Job, son of John, bpt. 23 Jul 1786
  Joel, son of Benjamin, bpt. 5 May 1822
  John, son of Wallis, bpt. 13 Jul 1746
  John, son of Job, bpt. Jun 1757
  John Henry, son of Richard, bpt. 5 Sep 1825
  Joseph Remick, son of Solomon, bpt. 24 Aug 1800
  Joshua, son of Job, bpt. 30 Aug 1761
  Joshua, son of William, bpt. 3 Oct 1790
  Joshua, son of Benjamin, bpt. 28 Dec 1816
  Katherine Babb, dau of Solomon, bpt. 13 Oct 1805
  Margora Teatherly, dau of Solomon, bpt. 4 Jul 1802
  Mark, son of Mark, bpt. 29 Oct 1749
  Martha Wentworth, dau of Solomon, bpt. 20 Aug 1815
  Mary, dau of Nathaniel, bpt. Feb 1745
  Mary, dau of Wallis, bpt. 12 Apr 1761
  Mary, dau of Job, bpt. 11 Feb 1764
  Mary Elizabeth, dau of Benjamin, bpt. 5 May 1822
  Molly, bpt. 3 Apr 1785
  Molly, dau of Samuel Dowrst, bpt. 10 Jul 1785
  Nathaniel, son of Mark, bpt. 22 Feb 1747
  Nathaniel, son of Nathaniel, bpt. 13 Jun 1756
  Nathaniel, son of Nathaniel Jr., bpt. 11 Dec 1796
  Oliver, son of Job, bpt. 5 Apr 1822
  Olly (twin), dau of John, bpt. 14 Jul 1793
  Olly, dau of Job, bpt. 30 Sep 1810
  Olly Rand, dau of Nathaniel, bpt. 5 Sep 1751
  Phinehas, son of Wallis, bpt. 16 Sep 1759
  Polly, dau of Samuel Dowrst, bpt. 22 Jun 1783
  Polly, dau of Nathaniel, bpt. 27 Mar 1791
  Rachel, dau of Wallis, bpt. 10 Jun 1750
  Rachel, dau of William, bpt. 6 Dec 1795
  Robert Shapleigh, son of Richard, bpt. 14 Sep 1825
  Robinson, son of John, bpt. 23 Nov 1788
  Sally, dau of William, bpt. 5 Feb 1792
  Sally, dau of Benjamin, bpt. 23 Aug 1818
  Samuel, son of Wallis, bpt. 28 Oct 1739
  Samuel, son of Nathaniel, bpt. 3 Jul 1762
  Samuel, son of Samuel Dowrst, bpt. 31 Aug 1777
  Samuel, son of Samuel, bpt. 22 Dec 1799
  Samuel Dowst, son of Wallis, bpt. 4 Aug 1754
  Samuel Wallis, son of Solomon, bpt. 27 Sep 1818
  Sarah, dau of Nathaniel, bpt. 20 Feb 1746/7
  Sarah, dau of Job, bpt. 4 Aug 1751

RYE BAPTISMS

FOSS, Sarah, dau of Samuel Dowrst, bpt. 3 Jul 1791
  Sarah, dau of Job, bpt. 5 Apr 1822
  Wallis, son of Wallis, bpt. 22 Sep 1765
  Wallis, son of Samuel Dowrst, bpt. 24 Sep 1775
  William, son of Nathaniel, bpt. 17 Apr 1748
  William, bpt. 3 Apr 1785
  William, son of Ebenezer, bpt. 17 Oct 1790
  William, son of Benjamin, bpt. 11 Jun 1815
FOYE, Aaron Seavey, son of William, bpt. 21 Apr 1817
  Anna Trefethern, dau of John, bpt. 3 Oct 1802
  Appia Little, dau of William, bpt. 22 Sep 1808
  Eliza, dau of John Jr., bpt. 9 Oct 1796
  Eliza Ann, dau of William, bpt. 18 Nov 1813
  Hannah Seavey, dau of William, bpt. 24 Nov 1805
  Joseph Stevens, son of William, bpt. 21 Apr 1817
  Lydia Stevens, dau of William, bpt. 19 Jun 1796
  Nathaniel Grow, son of John, bpt. 5 May 1799
  Stephen, son of William, bpt. 5 May 1799
  Thomas Fernald, son of William, bpt. Nov 1796
  William Little, son of William, bpt. 8 Nov 1801
FROST, Aaron, son of Aaron, bpt. 4 Aug 1771
FULLER, Christopher, son of Jeremiah, bpt. 15 Oct 1752
  David, son of Joseph, bpt. 10 Sep 1749
  David, son of Joseph, bpt. 7 Jul 1751
  Deborah, dau of Jeremiah, bpt. Mar 1756
  Elizabeth, dau of Joseph, bpt. 28 Sep 1740
  George, son of Jeremiah, bpt. 1 Jun 1746
  Hannah, dau of Joseph, bpt. 13 Jan 1745
  James, son of Joseph, bpt. 17 Apr 1743
  Jane, dau of Jeremiah, bpt. Nov 1757
  Jeremiah Scadgel, son of Jeremiah, bpt. 4 Mar 1760
  Margaret, dau of Jeremiah, bpt. 17 Mar 1751
  Mary, dau of Jeremiah, bpt. 14 Jul 1754
  Olly, dau of Joseph, bpt 30 Nov 1755
  Rachel, dau of Joseph, bpt. 25 Jan 1747
  Richard, son of Jeremiah, bpt. 30 Aug 1747
  Sarah, dau of Jeremiah, bpt. 10 Sep 1749
  Sarah, dau of Joseph, bpt. 12 May 1753
  Theodore Atkinson, son of Jeremiah, bpt. 2 May 1762
GARLAND, Abigail, dau of Peter, bpt. 27 Apr 1760
  Abigail, dau of Benjamin, bpt. 6 Mar 1763
  Abigail, dau of John 3rd, bpt. 5 Aug 1810
  Amos, son of Benjamin, bpt. 17 Jul 1768
  Amos Seavey, son of John Jr., bpt. 23 May 1791
  Anne, dau of Peter, bpt. 27 Jan 1771

RYE BAPTISMS

GARLAND, Benjamin, son of Benjamin, bpt. 22 Mar 1767
  Benjamin, son of Peter, bpt. 14 Nov 1772
  Benjamin, son of John, bpt. 6 Nov 1791
  Betty, dau of Joseph, bpt. 2 Dec 1787
  Betty Brown, dau of John, bpt. 6 Nov 1791
  Caroline Goodwin, dau of Amos, bpt. 24 Nov 1816
  Charlotte, dau of Benjamin Jr., bpt. 11 Dec 1803
  Data, dau of Benjamin, bpt. 16 Jul 1809
  Eliza, dau of Jonathan, bpt. 29 Aug 1807
  Elizabeth, dau of John, bpt. 3 Apr 1748
  Elizabeth, dau of Benjamin, bpt. 12 Oct 1760
  Elizabeth, dau of Simon, bpt. 6 Nov 1763
  Elizabeth, dau of Peter, bpt. Feb 1776
  Elizabeth Jenness, dau of Amos, bpt. 25 Oct 1801
  Emily, dau of Jonathan, bpt. 4 Jun 1809
  Gilman, son of Jonathan, bpt. 26 Sep 1802
  Hannah Perkins, dau of John 4th, bpt. 24 Oct 1802
  Harriet, dau of Jonathan, bpt. 25 Aug 1799
  Hitty, dau of Joseph, bpt. 14 Aug 1791
  Hitty Godfrey, dau of Joseph, bpt. 20 Jul 1794
  James, son of John, bpt. 13 Aug 1786
  John, son of John Jr., bpt. 30 Mar 1746
  John, son of Benjamin, bpt. 8 Oct 1758
  John, son of Peter, bpt. 2 May 1762
  John, son of Simon, bpt. 21 Jun 1767
  John, son of Joseph, bpt. 21 Aug 1785
  John Sanborn, son of Levi, bpt. 3 Apr 1796
  Jonathan, son of Peter, bpt. 14 Oct 1764
  Joseph, son of Simon, bpt. 11 May 1760
  Joseph, son of Joseph, bpt. 11 Aug 1805
  Joseph Parsons, son of John 4th, bpt. 30 Jun 1805
  Levi, son of Peter, bpt. 16 Nov 1766
  Levi, son of Levi, bpt. 4 Aug 1793
  Lucinda Rukesbury, dau of Amos S., bpt. 1 Nov 1818
  Mary, dau of John, bpt. 22 Jul 1744
  Mary, dau of Simon, bpt. Mar 1756
  Mary, dau of Benjamin, bpt. 22 Apr 1770
  Mary, dau of Benjamin 3rd, bpt. 30 Aug 1818
  Mary Ann, dau of John 4th, bpt. 21 Sep 1800
  Mary Leavitt, dau of Peter Jr., bpt. 29 Jun 1800
  Moses Leavitt, son of Peter Jr., bpt. 24 Mar 1801
  Nabby, dau of John, bpt. 1783
  Olive Shapleigh, dau of Amos, bpt. 13 Jul 1806
  Oliver, son of John 3rd, bpt. 1807

RYE BAPTISMS

GARLAND, Peter, son of Peter, bpt. 30 Oct 1768
  Reuel, son of John, bpt. 24 Feb 1799
  Sally, dau of Peter, bpt. 21 Feb 1779
  Sally, dau of Peter Jr., bpt. 10 Jun 1798
  Samuel Patten, son of Amos S., bpt. 31 Jul 1821
  Sarah, dau of Benjamin, bpt. 28 Oct 1764
  Sarah, dau of Benjamin, bpt. 19 Jul 1772
  Sarah Ann, dau of Amos, bpt. Oct 1812
  Sarah Ann, dau of Amos, bpt. 16 Jun 1815
  Simon, son of Simon, bpt. Jul 1758
  Simon (twin), son of John, bpt. 9 Mar 1794
  Thomas, son of Benjamin, bpt. 21 Sep 1777
  Thomas, son of Benjamin, bpt. 1 Oct 1820
  Thomas Leavitt, son of Peter Jr., bpt. 16 Jun 1793
  William, son of Benjamin, bpt. 25 Jun 1775
  William, son of Peter, bpt. 18 Oct 1795
  William Cutter, son of Jonathan, bpt. 17 Jun 1810
  William Seavey (twin), son of John, bpt. 9 Mar 1794
GODFREY, Abigail, dau of John, bpt. 16 Jul 1809
  Anna Brown, dau of John, bpt. 28 ___ 1806
  Joseph, son of John, bpt. 29 Sep 1802
  Susanna, dau of John Jr., bpt. 27 Nov 1803
GOSS, Andrua, son of Joseph, bpt. 27 Oct 1799
  Betsey, dau of Levi, bpt. 1 Jul 1798
  Daniel, son of Levi, bpt. 27 Nov 1803
  Daniel, son of John, bpt. 11 Aug 1798
  Dorcas Pitman, dau of Levi, bpt. 27 Nov 1803
  Elizabeth, dau of Jonathan, bpt. 23 Jul 1749
  Elizabeth, dau of Thomas, bpt. 10 Dec 1752
  Elizabeth, dau of Joseph, bpt. 14 Sep 1794
  Esther, dau of Jethro, bpt. 19 Jul 1741
  Hannah, dau of Thomas, bpt. Mar 1740
  James, son of Thomas, bpt. 8 Sep 1745
  James, son of Michael D., bpt. 16 Jun 1805
  James Madison, son of Michael D., bpt. 4 Dec 1809
  Jethro, son of Levi, bpt. 2 May 1773
  John, son of Levi, bpt. 2 Sep 1770
  John Sheridan, son of Thomas, bpt. 7 Dec 1817
  Jonathan, son of Jonathan, bpt. 17 Jul 1743
  Jonathan, son of Jonathan Jr., bpt. 24 Nov 1771
  Jonathan, son of Joseph, bpt. 5 Aug 1792
  Joseph, son of Jonathan, bpt. 21 Jan 1746
  Joseph, son of Jonathan Jr., bpt. 5 Nov 1769
  Joseph, son of John, bpt. 18 Oct 1795
  Joses, son of Esther, bpt. 4 Jul 1779

RYE BAPTISMS

GOSS, Joshua, son of Levi, bpt. Nov 1775
  Joshua, son of Levi, bpt. 23 Dec 1792
  Joshua, son of John, bpt. 18 Oct 1795
  Levi, son of Jethro, bpt. 11 Jan 1747
  Levi, son of Levi, bpt. 22 Apr 1770
  Mary, dau of Thomas, bpt. 24 Jul 1743
  Molly, dau of Nathan, bpt. 27 Aug 1775
  Nancy, dau of Levi, bpt. 5 Jan 1800
  Nathan, son of Thomas, bpt. 27 Sep 1741
  Richard, son of Jonathan, bpt. Nov 1738
  Richard, son of Thomas, bpt. 26 Aug 1750
  Richard, son of Jethro, bpt. 23 Jun 1751
  Richard, son of Nathan, bpt. Nov 1777
  Sally, dau of Nathan, bpt. 27 Aug 1775
  Sally, dau of Esther, bpt. 4 Jul 1779
  Sally, dau of Levi of Gilmanton, bpt. 9 Jan 1808
  Sally Blake, dau of Jonathan, bpt. 26 Aug 1798
  Salome, dau of Jonathan, bpt. 22 Feb 1741
  Samuel Rand, son of Levi of Gilmanton, bpt. 2 Feb 1806
  Sarah Ann, dau of Thomas Jr., bpt. May 1815
  Sarah Rand, dau of Jethro, bpt. 11 Jun 1797
  Sheridan, son of Thomas, bpt. 29 Oct 1809
  Simon, son of Nathan, bpt. 9 Aug 1771
  Susanna, dau of Jethro, bpt. 23 Sep 1744
  Thomas, son of Thomas, bpt. 13 Dec 1747
  Tobias Trundy, son of Michael D., bpt. 14 Jun 1801
  William, son of Thomas, bpt. 28 Aug 1803
  William Seavey, son of Joseph, bpt. 21 Oct 1805
GRANT, Dorothy Foss, bpt. 23 Jul 1809
GREEN, Ann Treadwell, dau of Stephen, bpt. 21 May 1809
  Charles, son of Richard, bpt. 7 Mar 1795
  Dorcas Marden, dau of Richard, bpt. 21 Apr 1793
  Elizabeth, dau of Stephen, bpt. 3 Sep 1826
  Ephraim, son of Mary, bpt. 10 Jun 1787
  John, son of Mary, bpt. 14 May 1786
  Joseph, son of Richard, bpt. 6 Aug 1798
  Mary Izette, dau of Stephen, bpt. 29 Jun 1823
  Molly, dau of Richard, bpt. 17 Jul 1791
  Richard, son of Mary, bpt. 14 May 1786
  Samuel Marden, son of Richard, bpt. 11 Aug 1799
  Silas, son of Stephen, bpt. 6 Jul 1817
GROW, Thomas Foy, son of Widow Grow, bpt. 13 Jan 1788
HALE, Benjamin, son of Benjamin, bpt. Mar 1741
HALL, Edward, son of Joseph, bpt. 19 Aug 1764
  Elizabeth, dau of Joseph, bpt. 9 Aug 1761

RYE BAPTISMS

HALL, Ephraim Rand, bpt. 9 Sep 1818
  Esther, dau of Joseph, bpt. 7 Oct 1781
  Joseph, son of Joseph, bpt. Jun 1754
  Joseph, son of Joseph, bpt. 30 Nov 1755
  Joseph, son of Widow Mary, bpt. 29 Jun 1806
  Mary Tucker, dau of Joseph, bpt. 6 Nov 1752
  Sarah, dau of Joseph, bpt. 16 Sep 1759
  Sarah Ann, dau of Ephraim, bpt. 13 Oct 1822
  William, son of Ephraim R., bpt. 27 Sep 1818
  William Tucker, son of Joseph, bpt. Nov 1757
HOBBS, Anne, dau of James, bpt. 26 Jul 1789
  Elizabeth Jenness, dau of Jonathan, bpt. 10 Sep 1780
  Jonathan, son of James, bpt. 22 Nov 1778
  Molly, dau of Jonathan (James is written beneath Jonathan's name), bpt. 10 Nov 1776
  Lucy, dau of James, bpt. Feb 1775
  Lucy, dau of James, bpt. Oct 1782
  Nathaniel, son of James, bpt. 13 Aug 1786
  Perna Judkins, dau of James, bpt. 17 Nov 1799
  Sally, dau of James, bpt. 12 May 1793
HOLMES, Anne, dau of Ephraim, bpt. 21 Sep 1746
  Elizabeth, dau of Ephraim, bpt. 10 Oct 1742
  Jacob, son of Widow Polly, bpt. 7 Sep 1800
  Joshua, son of Joseph, bpt. 28 Oct 1739
  Keziah, dau of Ephraim, bpt. 17 Mar 1736/7
  Phebe, dau of Ephraim, bpt. 28 Oct 1753
  Samuel, son of Ephraim, bpt. 11 Sep 1748
  Sarah, dau of Ephraim, bpt. 13 Jan 1745
  Tryphene, dau of Ephraim, bpt. 21 Oct 1750
HUNT, Elizabeth, dau of Zebedee, bpt. 10 Apr 1763
  Samuel, son of Zebedee, bpt. 2 Mar 1760
HUTCHINS, John, son of Samuel, bpt. 12 Mar 1769
HUTCHINSON, Samuel, son of Samuel, bpt. 17 May 1772
JENNESS, Abigail, dau of Francis, bpt. 3 May 1761
  Abigail, dau of Samuel, bpt. 9 Jul 1769
  Abigail, dau of Simon, bpt. 13 Nov 1785
  Abigail, dau of John Jr., bpt. 22 Aug 1779
  Abigail, dau of Peter, bpt. 3 Jul 1791
  Abigail Coffin, dau of Benjamin, bpt. 19 Feb 1797
  Abigail Locke, dau of Jonathan, bpt. 19 Jul 1801
  Adaline Shapleigh, dau of Simon, bpt. 17 Jun 1821
  Alexander Shapley, son of Simon, bpt. 17 May 1778
  Amos Coffin, son of Richard Jr., bpt. 14 Nov 1790

RYE BAPTISMS

JENNESS, Amos Seavey, son of Benjamin, bpt. 11 Oct 1801
  Anna, dau of Richard tert., bpt. Nov 1759
  Anna, dau of Francis, bpt. 30 Sep 1764
  Anna, dau of Richard of Deerfield, bpt. 23 Aug 1772
  Anna, dau of Simon, bpt. 5 Oct 1780
  Anna, dau of Joseph Jr., bpt. 21 Nov 1802
  Anna Yeaton, dau of Joseph Jr., bpt. 31 Jul 1814
  Benjamin, son of Richard tert., bpt. 19 Jun 1763
  Benjamin, son of Benjamin, bpt. 12 May 1765
  Benjamin, son of Joseph Jr., bpt. 24 Nov 1793
  Benjamin Garland, son of Jonathan, bpt. 12 Oct 1788
  Betsey, dau of Simon, bpt. Sep 1783
  Betsey, dau of Noah, bpt. 31 Aug 1794
  Betty, dau of Nathaniel, bpt. 23 Mar 1777
  Clarissa, dau of Nathaniel Jr., bpt. 16 May 1801
  Clarissa, dau of David, bpt. 30 Jun 1822
  Data, dau of Francis, bpt. 1 Jul 1781
  David Alexander, son of Simon Jr., bpt. 28 May 1815
  Deliverance, dau of Joshua, bpt. 10 May 1741
  Edwin, son of Benjamin Jr., bpt. 8 Nov 1818
  Elizabeth, dau of John, bpt. Aug 1736/7
  Elizabeth, dau of Francis, bpt. 27 Sep 1741
  Elizabeth, dau of Joshua, bpt. 13 May 1744
  Elizabeth, dau of Richard tert., bpt. 14 Oct 1753
  Elizabeth, dau of Samuel, bpt. 3 May 1761
  Elizabeth, dau of Joseph, bpt. 13 May 1821
  Elizabeth Mary, dau of Samuel, bpt. 29 Sep 1816
  Emily, dau of Jonathan, bpt. 26 Mar 1807
  Fanny, dau of Thomas, bpt. 14 Dec 1800
  Francis, son of Francis, bpt. 4 Mar 1753
  Francis, son of Isaac, bpt. 30 Oct 1774
  Francis, son of Francis, bpt. 18 Mar 1791
  Hall, son of Francis, bpt. 6 Sep 1788
  Hannah, dau of Joshua, bpt. 22 May 1736/7
  Hannah, dau of Nathaniel, bpt. Feb 1757
  Hannah, dau of Nathaniel, bpt. 29 Apr 1765
  Hannah, dau of John, bpt. Jul 1780
  Henry, son of Isaac, bpt. 18 Jun 1786
  Hezekiah, son of Joshua, bpt. 16 Jul 1749
  Isaac, son of Francis, bpt. 6 Jan 1745
  Isaac, son of Joseph, bpt. 26 May 1754
  Isaac, son of Joseph, bpt Oct 1755
  Isaac, son of Henry, bpt. 10 Jul 1814
  James, son of Thomas, bpt. 21 ____ 1806

RYE BAPTISMS

JENNESS, James Perkins, son of Samuel, bpt. 22 Nov 1818
Jeremiah, son of Samuel Jr., bpt. 9 Jun 1776
Joanna, dau of Benjamin, bpt. 12 May 1765
John, son of Francis, bpt. 20 Jan 1751
John, son of Nathaniel, bpt. 26 Apr 1752
John, son of Benjamin, bpt. 6 Mar 1763
John, son of Samuel, bpt. 10 Apr 1763
John, son of John B., bpt. 11 Jul 1790
John, son of John, bpt. 12 May 1793
Jonathan, son of Francis, bpt. 6 Feb 1743
Jonathan, son of Joseph, bpt. 27 Jul 1760
Jonathan, son of Richard, bpt. 11 Oct 1761
Jonathan, son of Jonathan, bpt. 1 May 1791
Jonathan, son of Nathaniel Jr., bpt. 25 Aug 1793
Jonathan, son of Thomas, bpt. 6 Jun 1802
Joseph, son of Joseph, bpt. 26 Feb 1771
Joseph, son of Isaac, bpt. 4 Oct 1772
Joseph, son of Richard, bpt. 18 Jun 1786
Joseph, son of Isaac, bpt. 19 Sep 1790
Joseph, son of Jonathan, bpt. 26 Jun 1796
Joseph, son of Joseph, bpt. 25 Feb 1815
Joseph Disco, son of Joseph, bpt. 8 Aug 1819
Joseph Tarlton, son of Nathaniel, bpt. 15 Jan 1772
Joseph Tarlton, son of Thomas, bpt. 10 Jun 1804
Joses, son of John, bpt. 18 Nov 1781
Joses, son of Noah, bpt. 11 Nov 1787
Josiah, son of Levi, bpt. 24 Sep 1797
Josiah Dearborn, son of Benjamin, bpt. 9 Mar 1817
Levi, son of Richard tert., bpt. Mar 1756
Levi, son of Samuel, bpt. 22 May 1757
Levi, son of Levi, bpt. 16 Jan 1791
Levi, son of Samuel, bpt. 24 Jul 1814
Mary, dau of John Jr., bpt. 6 Jul 1740
Mary, dau of Francis, bpt. 8 Mar 1747
Mary, dau of Joshua, bpt. 29 Mar 1747
Mary, dau of Samuel, bpt. 6 Nov 1749
Mary, dau of Nathaniel, bpt. Nov 1750
Mary, dau of Joseph, bpt. 19 Jan 1752
Mary, dau of Samuel, bpt. Feb 1759
Mary, dau of Isaac Jr., bpt. 16 Jul 1780
Mary, dau of Noah Jr., bpt. 10 Oct 1802
Mary Ann, dau of Henry, bpt. 22 Jun 1823
Mary Ann Elizabeth, dau of David, bpt. 9 Nov 1817
Mercy, dau of Isaac, bpt. 12 Aug 1787
Molly, dau of Isaac, bpt. 8 Jun 1777

RYE BAPTISMS

JENNESS, Molly, dau of Jonathan, bpt. 25 Jun 1786
Molly, dau of Nathaniel, bpt. 9 Aug 1778
Molly, dau of Peter, bpt. 12 Aug 1787
Molly, dau of Joseph Jr., bpt. 24 Nov 1793
Nabby, dau of John, bpt. 23 Jul 1786
Nancy, dau of Francis, bpt. 18 Nov 1781
Nancy, dau of Nathaniel Jr., bpt. 28 Jun 1795
Nathaniel, son of Nathaniel, bpt. 11 Oct 1760
Nathaniel Gilbert, son of Samuel Jr., bpt. 15 Jun 1823
Noah, son of Nathaniel, bpt 13 Apr 1755
Olive, dau of Simon, bpt. 2 Jun 1776
Oliver Peter, son of Samuel Jr., bpt. 17 Jun 1821
Olly, dau of Jno., bpt. 21 Jun 1778
Olly, dau of John B., bpt. 28 Jun 1795
Patty Wallis, dau of Levi, bpt. 25 Oct 1795
Peter, son of Samuel, bpt. 11 Jan 1756
Peter Mitchell, son of John, bpt. 7 Dec 1788
Peter Oliver, son of Jonathan Jr., bpt. 28 May 1815
Polly, dau of Thomas of Deerfield, bpt. 23 Jul 1775
Polly, dau of Francis, bpt. 1 Feb 1787
Polly, dau of Nathaniel, bpt. 26 Jul 1789
Polly Seavey, dau of Benjamin, bpt. 24 Oct 1790
Reuben Philbrick, son of Joseph Jr., bpt. 2 Jun 1805
Reuben Philbrick, son of Joseph Jr., bpt. 4 Jul 1808
Richard, son of Richard tert., bpt. 30 Nov 1746
Richard, son of Joseph, bpt. Jan 1758
Richard, son of Nathaniel, bpt. 18 Jun 1775
Richard, son of Nathaniel, bpt. 16 Jul 1780
Richard, son of John B., bpt. 11 Nov 1787
Sally, dau of Isaac, bpt. 19 Sep 1779
Sally, dau of Francis Jr., bpt. Jun 1783
Samuel, son of Samuel, bpt. 29 Oct 1752
Samuel, son of Levi, bpt. 9 Sep 1787
Samuel, son of Peter, bpt. 14 Sep 1794
Sarah, dau of John, bpt. Aug 1736/7
Sarah, dau of Francis, bpt. 9 Apr 1749
Sarah, dau of Joseph, bpt. 13 May 1764
Sarah, dau of John, bpt. 20 Jul 1777
Sarah, dau of Levi, bpt. 28 Jul 1793
Sarah Taylor, dau of Joseph Jr., bpt. 7 Aug 1796
Sheridan, son of Joseph, bpt. 29 Sep 1824
Simon, son of Richard tert., bpt. 12 May 1751
Simon, son of Noah, bpt. 3 Sep 1786

RYE BAPTISMS

JENNESS, Simon, son of Simon, bpt. 15 Mar 1787
  Simon, son of Simon, bpt. 18 Nov 1792
  Simon Lamprey, son of Henry, bpt. 21 Jun 1818
  Thomas, son of Richard, bpt. 27 Nov 1748
  Thomas, son of Richard of Deerfield, bpt. 7 Jun 1772
  Thomas, son of Nathaniel, bpt. 30 Jan 1774
  Warren, son of Samuel, bpt. 26 May 1811
  William, son of John Jr., bpt. 17 Sep 1780
  Yeaton, son of Benjamin Jr., bpt. 3 Dec 1820
JOHNSON, Edmond, bpt. 9 Oct 1791
  Edmond, son of Edmond, bpt. 18 Sep 1796
  John Batchelder, son of Peter Jr., bpt. 5 ___ 1806
  John Greenleaf, son of Edmond, bpt. 4 Jul 1802
  Polly, dau of Edmond, bpt. 30 Jan 1791
  Sally, bpt. 9 Oct 1791
  Sally, dau of Peter Jr., bpt. 26 Aug 1804
  Simon, son of Edmond, bpt. 14 Jul 1793
JONES, Abiah, dau of John, bpt. 27 May 1753
  Anne, dau of John, bpt. 22 Nov 1741
  John, son of John, bpt. 22 Oct 1752
  John, son of William, bpt. 4 Aug 1807
  Joseph, son of William, bpt. 20 Jun 1811
  Mary, dau of John, bpt. 17 Jan 1741
  Mary, dau of John, bpt. 30 May 1756
  Olly, dau of John, bpt. 1 Mar 1747
  Olly, dau of John, bpt. 22 Oct 1752
  Samuel, son of _____, bpt. 4 Sep 1748
JORDAN, Hepsibah, dau of Ithamar, bpt. 12 Aug 1750
  Jeremiah, son of Stilman, bpt. Feb 1753
  Sarah, dau. of Stilman, bpt. 15 Jun 1746
  Stilman, son of Stilman, bpt. 9 Oct 1748
KINGMAN, John, son of William, bpt. 22 May 1748
  Olive, dau of William, bpt. 8 Jul 1753
KNOWLES, Amos, son of Amos, bpt. Feb 1756
  Anne Brackett, dau of Samuel Jr., bpt. Dec 1773
  Comfort, dau of James, bpt. 26 Mar 1749
  Daniel, son of James, bpt. 30 Nov 1746
  David, son of David, bpt. 25 Aug 1751
  David, son of Amos, bpt. 3 Jun 1764
  Deliverance, dau of Joseph, bpt. 27 Oct 1751
  Deliverance, dau of Samuel, bpt. 19 Nov 1775
  Elizabeth, dau of Amos, bpt. Feb 1756
  Elizabeth, dau of Amos, bpt. 29 Nov 1761
  Ezekiel, son of Amos, bpt. 26 Feb 1749
  Ezekiel, son of Nathan, bpt. 4 Jan 1778
  Hannah, dau of Nathan, bpt. 15 Sep 1782
  Hannah, dau of Nathan Jr., bpt. 20 Nov 1808

RYE BAPTISMS

KNOWLES, Isaac, son of Amos, bpt. 17 Feb 1751
  John, son of John Jr., bpt. 27 Mar 1743
  John, son of Amos, bpt. 13 May 1759
  John, son of Joseph, bpt. Apr 1760
  John Clifford, son of Nathan, bpt. 23 Oct 1768
  John Langdon, son of Nathan Jr., bpt. 23 Jun 1805
  Joseph, son of Joseph, bpt., bpt. Jun 1758
  Love, dau of Joseph, bpt. Sep 1754
  Lydia, dau of Amos, bpt. 22 Feb 1747
  Mary, dau of James, bpt. 26 Mar 1749
  Nathan, son of Amos, bpt. 25 Aug 1745
  Nathan, son of Nathan, bpt. 10 Sep 1775
  Patty Brown, dau of Nathan, bpt. 5 Jul 1801
  Rachel Hobbs, dau of Joseph, bpt. 11 Jan 1756
  Samuel, son of Joseph, bpt. 29 Oct 1749
  Samuel, son of Samuel Jr., bpt. 24 Jul 1774
  Sarah, dau of John Jr., bpt. 27 Sep 1741
  Sarah, dau of Samuel, bpt. 21 Sep 1777
  Sarah Langdon, dau of Nathan Jr., bpt. 1807
  Seth, son of Amos, bpt. 13 Apr 1766
  Simon, son of Joseph, bpt. 10 Jul 1748
  Tryphene, dau of John Jr., bpt. 28 Jul 1745
LAMPREY, Betsey Brewster, dau of Simon Jr., bpt. 28 Oct 1792
  Charlotte, dau of Simon, bpt. 16 Mar 1794
LANE, David, son of John, bpt. Mar 1741
  Hannah, dau of John, bpt. 3 Mar 1745
  Mary, dau of John, bpt. 6 Mar 1743
  Nathan, son of John, bpt. 21 Jun 1747
LANG, Aaron, son of Mark, bpt. 10 Oct 1802
  Almira, dau of Richard, bpt. 4 Jul 1813
  Anna, dau of Thomas, bpt. Oct 1767
  Anna V., dau of Mark, bpt. 28 Dec 1794
  Anne, dau of Mark, bpt. 3 Apr 1763
  Benjamin, son of Benjamin, bpt. 4 Aug 1765
  Betty, dau of Benjamin, bpt. 1 Sep 1771
  Bickford, son of Bickford, bpt. 13 Nov 1774
  Billy, son of Bickford Jr., bpt. 20 Aug 1797
  Daniel, son of Mark, bpt. 20 May 1798
  Data, dau of John, bpt. 25 Sep 1796
  Dorothy, dau of Mary, bpt. 1 Sep 1765
  Ebenezer Wallis, son of Richard, bpt. 12 Sep 1802
  Eleanor, dau of Benjamin, bpt. 6 May 1759
  Elizabeth, dau of Mark, bpt. 17 May 1761
  Elizabeth, dau of Mark Jr., bpt. 24 Nov 1793
  Elizabeth Peverly, dau of William, bpt. 20 Oct 1799

RYE BAPTISMS

LANG, Elly Burley, dau of Jonathan, bpt. 20 Jan 1799
  Fanny Goldthwait, dau of Richard, bpt. 22 Jul 1798
  Francis, son of John, bpt. 15 Nov 1789
  Hannah, dau of Benjamin, bpt. Jan 1761
  Hannah, dau of Mark, bpt. 10 Nov 1765
  Hannah, dau of Bickford, bpt. Oct 1769
  Hannah, dau of Jonathan, bpt. 20 Jan 1799
  Hannah, dau of Mark Jr., bpt. 12 Mar 1801
  Harriot, dau of William, bpt. 20 May 1798
  Huldah, dau of John, bpt. 26 May 1793
  John, son of Bickford, bpt. 12 Apr 1767
  John Langdon, son of Mark, bpt. 14 Jan 1810
  Jonathan, son of Mark, bpt. 23 May 1773
  Leonard, son of William, bpt. 5 Feb 1804
  Levi, son of Thomas, bpt. Nov 1763
  Mark, son of William, bpt. 21 Jun 1741
  Mark, son of Mark, bpt. 9 Oct 1768
  Mark, son of Mark, bpt. 15 Sep 1799
  Martha, dau of Bickford, bpt. 16 Feb 1772
  Mary Ann, dau of William, bpt. 29 Jan 1797
  Mary Ann, dau of Richard, bpt. 5 Jun 1808
  Molly, dau of William, bpt. 18 Mar 1744
  Polly, dau of John, bpt. 28 Jun 1795
  Polly, dau of Mark, bpt. 21 Aug 1796
  Polly, dau of Mark Jr., bpt. 29 Jul 1804
  Richard, son of Thomas, bpt. 30 Sep 1770
  Sarah, dau of Thomas, bpt. 3 May 1774
  Sarah, dau of Bickford, bpt. 6 Oct 1776
  Sarah, dau of Richard, bpt. 5 Nov 1809
  Sarah Ann, dau of Mark Jr., bpt. 17 ___ 1806
  Susanna, dau of Thomas, bpt. Aug 1758
  William, son of Thomas, bpt. Feb 1761
  William, son of Bickford, bpt. 14 Apr 1782
  _____, children of Thomas, bpt. Sep 1783
  _____, dau of William, bpt. 13 Mar 1803
LANGMAID, Abigail, dau of William, bpt. 2 Dec 1750
  John, son of William, bpt. 6 Apr 1746
  Samuel, son of William, bpt. 12 Oct 1740
  Samuel, son of William, bpt. 3 Apr 1748
  William, son of William, bpt. 30 Jan 1743
LEAR, Alexander Salter, son of Samuel, bpt. 24 Nov 1793
  Deborah B., dau of John, bpt. 6 Apr 1777
  John, son of Nathaniel, bpt. 24 Jul 1748
  John, bpt. 24 Nov 1777
  Mehitable Odiorne, dau of Alexander, bpt. 28 Jun 1778

RYE BAPTISMS

LEAR, Molly, dau of Alexander, bpt. 6 Apr 1777
LEAVITT, Elizabeth, dau of Samuel Jr., bpt. 20 May 1759
  John, son of Samuel, bpt 20 Jul 1755
LIBBY, Aaron Seavey, son of Samuel, bpt. Jun 1782
  Abigail, dau of Abraham, bpt. 20 Nov 1763
  Abigail, dau of Benjamin, bpt. Jun 1768
  Abraham, son of Joseph, bpt. 17 Jul 1748
  Abraham, son of Joseph, bpt. 26 Aug 1750
  Abraham, son of Arter, bpt. 15 Jun 1766
  Abraham, son of Abraham, bpt. 23 Feb 1777
  Arthur Remick, son of Isaac Jr., bpt. 27 Jan 1754
  Benjamin, son of Jacob, bpt. 13 Mar 1736/7
  Benjamin, son of Abraham, bpt. 16 Jun 1782
  Billy, son of Samuel, bpt. 8 Jul 1787
  Daniel, son of Arter, bpt. 27 Jul 1760
  Daniel Rand, son of Samuel, bpt. 27 Jul 1800
  Deborah Smith, dau of Arthur, bpt. 24 Jun 1753
  Elias Tarlton, son of Abraham, bpt. 28 Nov 1773
  Elizabeth, dau of Isaac Jr., bpt. 5 Jan 1752
  Enoch, son of John, bpt. Apr 1755
  Ephraim, son of Joseph, bpt 30 Nov 1755
  Gloucester, negro child of Joseph Libby, bpt. 29 Oct 1749
  Hannah, dau of Samuel, bpt. 19 May 1751
  Hepsibah, dau of Jacob, bpt. 22 Aug 1742
  Hitty, dau of Samuel, bpt. 3 Sep 1792
  Isaac, son of Isaac, bpt. Apr 1750
  Isaac, son of Reuben, bpt. 3 Mar 1770
  Isaac, son of Arter, bpt. 2 May 1771
  Jacob, son of Samuel, bpt. 4 Oct 1747
  Jacob, son of Abraham, bpt. Mar 1762
  Jacob, son of Abraham, bpt. 23 Dec 1770
  Jacob, son of Arter, bpt. 3 Apr 1774
  James, son of Arter, bpt. 6 Jun 1756
  Jane, dau of Joseph, bpt. 11 Jan 1747
  Jane, dau of Benjamin, bpt. Jun 1768
  Jethro, son of Reuben, bpt. 9 Dec 1759
  John, son of John, bpt. 29 Mar 1746/7
  Jonathan, son of John, bpt. 14 Apr 1751
  Jonathan, son of Arter, bpt. 12 Feb 1758
  Joseph, son of Jacob, bpt. 13 Mar 1736/7
  Joseph, son of Joseph, bpt. 5 Nov 1752
  Joseph, son of Abraham, bpt. 17 Nov 1765
  Joseph, son of Joseph, bpt. 6 Nov 1791
  Josiah, son of Benjamin, bpt. 15 Sep 1776
  Keziah, dau of John, bpt. 20 May 1744
  Maria, dau of Samuel, bpt. 21 Oct 1804

RYE BAPTISMS

LIBBY, Mary, dau of Joseph, bpt. 23 Sep 1744
  Mary, dau of Isaac Jr., bpt. 18 Sep 1748
  Mary, dau of John, bpt. 25 Sep 1748
  Mary, dau of Joseph, bpt. Jan 1761
  Mary, dau of Joseph, bpt. 20 Mar 1763
  Mehitable, dau of Samuel, bpt. 10 May 1795
  Meribah Smith, dau of Arter, bpt. 14 Nov 1762
  Meshech, son of John, bpt. 5 May 1745
  Molly, dau of Benjamin, bpt. 30 Sep 1770
  Moses, son of Joseph, bpt. 29 Nov 1754
  Nancy Griffith, dau of Samuel, bpt. 15 Nov 1789
  Olive, dau of Reuben, bpt. 2 Feb 1755
  Olly, dau of Joseph, bpt. 30 Apr 1758
  Polly, dau of Joseph, bpt. 11 Apr 1790
  Reuben, son of Joseph, bpt. 13 Mar 1743
  Richard, son of Samuel, bpt. 1 Oct 1804
  Ruth Moses, dau of Samuel, bpt. 4 Jun 1797
  Samuel, son of Reuben, bpt. Jul 1757
  Samuel, son of Samuel, bpt. 1783
  Sarah, dau of Samuel, bpt. 27 Oct 1745
  Sarah, dau of Joanna, bpt. 29 Oct 1758
  Sarah, dau of Benjamin, bpt. 17 Aug 1760
  Sarah, dau of Reuben, bpt. 30 Aug 1767
  Sarah, dau of Abraham, bpt. 25 Jul 1779
  Sarah, dau of Samuel, bpt. 2 Oct 1785
  Susanna, dau of Isaac Jr., bpt. 19 Sep 1756
  _____, son of Samuel, bpt. 3 Jun 1754
LOCKE (LOCK), Abigail, dau of James, bpt. 29 Mar 1741
  Abigail, dau of William, bpt. 6 Mar 1743
  Abigail, dau of Jonathan Jr., bpt. 29 Jul 1764
  Abigail, dau of David, bpt. 29 Nov 1778
  Abigail, dau of William, bpt. 28 Oct 1781
  Abigail, dau of John Jr., bpt. 10 Feb 1793
  Abigail Jenness, dau of Samuel J., bpt. 19 Jan 1824
  Abigail Mace, dau of Simon, bpt. 15 Dec 1805
  Abigail Towle, dau of Joseph Jr., bpt. 26 Feb 1797
  Abner, son of Jonathan, bpt. 15 Aug 1742
  Abner, son of Richard, bpt. 13 Mar 1748
  Abner, son of Richard, bpt. 26 May 1754
  Abner, son of Jonathan Jr., bpt. 9 Nov 1760
  Abner, son of Simon, bpt. 12 May 1805
  Abraham, son of Francis, bpt. 28 Jun 1760
  Abraham, son of Richard Jr., bpt. 20 Aug 1775
  Alfred, son of Simon, bpt. 6 May 1819
  Anna, dau of David, bpt. 3 Apr 1774
  Anna, dau of Job, bpt. 25 Oct 1807

RYE BAPTISMS

LOCKE, Apphia, dau of Jeremiah, bpt. 29 Jun 1806
Asa, son of Richard Jr., bpt. 20 Aug 1775
Asa, son of Asa, bpt. 4 Nov 1801
Benjamin, son of Joseph, bpt. 16 Dec 1770
Benjamin, son of Joseph, bpt. 13 Jun 1776
Benjamin, son of David, bpt. 15 Apr 1781
Billy, son of Tryphena, bpt. 21 Oct 1796
Daniel, son of Elisha, bpt. 12 May 1745
Daniel, son of Jonathan Jr., bpt. 8 Nov 1772
Daniel, son of Job, bpt. 15 Apr 1787
Daniel Tredwell, son of Jethro, bpt. 28 Apr 1805
David, son of Jonathan, bpt. 13 May 1736/7
David, son of David, bpt. Dec 1765
David, son of David Jr., bpt. 17 Oct 1790
David, son of Simon, bpt. 13 Jul 1819
Deliverance, dau of Francis, bpt. 11 Apr 1754
Dorothy, dau of Jethro, bpt. 2 Sep 1750
Dorothy, dau of Jethro, bpt. 5 Sep 1751
Edwin, son of Simon, bpt. 13 Jul 1819
Elenore Dow, dau of James, bpt. 27 ___ 1806
Elijah, son of Elijah, bpt. 29 Sep 1746
Elijah, son of Elijah, bpt. Dec 1754
Elijah, son of Elijah, bpt. 1 Jul 1781
Elis, dau of Jethro, bpt. 15 Apr 1759
Elisha, son of Elisha, bpt. 24 Oct 1743
Elizabeth, dau of William, bpt. 13 Apr 1740
Elizabeth, dau of Elijah, bpt. 15 Jan 1749
Elizabeth, dau of Francis, bpt 4 May 1755
Elizabeth, dau of Jethro, bpt. 12 Feb 1758
Elizabeth, dau of James Jr., bpt. 17 Apr 1763
Elizabeth, dau of Richard, bpt. 10 Apr 1768
Elizabeth, dau of John Jr., bpt. 30 Nov 1788
Elizabeth, dau of Joseph 3d, bpt. 26 Jun 1808
Elizabeth, dau of Simon, bpt. Aug 1811
Elizabeth Emerett, dau of Samuel J., bpt. 2 Jul 1826
Elizabeth Garland, dau of Job, bpt. 24 Sep 1797
Elizabeth Garland (twin), dau of Simon, bpt. 16 Apr 1801
Elvin, son of John, bpt. 2 Apr 1809
Emmaline, dau of John Jr., bpt. 14 Nov 1802
Ephraim, son of Ephraim, bpt. Aug 1757
Francis, son of Francis, bpt. 16 Oct 1757
George Washington, son of John, bpt. 2 Mar 1777
Gordon Henry, son of Richard 3d, bpt. 2 Aug 1812
Hall Jackson, son of Jonathan, bpt. 14 Dec 1777
Hannah, dau of Joseph, bpt. 22 Feb 1741
Hannah, dau of Jonathan, bpt. 21 Dec 1746
Hannah, dau of Jethro, bpt. 13 Nov 1748

RYE BAPTISMS

LOCKE, Hannah, dau of James Jr., bpt 13 Apr 1755
  Hannah, dau of Elisha, bpt Jun 1755
  Hannah, dau of Francis, bpt. 9 Jan 1763
  Hannah, dau of Richard Jr., bpt. Oct 1767
  Hannah, dau of Joseph, bpt. 4 Apr 1773
  Hannah, dau of Job, bpt. 21 Jul 1793
  Hannah, bpt. 20 Jun 1816
  Hannah Dow, dau of Jeremiah, bpt. 7 Aug 1808
  Hannah Jenness, dau of Richard Jr., bpt. 11 Jun 1769
  Hannah Wallis, dau of Joseph, bpt. 3 Feb 1796
  Henry, son of Joseph Jr., bpt. 31 Aug 1780
  Henry, son of Jeremiah Jr., bpt. 28 Jun 1801
  Hiram, son of Jethro, bpt. 15 Jul 1802
  Hiram, son of William, bpt. 15 Aug 1802
  Huldah, dau of Elijah, bpt. 28 Jun 1741
  Huldah, dau of William, bpt. 11 Oct 1783
  Ira, son of Jeremiah, bpt. 11 Jul 1802
  Jacob, son of Richard, bpt. 23 Feb 1752
  Jacob, son of Richard, bpt. 22 Jan 1757
  James, son of James Jr., bpt. 27 May 1753
  James, son of James, bpt. 21 Sep 1777
  James, son of Richard 3d, bpt. 5 Nov 1809
  James Hobbs, son of Richard Jr., bpt. 6 Jun 1773
  James Hobbs, son of Asa, bpt. 19 May 1805
  James William, son of Widow Abigail, bpt. 25 Oct 1816
  Janney, dau of Joseph 3d, bpt. 30 Oct. 1796
  Jeremiah, son of John Jr., bpt. 14 Jul 1771
  Jeremiah, son of Jeremiah, bpt. 16 Sep 1804
  Jeremiah, son of Jeremiah, bpt. 25 Aug 1811
  Jesse, son of Joseph 3d, bpt. 8 Mar 1807
  Jethro, son of Jonathan, bpt. 2 Jul 1775
  Jethro, son of John Jr., bpt. 20 May 1798
  Job, son of Richard, bpt. 26 Sep 1762
  Job, son of Job, bpt. 5 May 1799
  John, son of Francis, bpt. 23 Oct 1736/7
  John, son of Richard, bpt. 19 Oct 1746
  John, son of Jonathan, bpt. 11 Dec 1748
  John, son of James Jr., bpt. Apr 1757
  John, son of Jonathan, bpt. 19 Jul 1767
  John, son of John Jr., bpt. 1 Apr 1770
  John, son of David, bpt. 31 May 1772
  John, son of William, bpt. 27 May 1781
  John, child under the care of John Locke, bpt. 27 Mar 1787
  John, son of Jeremiah, bpt. 4 Sep 1796
  John Odiorne (twin), son of Hannah, bpt. 12 Oct 1802

RYE BAPTISMS

LOCKE, John Oliver, son of Asa, bpt. 12 Aug 1822
John Webster, son of Jethro, bpt. 7 Aug 1808
John Wilkes Parsons, son of Job, bpt. 10 Apr 1803
Jonathan, son of Jonathan Jr., bpt. 29 Jul 1759
Jonathan, son of David, bpt Mar 1768
Jonathan, son of Jonathan Jr., bpt. 18 Nov 1787
Jonathan, son of John Jr., bpt. 27 Jul 1800
Jonathan (twin), son of Joseph Jr., bpt. 29 Aug 1813
Jonathan Dearborn, son of Asa, bpt. 31 May 1812
Jonathan Marden, son of Joseph 3d, bpt. 29 Apr 1810
Jonathan Hobbs, son of James, bpt. 13 Jun 1802
Joseph, son of Joseph, bpt. 4 Apr 1742
Joseph, son of Joseph, bpt. 21 Jul 1751
Joseph, son of Jeremiah, bpt. 28 Apr 1754
Joseph, son of Joseph, bpt. 18 Dec 1768
Joseph, son of Jonathan, bpt. 1 Apr 1770
Joseph, son of Richard tert., bpt. 4 Jun 1775
Joseph, son of Joseph, bpt. 1 Jul 1787
Joseph, son of Joseph 3d, bpt. 4 May 1800
Joseph (twin), son of Hannah, bpt. 12 Oct 1802
Joseph, son of Joseph, bpt. 1806
Joshua, son of Joseph, bpt. 28 Apr 1754
Joshua, son of Richard Jr., bpt. 20 Aug 1775
Leacada, dau of Joseph 3d, bpt. 18 Jun 1804
Lemuel, son of Asa, bpt. 1807
Levi, son of Elijah, bpt. 9 Dec 1750
Levi, son of David, bpt. Feb 1770
Lucy Ann, dau of Joseph Jr., bpt. 7 Jul 1820
Luiretia, dau of Joseph, bpt. 26 Jun 1803
Margaret, dau of Jonathan, bpt. 20 Jul 1740
Martha, dau of Elijah, bpt. 3 Jan 1742
Martha, dau of Jeremiah, bpt. 13 Nov 1814
Mary, dau of Elijah, bpt. 23 Nov 1744
Mary, dau of Elisha, bpt. 5 Apr 1747
Mary, dau of William, bpt. 14 Apr 1751
Mary, dau of Jeremiah, bpt Jul 1755
Mary, dau of Joseph, bpt. 21 Nov 1756
Mary, dau of Jonathan Jr., bpt. 12 Jun 1763
Mary, dau of David, bpt. 20 May 1764
Mary, dau of John, bpt. 15 May 1803
Mary, dau of Joseph Jr., bpt. 8 Oct 1809
Mary Elizabeth, dau of Asa, bpt. 21 Oct 1824
Mary White, dau of Jeremiah Jr., bpt. 22 May 1803
Mary Olivia, dau of Samuel J., bpt. 23 Jul 1828
Mehitable Berry, dau of Simon, bpt. 30 Sep 1792

RYE BAPTISMS

LOCKE, Mercy, dau of Joseph, bpt. Mar 1783
  Meribah, dau of Jethro, bpt. Jan 1756
  Molly, dau of John Jr., bpt. 8 Aug 1773
  Molly, dau of Elijah, bpt. Mar 1784
  Moses, son of James Jr., bpt. 24 Mar 1751
  Nabby, dau of Joshua, bpt. 15 Apr 1792
  Nabby, dau of Jno. Jr., bpt. 23 Sep 1792
  Nancy, dau of David, bpt. 5 Jun 1785
  Nathaniel, son of Joseph 3d, bpt. 10 Jun 1798
  Olly Shapleigh, dau of John Jr., bpt. 12 Jul 1795
  Patty, dau of Joseph, bpt. 24 May 1801
  Perna Towle, dau of Asa, bpt. 1 Oct 1809
  Perna Towle, dau of Asa, bpt. 21 Oct 1813
  Prudence, dau of Ephraim, bpt. 30 Dec 1753
  Rachel Berry (twin), dau of Simon, bpt. 16 Apr 1801
  Rachel Dowrst, dau of Charity, bpt. 23 Oct 1791
  Reuben, son of David, bpt. Aug 1758
  Reuben, son of David, bpt. 6 Apr 1760
  Reuben, son of William, bpt. 20 Mar 1791
  Richard, son of Joseph, bpt. 9 Sep 1744
  Richard, son of Richard, bpt. 7 Jan 1750
  Richard, son of Richard tert., bpt. 20 Jun 1773
  Richard, son of John Jr., bpt. 8 Aug 1773
  Richard, son of Simon, bpt. 1 Mar 1794
  Richard, son of Joseph 3d, bpt. 4 Aug 1805
  Robert Waldron, son of Samuel, bpt. 5 Aug 1821
  Ruth, dau of James Jr., bpt. 8 Mar 1752
  Sally, dau of Job, bpt. 29 May 1791
  Sally, dau of Tryphena, bpt. 14 Oct 1792
  Sally Hobbs, dau of Asa, bpt. 7 Sep 1800
  Sally Hobbs, dau of Asa Jr., bpt. 13 Dec 1825
  Sally Wood, dau of Job, bpt. 21 Jul 1793
  Samuel, son of William, bpt. 14 Aug 1748
  Samuel, son of James Jr., bpt. Oct 1761
  Samuel Jenness, son of John Jr., bpt. 11 Jul 1790
  Sarah, dau of Jonathan, bpt. 9 Sep 1744
  Sarah, dau of Francis Jr., bpt. 13 Oct 1751
  Sarah, dau of James Jr., bpt. 8 Jul 1759
  Sarah, dau of David, bpt. 29 Nov 1761
  Sarah, dau of Richard, bpt. 8 Sep 1765
  Sarah, dau of Richard Jr., bpt. 17 Mar 1771
  Sarah, dau of James, bpt. 1 Jun 1777
  Sarah Ann, dau of Joseph, bpt. 14 Apr 1799
  Sarah Frost, dau of Simon, bpt. 12 Jun 1796
  Sheridan Porter, son of Richard, bpt. 13 Nov 1814

RYE BAPTISMS

LOCKE, Simeon Prescott, son of Levi, bpt. 20 Jan 1799
Simon, son of Jethro, bpt. 23 Sep 1753
Simon, son of Richard, bpt. 23 Sep 1770
Simon, son of Simon, bpt. 5 Nov 1797
Thomas Dockum, son of Simon, bpt. 7 Aug 1808
Thomas Lemuel, son of Asa Jr., bpt. 3 Sep 1826
Tryphene, dau of Richard, bpt May 1759
William, son of William, bpt. 15 Sep 1745
William, son of Elijah, bpt. 8 Apr 1753
William, son of Elijah, bpt. Jun 1758
William, son of David, bpt. 21 Apr 1776
William, son of William, bpt. 9 Oct 1785
William, son of Jona. Jr., bpt. 23 Sep 1792
William, son of Simon, bpt. 6 Oct 1799
William (twin), son of Joseph Jr., bpt. 29 Aug 1813
Worthy Dearborn, son of Richard 3d, bpt. 20 Dec 1807

MACE, Abigail, dau of Ithamar, bpt. 1 Feb 1767
John, son of Ithamar, bpt. 23 Jul 1769
John, son of John, bpt. 4 Mar 1798
John Alphius, son of John (deceased), bpt. 24 Nov 1822
Joseph, son of Widow Mace, bpt. 9 Jan 1798
Joshua, son of Levi, bpt. 23 Dec 1792
Levi, son of Levi, bpt. 23 Dec 1792
Molly, bpt. 24 Nov 1822
Sally Brown, dau of Sarah, bpt. 17 Nov 1805
Sally Goss, dau of John, bpt. 19 Feb 1794
Sarah, dau of Ithamar, bpt. 1 Dec 1765

MARDEN, Abiel, dau of Benjamin Jr., bpt. 1 Mar 1767
Abigail, dau of Joseph, bpt. 30 Apr 1758
Abigail, dau of Stephen Jr., bpt. 12 Apr 1761
Abigail, dau of William, bpt. 9 Aug 1776
Abigail, dau of Solomon, bpt. 11 Jan 1807
Abigail, dau of Solomon, bpt. 29 Aug 1813
Almira, dau of Solomon, bpt. 28 Dec 1817
Anna Brown, dau of Reuben, bpt. 13 Oct 1811
Anna Tredwell, dau of Benjamin tert., bpt. 23 Mar 1777
Anna Yeaton, dau of _____ Jr., bpt. 11 Oct 1813
Becky, dau of Benjamin tert., bpt. 9 Feb 1773
Benjamin, son of Benjamin, bpt. 11 Feb 1750
Benjamin, son of Benjamin Jr., bpt. 18 Jun 1769
Benjamin, son of Benjamin tert., bpt. 23 Jul 1775

RYE BAPTISMS

MARDEN, Benjamin, son of Solomon, bpt. 29 May 1808
  Benjamin Whidden, son of Samuel, bpt. 21 Sep 1800
  Betty, dau of Timothy, bpt. 16 Sep 1761
  Betty, dau of Nathaniel, bpt. 11 Jan 1778
  Charity, dau of Benjamin Jr., bpt. Mar 1759
  Charles, son of Samuel Jr., bpt. 17 Mar 1828
  Clarrisa Davis, dau of Samuel, bpt 14 Jul 1816
  Daniel, son of Samuel, bpt. 1 Apr 1813
  David Smith, son of Stephen, bpt. 17 Oct 1790
  Elizabeth, dau of Ebenezer, bpt. 1743
  Elizabeth, dau of William, bpt. 19 Jan 1746
  Elizabeth, dau of Benjamin, bpt. Aug 1755
  Elizabeth, dau of Jonathan Jr., bpt. Jun 1758
  Elizabeth, dau of Benjamin Jr., bpt. 14 Feb 1762
  Elizabeth, dau of Nathaniel, bpt. 16 Mar 1788
  Elizabeth, dau of Solomon, bpt. 3 Jul 1803
  Elizabeth Moulton, dau of Ebenezer, bpt. 21 Oct 1810
  Esther, dau of Nathaniel Jr., bpt. 7 Aug 1785
  Francis, son of Israel, bpt. 17 Jul 1763
  Francis, son of Francis, bpt. 31 Aug 1794
  George, son of Ebenezer, bpt. 19 Jul 1741
  George, son of Josiah, bpt. 4 Nov 1804
  Hannah, dau of Joseph, bpt. 8 Apr 1764
  Hannah, dau of Nathaniel Jr., bpt. 12 Jan 1772
  Hannah, dau of Nathaniel, bpt. 23 Jul 1780
  Hannah, dau of William, bpt. 15 Apr 1781
  Hannah, dau of Samuel, bpt. 1807
  Hannah, dau of David, bpt. 27 Jul 1817
  Hepsibah, dau of Jonathan, bpt. 7 Nov 1742
  Hepsibath, dau of Jonathan Jr., bpt. 2 Apr 1756
  Hepsibah, dau of Joseph, bpt. 1 Nov 1767
  Hepsibah, dau of Samuel, bpt. 9 Jul 1775
  Israel, son of Israel, bpt. 4 Aug 1765
  Israel, son of Francis, bpt. 11 Oct 1789
  James, son of Nathan, bpt. 2 Nov 1746
  James, son of Ebenezer, bpt. 10 Apr 1748
  James, son of Nathaniel Jr., bpt. 27 May 1781
  James, son of William, bpt. Mar 1784
  James, son of Francis, bpt. 21 May 1786
  Jane, dau of Joseph, bpt. 8 Sep 1765
  Jesse, son of Josiah, bpt. 14 ___ 1806
  John, son of John, bpt. 6 Dec 1747
  John, son of Benjamin, bpt. 22 Aug 1762
  Jonathan, son of Nathaniel Jr., bpt. 29 Jul 1770
  Jonathan, son of Samuel Jr., bpt. 13 Jun 1773
  Jonathan, son of Joseph, bpt. Oct 1779
  Jonathan Towle, son of Nathaniel, bpt. Feb 1796

RYE BAPTISMS

MARDEN, Joses, son of Benjamin, bpt. 13 Oct 1766
Joseph, son of Joseph, bpt. 23 Aug 1769
Joseph, son of Joseph, bpt. 19 Sep 1774
Judith, dau of James, bpt. 19 Jul 1741
Judith, dau of Nathan, bpt. 5 Nov 1752
Keziah, dau of Nathaniel, bpt. 10 Mar 1770
Lavinia, dau of James, bpt. 17 Jun 1810
Lovey Brackett, dau of Ebenezer, bpt. 7 Aug 1808
Lowell Sanborn, son of Samuel, bpt. 18 Jul 1819
Lucia, dau of Nathaniel Jr., bpt. 6 Oct 1776
Martha, dau of Timothy, bpt. 16 Sep 1759
Mary, dau of William, bpt. 3 Apr 1737
Mary, dau of Samuel, bpt. 12 Dec 1742
Mary, dau of Ebenezer, bpt. 4 Feb 1750
Mary, dau of Joseph, bpt. 7 Jun 1761
Mary, dau of Benjamin Jr., bpt. 4 Apr. 1779
Mary, dau of Ebenezer, bpt. 24 Jul 1814
Mary, dau of David S., bpt. 2 Oct 1814
Mary, dau of Solomon, bpt. 8 Sep 1816
Mehitable, dau of Samuel Jr., bpt. May 1770
Molly, dau of Benjamin, bpt. 29 Sep 1758
Molly, dau of Benjamin, bpt. 27 May 1770
Moses, son of Solomon, bpt. 28 Jun 1809
Nathan, son of Nathan, bpt. Dec 1754
Nathaniel, son of Jonathan, bpt. 28 Jul 1745
Nathaniel, son of Ebenezer, bpt. 23 Mar 1746
Nathaniel, son of Nathaniel, bpt. 6 May 1792
Nathaniel, son of Reuben, bpt. 19 Jul 1817
Olly, dau of James, bpt. 11 Jan 1746/7
Olly, dau of Nathaniel Jr., bpt. 4 Sep 1774
Patience, dau of Francis, bpt. 21 Aug 1796
Prudence, dau of Israel, bpt. 15 Jan 1769
Prudence Perry, dau of Nathaniel, bpt. 26 Feb 1769
Rachel, dau of William, bpt. 27 Sep 1741
Reuben, son of Nathaniel, bpt. 1783
Rhoda, dau of James, bpt. 23 Oct 1803
Sally, dau of Timothy, bpt. 25 Dec 1787
Samuel, son of Jonathan, bpt. 13 Sep 1747
Samuel, son of Benjamin, bpt. 22 May 1748
Samuel, son of Samuel Jr., bpt. 1 Dec 1771
Samuel, son of Benjamin, bpt. 13 Jun 1773
Samuel, son of Benjamin Jr., bpt. 6 Oct 1776
Samuel Brackett, son of Josiah, bpt. 6 Nov 1808
Samuel Hunt, son of Joseph, bpt. 1 Jun 1777
Sarah, dau of Nathan, bpt. 25 Nov 1744
Sarah, dau of Israel, bpt. Mar 1759
Sarah, dau of Joseph, bpt. 5 Aug 1759
Sarah, dau of Israel, bpt. 22 Mar 1761

RYE BAPTISMS

MARDEN, Sarah, dau of Benjamin Jr., bpt. 24 Nov 1771
  Sarah, dau of William, bpt. 8 Nov 1778
  Simon, son of Francis, bpt. 18 Nov 1787
  Solomon, son of Benjamin Jr., bpt. 29 Mar 1774
  Solomon Dowrst, son of Benjamin Jr., bpt. 2 Oct 1757
  Stephen, son of Benjamin Jr., bpt. 4 Nov 1764
  Stephen, son of Stephen, bpt. 5 Feb 1795
  Thomas, son of Israel, bpt. Jul 1756
  Thomas, son of Israel, bpt. 22 Jul 1770
  Thomas, son of Francis, bpt. 14 Oct 1792
  Thomas, son of Stephen, bpt. 8 Nov 1801
  Thomas, son of Solomon, bpt. 20 Apr 1804
  Timothy, son of Joseph, bpt. 25 Mar 1787
  William, son of James, bpt. 3 Jun 1744
  William Gould, son of Benjamin, bpt. 15 Oct 1752
  William, son of Benjamin, bpt. Sep 1759
  William, son of Jonathan Jr., bpt. Apr 1760
  William, son of James Jr., bpt. 25 Aug 1811
  _____, dau of Israel, bpt. 20 Oct 1754
MARSTON, Catherine Elkins, dau of John, bpt. 24 Nov 1799
  Huldah Locke, dau of John, bpt. 29 Aug 1813
  Jane, dau of Reuben, bpt. 26 Mar 1749
  Mary, dau of John, bpt. 1 Oct 1809
  Mary Berry, dau of John, bpt. 1807
  Reuben, son of Reuben, bpt. May 1746
  William Smith, son of John, bpt. 4 Jul 1802
MASON, Betsey, dau of Daniel, bpt. 27 Jun 1790
  Elizabeth Ruhamah, dau of Daniel Jr., bpt. 5 Jun 1808
  Florinda, dau of Samuel, bpt. 26 May 1811
  Joseph Locke, son of Samuel, bpt. 22 May 1803
  Lucy Maria, dau of Nicholas, bpt. 26 Jun 1808
  Martha Neal, dau of Samuel, bpt. 27 ___ 1806
  Martha Wentworth, dau of Joseph (deceased), bpt. 30 Jul 1811
  Mary, dau of Samuel, bpt. 7 Aug 1808
  Mary Jenness, dau of Daniel Jr., bpt. 15 Jul 1810
  Nicholas, child of Mr. Mason, bpt. 1783
  Ruhamah, dau of Daniel, bpt. 27 Nov 1785
  Samuel Jenness, son of Samuel, bpt. 29 May 1812
MATHES (MATTHEWS), Abraham, son of Abraham, bpt. 9 Jul 1780
  Abraham, son of Robert, bpt. 22 Apr 1810
  Elizabeth, dau of Abraham, bpt. 20 Mar 1785
  Molly, dau of Abraham, bpt. 21 May 1775

RYE BAPTISMS

MATHES, Robert, son of _____, bpt. 1783
   Robert, son of Robert, bpt. 17 Feb 1812
   Sarah, dau of Abraham, bpt. 22 Nov 1777
   William Saunders, son of Robert (deceased), bpt.
     25 Jan 1814
   William Thomas, son of Abraham, bpt. 16 Jan 1792
MATHESON, Edward Randal, son of Robert, bpt. 28
   Feb 1808
MELCHER, Olly, dau of _____, bpt. 20 Nov 1748
MORRISON, Alexander, son of Alexander, bpt. 9 Jun
   1781
   Anna, dau of Alexander, bpt. 26 Jun 1774
   Becka, dau of Alexander, bpt. 1 Mar 1778
   Elizabeth, dau of Alexander, bpt. 23 Jul 1780
   John Rand, son of Alexander, bpt. 26 Sep 1790
   Molly, dau of Alexander, bpt. 1784
   Rachel, dau of Samuel, bpt. 25 Apr 1779
   Rachel, dau of Alexander, bpt. 8 Feb 1789
   Robert, son of Samuel, bpt. 25 Apr 1779
   Samuel, son of Samuel, bpt. 15 Jan 1788
   William Rogers, son of William, bpt. Nov 1781
MOULTON, Anna, dau of Nehemiah, bpt. 12 Sep 1762
   Bethiah, dau of Nehemiah, bpt. 9 Jun 1776
   Daniel, son of Daniel Jr., bpt. 29 Jan 1749
   Daniel, son of Daniel Jr., bpt. 13 Apr 1755
   Daniel, son of Noah, bpt. Dec 1761
   Elizabeth, dau of Reuben, bpt. 8 Mar 1752
   Hannah, dau of Daniel Jr., bpt. 18 Aug 1751
   Job, son of Noah, bpt. 20 Sep 1752
   John, son of Daniel, bpt. 12 Jun 1743
   John, son of Daniel, bpt. 7 Sep 1745
   John, son of Daniel Jr., bpt. 15 Apr 1753
   Lucy, dau of Reuben, bpt. Aug 1757
   Lydia, dau of Daniel, bpt. 14 Aug 1740
   Mary, dau of Noah, bpt. 22 Sep 1754
   Mary, dau of Nehemiah, bpt. 14 Apr 1765
   Michael, son of Daniel Jr., bpt. 29 May 1757
   Nathan, son of Daniel, bpt. 30 Apr 1737/8
   Noah, son of Daniel, bpt. 7 Sep 1746
   Noah, son of Noah, bpt. 30 Dec 1759
   Noah, son of Daniel Jr., bpt. 19 Jul 1761
   Reuben, son of Daniel, bpt. 9 Sep 1764
   Sally, dau of Nehemiah, bpt. 28 Jan 1770
   Samuel, son of Daniel Jr., bpt. 8 Jul 1759
   Sarah, dau of Noah, bpt. 14 Apr 1751
   Sarah, dau of Daniel, bpt. 30 Aug 1767
MOW (MOWE), Hannah, dau of Ephraim, bpt. 16 Mar
   1760
   Mary, dau of Ephraim, bpt. 24 Dec 1757

RYE BAPTISMS

MOW, Samuel, son of Dorcas, bpt. 13 Dec 1772
MURRAY, Eliza, dau of Samuel, bpt. Aug 1770
  John, son of Samuel, bpt. 2 Mar 1777
  Josiah, son of Samuel, bpt. 22 Jan 1775
  Samuel, son of Samuel, bpt. 5 Feb 1757
  Susanna, dau of Samuel, bpt. 8 Apr 1759
  William, son of Samuel, bpt. 21 Dec 1772
NORTON, Abigail M., dau of Dudley, bpt. 16 Jul 1797
  Hannah Bartlett, dau of Dudley, bpt. 30 Apr 1786
  Lucy, dau of Dudley, bpt. 21 Jul 1793
  Polly (twin), dau of Dudley, bpt. 19 Dec 1790
  Sally (twin), dau of Dudley, bpt. 19 Dec 1790
  William, son of Dudley, bpt. 9 Nov 1788
NUTE, Sarah, dau of James, bpt. May 1736/7
ODIORNE, Abigail, dau of John, bpt. 15 Apr 1750
  Abigail, dau of Ebenezer, bpt. 3 Oct 1802
  Benjamin, son of Ebenezer, bpt. 26 May 1805
  Ebenezer Lewis, son of Ebenezer, bpt. 24 Aug 1800
  Hannah, dau of John, bpt. 7 Feb 1745
  James, son of Ebenezer, bpt. 30 Sep 1810
  John Seavey, son of Ebenezer, bpt. 16 Oct 1808
  Jonathan, son of Mary, bpt. 31 Sep 1775
  Samuel, son of John, bpt. 13 Nov 1748
  Samuel, son of John, bpt. 20 Nov 1748
  William Seavey, son of Ebenezer, bpt. 15 Jul 1798
OZEL, Cesar, son of Phebe, bpt. 13 Sep 1767
PAGE, Mary, bpt. 9 Oct 1803
  Reuben, son of Jeremiah of Epsom, bpt. 28 Jul 1776
PAIN, Abner, son of William, bpt. 4 Aug 1754
  Amos, son of William, bpt. 13 Sep 1740
  Amos, son of William, bpt. 7 Jun 1752
  Benjamin, son of William, bpt. 26 Aug 1750
  Christian, dau of John, bpt. 22 Jun 1740
  Deborah, dau of Amos, bpt. 11 Sep 1763
  Dorothy, dau of Amos, bpt. 4 Apr 1762
  Hannah, dau of William, bpt. Feb 1757
  Joanna, dau of Amos, bpt. 14 Sep 1760
  John, son of John, bpt. 3 Jan 1742
  John, son of Amos, bpt. 13 Oct 1754
  Lydia, dau of Amos, bpt. 8 Apr 1759
  Mary, dau of William, bpt. 3 Jul 1748
  Philip, son of William, bpt. 19 Jul 1741
  Richard, son of Amos, bpt. Mar 1757
  Sarah, dau of Amos, bpt. Oct 1755
  William, son of William, bpt. 18 Sep 1743

RYE BAPTISMS

PALMER, Abigail, dau of Jonathan, bpt. 12 Oct 1740
  Abigail, dau of Jonathan, bpt. 29 Jan 1749
  Anna, dau of Jonathan, bpt. 17 Apr 1743
  Hannah, grandau of William, bpt. 26 Sep 1773
  James, son of Jonathan, bpt. May 1753
  Jenny, dau of William, bpt. 14 Apr 1745
  Jeremiah, son of Jonathan, bpt. 21 Aug 1763
  John, son of Jonathan, bpt. 30 Nov 1755
  Jonathan, son of Jonathan, bpt. 22 Feb 1746/7
  Joseph, son of William, bpt. 29 Jun 1740
  Joseph, son of Jonathan, bpt. 10 Feb 1745
  Keziah, dau of Ephraim, bpt. 17 Mar 1736/7
  Mary, dau of Jonathan, bpt. 10 Feb 1745
  Samuel, son of Jonathan, bpt. 25 Apr 1736/7
  Sarah, dau of William, bpt. 7 Nov 1742
  Sarah, dau of Jonathan, bpt. 6 Jan 1751
  Simon, son of Jonathan, bpt. 3 Aug 1760
  William, son of Jonathan, bpt. Feb 1758
PARSONS, Abigail, dau of John W., bpt. 11 Mar 1816
  Almira, dau of Amos S., bpt. 9 Jul 1809
  Amos Seavey, son of Joseph, bpt. 16 Oct 1768
  Anna Seavey, dau of Amos S., bpt. 22 Mar 1807
  Anne, dau of William, bpt. 10 Jun 1750
  Betty, dau of Joseph, bpt. 27 Dec 1776
  Charles Grandison, son of John W., bpt. 16 Oct 1808
  Elizabeth, dau of Amos S., bpt. 11 Jan 1801
  Emily, dau of John W., bpt. 13 Jul 1806
  Isaac Dow, son of Amos S., bpt. 15 Sep 1799
  James Monroe, son of Amos S., bpt. 30 Mar 1817
  John Wilkes, son of Joseph, bpt. 3 Oct 1779
  Joseph, son of Joseph, bpt. 25 Sep 1774
  Joseph, son of Amos S., bpt. 8 Sep 1811
  Lovina, dau of Amos S., bpt. 4 Sep 1814
  Mary, dau of Joseph, bpt. 2 Sep 1770
  Patty, dau of Amos, bpt. 24 Apr 1803
  Polly Dow, dau of Amos S., bpt. 8 Feb 1797
  Samuel, son of Joseph, bpt. 12 Jul 1772
  Samuel, son of Amos S., bpt. 23 Jun 1805
  Thomas Jefferson, son of John W., bpt. 5 Aug 1804
PERKINS, Abigail, dau of James Jr., bpt. 12 Oct 1760
  Anna, dau of James Jr., bpt. 24 May 1767
  Eliza James, dau of James, bpt. 1807
  Hannah, dau of James, bpt. 16 Jul 1780
  Hannah, dau of James Jr., bpt. 21 Aug 1796
  Huldah, dau of James, bpt. 25 May 1777
  Huldah, dau of James Jr., bpt. 13 May 1804

RYE BAPTISMS

PERKINS, James, son of James, bpt. Apr 1769
  James, son of James Jr., bpt. 2 Aug 1801
  Jane Moulton, dau of James Jr., bpt. 2 Sep 1798
  John, son of John, bpt. 9 Dec 1750
  John, son of James Jr., bpt. 18 Nov 1764
  John, son of James, bpt. 14 May 1809
  Jonathan, son of John, bpt. 14 May 1749
  Jonathan, son of James Jr., bpt. 16 Feb 1772
  Josiah, son of James, bpt. 30 Jun 1774
  Mary, dau of James Jr., bpt. 24 Jun 1759
  Molly, dau of James Jr., bpt. 17 Nov 1793
  Sarah, dau of James Jr., bpt. 12 Sep 1762
PHILBRICK, Abigail, dau of Ebenezer, bpt. 17 May 1761
  Abigail, dau of Joseph, bpt. 9 Oct 1768
  Abigail, dau of Jonathan, bpt. 10 Nov 1776
  Abigail, dau of Jonathan, bpt. 5 Nov 1780
  Abigail, dau of Joses Jr., bpt. 1807
  Anne, dau of Joseph, bpt. 15 Apr 1764
  Anne T., dau of James, bpt. Oct 1755
  Benjamin, son of James, bpt. Feb 1761
  Benjamin, son of James, bpt. Aug 1770
  Bethiah, dau of Ebenezer Jr., bpt. 12 Jul 1752
  Daniel, son of Joses, bpt. Feb 1740
  Daniel, son of Joseph, bpt. 10 Mar 1776
  Daniel, son of Joses Jr., bpt. 17 Jul 1791
  Daniel, son of Jonathan, bpt. 13 Oct 1805
  David, son of Joses, bpt. 11 Jun 1797
  Deborah, dau of James Jr., bpt. 2 Oct 1768
  Elizabeth Thompson, dau of Daniel, bpt. 11 Jun 1797
  Hannah, dau of Reuben, bpt. 7 Oct 1764
  Hannah, dau of Joseph, bpt. 30 Dec 1770
  Hannah, dau of Reuben, bpt. 14 Apr 1776
  Harriot Noyes, dau of James, bpt. 10 Jun 1804
  Huldah, dau of James, bpt. 25 May 1777
  Ira, son of Jonathan Jr., bpt. 27 Nov 1808
  James, son of James, bpt. 5 Nov 1736/7
  James, son of Joseph, bpt. 13 Aug 1780
  John, son of Ebenezer, bpt. 26 Feb 1749
  John, son of Ebenezer, bpt. 26 Aug 1750
  John, son of Joses Jr., bpt. 11 Nov 1804
  Jonathan, son of James, bpt. 11 Apr 1741
  Jonathan, son of Joses, bpt. 1 Dec 1745
  Jonathan, son of Ebenezer Jr., bpt. 29 Apr 1759
  Jonathan, son of Jonathan, bpt. 11 Oct 1772
  Jonathan, son of Joseph, bpt. 19 Sep 1773
  Jonathan, son of Jonathan Jr., bpt. 14 Nov 1802
  Joseph, son of Joseph, bpt. 1783

RYE BAPTISMS

PHILBRICK, Joseph, son of Jonathan, bpt. 31 Aug 1788
  Joseph, son of Jonathan Jr., bpt. 10 Jun 1798
  Joseph, son of Joses 3d, bpt. 4 Aug 1807
  Joses, son of James, bpt. 11 Mar 1758
  Joses, son of Joseph, bpt. 8 Nov 1761
  Joses, son of Daniel, bpt. 10 Aug 1766
  Joses, son of Reuben, bpt. 22 Jul 1781
  Josiah Webster, son of Ephraim, bpt. 7 Aug 1808
  Langdon, son of James, bpt. 29 Jun 1806
  Levi, son of Joseph, bpt. 28 Jun 1778
  Mary, dau of James, bpt. Jun 1753
  Mary Marden, dau of Jonathan Jr., bpt. 31 Dec 1797
  Mary May, dau of Joses, bpt. 12 May 1805
  Mercy, dau of Daniel, bpt. 13 Mar 1763
  Mehitable, dau of James, bpt. 31 May 1772
  Molly, dau of Joses, bpt. 15 Jul 1792
  Nathaniel, son of James, bpt. 29 Mar 1747
  Newhall, son of Jonathan Jr., bpt. 12 Aug 1810
  Oliver, son of James, bpt. 10 Jun 1804
  Polly Shapleigh, bpt. 11 Oct 1796
  Rebecca, dau of Ebenezer Jr., bpt. 5 Dec 1756
  Reuben, son of Joses, bpt. 5 Nov 1736/7
  Reuben, son of Reuben, bpt. 12 Sep 1773
  Reuben, son of Reuben, bpt. 21 Jun 1795
  Reuben, son of Joses, bpt. 11 Sep 1798
  Ruth, dau of James, bpt. 14 Apr 1751
  Sally, dau of Joseph, bpt. 1 Sep 1788
  Sally, dau of Joses, bpt. 5 Jul 1795
  Sally, dau of Jonathan Jr., bpt. 6 Jul 1800
  Sarah, dau of James, bpt. 14 Jul 1745
  Sarah, dau of Daniel, bpt. 5 Aug 1764
  Sarah, dau of Reuben, bpt. 31 May 1778
  Sarah, dau of Reuben Jr., bpt. 12 May 1805
  Sheridan, son of Jonathan Jr., bpt. 15 Mar 1816
  Stephen, son of James, bpt. 26 Jun 1763
  Thomas, son of Joses, bpt. 15 Aug 1799
  Titus, son of James, bpt. 10 Apr 1743
POORE (see POWERS)
PORTER, Caroline, bpt. 15 Dec 1793
  Charles Henry, bpt. 18 Aug 1816
  Charles Henry (twin), son of Huntington, bpt. 21 Sep 1817
  Eliphalet, bpt. 4 May 1800
  Elvina, dau of Huntington, bpt. 19 Mar 1820
  Emery Moulton, son of Huntington, bpt. 24 Sep 1815
  Huntington, son of Huntington, bpt. 7 Feb 1813

RYE BAPTISMS

PORTER, John, bpt. 9 Oct 1791
  Louisa, bpt. 29 May 1803
  Maria, bpt. 18 Feb 1798
  Martha Ruggles, dau of Huntington, bpt. 23 Jun 1805
  Nathaniel Sargent, son of Huntington, bpt. 7 Jun 1789
  Oliver, bpt. 14 Mar 1802
  Olivia, dau of Huntington, bpt. 17 Mar 1811
  Samuel Huntington, bpt. 15 Jul 1787
  Sarah Emery, dau of Huntington, bpt. 25 Jun 1809
  Susanna Sargent, dau of Huntington, bpt. 26 Mar 1807
  William Henry (twin), son of Huntington, bpt. 21 Sep 1817
POWERS (POORE), Betsey, dau of Robert, bpt. 9 Nov 1794
  Daniel Sheafe, son of Robert, bpt. 4 Nov 1804
  George, son of Robert, bpt. 22 Apr 1798
  Judith, dau of Robert, bpt. 22 Nov 1789
  Nabby Daniels, dau of Robert, bpt. 3 May 1801
  Sally, dau of Robert, bpt. 27 Nov 1791
RAND, Aaron, son of Samuel Jr., bpt. 21 Sep 1794
  Abigail, dau of Benjamin, bpt. 30 Nov 1755
  Abigail, dau of Samuel, bpt. 8 Oct 1758
  Abigail Moses, dau of Billy, bpt. 16 Oct 1808
  Adaline, dau of Daniel, bpt. 23 Feb 1817
  Affia, dau of Nathaniel, bpt. 1784
  Anna Trefethern, dau of Daniel, bpt. 13 Dec 1812
  Anne, dau of John, bpt. May 1758
  Benjamin, son of Benjamin, bpt. 22 Sep 1765
  Bethiah, dau of Joshua, bpt. 13 Jun 1742
  Betty, dau of John Jr., bpt. 13 Jun 1773
  Betty, dau of George, bpt. 19 May 1776
  Betty, dau of Richard, bpt. 9 Jun 1776
  Billy, son of Samuel, bpt. 16 Nov 1766
  Billy, son of Dowrst, bpt. 11 Jan 1789
  Daniel, son of Reuben, bpt. 15 Mar 1767
  Daniel, son of Joshua, bpt. 9 Aug 1778
  Daniel, son of Daniel, bpt. 5 Aug 1810
  David, son of Ephraim, bpt. 1 Nov 1772
  David, son of David, bpt. 30 Nov 1800
  David Lang, son of John, bpt. 16 Nov 1817
  Deborah, dau of Joseph, bpt. 8 Sep 1765
  Dowst, son of Samuel, bpt. 1 Jul 1764
  Edward, son of Thomas, bpt. 12 Jan 1806
  Eliza, dau of John, bpt. 15 Sep 1811
  Elizabeth, dau of Joshua, bpt. 17 Mar 1751
  Elizabeth, dau of Samuel, bpt. 22 Jan 1757

RYE BAPTISMS

RAND, Elizabeth, dau of Joseph Jr., bpt. 2 Dec 1804
  Elizabeth Martha, dau of John T., bpt. 26 Aug 1821
  Ellie Morrison, dau of Samuel Jr., bpt. 6 Sep 1789
  Elvin, son of Daniel, bpt. 19 Mar 1815
  Ephraim, son of Thomas, bpt. 17 Mar 1736/7
  Ephraim, son of Ephraim, bpt. 19 Nov 1769
  Florinda, dau of Thomas, bpt. 12 Mar 1801
  George, son of Joshua, bpt. 8 Apr 1744
  George, son of George, bpt. 19 May 1776
  Hannah, dau of John, bpt. Aug 1781
  Hannah, dau of Dowrst, bpt. 14 Oct 1804
  Hannah Moses, dau of Joshua Jr., bpt. 15 Oct 1752
  Harriet Jane, dau of John, bpt. 12 Nov 1809
  Harry, son of Joshua, bpt. 23 Oct 1803
  Hepsibah, dau of Joshua, bpt. 15 Jun 1746
  Ira, son of Joseph, bpt. 8 Sep 1816
  Isabella, dau of Olive, bpt. 14 Aug 1803
  Israel, son of Ephraim, bpt. 19 Jul 1761
  James, son of Daniel, bpt. 16 Oct 1808
  Jeremiah, son of John, bpt. 12 Apr 1761
  John, son of Joshua, bpt. 14 Feb 1742
  John, son of John, bpt. 10 Sep 1749
  John, son of George, bpt. 3 May 1772
  John, son of John Jr., bpt. 24 May 1778
  John, son of Samuel Jr., bpt. 4 Oct 1801
  John Tuck, son of Thomas, bpt. 6 May 1792
  Jonathan, son of Ephraim, bpt. Oct 1767
  Joseph, son of Joshua, bpt. 15 Sep 1739
  Joseph, son of Joseph, bpt. 30 Nov 1755
  Joseph, son of Joseph, bpt. 30 Oct 1796
  Joshua, son of Joshua Jr., bpt. Jan 1758
  Joshua, son of Joseph, bpt. Mar 1768
  Joshua, son of Nathaniel Jr., bpt. 29 Oct 1769
  Joshua, son of Joshua, bpt. 9 Jul 1780
  Joshua, son of John, bpt. 1784
  Levi, son of Joseph, bpt. 21 Jun 1782
  Levi, son of Joseph Jr., bpt. 20 Oct 1811
  Levi Moses, son of Billy, bpt. 8 Mar 1819
  Louisa, dau of Daniel, bpt. 22 Jun 1806
  Lucy, dau of John, bpt 19 Apr 1746/7
  Lucy, dau of Benjamin, bpt. 31 Jul 1757
  Margaret, dau of George, bpt. 12 Feb 1769
  Mary, dau of Joshua Jr., bpt. 1 Jul 1744
  Mary, dau of Joseph, bpt. Apr 1759
  Mary, dau of Temperance, bpt. 12 Apr 1761

RYE BAPTISMS

RAND, Mary, dau of Nathaniel, bpt. 3 Jun 1764
Mary, dau of John Jr., bpt. Feb 1776
Mary, dau of Joseph Jr., bpt. 10 Jul 1808
Mary, dau of Samuel H., bpt. 6 Mar 1809
Mary Ann, dau of David, bpt. 19 Jan 1806
Mary Jones Wallis, dau of Thomas, bpt. 14 Jul 1793
Mary Moses, dau of Widow Mary, bpt. 30 May 1790
Mehitable, dau of Nathaniel, bpt. Jan 1771
Mehitable, dau of Joshua, bpt. 15 Jun 1788
Mercy, dau of William, bpt. 6 Dec 1772
Mercy, bpt. 9 Oct 1803
Micah, son of Joshua, bpt. 18 Dec 1748
Molly, dau of Nathaniel, bpt. 25 Nov 1764
Molly, dau of Joseph, bpt. 31 Mar 1771
Molly, dau of Nathaniel, bpt. 4 Jul 1782
Molly, dau of Zebedee, bpt. 1 Jul 1798
Moses, son of Joshua, bpt. 30 Aug 1789
Moses, son of Daniel, bpt. 10 Jun 1804
Nancy, dau of John, bpt. 14 Sep 1794
Nancy, dau of Nathaniel, bpt. 5 Oct 1794
Nathaniel, son of Richard, bpt. 13 Mar 1736/7
Nathaniel, son of Amos, bpt. 14 Aug 1740
Nathaniel, son of John, bpt. 31 Mar 1754
Nathaniel Marden, son of Joseph Jr., bpt. 1807
Obed, son of Joshua, bpt. 7 Oct 1804
Olive, dau of Richard, bpt. 13 Jul 1740
Oliver, son of Dowrst, bpt. 10 Jun 1802
Oliver Porter, son of Dowrst, bpt. 15 Nov 1807
Olly, dau of Nathaniel, bpt. 15 Apr 1762
Olly, dau of Joseph, bpt. 21 May 1775
Olly, dau of John, bpt. 11 Jul 1789
Olly, dau of Joseph Jr., bpt. 11 Oct 1801
Patty, dau of Daniel, bpt. 4 Nov 1801
Philbrick, son of Joseph, bpt. 29 Mar 1761
Rachel, dau of John, bpt. 1 Dec 1745
Rachel, dau of Samuel, bpt. 25 Apr 1762
Reed Venard, son of Samuel Jr., bpt. 9 Sep 1798
Reuben, son of Reuben, bpt. 4 Mar 1764
Reuben, son of David, bpt. 30 Dec 1798
Richard, son of William Jr., bpt. 5 Jul 1753
Richard, son of Nathaniel, bpt. Jun 1758
Ruth, dau of Nathaniel, bpt. 15 Sep 1776
Sally, dau of Nathaniel, bpt. 17 Jan 1773
Sally, dau of Richard, bpt. 2 Jul 1775
Sally, dau of Abigail, bpt. 31 Aug 1778
Sally, dau of Nathaniel Jr., bpt. 25 Jul 1779
Sally, dau of Joseph, bpt. 2 Oct 1785
Sally, dau of John, bpt. 2 Sep 1787

RYE BAPTISMS

RAND, Samuel, son of Thomas, bpt. 15 Nov 1741
   Samuel, son of Samuel, bpt. 23 Dec 1753
   Samuel, son of John, bpt. 18 Aug 1751
   Samuel, son of John, bpt. May 1758
   Samuel, son of Ephraim, bpt. 28 May 1758
   Samuel, son of Nathaniel, bpt. 10 Feb 1760
   Samuel, son of Joshua Jr., bpt. 11 Apr 1762
   Samuel, son of William, bpt. 30 Apr 1769
   Samuel, son of Nathaniel, bpt. 12 Aug 1781
   Samuel, son of Joshua, bpt. 22 Jun 1783
   Samuel, son of Samuel, bpt. 12 Feb 1787
   Samuel, son of Thomas, bpt. 17 Jul 1796
   Samuel Hunt, son of Joseph, bpt. 25 May 1777
   Samuel Hunt, son of Joseph, bpt. 3 Jul 1803
   Samuel Moses, son of Billy, bpt. 21 Aug 1803
   Sarah, dau of Joshua, bpt. 13 Apr 1740
   Sarah, dau of Joshua Jr., bpt. 15 Jan 1749
   Sarah, dau of Samuel, bpt. 17 Nov 1751
   Sarah, dau of Ephraim, bpt. 18 Nov 1764
   Sarah, dau of Nathaniel, bpt. 5 Aug 1774
   Sarah, dau of Samuel Jr., bpt. 16 Oct 1774
   Sarah, dau of Billy, bpt. 14 Jun 1801
   Sarah, dau of David, bpt. 5 Sep 1813
   Simeon, son of Ephraim, bpt. May 1775
   Simon, son of Nathaniel, bpt. 5 Nov 1772
   Stephen, son of William, bpt. 17 Dec 1748
   Stephen, son of William, bpt. 5 Mar 1749
   Stephen, son of Elis, bpt. Jan 1756
   Stephen Dolbear, son of Samuel, bpt. 26 Jun 1785
   Susannah Goss, dau of Joses, bpt. 1 Jul 1810
   Tabitha, dau of Nathaniel, bpt. Aug 1777
   Temperance, dau of Joshua, bpt. 3 Aug 1738
   Theodore, son of Joshua, bpt. 15 Apr 1787
   Thomas, son of Samuel, bpt. 2 Apr 1749
   Thomas, son of Samuel, bpt. Jun 1760
   Thomas, son of Reuben, bpt. Feb 1761
   Thomas, son of Thomas, bpt. 23 Jun 1799
   Thomas, son of Thomas, bpt. 7 Aug 1803
   Thomas Jefferson, son of John, bpt. 23 Oct 1814
   Trundy, son of Dowrst, bpt. 29 Jun 1800
   William, son of John, bpt. 25 May 1755
   William, son of William Jr., bpt. 16 Oct 1774
   William Hodskins, son of William Jr., bpt. 5 Jul 1753
   William Seavey, son of Joshua, bpt. Aug 1781
   Zeb, son of Joseph, bpt. 12 May 1765
   Zebedee, son of Joseph, bpt. 2 May 1773
   Zebedee, son of Joseph Jr., bpt. 6 Jul 1800
   _____, child of Joshua, bpt. 1783

RYE BAPTISMS

RANDALL (RENDALL), Abigail, dau of John, bpt. Nov 1749
  Abigail, dau of Mark, bpt. 1 Apr 1750
  Abigail, dau of Paul, bpt. 11 Apr 1762
  Abigail, dau of George, bpt. 9 Jul 1769
  Abigail, dau of George, bpt. 11 Dec 1796
  Alexander Shapleigh, son of William B., bpt. 3 Aug 1805
  Amelia Berry, dau of George, bpt. 28 Sep 1760
  Benjamin, son of Benjamin, bpt. 20 Aug 1817
  Daniel, son of Mark, bpt. 5 Nov 1769
  Deborah, dau of Mark, bpt. 29 Jul 1764
  Dolly Sherburne Wendal, dau of Benjamin, bpt. 7 Oct 1804
  Edward, son of George, bpt. Aug 1758
  Edward, son of George, bpt. 3 Apr 1785
  Elizabeth, dau of Mark, bpt. 22 Jun 1755
  George, son of George, bpt. Mar 1762
  George Sanders, son of Benjamin, bpt. 7 Jul 1799
  Hannah, dau of Paul, bpt. Apr 1757
  Hannah, dau of Mark, bpt. Sep 1778
  Hannah, dau of Benjamin, bpt. 30 Aug 1801
  James Marston, son of William, bpt. 1 Jun 1746
  John, son of John, bpt. 20 Apr 1746
  John, son of Mark, bpt. 23 Jul 1762
  Jonathan, son of William, bpt. 8 Apr 1759
  Joseph, son of William, bpt. Apr 1756
  Joseph Yeaton, son of William, bpt. 25 Apr 1802
  Lovey Brackett, dau of George, bpt. 2 Nov 1794
  Lucy, dau of William, bpt. 17 Jan 1768
  Mark, son of Mark, bpt. 23 Jul 1757
  Mary, dau of William, bpt. 23 Sep 1750
  Mary Elizabeth, dau of Reuben, bpt. 6 Feb 1820
  Mary Saunders, dau of Benjamin, bpt. 23 Mar 1817
  Molly, dau of George, bpt. 3 Apr 1785
  Moses, son of Mark, bpt. 12 May 1751
  Nancy, dau of William, bpt. 8 Nov 1795
  Paul, son of Paul, bpt. 25 May 1755
  Rachel, dau of George, bpt. 16 Jan 1765
  Reuben, son of Benjamin, bpt. 5 Oct 1794
  Reuben, son of Benjamin, bpt. 3 Jan 1802
  Sally, dau of Mark, bpt. 14 Nov 1772
  Sally, dau of William B., bpt. 24 Dec 1807
  Samuel, son of Mark, bpt. 12 Jul 1767
  Samuel, son of Benjamin, bpt. 3 Dec 1810
  Samuel Sanders, son of Benjamin, bpt. 4 Dec 1796
  Sarah, dau of George, bpt. 13 Sep 1752
  Sarah, dau of George, bpt. 7 Apr 1754
  Sarah, dau of Benjamin, bpt. 20 Aug 1817

RYE BAPTISMS

RANDALL, Simeon, son of Mark, bpt. 6 Apr 1760
  Stephen, son of William, bpt. 29 Jul 1753
  Susanna Lang, dau of William, bpt. 17 Sep 1797
  Thomas, son of William, bpt. 27 Oct 1770
  William, son of William, bpt. 3 Jul 1748
  William, son of William B., bpt. 4 May 1800
  William Bates, son of George, bpt. 27 Jun 1771
  William Saunders, son of Benjamin, bpt. 1806
REMICK, David, son of Isaac, bpt. Mar 1759
  Elizabeth, dau of Isaac, bpt. Jun 1771
  Hannah, dau of Isaac, bpt. 3 May 1774
  Huldah, dau of Isaac, bpt. 6 Oct 1776
  Isaac, son of Isaac, bpt. Oct 1769
  Jane Foss, dau of Isaac, bpt. 13 Mar 1803
  Jane Kitson, dau of Isaac, bpt. 19 Jul 1778
  John Yeaton, bpt. 9 Sep 1818
  Joseph, son of Isaac, bpt. Oct 1769
  Mary, dau of Isaac, bpt. 1 Dec 1765
  Meribah, dau of Isaac, bpt. Nov 1760
  Moses, son of Widow Remick, bpt. 7 Oct 1781
  Nancy, dau of Joseph, bpt. 20 Jun 1805
  Sarah, dau of Isaac, bpt. 7 Nov 1756
  Thomas, son of Isaac, bpt. Sep 1762
  _____, dau of Moses, bpt. 13 Jul 1806
ROLLINS, Martha, dau of Henry, bpt. 9 Jul 1775
RUGG, Juda Mace, dau of William, bpt. 6 Nov 1793
SALTER, Alexander, son of Alexander, bpt. 7 Oct 1744
  Alexander, son of Alexander, bpt. 7 Jun 1778
  Elizabeth, dau of Alexander, bpt. 13 Jul 1746
  John, son of Alexander, bpt. 27 Jun 1742
  John, son of Alexander, bpt. 25 Sep 1748
  John, son of Alexander, bpt. 14 ___ 1806
  Joseph Jenness, son of Alexander, bpt. 30 Aug 1812
  Lois Ann, dau of Alexander, bpt. 8 Jul 1804
  Lucy, dau of Alexander, bpt. 23 Jun 1751
  Lucy, dau of Alexander, bpt. 5 Nov 1769
  Mary, dau of Alexander, bpt. 20 Apr 1741
  Sally Goss, dau of Alexander, bpt. 30 Oct 1808
  Sarah, dau of Alexander, bpt. 1 Sep 1771
  Webster, son of Alexander, bpt. 27 Jan 1783
SANBORN, Hannah Moses, dau of _____, bpt. 25 Sep 1802
  Nathan, son of Samuel, bpt. 17 Jan 1768
  Sarah, dau of John, bpt. 8 Jul 1770
SANDAY, John, a negro man, bpt. 18 Oct 1772
SAUNDERS (SANDERS), Abigail, dau of John, bpt. 12 Oct 1760

RYE BAPTISMS

SAUNDERS, Betsey, dau of William, bpt. 20 Nov 1785
  Dorothy Wallis, dau of Robert 3d, bpt. 8 Mar 1795
  Elijah, son of Robert Jr., bpt. 20 Aug 1769
  Elizabeth, dau of Samuel, bpt. 21 Oct 1753
  Esther, dau of John, bpt. 27 Sep 1741
  George, son of Samuel, bpt. 3 Aug 1760
  George, son of George, bpt. 2 Sep 1764
  George, son of George, bpt. 23 Jul 1769
  George, son of George, bpt. 23 Dec 1792
  George Berry, son of John, bpt. 11 Sep 1748
  Hannah, dau of Samuel, bpt. 28 Aug 1749
  Hannah, dau of George, bpt. 15 Aug 1779
  Henry Shapley, son of George, bpt. 6 Mar 1791
  Job, son of Robert 3d, bpt. 26 May 1793
  John, son of John, bpt. 9 Nov 1746
  John, son of Samuel, bpt. 28 May 1758
  John, son of Widow Dorcas, bpt. 9 Jun 1771
  John, son of Robert Jr., bpt. 10 Apr 1774
  Levi Dearborn, son of Samuel, bpt. 9 Mar 1766
  Martha, dau of George, bpt. 22 Jun 1766
  Mary, dau of Samuel, bpt. 8 Jan 1744
  Mary, dau of John, bpt. 20 Oct 1744
  Mary, dau of Robert Jr., bpt. 16 Aug 1767
  Mary, dau of John Jr., bpt. 14 May 1769
  Mary, dau of George, bpt. 3 Nov 1776
  Mary Mead, dau of George, bpt. 16 Jul 1794
  Mercy Haines, dau of George, bpt. 30 Aug 1767
  Molly, dau of George Jr., bpt. 10 May 1772
  Molly, dau of Widow Amelia, bpt. 5 Oct 1794
  Nathaniel, son of Robert Jr., bpt. 29 Nov 1778
  Patience Lock, dau of Elijah, bpt. 29 Jun 1794
  Robert, son of Robert, bpt. 30 Mar 1742
  Robert, son of John, bpt. 3 Jul 1743
  Robert, son of Samuel, bpt. 7 Dec 1755
  Robert, son of Robert Jr., bpt. 12 Oct 1766
  Robert, son of Robert, bpt. 31 Oct 1790
  Sally, dau of Robert 3d, bpt. 23 Nov 1788
  Samuel, son of Samuel, bpt. 14 Jul 1745
  Samuel, son of George, bpt. 8 Dec 1771
  Samuel, son of Widow Amelia, bpt. 5 Oct 1794
  Sarah, dau of Samuel, bpt. 4 Oct 1747
  Sarah, dau of George, bpt. 18 Sep 1757
  Sarah, dau of John, bpt. Aug 1763
  Sarah, dau of George, bpt. 10 Oct 1773
  William, son of George, bpt. 11 Nov 1759
  William, son of John, bpt. 19 Jun 1763
  William, son of William, bpt. 20 Mar 1785
SCADGEL, Abigail, dau of Benjamin, bpt. May 1754

RYE BAPTISMS

SCADGEL, Abigail, dau of Benjamin, bpt. 19 Jul 1761
  Benjamin, son of Benjamin, bpt. Feb 1757
  Hannah, dau of Benjamin, bpt. 25 Jul 1752
  Mary, dau of Benjamin, bpt. 7 Aug 1748
  Sarah, dau of Benjamin, bpt. 20 May 1750
SCOTT, George Silvanus, son of Samuel, bpt. 12 Mar 1749
SEAVEY (SEAVY), Aaron, son of William, bpt. Aug 1759
  Aaron, son of Daniel, bpt. 22 May 1785
  Abigail, dau of Amos, bpt. 10 Jun 1764
  Abigail, dau of Moses, bpt. May 1770
  Abigail, dau of William, bpt. 3 Jul 1791
  Alfred, son of Joseph Jr., bpt. 22 Jun 1806
  Amos, son of William, bpt. 20 May 1787
  Amos, son of Amos, bpt. 21 Jun 1818
  Anna, dau of William Jr., bpt. 19 Apr 1772
  Anna Towle, dau of Ebenezer, bpt. 1 Jul 1798
  Anna Trefethern, dau of Amos, bpt. 12 Oct 1827
  Anne, dau of Amos, bpt. 16 Nov 1755
  Asa, son of William, bpt. Nov 1775
  Benjamin, son of Samuel Jr., bpt. 2 Oct 1778
  Betsey, dau of Ebenezer, bpt. 28 Dec 1794
  Betty, dau of Joseph Langdon, bpt. 15 Sep 1782
  Catherine, dau of Henry Jr., bpt. 29 Sep 1746
  Clarrisa Bryant, dau of Amos, bpt. 12 Oct 1827
  Comfort, dau of Jonathan, bpt. Apr 1756
  Daniel, son of William, bpt. 1 May 1763
  Deborah, dau of Samuel Jr., bpt. Jan 1737/8
  Deborah, dau of Samuel Jr., bpt. 11 Mar 1764
  Deborah, dau of Paul, bpt. 22 Feb 1767
  Dinah, negro woman of James Seavey, bpt. 31 Jul 1757
  Dinah, negro child of James Seavey, bpt. 13 Sep 1772
  Dolly, dau of William, bpt. Aug 1781
  Dorothy, dau of Amos, bpt. 27 Sep 1761
  Ebenezer, son of Paul, bpt. 9 Jun 1765
  Ebenezer Wallis, son of Ebenezer, bpt. 30 Jun 1796
  Edward, son of Joseph, bpt. 21 Oct 1810
  Elijah, son of Henry, bpt. 15 Aug 1742
  Elijah, son of Moses, bpt. 22 May 1774
  Eliza Ann, dau of William Jr., bpt. 22 Mar 1807
  Eliza Mary Langdon, dau of Joseph Jr., bpt. 13 May 1804
  Emmaline, dau of William Jr., bpt. 3 Mar 1805
  Ephraim, son of Joseph, bpt. 19 Feb 1792

RYE BAPTISMS

SEAVEY, George, son of Joseph Jr., bpt. 22 May 1748
George, negro of Amos Seavey, bpt. 5 Apr 1753
Hannah, dau of Samuel Jr., bpt. 5 Apr 1746/7
Hannah, dau of Amos, bpt. 9 Apr 1749
Hannah, dau of Henry, bpt. 20 May 1750
Hannah, dau of William, bpt. 20 May 1753
Hannah, dau of Paul, bpt. 7 May 1769
Hannah, dau of Joseph, bpt. 29 Mar 1774
Hannah, dau of William, bpt. 3 May 1774
Hannah, dau of William Jr., bpt. 10 Nov 1776
Hannah, dau of Ebenezer, bpt. 13 May 1792
Hannah Whidden, dau of Joseph, bpt. 19 Mar 1815
Henry Dow, son of Samuel Jr., bpt. 14 Nov 1773
Huldah, dau of Moses, bpt. 22 Jul 1763
Isaac, son of Samuel Jr., bpt. 30 Jan 1749
Isaac, son of Samuel Jr., bpt. 12 Apr 1752
James, son of James, bpt. 14 Nov 1756
James, son of Joseph, bpt. 25 Jul 1813
Jenny, negro child of Amos Seavey, bpt. 12 Oct 1760
Jesse, son of Joshua of Farmington, bpt. 27 Jan 1811
John, son of Henry, bpt. 16 Aug 1741
John, son of James, bpt. 4 Mar 1760
John, son of Noah, bpt. 11 Feb 1764
John Langdon, son of William, bpt. 8 Sep 1793
Jonathan, son of Jonathan, bpt. Aug 1758
Joseph, son of Henry Jr., bpt. 7 Oct 1744
Joseph, son of Henry Jr., bpt. 30 Mar 1746
Joseph, son of Solomon, bpt. 26 Mar 1759
Joseph, son of James, bpt. Dec 1767
Joseph, son of Joseph, bpt. 25 Nov 1770
Joseph, son of Joseph, bpt. 6 Jul 1788
Joseph Langdon, son of Amos, bpt. 9 Jun 1751
Joseph Langdon, son of Joseph Langdon, bpt. 30 Dec 1798
Joseph Mason, son of Isaac, bpt. 14 Aug 1785
Joseph Whidden, son of Joseph Jr., bpt. 19 Jun 1808
Lettice Stillson, dau of Amos, bpt. 13 May 1810
Levi, son of Jonathan, bpt. Dec 1760
Levi, son of Moses, bpt. 6 Apr 1766
Lucy Wainwright, dau of Daniel, bpt. 4 Jun 1797
Lyman, son of William Jr., bpt. 27 Feb 1803
Margaret, dau of Samuel Jr., bpt. 4 Feb 1750
Mark, son of William, bpt. 4 Jul 1742
Mark, son of William, bpt. 7 Dec 1766
Martha, dau of William, bpt. 15 Dec 1754

RYE BAPTISMS

SEAVEY, Martha, dau of Amos, bpt. Jun 1758
  Mary, dau of Amos, bpt. 25 Jan 1746/7
  Mary, dau of William Jr., bpt. 24 Nov 1769
  Mary, dau of Amos, bpt. 30 Oct 1814
  Mary Jenness, dau of Amos, bpt. 29 May 1808
  Mary Meder, dau of Ebenezer, bpt. 9 Feb 1805
  Mary Moses, dau of Joshua, bpt. 20 Nov 1803
  Mehitable, dau of William, bpt. 12 Feb 1758
  Mehitable, dau of Paul, bpt. 5 Mar 1775
  Mehitable, dau of Daniel, bpt. 14 Feb 1802
  Molly, dau of Joseph, bpt. 12 Jan 1777
  Molly, dau of Joseph L., bpt. 21 Jul 1793
  Moses, son of William, bpt. 31 Mar 1765
  Moses, son of Moses, bpt. 29 Nov 1767
  Nabby, dau of Joseph, bpt. 22 Sep 1782
  Nabby, dau of Joshua, bpt. 28 Apr 1805
  Noah, son of Noah, bpt. 12 Jul 1778
  Olly, dau of Henry Jr., bpt. 18 Sep 1748
  Olly, dau of Joshua, bpt. 21 Sep 1800
  Patience, negro child of Amos Seavey, bpt. 21 Aug 1768
  Peggy, negro child of Amos Seavey, bpt. May 1754
  Polly, dau of Joseph Langdon, bpt. 11 Jun 1780
  Polly, dau of Joseph Langdon, bpt. 15 Sep 1782
  Ruth, dau of Henry, bpt. 14 Oct 1744
  Ruth, dau of William, bpt. 30 May 1756
  Ruth, dau of Noah, bpt. 6 Apr 1766
  Ruth Tarlton, dau of Samuel Jr., bpt. 13 Jul 1766
  Sally, dau of _____, bpt. 1784
  Sally, dau of Joseph Langdon, bpt. 17 May 1778
  Sally, dau of Joseph, bpt. 13 Aug 1786
  Sally, dau of Daniel, bpt. 8 Jul 1787
  Sally, dau of Ebenezer, bpt. 13 May 1792
  Sally, dau of Joshua, bpt. 21 Jul 1799
  Samuel, son of Samuel Jr., bpt. 30 Sep 1739
  Samuel, son of Moses, bpt. 24 Oct 1762
  Samuel, son of Joseph, bpt. 11 Jun 1780
  Samuel Wallis, son of Paul, bpt. Oct 1779
  Sarah, dau of Joseph, bpt. 27 Oct 1745
  Sarah, dau of Samuel Jr., bpt. Feb 1756
  Sarah, dau of Noah, bpt. 26 Feb 1771
  Sarah, dau of Paul, bpt. 14 Jun 1772
  Sarah Drake, dau of Amos, bpt. 27 Jul 1823
  Shadrach, son of William, bpt. 24 Dec 1769
  Simon, son of William, bpt. 31 May 1772
  Susan Hart, dau of William Jr., bpt. 8 Sep 1811
  Sydna Sargent, dau of Joseph L., bpt. 7 May 1797
  Temperance, dau of Noah, bpt. 23 Oct 1768

RYE BAPTISMS

SEAVEY, Theodore Jackson, son of Joseph L., bpt. 3 Jul 1785
  Thomas, son of Noah, bpt. 12 Jul 1778
  Titus, negro child of James Seavey, bpt. 13 Sep 1772
  William, son of Amos, bpt. 11 Aug 1745
  William, son of William, bpt. 14 Jun 1761
  William, son of William Jr., bpt. 29 May 1774
  William, son of Paul, bpt. 26 Mar 1782
  William, son of Daniel, bpt. 10 Oct 1790
  William, son of Joseph, bpt. 9 Oct 1791
  William, son of Ebenezer, bpt. Dec 1800
  William Darren, son of William Jr., bpt. 31 Jan 1808
  William Lyman, son of William Jr., bpt. 4 Nov 1801
  Winthrop, son of Joshua, bpt. 12 Dec 1802
  _____, dau of Solomon, bpt. Mar 1762
SHANNON, Bette, dau of Thomas, bpt. 17 Feb 1754
  John, son of Thomas, bpt. Sep 1757
  Samuel, son of Thomas, bpt. 5 Sep 1762
  Thomas, son of Thomas, bpt. 21 Oct 1759
  William, son of Thomas, bpt. 31 Aug 1755
SHAPLEY (SHAPLEIGH), Benjamin, son of James, bpt. 17 Jan 1790
  Dorcas Pitman, dau of Henry, bpt. 21 Apr 1793
  Eliza, dau of Henry, bpt. 5 Jan 1800
  Elizabeth, dau of James, bpt. 17 Jan 1790
  Henry Carter, son of Henry, bpt. 30 Apr 1797
  James, son of Widow Hepsibah, bpt. 23 Jan 1790
  Joshua, son of Samuel, bpt. 2 Aug 1817
  Jotham Berry, son of Henry, bpt. 14 Dec 1794
  Judith, dau of Henry, bpt. 30 Jun 1774
  Reuben, son of Henry, bpt. 30 Jun 1774
  Reuben, son of Henry, bpt. 3 Nov 1805
  Robert, son of Widow Hepsibah, bpt. 2 Nov 1788
  Robert Powers, son of Henry, bpt. 11 Jun 1809
  Sally, dau of Henry, bpt. 30 Jun 1774
  Samuel, son of Henry, bpt. 21 Apr 1793
  Sarah, dau of Widow Hepsibah, bpt. 2 Nov 1788
SHERBURNE, Andrew, son of Andrew, bpt. 6 Oct 1765
  Elizabeth, dau of Andrew, bpt. 27 Nov 1768
  Martha, dau of Andrew, bpt. 11 Jul 1762
  Martha, dau of Andrew, bpt. 11 Mar 1764
  Samuel, son of Andrew, bpt. 24 May 1767
  Thomas, son of Andrew, bpt. 12 Jul 1761
SLEEPER, Benjamin, son of Tristram, bpt. 9 May 1779
  Eliphalet, son of Tristram, bpt. 25 Nov 1770

RYE BAPTISMS

SLEEPER, Mary Wedgewood, dau of Eliphalet, bpt. 1807
  Molly, dau of Tristram, bpt. 20 Dec 1772
  Nancy, child living with William Sleeper, bpt. 22 May 1796
  Richard, son of Eliphalet, bpt. 13 Jun 1802
  Ruth Tarlton, dau of Thomas, bpt. 2 Nov 1800
  Sally Johnson, dau of Eliphalet, bpt. 5 ___ 1806
  Sarah Ann Gilman, dau of William, bpt. 6 Nov 1808
  Theophilus William, son of William, bpt. 6 Nov 1808
  Thomas, son of Tristram, bpt. 20 Sep 1767
  William, son of Tristram, bpt. 12 May 1776
SMITH, Betsey, dau of Samuel, bpt. 18 Oct 1795
  Billy, son of Samuel, bpt. 4 Sep 1790
  David, son of David, bpt 17 Jan 1741
  Esther, dau of Samuel, bpt. 4 Sep 1790
  Hannah, dau of David, bpt. 20 Dec 1742
  Israel, son of David, bpt. 31 Dec 1749
  Joanna, dau of David, bpt. 22 Feb 1747
  John, son of Samuel, bpt. 9 Oct 1791
  Jonathan, son of David, bpt. 29 Dec 1737/8
  Jonathan, son of David, bpt. 13 Jan 1745
  Joseph Hall, son of Samuel, bpt. 19 Nov 1797
  Mary, dau of David, bpt. 13 Aug 1769
  Sarah, dau of David Jr., bpt. 11 Oct 1772
TARLTON, Mercy, bpt. 5 Oct 1794
  Peggy, bpt. 5 Oct 1794
  Ruth, dau of Mary, bpt. 17 Oct 1762
TAYLOR, Darius, son of Thomas, bpt. 1807
  John, son of Thomas, bpt. 12 May 1805
  Lydia Lovering, dau of Thomas, bpt. 11 Dec 1803
  Sarah Ann, dau of Ebenezer, bpt. 20 Aug 1809
  William Norton, son of Ebenezer, bpt. 11 Dec 1803
THOMAS, James, son of William, bpt. 18 Nov 1764
  John Sanders, son of William, bpt. Jul 1768
  Robert Sanders, son of Widow Mary, bpt. 16 Dec 1770
  William, son of William, bpt. 12 Oct 1766
TIBBIT (TIBBETS), Edward Randall, son of Jacob, bpt. 8 Aug 1778
  Mary, dau of Jacob, bpt. 13 Sep 1767
  Molly, dau of Jacob, bpt. 17 Oct 1773
  Samuel, son of Jacob, bpt. 8 Dec 1771
  Thomas, son of Jacob, bpt. 14 Apr 1776
TOWLE (TOWL), Benjamin, son of Jonathan Jr., bpt. 7 May 1769

RYE BAPTISMS

TOWLE, Benjamin Marden, son of Simon, bpt. Oct 1782
    Dolly, dau of Samuel, bpt. 16 Oct 1774
    Elizabeth, dau of Jonathan Jr., bpt. 15 Jul 1764
    Esther, dau of Samuel, bpt. 11 Oct 1772
    Hannah, dau of Jonathan Jr., bpt. 3 Jul 1762
    Job, son of Samuel, bpt. Jan 1771
    Jonathan, son of Levi, bpt. 24 Mar 1754
    Jonathan, son of Nathan, bpt. 22 May 1774
    Joseph, son of Jonathan Jr., bpt. 14 Dec 1766
    Levi, son of Jonathan Jr., bpt. Mar 1757
    Lucy, dau of Nathan, bpt. 13 Sep 1767
    Mary, dau of Jonathan Jr., bpt. Apr 1755
    Molly, dau of Samuel, bpt. 7 Jun 1767
    Nabby, dau of Samuel, bpt. 16 Aug 1778
    Nathan, son of Nathan, bpt. 24 Nov 1771
    Olly, dau of Samuel, bpt. 25 Sep 1763
    Sally, dau of Jonathan Jr., bpt. 14 Jan 1776
    Sarah, dau of Samuel, bpt. 14 Apr 1765
    Simeon, son of Jonathan Jr., bpt. 4 Feb 1753
TREFETHERN, Abigail, dau of Robinson, bpt. 17 Aug 1755
    Abigail, dau of _____, bpt. 7 Oct 1780
    Benjamin Bailey, son of William, bpt. 12 May 1805
    Betty, dau of William, bpt. 1783
    Hanson Hoyt, son of William Jr., bpt. 6 Oct 1822
    Henry, son of Robinson, bpt. 24 Jul 1774
    Henry, son of William, bpt. 8 Mar 1795
    John Adams, son of William, bpt. 11 Aug 1799
    Joseph, son of William, bpt. 29 Mar 1788
    Mary, dau of Robinson, bpt. 24 Jul 1748
    Mary Shaddock, dau of Henry, bpt. 9 Jul 1826
    Nancy, dau of William, bpt. 14 Nov 1790
    Naphtili Tucker, son of William, bpt. 15 May 1785
    Nathaniel, son of William, bpt. 2 Oct 1777
    Polly, dau of William, bpt. 18 Nov 1792
    Robinson, son of Robinson, bpt. 8 Apr 1753
    Sabrina, dau of William Jr., bpt. 11 Jul 1813
    Salome, dau of Robinson, bpt. 24 Jul 1774
    Thomas, son of William, bpt. 13 Jun 1802
    William, son of Robinson, bpt. 7 Jul 1751
    William, son of William, bpt. 18 Jun 1775
    William, son of William Jr., bpt. 2 Dec 1810
TUCKER, Elizabeth, dau of Nathaniel, bpt. 17 Feb 1754
    Elizabeth Hall, dau of Joseph, bpt. 29 May 1803
    Huldah, dau of Widow Sarah, bpt. 8 Oct 1758

RYE BAPTISMS

TUCKER, John, son of William, bpt. 23 Nov 1788
  John, son of Joseph, bpt. 12 Oct 1800
  Joseph, son of Nathaniel, bpt. 5 Jun 1774
  Joseph Parsons, son of Joseph, bpt. 10 Jun 1798
  Mary, dau of William, bpt. 17 Jan 1741
  Molly, dau of Widow Sarah, bpt. Oct 1758
  Molly, ____ Nathaniel took to bring up, bpt. 5 Jun 1774
  Nathaniel, son of Nathaniel, bpt. 8 Oct 1758
  Nathaniel, son of Joseph, bpt. 4 Sep 1796
  Olly, dau of William, bpt. 2 Nov 1794
  Richard, son of Nathaniel, bpt. 17 Mar 1765
  Richard, son of William, bpt. 21 Mar 1790
  Sarah, dau of William, bpt. May 1737
  Sarah, dau of Nathaniel, bpt. 20 Jun 1756
  William, son of Nathaniel, bpt. 14 Feb 1762
  William, son of William, bpt. 4 Dec 1791
VARRELL (VERRILL), Abigail Locke, dau of Joseph, bpt. 5 Nov 1803
  Betty, dau of Edward, bpt. 9 Jun 1776
  Deborah, dau of Solomon, bpt. 20 May 1759
  Edward, son of Edward, bpt. 3 Apr 1785
  Elizabeth, dau of Solomon, bpt. 20 May 1759
  Hannah, dau of Solomon, bpt. 20 May 1759
  John, son of Solomon, bpt. 20 May 1759
  John, son of Edward, bpt. 9 Mar 1794
  John, son of John, bpt. 1 Aug 1795
  Joseph (twin), son of Joseph, bpt. 19 Dec 1794
  Joseph, son of Joseph, bpt. 4 Dec 1796
  Joseph, son of Edward, bpt. 19 Apr 1801
  Joses Philbrick (twin), son of Joseph, bpt. 19 Dec 1794
  Maria, dau of Richard T., bpt. 17 Jun 1804
  Martha Lang, dau of Samuel, bpt. 10 Nov 1822
  Mary, dau of Solomon, bpt. 9 Jun 1765
  Nancy, dau of William, bpt. Nov 1796
  Nathaniel, son of John, bpt. 30 Apr 1786
  Polly, dau of Edward, bpt. 10 Apr 1791
  Rachel, dau of Edward, bpt. 13 Nov 1774
  Richard Tucker, son of Edward, bpt. 3 Apr 1785
  Robert Waldron, son of Samuel, bpt. 27 Aug 1826
  Sally, dau of John, bpt. 21 Jun 1789
  Sally, dau of Edward, bpt. 11 Aug 1799
  Samuel, son of Edward, bpt. 10 Jun 1787
  Samuel Hervey, son of Samuel, bpt. 7 Feb 1819
  Sarah, dau of Solomon, bpt. 17 Jul 1768
  Tryphena Philbrick, dau of William, bpt. 9 Aug 1801
  Washington, son of John, bpt. 21 Dec 1800

RYE BAPTISMS

VARRELL, William, son of Solomon, bpt. 29 May 1763
  William, son of Edward, bpt. 12 Jul 1778
WALDRON, Elizabeth Saunders, dau of Jonathan B.,
    bpt. 27 Feb 1791
  George, son of Jonathan B., bpt. 25 Apr 1802
  Joshua Foss, son of Jonathan B., bpt. 9 Apr 1797
  Polly Westbrook, dau of Jonathan B., bpt. 26 Aug
    1792
  Richard Harvey, son of Jonathan B., bpt. 4 Nov
    1798
  Robert Saunders, son of Jonathan B., bpt. 29 Jun
    1794
WALKER, Eliza Ann Maria, dau of Samuel, bpt. 18
    Oct 1812
  Jesse Merril, son of Samuel Jr., bpt. 27 Apr
    1800
  Levi Towle, son of Samuel, bpt. 19 Nov 1809
  Nathaniel Marden, son of Samuel, bpt. 24 May
    1818
  William, son of Samuel, bpt. 1807
WALLIS, Betsey, dau of Samuel, bpt. Mar 1762
  Deborah, dau of Samuel, bpt. 28 Oct 1759
  Hannah, dau of George, bpt. 29 Jun 1740
  Hannah, dau of Samuel, bpt. 11 Aug 1745
  James, son of Samuel, bpt. 15 Aug 1756
  Margaret, dau of George, bpt. 22 Jul 1744
  Martha, dau of George, bpt. 19 Sep 1742
  Martha, dau of Samuel, bpt. 29 Mar 1752
  Mary, dau of Samuel, bpt. 7 Jan 1750
  Mary Jones, dau of Samuel, bpt. 1 Jun 1777
  Samuel, son of Samuel, bpt. 16 Aug 1746/7
  Sarah, dau of Samuel Jr., bpt. 20 Mar 1777
WATER, Margaret, dau of Thomas, bpt. 18 Feb 1750
WATSON, Hannah, dau of Widow Watson, bpt. 25 Dec
    1769
  John, son of Thomas, bpt. 28 Jun 1741
  Samuel, son of Thomas, bpt. 10 May 1739
WEBSTER, Abiah, dau of Joseph, bpt. 12 Sep 1742
  Abigail, dau of John, bpt. Aug 1777
  Abigail, dau of Richard, bpt. 5 Nov 1779
  Abigail, dau of Richard, bpt. 7 Oct 1780
  Abigail, dau of Richard, bpt. 11 Oct 1783
  Anne, dau of John, bpt. 2 Sep 1787
  Daniel, son of Richard Jr., bpt. 14 May 1815
  David, son of Josiah, bpt. 1784
  Dolly, dau of John, bpt. 1784
  Elizabeth, dau of Josiah, bpt. 13 Apr 1740
  Fanny, dau of Josiah, bpt. 27 Jun 1790
  Hannah, dau of Richard, bpt. 20 Feb 1785

RYE BAPTISMS

WEBSTER, Jeremy, son of John, bpt. 27 Jun 1790
  Jeremy, son of John, bpt. 15 Jul 1792
  John, son of Josiah, bpt. 28 Oct 1739
  John, son of Josiah, bpt. 20 Jan 1751
  John, son of Josiah, bpt. 27 Jul 1788
  John Hobbs, son of John, bpt. Sep 1795
  Josiah, son of Josiah, bpt. 10 Jul 1748
  Josiah, son of Josiah, bpt. 22 May 1757
  Josiah, son of Josiah, bpt. 27 Jan 1783
  Levi Locke, son of Josiah, bpt. 23 May 1797
  Mark, son of Richard, bpt. 26 Jun 1791
  Martha, dau of Josiah, bpt. Feb 1755
  Martha, dau of John, bpt. Aug 1781
  Martha, dau Richard, bpt. Feb 1782
  Mary, dau of John, bpt. 25 Apr 1779
  Mary, dau of Josiah, bpt. 21 Oct 1781
  Mary, dau of John, bpt. 8 Jul 1798
  Nathaniel, son of Josiah, bpt. 14 Apr 1793
  Olly, dau of Richard, bpt. 7 Jan 1787
  Richard, son of Josiah, bpt. Jan 1754
  Sarah, dau of Josiah, bpt. 25 Jun 1786
WEDGEWOOD, Betsey, dau of Jonathan, bpt. 12 Jul 1795
  David, son of Jonathan, bpt. 11 Nov 1792
  Elizabeth Sleeper, dau of David, bpt. 15 Jul 1798
  Hannah, dau of David, bpt. 28 Jun 1795
  Hannah, dau of Jonathan, bpt. 27 Jul 1800
  Sarah Wallis, dau of Jonathan, bpt. 24 Sep 1797
WEEKS, Abigail, dau of Jotham, bpt. Mar 1771
  Abigail, dau of Widow Weeks, bpt. 10 Nov 1776
  Betty, dau of Joshua, bpt. 19 Mar 1769
  John, son of Joshua, bpt. 10 Jun 1764
  Molly, dau of Joshua, bpt. 14 Jun 1767
  Sarah, dau of Joshua, bpt. 21 Jun 1761
WELLS, Anne, dau of Samuel, bpt. 12 Aug 1750
  Deborah, dau of Samuel, bpt. 12 Oct 1740
  Deborah, dau of Samuel, bpt. 29 Jul 1781
  Elizabeth, dau of Samuel, bpt. Dec 1773
  Isiah, son of Samuel, bpt. 17 Apr 1743
  Jeremiah, son of Samuel, bpt. 9 Oct 1757
  John, son of Samuel, bpt. 27 Oct 1745
  Molly, dau of Samuel, bpt. 2 Aug 1778
  Olly, dau of Samuel, bpt. 29 Jul 1770
  Samuel, son of Samuel, bpt. 2 Jun 1776
  Sarah, dau of Samuel, bpt. 19 Mar 1748
  Sarah, dau of Samuel, bpt. 24 Nov 1765
  Simon, son of Samuel, bpt. 17 Jun 1768
WEYMOUTH, Eunice, dau of _____ , bpt. 21 Nov 1756

RYE BAPTISMS

WEYMOUTH, James, son of Shadrach, bpt. Mar 1759
  Samuel, son of Shadrach, bpt. 19 Apr 1761
  Thomas Cotton, son of _____ , bpt. Oct 1758
WOODMAN, Mary, dau of Jonathan, bpt. 31 Mar 1771
WORMWOOD, Esther Philbrick, dau of William, bpt. 7 Apr 1771
  James, son of William, bpt. 25 Oct 1772
  Mary, dau of William, bpt. 17 Mar 1751
  William, son of William, bpt. 21 Aug 1748
YEATON, Anne, dau of Joseph, bpt. 23 Dec 1753
  Billy, son of William, bpt. 1783
  Elizabeth, dau of Joseph, bpt. Sep 1758
  Elizabeth, dau of John, bpt. 12 Oct 1766
  Esther, dau of John, bpt. 9 Jul 1769
  Hannah, dau of Joseph, bpt. 19 Jun 1763
  John, son of John, bpt. 17 Aug 1760
  John, son of Joseph, bpt. 29 Mar 1761
  John, son of William, bpt. 12 Aug 1781
  Joseph, son of Joseph Jr., bpt. 12 Jul 1752
  Mary, dau of John, bpt. 22 Aug 1762
  Mary, dau of John, bpt. 18 Nov 1764
  Philip, son of Joseph, bpt. 17 Jun 1768
  Samuel, son of Joseph Jr., bpt. 25 Jan 1777
  Sarah, dau of Joseph, bpt. 27 Nov 1748
  Sarah, dau of Joseph, bpt. 30 Sep 1750
  Susanna, dau of Joseph, bpt. May 1765
  William, son of Joseph, bpt. Jul 1756

RYE MARRIAGES

ABBOTT, Charles P., of Portsmouth, and Mary C. Webster, 24 Apr 1862
 Elizabeth, of Greenland, and Daniel Welch, 29 Feb 1744
 Esther, of Greenland, and John Rawlins, 29 Jul 1754
 Samuel and Ruth Ayers of Greenland, 3 Dec 1764
 Sarah, of Portsmouth, and Theodore Fuller, 13 Nov 1780
ADAMS, Charles, of Stratham, and Sarah E. Porter, 31 Jul 1833
 Hannah and Paul Rendall, 4 Feb 1752
 John W. and Lydia M. Trefethern, 1858
 L. Viola, a.21y, and Lewis H. Foss, a.27y, 15 Mar 1881
 Olive and Jonathan Goss Jr., 20 Dec 1812
 Oliver, of Portsmouth, and Mary Jane Foss, 30 Sep 1855
 Sarah E. and Daniel Conner, both of Exeter, at Hampton, 1 Sep 1805
 Thomas and Mary Pickering, both of Portsmouth, 11 Mar 1812
AKERMAN, Benjamin, of Farmington, and Sally Philbrick, 5 Mar 1821
 Peter and Rachel Foss, 28 Nov 1779
 Peter, of Epsom, and Mrs. Charity Locke, 19 Oct 1797
ALDRICH, Sarah Pauline, a.22y, and Rev. George Walker Christie, a.34y, of Kittery, ME, 29 Apr 1875
ALLARD, Sarah and Edward Johnson, 25 Feb 1743
ALLEN, Elizabeth L. and Simon Locke, 10 Nov 1803
 John, of Stratham, and Elizabeth Cate of Greenland, 21 Nov 1738
 Joseph and Susannah Jones, 8 Nov 1781
 Jude, of Stratham, and Elizabeth Locke, 6 Jan 1743
 Jude, of Stratham, and Dorcas Mow, 4 Oct 1776
 Sally (Mrs.) and James H. Locke, 19 Aug 1827
 Salome and John Brown, 4 Feb 1779
 Samuel and Sally Mowe, 8 Apr 1824
AMAZEEN, Abigail and Hall J. Locke, (Newcastle Record), 11 Jan 1809
 Henry, of Newcastle, and Louisa Rand, Sep 1826
 Sally and Joseph Rand, 13 Aug 1791
AMY, Joel and Elizabeth Dowrst, 22 Jan 1776
APPLETON, Peggy and John F. Williams, 4 Jul 1790

RYE MARRIAGES

ASPINALL, Maria and Jonathan L. Kennison, both of
Portsmouth, 19 Apr 1807
ATKINS, Harriet and James Tarlton, both of Portsmouth, 20 Dec 1806
ATWOOD, Joshua, of Bradford, and Mehitable Seavey,
6 Jan 1745
  Mary, of Ipswich, and David Nelson, 26 Sep 1740
  William and Sarah Marden of Bradford, 29 Dec
1743
AYERS, Eliza W., of Greenland, and Andrew French
of Dover, 25 Oct 1813
  John, of Greenland, and Anna Drake of Hampton, 7
Jan 1812
  John and Mercy Tarlton, both of Portsmouth, 18
Mar 1796
  John and Polly Patterson, both of Greenland, 12
Mar 1793
  Levi and Ruhamah Norton, 10 Dec 1778
  Lizzie A., of Portsmouth, and Thomas Green, 1874
  Nathaniel, of Portsmouth, and Ruth Shapley of
the Shoals, 23 Nov 1750
  Phebe, of Greenland, and Jacob Johnson of Portsmouth, 4 Jun 1789
  Ruth, of Greenland, and Samuel Abbot, 3 Dec 1764
  Samuel and Nancy Trefethern, both of Greenland,
28 Mar 1819
BABB, Thomas, of Barrington, and Mrs. Susanna
Locke, 22 Apr 1810
BAILEY, Joseph and Mary Ann Nutter, both of Portsmouth, 10 Jul 1816
BALCH, Grace E., and John H. Jenness of No. Hampton, 29 Nov 1882
  Martha Ellen, a.27y, of Portsmouth, and Charles
Elvin Trefethern, a.28y, Sep 1877
BALLARD, Elizabeth, of Boston, and Ebenezer Swan,
7 Jul 1753
BANFIELD, Addison W., of Wolfborough, and Jeanette
Huntress, 7 Sep 1872
BARBER, Daniel W., of Methuen, MA, and Adeline H.
Lang, 28 Feb 1847
  Rufus C., of Methuen, MA, and Nancy Carr of
Boston, MA, 28 Feb 1847
BARKER, Elizabeth and Thomas Boyd, both of Hampton, 10 Sep 1740
  Mary, of Hampton, and John Ruswick, Dec 1739
BARNES (BARNS), Dorcas and Benjamin Scadgel, 20
Oct 1747
  Margaret, of Portsmouth, and Ebenezer Johnson,
19 Feb 1749

RYE MARRIAGES

BARNES, Mary and Samuel Sanborn, 18 Mar 1767
  Peter and Abigail Lang, 21 Jun 1759
BATCHELDER, Abigail Dalton, of No. Hampton, and
    Peter Johnson Jr., 26 Nov 1801
  Angelina E., of No. Hampton, and Benjamin Philbrick, 29 Dec 1844
  Betsey, of No. Hampton, and Josiah Perkins,
    Spring 1807
  Charles E. and Martha M. Brown, both of No.
    Hampton, 1 Jan 1863
  Charlotte, of No. Hampton, and Billy Rand Jr.,
    28 Feb 1811
  Comfort, of No. Hampton, and John Lamprey of
    Kensington, 1811
  Dearborn, of Hampton, and Mary Jenness, 1833
  Dearborn, of Hampton, and Abby O. Jenness, Mar
    1841
  Edmund and Nancy Philbrick, both of No. Hampton,
    1810
  Huldah, of Hampton, and Jonathan Garland Jr., 20
    Oct 1777
  James L., of No. Hampton, and Mary M. Philbrick,
    Dec 1828
  Jeremiah, of No. Hampton, and Caroline M. Chesley, 10 Sep 1823
  John, of No. Hampton, and Nancy Knowles, 12 Mar
    1795
  John and Martha Fogg, both of No. Hampton, 30
    Apr 1815
  John and Betsey Burleigh of Newmarket, 8 Apr
    1825
  John Jr., of No. Hampton, and Mary Ann Philbrick, 26 Dec 1842
  Jonathan C. and Abigail Varrell, 1 Mar 1827
  Josiah and Olive Wells, Feb 1799
  Lucinda, of No. Hampton, and Simon Brown Jr. of
    Hampton, 29 Apr 1824
  Lucy A. and Josiah D. Prescott, 3 Jun 1865
  Mary and Bradbury C. French, 7 Jan 1827
  Nancy, of No. Hampton, and Stacy W. Brown of
    Hampton, 28 Feb 1841
  Nathaniel, of Deerfield, and Molly Libby of
    Hampton, 10 Jun 1781
  Ruth L., of No. Hampton, and William Blake of
    Hampton, 10 Aug 1838
  Samuel, of Greenland, and Abigail Norton of
    Portsmouth, 3 Aug 1815
  Susan L., of No. Hampton, and Joseph Blake of
    Hampton, 28 Nov 1837

RYE MARRIAGES

BATES, Mary and Jotham Berry, 11 Nov 1731
BEAN, John W., of Moultonborough, and Huldah
    Berry, 23 Dec 1806
BECK, Henry and Eliza Thompson of Greenland, 20
    Jan 1763
  James, of Portsmouth, and Deborah B. Lear, 13
    Nov 1794
  John and Betsey Odiorne, both of Portsmouth, 16
    Sep 1798
  Molly and Reuben Philbrick, 9 Sep 1806
  Thomas, of Portsmouth, and Hannah Elkins, 28 May
    1761
BELL, Lucretia, and William Tredick Jr., both of
    Newcastle, 9 Jan 1785
  Shadrach and Grace Tucker, Dec 1739
BENSON, Jane C., of Portsmouth, and Thomas W.
    Philbrick, 4 Jul 1852
BERRY, Abigail and Edmund Johnson, 9 Aug 1789
  Abigail, of Greenland, and Jacob Brown of Hampton Falls, 29 Aug 1792
  Abigail, of Greenland, and Capt. James B. Rand,
    (int.) 13 Oct 1838
  Abigail and Langley B. Lewis of Charlestown,
    MA, 26 Oct 1847
  Anna J. and William Varrell, 22 May 1825
  Benjamin, of Moultonborough, and Abigail Locke,
    31 Aug 1815
  Betsey and Joseph Berry, 3 Oct 1821
  Betsey and William Goss, 14 Sep 1823
  Betsey M. and Abram Mathes, 23 Oct 1830
  Charlotte and Joseph Caswell, 26 Oct 1843
  Deborah and William Langmaid, 13 Dec 1739
  Ebenezer and Mary Kingman, 14 Nov 1727
  Ebenezer and Polly Garland, 10 Nov 1786
  Eleanor and John Libby, 26 Jun 1743
  Eleanor and James Locke Jr. of Portsmouth, 18
    Feb 1808
  Elizabeth and George Rendall, 14 Nov 1782
  Elizabeth M. and Reuben S. Randall, 26 Nov 1818
  Ester and Ebenezer Marden, 17 Jan 1735
  Florence L. and Martin H. Rand, 25 Nov 1875
    (divorced 1886)
  Francis A., of Greenland, and Martha A. Brown, 1
    Feb 1854
  Geneva D., a.18y, and James F. Brown, a.30y, 23
    Dec 1890
  Gilman C. and Elizabeth J. Caswell, 28 Dec Nov
    1841
  Gilman Woodbury and Julia Abby Butter of Bay

RYE MARRIAGES

View, MA, 4 Jan 1873
BERRY, Hannah and Nathaniel Marden, 21 Jul 1768
  Hannah and James Locke, 17 Apr 1801
  Hannah and Josiah Marden, 24 Dec 1801
  Hannah and Joseph Trefethern, 29 Jan 1810
  Hannah and Joseph Locke 3rd, 11 Sep 1814
  Hannah and John Foye Jr., 24 Sep 1822
  Huldah and John W. Bean of Moultonborough, 23 Dec 1806
  Huldah and Stacy Page of No. Hampton, 12 Oct 1828
  Isaac and Temperance Trefethern, 17 Oct 1790 (Record at Great Island, NH)
  Jeremiah and Hannah Locke, 3 Oct 1745
  Jeremiah and Eleanor Brackett, 8 Sep 1771
  Jeremiah Jr. and Sally Foss, 22 Jun 1808
  John and Sarah Symes, May 1746
  John and Betty Yeaton, 27 Jul 1757
  John and Sarah A. Shapley, 11 Aug 1844
  John O. and Adelia French of Portsmouth, 7 Nov 1871
  Joseph and Betsey Berry, 3 Oct 1821
  Joseph J. and Hannah W. Locke, 18__
  Joseph W. and Permelia A. Locke, 1854
  Joseph William and Mary Adelaide Green, 20 Dec 1872
  Jotham and Mary Bates, 11 Nov 1731
  Jotham and Tryphene Saunders, 16 Apr 1780
  Levi and Sally Jenness, 13 Nov 1785
  Louisa and Elvin Locke, 2 Apr 1835
  Lovey and Ebenezer Marden, 26 Jun 1806
  Lydia and William Trefethern Jr., 20 Jan 1801
  Mary and John Sanders of Gosport, 17 Apr 1740
  Mary and Jonathan Hobbs of Hampton, 28 Mar 1745
  Mary and Samuel Dowrst Foss, 13 Jan 1774
  Mary and Edward Verril, 19 Nov 1784
  Mary and Henry Shapley, 16 Sep 1790
  Merrifield and Huldah Towle of Hampton, 17 Aug 1756
  Molly and Jonathan Edmonds, 21 Dec 1799
  Molly and Alexander Salter, 18 Mar 1803
  Molly and John Mace Jr., 18 Oct 1821
  Nathaniel and Abigail Rand, 21 Apr 1747
  Nathaniel Jr. and Betsey Lang, 9 Feb 1797
  Nathaniel Jr. and Esther Hall, 26 Jan 1804
  Nathaniel F. and Rebecca Caswell of Gosport, 1827
  Nehemiah and Alice Locke, 14 Mar 1705
  Olive and John Bean Jenness, 22 Jun 1786

RYE MARRIAGES

BERRY, Oliver, of Kittery, and Elizabeth G. Dalton, 5 Mar 1839
  Oliver, of Greenland, and Abigail Brown, 21 Nov 1848
  Patience and James Seavey Jr., 23 May 1780
  Patty and Job Foss, 22 Mar 1809
  Rachel and Hinckson Foss, 7 Jun 1733
  Rachel and Ithamar Mace of the Shoals, 6 Dec 1764
  Richard and Olive Holmes of Portsmouth, 30 Mar 1805
  Sally and Thomas Sleeper, 1798
  Sally and Simon Goss, 27 Apr 1806
  Sally and Joseph Caswell of Gosport, 22 Oct 1820
  Samuel and Joanna Jenness, 27 Dec 1750
  Samuel and Molly Foss, 26 Aug 1762
  Samuel and Eliza Marden, 13 Nov 1780
  Samuel B. and Abigail Webster, Feb 1798
  Samuel F. and Mary Caswell of Star Island (Shoals), 6 Mar 1836
  Sarah and George Randall, 18 Jul 1751
  Sarah and Elijah Seavey of Barrington, 4 Sep 1764
  Sarah and Aaron Jenness of Rochester, 17 Oct 1776
  Simon and Phebe Moulton, 29 Nov 1757
  Solomon and Martha Kate, both of Greenland, 5 Oct 1794
  Susanna and Nathan Marden, 7 Oct 1743
  Susannah and Richard Fitzgerald of Portsmouth, 21 Apr 1811
  Thomas J., of Greenland, and Lettis Seavey, 16 Apr 1828
  Timothy and Mary Tucker, 19 May 1760
  William and Judith Locke, 8 Jul 1678
  William and Love Brackett, 10 Nov 1774
  William and Elizabeth Wendall, 6 Mar 1796
  William, of Greenland, and Olive S. Locke, 12 Feb 1818
  Zachariah and Charity Webster, 23 Oct 1734
BICKFORD, Henry C., of Deerfield, and Julia Rand, 23 May 1868
  Joseph and Ruth Rand, Jul 1760
  Mary, of Epsom, and Nathaniel Morgan, 9 Mar 1777
  Mary, of Deerfield, and Emery Woodman, 1860
BILLINGS, Mary and Samuel Morrison, 25 Dec 1775
  Richard and Hannah Newmarch of Portsmouth, 22 Aug 1777
BLAKE, Clarissa and Dearborn T. Shaw, both of

RYE MARRIAGES

    Hampton, 4 May 1828
BLAKE, Dearborn, of Epping, and Elizabeth Shaw of Hampton, 23 Oct 1777
    Elisha and Mary Saunders, 11 Dec 1766
    John, of Greenland, and Jemima Locke, May 1740
    Joseph, of Hampton, and Susan L. Batchelder of No. Hampton, 28 Nov 1837
    Moses, of Hampton, and Sarah Ann Goss, 1836
    Samuel and Sarah Libbee, 24 Nov 1743
    William, of Hampton, and Ruth L. Batchelder of No. Hampton, 10 Aug 1838
BLAZO, Ivory and Adeline E. Brown, both of Stratham, 7 Nov 1862
    Thankful and John Locke, 18 Aug 1796
BLUE, Edward and Mehitable Seavey, 4 Jan 1753
BOARDMAN, Sarah Jane, of Stratham, and Theophilus Wm. Sleeper, (int.) 10 Nov 1838
BOND, John and Esther Rand, 17 Aug 1752
BOSS, George, of Portsmouth, and Mima Varrell, 2 Dec 1882
BOWERS, Phillip and Mary Gove of Portsmouth, 15 Aug 1828
BOYCE, Jeremiah, of Concord, and Azolia M. Foye, 30 Jun 1851
BOYD, Ann Morrison and Samuel Johnson, both of Londonderry, 15 Aug 1805
    Thomas and Elizabeth Barker, both of Hampton, 10 Sep 1740
BRACKETT, Eleanor and Jeremiah Berry, 8 Sep 1771
    Love and Joseph Knowles, 3 Mar 1748
    Love and William Berry, 10 Nov 1774
    Prudence, of Greenland, and Richard Haines, 25 May 1774
BRAGG, Anna and William Caswell, both of Gosport, 22 Sep 1805
    Hannah and John Randall, 6 Jul 1816
    John and Amelia Saunders, 7 Jun 1796
BREWSTER, Caleb and Elizabeth Lear of Portsmouth, 28 Dec 1766
    John G. and Deborah Muchmore of Portsmouth, 7 Aug 1808
BRIAR, Peter and Rachel Briar of Stratham, 23 Oct 1758
    Rachel, of Stratham, and Peter Briar, 23 Oct 1758
BROUGHTON, Benjamin, of Marblehead, and Elizabeth Rand of Hampton, 27 Jan 1851
BROWN, Abigail and Samuel Davis, 20 Jan 1782
    Abigail and Jonathan Philbrick Jr., 26 Feb 1834

RYE MARRIAGES

BROWN, Abigail and Oliver Berry of Greenland, 21 Nov 1848
  Abigail L., of No. Hampton, and Amos T. Leavitt of Hampton, 14 Jun 1829
  Ada B., a.22y, of Raymond, and Clarence K. Caswell, a.27y, 9 Nov 1878
  Adeline E. and Ivory Blazo, both of Stratham, 7 Nov 1862
  Adna, of No. Hampton, and Mrs. Sarah E. Jenness, 1 Jul 1853
  Almira and Jonathan Locke, 2 Dec 1838
  Amos and Sarah Philbrick, Jun 1784
  Amos P. and Anna M. Jenness, 1857
  Amos P. and Calvena E. Seavey, 27 Jan 1867
  Amos S. and Martha E. Mudge of Lynn, MA, at Lynn, MA, 29 Sep 1869
  Angelina and James H. Dow, 5 Jun 1849
  Annie Eliza and C. Austin Jenness, 24 May 1870
  Artimissa R. and Daniel Marden, 29 May 1842
  Benjamin and Janey Locke, 31 Mar 1817
  Betsey (Mrs.) and Richard Jenness Jr., 18 Dec 1809
  Caleb and Phila Fellows of Kensington, 9 Apr 1822
  Charles J. and Mary L. Drake, 30 Nov 1855
  Charles Woodbury and Mrs. Eliza A. Frost of No. Hampton, 1876
  Clarissa and Nathan Brown of No. Hampton, 4 Aug 1836
  Data and Samuel Whidden of Portsmouth, 22 Dec 1842
  David P., of No. Hampton, and Nancy Perkins, 2 Aug 1828
  Dorothy, of Portsmouth, and John R. Cronk, 29 Nov 1827
  Eleck, of Epsom, and Mary Dalton, 2 Sep 1813
  Elihu and Mehitable B. Locke of Chichester, 1856
  Eliza and Thomas J. Parsons, (no date)
  Elizabeth and Simon Garland, 3 Jan 1754
  Elizabeth and Jonathan Goss Jr., 16 Feb 1769
  Elizabeth and Elijah Locke Jr., 21 Nov 1776
  Elizabeth F., of No. Hampton, and John Kinsman Jr. of Portsmouth, 1828
  Emeret A. and Job Rienza Jenness, 1866
  Emily B., dau of Chas J., and Charles M. Remick, 24 Dec 1884
  George Henry, a.21y, and Cora Jane Moulton, a.21y, of No. Hampton, Dec 1876
  Hannah and Joseph B. Dalton, 14 Mar 1833

RYE MARRIAGES

BROWN, Hannah (Mrs.) and Eliphalet Wedgewood, 15 Apr 1861
  Horace, of No. Hampton, and Vianna Garland, 11 Nov 1868
  Ira and Jane M. Perkins, 6 Sep 1820
  Ira Jr. and Hannah Garland, at Lamp River, 27 Oct 1834
  Ivory and Mary C. Johnson, 8 May 1845
  Jacob, of Hampton Falls, and Abigail Berry of Greenland, 29 Aug 1792
  James and Martha Webster, 9 Dec 1819
  James Jr. and Margaret V. Green, 1855
  James F., a.30y, and Geneva D. Berry, a.18y, 23 Dec 1890
  Jeremiah and Sarah Dalton, 20 Mar 1785
  Jessie M. and Charles W. Julyn of Salem, MA, 29 Apr 1877
  John and Salome Allen, 4 Feb 1779
  John and Comfort Jenness, 25 Oct 1789
  John and Mary Gould, 1796
  John and Sally Foss, 29 Jul 1802
  John and Polly Rand, 9 Dec 1839
  John and Abba L. Yeaton, both of Portsmouth, 14 Aug 1863
  John 3d and Nancy Jenness, 28 Apr 1807
  John A., of Gloucester, MA, and Susan H. Seavey, 22 Jan 1832
  John Henry and Mrs. Mary Abby Davis of No. Hampton, 1873
  Jonathan and Mary Garland, 3 Jan 1753
  Jonathan, of No. Hampton, and Hannah Drake, 7 Oct 1802
  Jonathan and Almira Parsons, 3 Jan 1832
  Jonathan Jr. and Polly Locke, 5 Nov 1805
  Jos. Arthur, a.22y, and Olive A. Goss, a.20y, Oct 1878
  Joseph and Abigail Goss, 27 Nov 1746
  Joseph and Abigail Dolbear, 28 Mar 1780
  Joseph, of Epsom, and Rachel Locke, 15 Mar 1810
  Joseph and Mary D. Foss, 13 Sep 1843
  Joseph 3d, (alias Joseph Ward Brown), and Emily Parsons, 24 Mar 1829
  Joseph Jr., of No. Hampton, and Betsey Seavey, 26 Apr 1804
  Joseph Ira and Augusta E. Hanson of Portsmouth, 1857
  Joseph Ward (see Joseph Brown 3d)
  Langdon and Elizabeth S. Dow, 20 May 1837
  Lydia, of No. Hampton, and Pepperall Frost of

RYE MARRIAGES

 Parsonfield ME, 4 Jul 1846
BROWN, Lydia (Mrs.), of No. Hampton, and Ebenezer Fogg, 22 Dec 1846
 Mahala, of Kensington, and Joel Lane, 2 Jan 1814
 Martha and Daniel Dalton, 4 Jul 1842
 Martha A. and Francis Berry of Greenland, 1 Feb 1854
 Martha H. and Uri H. Jenness, 25 May 1851
 Martha M. and Charles E. Batchelder, both of No. Hampton, 1 Jan 1863
 Mary and Joseph Locke Jr., 16 Nov 1794
 Mary and Ebenezer L. Odiorne, 27 Nov 1825
 Mary Esther and Jonathan Walker, 12 Jul 1831
 Minerva A., of Hampton, and Phineas Coleman of Greenland, 14 Mar 1867
 Molly, of No. Hampton, and Daniel Moulton, 9 Aug 1818
 Moses and Henrietta Garland of No. Hampton, 11 Dec 1869
 Nathan and Molly Jenness, both of North Hill, 11 Apr 1801
 Nathan, of No. Hampton, and Clarissa Brown, 4 Aug 1836
 Patty and Daniel P. Dalton, 2 Oct 1809
 Rachel, of Hampton, and Daniel Dow, 27 Nov 1749
 Richard and Sarah Jenness, 12 Jan 1773
 Sally and John Philbrick, 25 Dec 1831
 Samuel and Susannah Knowles, 18 Jul 1745
 Sarah and Moses Lufkins of Ipswich, 30 Jun 1756
 Sarah Ann and Thomas Rand Jr., 24 Nov 1831
 Sarah Ann and Josiah W. Philbrick, 25 Jun 1833
 Semira and George Lougee of Exeter, 1859
 Simon and Polly Seavey, 16 Mar 1806
 Simon and Mrs. Abigail Hall, 7 Apr 1833
 Simon Jr., of Hampton, and Lucinda Batchelder of No. Hampton, 29 Apr 1824
 Simon Jr. and Mary Seavey, 4 Jan 1837
 Sophia and Charles Rand, 20 Feb 1848
 Stacy W., of Hampton, and Nancy M. Batchelder of No. Hampton, 28 Feb 1841
 Zacheus, of Hampton, and Martha Davison, 28 Oct 1781
BUCKINAN, William and Deborah Locke, 19 Oct 1720
BUNKER, Addie P. and George D. Cotton, 27 Oct 1868
 James and Ann Langley of Lee, 1862
 James L., of Barnstead, and Nancy Hobbs, 27 Sep 1820
 Lemuel J. and Isette Garland, 7 Mar 1848
BURBANK, Enoch, of Deerfield, and Elizabeth Jen-

ness, 5 Oct 1784
BURGIN, Joseph T. and Charity Grover, both of
    Portsmouth, 4 Apr 1811
BURLEIGH, Betsey, of Newmarket, and John Batchelder, 8 Apr 1825
BURTON, Mary O., of No. Hampton, and Charles C.
    Marden, 12 Dec 1875
BUTLER, Edward and Elizabeth Langdon of Portsmouth, 5 Oct 1759
BUTTER, Julia Abby, of Bay View, MA, and Gilman
    Woodbury Berry, 4 Jan 1873
BUTTERFIELD, John and Sarah Dolbee of Chester, 28
    Sep 1767
CALL, Edward, of Portsmouth, and Eleanor Marston of
    Greenland, 9 Oct 1809
CARR, Benjamin, of Salisbury, MA, and Sarah Shaw
    of Kensington, 1816
  Nancy, of Boston, MA, and Rufus C. Barber of
    Methuen, MA, 28 Feb 1847
CARLETON, Isaac, of Pelham, ME, and Lydia H. Lord
    of Berwick, ME, 26 Mar 1856
CARYL, John and Sally Goss, 31 Oct 1793
CASWELL, Angelina E. and John Pool of Kittery,
    ME, 25 Jun 1860
  Augustus and Lelia Jenness, 19 Mar 1868
  Charles R. and Mary E. Varrell, 9 Nov 1853
  Charles R. and Sarah E. Robinson, 16 Sep 1863
  Clarence K., a.27y, and Ada B. Brown, a.22y, of
    Raymond, 9 Nov 1878
  Edward, of the Shoals, and Sarah Locke, 13 Jun
    1819
  Eliza G. and William Randall, 11 Dec 1827
  Elizabeth A. and John Mace, Jul 1855
  Elizabeth J. and Gilman C. Berry, 28 Nov 1841
  Henry N. and Lydia Randall of Gosport, 15 Mar
    1871
  Henry N., a.32y, and Molly Eaton, a.21y, of So.
    Seabrook, 5 Dec 1879
  John Jr., of the Shoals, and Elizabeth Locke, 2
    Nov 1816
  John W. and Hattie Mathes, 10 Jul 1864
  Joseph, of Gosport, and Sally Berry, 22 Oct 1820
  Joseph and Charlotte Berry, 26 Oct 1843
  Lemuel, of Gosport, and Sarah Palmer Locke, 4
    Apr 1823
  Mary and Mark Newton, both of the Isles of
    Shoals, 31 Mar 1817
  Mary, of Star Island (Shoals), and Samuel F.
    Berry, 6 Mar 1836

RYE MARRIAGES

CASWELL, Mary and Benjamin L. Varrell, 9 Jan 1850
  Mary H. and John Randall of Gosport, 19 Feb 1850
  Michael, of the Isles of Shoals, and Dorcas Green, 24 Oct 1816
  Polly (Mrs.) and William Caswell Jr. of the Shoals, 15 Aug 1819
  Rebecca, of Gosport, and Nathaniel F. Berry, 1827
  Richard G. and Anna B. Marden, at Greenland, 22 Jun 1828
  Sally and Henry C. Shapley, 22 Sep 1811
  Samuel and Betty Randall of Gosport, 25 Sep 1783
  Samuel, of Gosport, and Polly Green, 28 Apr 1808
  Sarah A. and Nathaniel Gilman Varrell, 4 Dec 1856
  Sarah E., a.18y, and Wallace Goss, a.23y, 22 May 1880
  Tammy, of Gosport, and Robert Robinson, 18 May 1826
  Warren and Sarah E. Knowles, 26 Jun 1861
  William and Anna Bragg, both of Gosport, 22 Sep 1805
  William, of Gosport, and Catherine Marston, 1817
  William Jr., of the Shoals, and Mrs. Polly Caswell, 15 Aug 1819
CATE (KATE), Deborah, of Sanbornton, and John Dearborn of Hampton, 6 Jan 1827
  Elizabeth, of Greenland, and John Allen of Stratham, 21 Nov 1738
  Elizabeth and John Jenness, 11 Jul 1774
  Joseph, of Nottingham, and Prudence Marden of Portsmouth, 7 May 1789
  Lucy A. and Joseph S. Foss, Mar 1858
  Martha and Solomon Berry, both of Greenland, 5 Oct 1794
  Olive, of Portsmouth, and Jonathan Jenness, 9 Jan 1777
  Olive, of Greenland, and John Snell of Portsmouth, 2 Mar 1797
  Richard, of Barrington, and Polly Rand, 16 Nov 1790
  Samuel, of Barrington, and Ruthy Rand, 28 Sep 1801
CATER, Anna and William Walker, both of Portsmouth, 21 Apr 1804
  Lydia, of Greenland, and David Haines, 17 Feb 1743
  Robert and Mary Edmonds, 19 Jul 1774
CATHERTON, James and Annie Haines, both of Green-

RYE MARRIAGES

land, (no date)
CAVERLY, Phebe and Elisha Hart, both of Portsmouth, 4 May 1794
CHAMBERLAIN, Louise, of Auburn, ME, and B. N. Marden of Lewiston, 1 Jan 1866
  William and Mary Rand, 27 Nov 1729
CHANDLER, Benjamin, of Kittery, and Mary Rand, 16 Mar 1749
CHAPMAN, James and Abigail Philbrick of No. Hampton, 10 Dec 1801
  Job, of Hampton, and Rachel Goss, 6 Jun 1737
  Pennel and Sarah Libby, 17 Jan 1744
  Samuel Jr., of No. Hampton, and Patty W. Jenness, 15 Apr 1819
CHASE, Elisha and Betsey L. Merril, both of Stratham, 13 Sep 1809
  Hiram, of Stratham, and Clara A. Philbrick, 1859
  Moses, of Stratham, and Lucia Moulton, 22 Dec 1755
CHESLEY, Caroline M. and Jeremiah Batchelder of Hampton, 10 Sep 1823
  Eliza B. and Samuel Coleman of Portsmouth, 1 Dec 1841
  Frank E. and Ella C. Moulton of No. Hampton, 27 Nov 1884
  Hannah P. and James Locke of Seabrook, 11 Jan 1841
  Simon and Olive Elkins, 29 Apr 1807
  Simon L. and Susan N. Green, 22 Mar 1859
CHICKERING, Henrietta, of Kittery, ME, and James Varrell, 21 Jul 1861
  Zachariah (Sergt), of Ft. Constitution, and Sally J. Sleeper, 24 Dec 1826
CHRISTIE, George Walker (Rev.), a.34y, of Kittery, ME, and Sarah Pauline Aldrich, a.22y, 29 Apr 1875
CLARK (CLARKE), Alice, of Newcastle, and Robert Neal, 19 Apr 1750
  Alice and John Watson, 25 Oct 1767
  Andrew and Hannah Remick, 23 Nov 1797
  Ann M. and Horace L. Trefethern, 1 Oct 1856
  Charles and Mary Fanguar of Lower Canada, 1854
  Elizabeth H. and John Webster, 20 Sep 1827
  Hannah and John Gordon of Brentwood, 5 Jan 1756
  Hannah R. and Seth Sprague of Green, ME, 27 Nov 1845
  Hattie A., of Kittery, ME, and James M. Haley of Gosport, 3 Jul 1866
  John and Mary Mace, 19 Jun 1766

RYE MARRIAGES

CLARK, Judith and Thomas Cotton, 1 Apr 1790
  Levi, of Stratham, and Lovey Wiggin of Greenland, 6 Jun 1790
  Levi and Mary Hutchins, 2 Jan 1876
  Lucy A. and Joseph S. Foss, Mar 1858
  Marcia B. and Edwin H. Drake, 6 Aug 1884
  Mary E. and Supply Trefethern, 13 Jun 1862
  Mary F. and David C. Page, 18 Oct 1848
  Moses L. and Susan A. Tucker of Portsmouth, 1858
  Samuel and Hannah Marden, 30 Mar 1758
CLIFFORD, Abraham and Abigail Seavey, May 1746
  Elizabeth and John Dolbeer, 3 Mar 1742
  Peter and Hannah Dolbee, 25 Jul 1738
CLOUGH, Alveda H. and Oliver Winslow Trefethern, 27 Oct 1874
  Nathan, of Seabrook, and Abigail Marden, 29 Oct 1837
COE, John A. and Florence J. Perkins, 16 Apr 1882
COCHRAN, Mary, of Portsmouth, and Charles Hardy, 14 Aug 1802
COLCORD, Frederick, of Brentwood, and Elizabeth M. Jenness, (int). 6 Oct 1838
COLE, Eli, of Elliot, ME, and Olly Foss, 27 Apr 1830
COLEMAN, Nathaniel and Mrs. Mercy Saunders, 7 Aug 1796
  Phineas, of Greenland, and Minerva A. Brown of Hampton, 14 Mar 1867
  Samuel, of Portsmouth, and Eliza B. Chesley, 1 Dec 1841
CONNER, Daniel, and Sarah E. Adams, both of Exeter, at Hampton, 1 Sep 1805
  Fanny, of Portsmouth, and Richard Webster, 1854
  Joseph and Mary Seavey, 25 Jan 1738
CORNELIUS, Joseph and Emily Frances Howe, both of Portsmouth, 1859
COTTON, Comfort, of Portsmouth, and William Wallis, 15 Aug 1738
  Comfort and Joseph Tarlton, both of Portsmouth, 30 Dec 1784
  George D. and Addie P. Bunker, 27 Oct 1868
  Mary and Richard Tarlton, 2 Nov 1752
  Sarah A., of No. Hampton, and Nathaniel Abraham Jenness, 15 Apr 1849
  Thomas and Judith Clark, 1 Apr 1790
COX, Joanna and Reuben Frost, both of Portsmouth, 21 Mar 1816
CRIMBLE, Hannah, of Stratham, and Noah Piper, 12 Mar 1837

RYE MARRIAGES

CRIMBLE, Mary, of No. Hampton, and Noah Piper of Stratham, 12 Apr 1820
CRITCHET, Reuben H., of Greenland, and Thankful Whidden of Portsmouth, 17 Jan 1813
CROCKETT, Pelahah and Mary Marden of Stratham, Dec 1760
CRONEE, Mary Butler, a.23y, of Lawrence, MA, and Charles Wilson Jenness, a.23y, 8 Feb 1875
CRONK, John R. and Dorothy Brown of Portsmouth, 29 Nov 1827
CROSBY, John and Elizabeth Woodman of Greenland, 15 Oct 1778
CUNNINGHAM, Harriet, of Beverly, MA, and John Jenness, 1868
CURRIER, Thomas and Mary Ring of Portsmouth, 3 Dec 1772
 William, of Epping, and Eliza Robey of Hampton, 31 May 1770
CURTIS, Elizabeth and Daniel Marden, both of Portsmouth, 28 Aug 1828
CUSHING, Hannah, of Portsmouth, and Benjamin Thomas, 1812
CUTT, Ann, of Portsmouth, and Henry Saymore, 13 Sep 1750
DALTON, Abigail and Moses Shaw of Hampton, 12 Feb 1799
 Benjamin and Sally Garland 2d, 3 Dec 1805
 Daniel and Martha Brown, 4 Jul 1842
 Daniel and Emily A. Shapley, 16 Nov 1876
 Daniel P. and Patty Brown, 2 Oct 1809
 Daniel Woodbury, a.27y, and Belle O. Lane, a.22y, of Portsmouth, Mar 1877
 Eben H. and Celia Haines, both of No. Hampton, 6 Nov 1864
 Elizabeth G. and Oliver Berry of Kittery, 5 Mar 1839
 Elvira and Edward L. Garland, 2 Jul 1845
 Emily B. and David Jenness, 7 Mar 1854
 Hannah and Samuel Murey, 4 May 1769
 Joseph (Dr.), of Brentwood, and Mary D. Parsons, 9 Jan 1825
 Joseph B. and Hannah Brown, 14 Mar 1833
 Louisa and William Leavitt of No. Hampton, 20 Jun 1837
 Mary and Richard Jenness, 4 Jan 1770
 Mary and Eleck Brown of Epsom, 2 Sep 1813
 Michael 2d and Elizabeth W. Scammon of Stratham, 28 Apr 1839
 Morris and Ursula Leavitt of No. Hampton, 13 Jan

RYE MARRIAGES

1827

DALTON   Sarah and Jeremiah Brown, 20 Mar 1785
  Timothy and Elizabeth Marden, 29 Dec 1763
  Vienna M., of No. Hampton, and Emmons B. Philbrick, 1859
DAMRELL, Mary and Thomas Disco, 6 Dec 1753
DANIELS, Minas and Elizabeth Odiorne, 26 Mar 1753
  Olive, of Portsmouth, and Nathaniel Dodge, 22 Apr 1809
DAVIDSON (DAVISON), Josiah and Abigail Shaw of Hampton, 28 Oct 1794
  Martha and Zacheus Brown of Hampton, 28 Oct 1781
  Patty and Jonathan Goss, 10 Jan 1796
DAVIS, Lydia, of No. Hampton, and Edson Littlefield, 7 Dec 1837
  Mary Abby (Mrs.), of No. Hampton, and John Henry Brown, 1873
  Samuel and Abigail Brown, 20 Jan 1782
DAY, Lovina, of Parsonfield, ME, and James Jenness, 1856
DEAN, Benjamin Woodbridge, of Exeter, and Eunice Libby, 26 Sep 1765
  Eliza Ann and William Miller, 18 Feb 1813
DEARBORN, Anna and Lemuel Ordway, both of Loudon, 14 Nov 1802
  Clarence M., of Hampton, and John Oren Drake, 4 Aug 1876
  John, of Hampton, and Mrs. Deborah Cate of Sanbornton, 6 Jan 1827
  Jonathan, of Hampton, and Sarah Wait of Amesbury, 24 Apr 1746
  Joseph and Mary Dearborn of No. Hampton, 29 Jan 1776
  Mary, of No. Hampton, and Joseph Dearborn, 29 Jan 1776
  Mary, of Greenland, and Edward Varrill of Salem, 3 Aug 1809
  Olive and John Kerseys, both of Greenland, 19 Jul 1812
  Samuel Jr. and Sarah Meserve, both of Greenland, 7 Jan 1807
DENNETT, William Jr. and Olive Paul, both of Portsmouth, 16 Jun 1816
DISCO, Mary and Isaac Remick, 23 Aug 1759
  Thomas and Mary Damrell, 6 Dec 1753
DODGE, Nathaniel and Olive Daniels of Portsmouth, 22 Apr 1809
DOLBER (DOLBEE), Abigail and Joseph Brown, 28 Mar 1780

RYE MARRIAGES

DOLBER, Daniel, of Chester, and Margaret Haine,
   25 May 1767
  Hannah and Peter Clifford, 25 Jul 1738
  Hannah and Samuel Rand, 5 Jan 1784
  Israel and Sarah Lamprey, 11 Nov 1736
  John and Elizabeth Clifford, 3 Mar 1742
  Jonathan and Hannah Marden, 21 Dec 1744
  Nicholas and Mary Randall, 27 May 1773
  Sarah, of Chester, and John Butterfield, 28 Sep
   1767
DORR, Nancy M. and Wentworth Ricker, both of
   Portsmouth, 9 Apr 1860
DOW, Albert and Ann E. Seavey, 21 Nov 1847
  Benjamin W., of Exeter, and Sarah A. Locke of
   No. Hampton, 8 Apr 1857
  Betsey and John T., Rand, 4 May 1820
  Daniel and Rachel Brown of Hampton, 27 Nov 1749
  Elizabeth S. and Langdon Brown, 20 May 1837
  Hannah and Isaac Jenness, 20 Aug 1778
  Harriet A. and Levi Walker, 5 Sep 1855
  Isaac and Elizabeth Seavey, 21 Aug 1777
  James Jr. and Data Drake, 6 Feb 1812
  James H. and Angelina Brown, 5 Jun 1849
  John T. and Mrs. Betsey Newman of No. Hampton,
   16 Jun 1822
  Margaret, of No. Hampton, and John D. Lane, 30
   Nov 1843
  Martha and Joseph Locke Jr., 25 Jun 1778
  Martha L. and Nathaniel Foye, 10 Aug 1820
  Mary and Joseph Jenness, 25 Dec 1750
  Mary and John Dowrst, 25 Oct 1781
  Patty and Amos Seavey Parsons, 3 Aug 1796
  Rhoda and Josiah Shaw Jr., both of Hampton, 23
   Dec 1816
  Sarah Ann and Warren Parsons, 1 Jan 1845
  Simon Jr., of Hampton, and Patty Lang Rand, 11
   Nov 1813
DOWNING, Nettie and Jacob Godfrey of Hampton, 20
   Nov 1869
  Thomas and Martha Norris, both of Greenland, 14
   Aug 1796
DOWNS (DOWN), Abner and Sarah Down, both of Gos-
   port, 13 Oct 1810
  Amanda and Augustus Yeaton Rand, 26 Jun 1870
  Betsey, of Gosport, and George Randall, 15 Nov
   1832
  Dorcas, of Gosport, and Richard Rendall, 20 Sep
   1781
  Effie A. and Charles W. Towle, 6 Feb 1867

RYE MARRIAGES

DOWNS, Hannah, of No. Hampton, and Thomas Moulton, 1 Aug 1750
  Henry, of Gosport, and Elizabeth Foss, 1828
  John and Betsy Mathes, 21 Jun 1815
  John B., of Gosport, and Olive Foss, 27 Nov 1834
  John L. and Susan M. Marten, both of Portsmouth, 25 Apr 1858
  John O., of Gosport, and Sarah Lear, 4 Mar 1863
  John W. and Hannah J. Foss, 1855
  Mary B. and Asa C. Robinson of Stratham, 12 Feb 1824
  Mary C. and William Randall, Nov 1834
  Nancy, of Gosport, and John Lear, 1827
  Sally (Mrs.) and James Robinson, 27 Feb 1821
  Sally, of Hampton, and Darius Towle, 1836
  Samuel and Mrs. Betsey Tucker, 16 Aug 1814
  Sarah and Abner Down, both of Gosport, 13 Oct 1810
DOWRST (DOUST), Abiel and Samuel Leavitt Jr., 5 Dec 1757
  Comfort and Ephraim Locke, 14 May 1752
  Elizabeth and Joel Amy, 22 Jan 1776
  John and Mary Dow, 25 Oct 1781
  Mary and Wallis Foss, 25 Jan 1739
  Ozem and Elizabeth Jenness, 29 Oct 1761
  Ozem, of Deerfield, and Martha Webster, 3 Nov 1796
  Rachel and Benjamin Marden, 31 Jan 1754
  Samuel and Elizabeth Shannon, 8 Jan 1754
  Sarah and Samuel Rand, 10 May 1748
DRAKE, Abba and Dudley Littlefield of Greenland, 25 Feb 1862
  Abraham and Mary Jenness, 23 Jul 1767
  Abraham and Mary Jenness, 21 Mar 1811
  Abraham J. and Emma A. Philbrick, 20 Oct 1870
  Adams and Laura Marden, 23 Jun 1871
  Anna, of Hampton, and John Ayers of Greenland, 7 Jan 1812
  Anna and Hiram Fuller of Boston MA, 27 Nov 1855
  Anna and Joseph William Garland, 22 Oct 1860
  Augusta M., a.23y, and Charles M. Rand, a.24y, 19 Nov 1879
  Charles A. and Helen A. Weeks of Greenland, 1859
  Cotton W. and Martha Parsons, 14 Jul 1822
  Data and James Dow Jr., 6 Feb 1812
  Edwin H. and Marcia B. Clark, 6 Aug 1884
  Eliza Ann and Benjamin Jarvis of Nova Scotia, 5 Feb 1856
  Elizabeth (Mrs.) and Benjamin W. Marden, 28 Dec

RYE MARRIAGES

DRAKE, Elizabeth Dow and Oliver P. Jenness, 21 Jun 1834
  Hannah and Jonathan Brown of No. Hampton, 7 Oct 1842
  John Oren and Clarence M. Dearborn of Hampton, 4 Aug 1802
  Jonathan Jr. and Elizabeth J. Garland, 14 May 1876
  Joseph and Clarissa D. Knowles, 12 Oct 1838
  Mary (Mrs.) and David W. Jenness, 23 Aug 1827
  Mary J. and Alfred V. Seavey, 17 Feb 1870
  Mary L. and Charles J. Brown, 30 Nov 1855
  Morris Abraham and Laura Frances Trefethern, 1872
  Nathaniel, of Hampton, and Abigail Foss, 22 Nov 1744
  Nathaniel and Elizabeth Jenness, 20 Nov 1783
  Oren and Mary Abby Odiorne, 30 Apr 1848
  Oren, a.56y, and Izette Trefethern, a.44y, 1 Feb 1880
  Samuel, of Hampton, and Mary Jenness, 19 Sep 1782
  Sarah and Amos Seavey, 16 Jun 1807
  Sarah and Jacob Marston of Greenland, 27 Jan 1851
  Sarah Ward and David A. Jenness, 15 Apr 1841
DURGINS, Mary, of Portsmouth, and David Young, Jun 1834
EATON, Chester W. and Emma Giles Leach, 14 May 1868
  Molly, a.21y, of So. Seabrook, and Henry N. Caswell, a.32y, 5 Dec 1879
EDMONDS, Benjamin, of Wolfborough, and Hannah Merril of So. Hampton, 1812
  Edward and Susannah Tucker, 21 Dec 1744
  Jonathan and Molly Berry, 21 Dec 1799
  Joseph and Ruth Libby, 27 Sep 1753
  Mary and Robert Cater, 19 Jul 1774
  Mehitable and Edmund Rand Leavitt of Hampton, 19 Oct 1769
  Polly J. and Samuel Jenness, 19 Jul 1835
ELKINS, Abigail, of Portsmouth, and Hartwell Hall of Lee, 1823
  Catherine and Paul Smith Marston, 15 Feb 1763
  Hannah and Thomas Beck of Portsmouth, 28 May 1761
  Henry and Mary Webster, 1806
  James and Mehitable Rand, 7 Mar 1809

RYE MARRIAGES

ELKINS, Joanna and William Emery of New Brittian, 8 Oct 1766
  Mary and Jeremiah Locke, 15 Feb 1753
  Mary and Josiah Philbrick of No. Hampton, 10 Dec 1801
  Olive and Simon Chesley, 29 Apr 1807
  Olive (Mrs.) and David Locke, 24 May 1809
  Rachel, of Hampton, and Samuel Towle, 21 Aug 1760
  Samuel and Olly Marden, 24 Jun 1773
EMERY, John and Sarah A. Wiggin, both of Stratham, 30 Jun 1861
  Nathaniel, of Hampton, and Mary Perkins, 1 Apr 1777
  Sally (Mrs.), of Bartlett, and Joseph Philbrick, 9 Mar 1813
  William, of New Brittian, and Joanna Elkins, 8 Oct 1766
FANGUAR, Mary, of Lower Canada, and Charles Clark, 1854
FELKER, Elizabeth, of Barrington, and John H. Foss, 1856
FELLOWS, John, of Deerfield, and Lois Fellows of Kensington, 21 Nov 1811
  Lois, of Kensington, and John Fellows of Deerfield, 21 Nov 1811
  Phila, of Kensington, and Caleb Brown, 9 Apr 1822
FIELDS, Stephen and Hannah Seavey, 7 Jul 1799
FITZGERALD, Mary and Joseph Plaisted, 13 Nov 1780
  Richard, of Portsmouth, and Susannah Berry, 21 Apr 1811
FLANDERS, Christopher, of Hawke, and Joanna Smith, 21 Nov 1771
FOGG, Abigail, of No. Hampton, and Joseph Mace of Hampton, 15 Nov 1796
  Daniel and Sarah Page, 22 Oct 1754
  Ebenezer and Jemima Philbrick of No. Hampton, 17 May 1824
  Ebenezer and Mrs. Lydia Brown of No. Hampton, 22 Dec 1846
  Hannah (widow) and Thomas Marden, 9 Jun 1761
  Harriet and Morris Moulton, both of No. Hampton, 17 Sep 1860
  Jeremiah, of No. Hampton, and Patty Lang, 19 Jul 1795
  Martha and John Batchelder, both of No. Hampton, 30 Apr 1815
  Mary, of No. Hampton, and Benjamin Page, 30 May

RYE MARRIAGES

1781
FOGG, Sarah and Stephen Rand, 17 May 1781
FOLSOM, Ann, of Lowell, MA, and Lowell Jenness, 19 Oct 1845
   Betsey and John Shaw, both of Exeter, 19 Jun 1785
FOSS, Abigail and Nathaniel Drake of Hampton, 22 Nov 1744
   Alice E. and Cotton W. D. Jenness, 10 Feb 1881
   Annie Julia and Lewis Everett Walker, 13 May 1873
   Benjamin and Dorcas Shapley, 17 Feb 1814
   Betsey and Thomas Taylor of No. Hampton, 1803
   Caroline R. and J. Calvin Garland, 1854
   Chalcedonia S. and Daniel M. Foss, 28 Nov 1858
   Charlotte and James E. Seavey, 13 Jun 1869
   Comfort and Richard Lang of Portsmouth, 28 Sep 1797
   Daniel M. and Chalcedonia S. Foss, 28 Nov 1858
   David Tenny, of Barrington, and Betsey Sargeant of Haverhill, MA, 7 Jan 1793
   Dorothy and John Grant, 20 Apr 1775
   Ebenezer and Molly Foss, 26 Nov 1789
   Eliza Esther and Robert W. Varrell, 16 Apr 1848
   Elizabeth and Jonathan Belcher Waldron, 24 Sep 1789
   Elizabeth and William Mathes, 17 Feb 1812
   Elizabeth and Henry Downs of Gosport, 1828
   Emily J. and Joseph Wm Rand, 1884
   Esther Y. and John Jones, 12 Nov 1827
   Francis P. and Thomas Whidden of Portsmouth, 3 Jan 1830
   George and Mary Marden, 3 Apr 1746
   Hannah and Samuel Saunders of the Shoals, 21 Aug 1741
   Hannah J. and John W. Downs, 1855
   Hardison and Elvira Holmes, 16 Jul 1843
   Henry D. and Clara E. Mathes, 5 Oct 1858
   Hinckson and Rachel Berry, 7 Jun 1733
   Jane and William Palmer, 27 Jun 1736
   Jane and Isaac Remick, 19 Nov 1790
   Jane and Daniel Page of No. Hampton, 24 Dec 1812
   Job and Sarah Lang of Greenland, 1 Nov 1750
   Job and Patty Berry, 22 Mar 1809
   John and Sarah Tucker, 6 Mar 1783
   John and Hannah M. Odiorne, 10 Dec 1855
   John H. and Elizabeth Felker of Barrington, 1856
   John O. and Amanda Marden, 24 May 1866
   Joseph R. and Joanna Seward of Kittery, 6 Dec

RYE MARRIAGES

1826
FOSS, Joseph S. and Lucy A. Clark, Mar 1858
  Joshua and Rachel Marden, 29 Nov 1762
  Joshua M. and Mehitable I. Foss, 14 Jan 1841
  Lewis H., a.27y, and L. Viola Adams, a.21y, 15 Mar 1881
  Lucy B., of So. Newmarket, and John E. Odiorne, 26 Jun 1859
  Margaret E. and John A. Yeaton of Portsmouth, 10 Jul 1864
  Margery T. and David Nason of So. Berwick, 12 Nov 1822
  Mark and Amy Thompson, 28 Nov 1745
  Mark, of Barrington, and Sarah Foss, 6 Jun 1776
  Mary and Robert Saunders 3d, 12 Apr 1787
  Mary D. and Joseph Brown, 13 Sep 1843
  Mary Jane and Oliver Adams of Portsmouth, 30 Sep 1855
  Mehitable I. and Joshua M. Foss, 14 Jan 1841
  Molly and Samuel Berry, 26 Aug 1762
  Molly and Ebenezer Foss, 26 Nov 1789
  Nathaniel and Mary Tucker, 16 Oct 1740
  Olive and John B. Downs of Gosport, 27 Nov 1834
  Olly and Joseph Locke, 16 Jul 1804
  Olly and Eli Cole of Elliot, ME, 27 Apr 1830
  Patience Seavey and James Newton of Gosport, 1 Nov 1815
  Patty W. and Joseph Mason, 25 Jan 1809
  Polly and Richard Goss, 4 Apr 1811
  Priscilla and James Marden, 2 Jan 1751
  Rachel and Peter Akerman, 28 Nov 1779
  Rachel and Samuel Shapley, 17 Apr 1817
  Richard and Eliza Shapley, 17 Oct 1819
  Robinson and Mrs. Patty W. Mason, 12 Nov 1818
  Sally and John Brown, 29 Jul 1802
  Sally and Jeremiah Berry Jr., 22 Jun 1808
  Samuel Dowrst and Mary Berry, 13 Jan 1774
  Samuel Wallis and Sula Ann Locke, 10 Aug 1845
  Sarah and Mark Foss of Barrington, 6 Jun 1776
  Sarah G. and Albert A. White of Newcastle, 21 Oct 1841
  Sula A. (Mrs.) and John S. Goss, 7 Oct 1855
  Sylvanus W., a.34y, and Ella Frances Philbrick, a.26y, 3 Apr 1879
  Thomas, of Barrington, and Meribah Rand, 18 Sep 1760
  Wallis and Mary Doust, 25 Jan 1739
  William and Abiel Marden, 11 Mar 1790
FOSTER, Sarah and H.A. Jenness, both of Newmarket,

RYE MARRIAGES

FOYE, Azolia M. and Jeremiah Boyce of Concord, 30 Jun 1851
    12 Oct 1860
  Cecelia A. and Samuel Marden 3d, 7 Jun 1842
  Hannah (Mrs.) and John Y. Randall, 19 Oct 1828
  Harold and Lizzie Odiorne, both of Portsmouth, 20 Jan 1859
  John and Mrs. Martha Odiorne, 5 Nov 1829
  John Jr. and Mrs. Hannah Rand, 1 Dec 1805
  John Jr. and Hannah Berry, 24 Sep 1822
  John Wesley and Martha J. Seavey, 22 Feb 1871
  Lydia and Hopley Yeaton, 7 Nov 1813
  Mary Elizabeth and Joseph Drisco Jenness, 9 Dec 1841
  Nathaniel and Martha L. Dow, 10 Aug 1820
  Stephen and Hannah Neal Mason, 1 Apr 1804
  Thomas, of Boston, and Mary Rand, 10 Nov 1808
  Thomas and Clarissa Willey, 28 Nov 1822
  William and Hannah Seavey, 23 Feb 1795
  William and Hannah Rand, 15 Nov 1804
  William L. and Eunice D. Weeks, 7 Nov 1822
FRASER, John, a.26y, of Scotland, and Ella M. Parsons, a.20y, 29 Sep 1880
FRENCH, Adelia, of Portsmouth, and John O. Berry, 7 Nov 1871
  Andrew, of Dover, and Eliza W. Ayers of Greenland, 25 Oct 1813
  Bradbury C. and Mary Batchelder, 7 Jan 1827
  David and Irena Jewell, 13 Feb 1861
  Martha, of Stratham, and Jonathan Locke, 1862
FRISBEE, Hannah Jane (Mrs.), of Kittery, ME, and James Locke, 4 Mar 1847
FROST, Eliza A.(Mrs.), of No. Hampton, and Charles Woodbury Brown, 1876
  John N., of Newcastle, and Emaline Seavey, 29 Dec 1824
  Pepperall, of Parsonsfield, ME, and Lydia Brown of No. Hampton, 4 Jul 1843
  Reuben and Joanna Cox, both of Portsmouth, 21 Mar 1816
FULLER, Deborah and Benjamin Wallis, both of Greenland, 18 Mar 1785
  Elizabeth and Henry Seavey, 28 Sep 1745
  Hiram, of Boston, MA, and Anna Drake, 27 Nov 1855
  Jeremiah and Mary Scadgel, 26 Jul 1745
  Joseph and Joanna Seavey, 8 Mar 1733
  Love and William Wormwood, 26 Oct 1747
  Margaret, of Greenland, and Joseph Wallis, 23

RYE MARRIAGES

Nov 1769
FULLER, Theodore and Sarah Abbot of Portsmouth, 13 Nov 1780
_____, and Solomon Seavey, 30 Mar 1758
FULLINGTON, Abigail, of No. Hampton, and Simon Ward, 2 Mar 1784
GARDNER, Abigail, of Portsmouth, and Isaac Seavey, 6 Apr 1785
  John and Emeline Locke, both of Portsmouth, 29 Apr 1849
  Sukey and Abraham Wendall, both of Portsmouth, 24 Oct 1809
GARLAND, Abigail and Samuel Jenness, 15 Nov 1748
  Abigail and Isaac Lane of Chester, 8 Jun 1780
  Abigail and John W. Parsons, 11 Aug 1803
  Amos (Lieut.) and Olive Jenness, 18 Nov 1800
  Amos S. and Martha Seavey, 28 Nov 1816
  Anna L. and Joseph Smith Jr. of Chester, 13 Nov 1798
  Anna (Mrs.) and Gardner T. Locke, 3 Jan 1876
  Annah, of No. Hampton, and Charles Knowles, 2 Feb 1868
  Benjamin and Sarah Jenness, 5 Dec 1757
  Benjamin and Fanny Seavey, 15 May 1803
  Betsey and Ephraim Seavey, 1823
  Caroline and Jonathan D. Locke, 23 Dec 1838
  Charles D. and Eliza J. Garland, 3 Nov 1869
  Charlotte and William Garland, 1827
  Charlotte A. and Alfred V. Seavey, 31 Jan 1861
  Clara D. and Thomas W. Marston of Portsmouth, 1860
  Clara J. and Albert Dana Jenness, 1863
  Data and Leonard Lang, 1829
  Edward L. and Elvira Dalton, 2 Jul 1845
  Eliza J. and Charles D. Garland, 3 Nov 1869
  Elizabeth and Joseph Langdon Seavey, 17 Jul 1777
  Elizabeth J. and Jonathan Drake Jr., 14 May 1818
  Elvira L. and Joseph G. Jenness, Apr 1857
  Emily and Richard J. Sleeper, 6 Jun 1829
  Estella and John Warner of No. Hampton, 28 Jan 1869
  Fidelia and Charles E. Seavey, 31 Jan 1861
  Hannah and Reed V. Rand, 6 May 1824
  Hannah and Ira Brown Jr., at Lamp River, 27 Oct 1834
  Hannah and William Trefethern Jr., 24 Aug 1837
  Henrietta, of No. Hampton, and Moses Brown, 11 Dec 1869
  Horace W. and Nettie R. Whidden of Portsmouth,

RYE MARRIAGES

27 Dec 1869
GARLAND, Irving W., a.27y, and Anna Whidden,
   a.21y, of Portsmouth, 17 Dec 1877
Isette and Lemuel J. Bunker, 7 Mar 1848
J. Calvin and Caroline R. Foss, 1854
John and Mary Rand, 14 Feb 1744
John and Abigail Perkins, 18 Oct 1778
John and Betsey Parsons, 15 Aug 1799
Jonathan and Betsey Woodman, 14 May 1797
Jonathan Jr. and Huldah Batchelder of Hampton,
   20 Oct 1777
Joseph William and Anna Drake, 22 Oct 1860
Julia A., of No. Hampton, and Gardner T. Locke,
   28 Dec 1844
Levi and Lucy Salter, 24 Nov 1789
Levi Jr. and Polly Perkins, 21 Nov 1811
Levi Jr. and Mary Watson of Nottingham, 29 May
   1838
Lucinda R. and Alfred G. Jenness, 3 Jul 1850
Lucy Ann and William Marden, 1832
Martha A. and Alfred G. Jenness, 7 Jun 1843
Mary and Jonathan Brown, 3 Jan 1753
Mary and John Robey of No. Hampton, 13 Dec 1781
Mary and Joseph Jenness Jr., 19 Dec 1824
Mary A. and Jenness Marden, 1860
Mary Ann, of No. Hampton, and Simon Garland, 11
   Sep 1825
Mary Jane and John Ira Rand, 15 Nov 1849
Mehitable (Mrs.) and Lieut. James Perkins, 14
   Jun 1812
Moses and Adeline Jenness, 8 Mar 1840
Moses L. and Lucretia Locke, 18 Jul 1822
Nabby and Jonathan Jenness, 14 Aug 1785
Olive and Simon Moulton of Hampton, 23 Jun 1825
Orlando, of Gloucester, MA, and Lizzie Rand, 19
   Oct 1862
Peter Jr. and Mehitable Seavey, 30 Sep 1792
Polly and Ebenezer Berry, 10 Nov 1786
Reul and Patty Locke, 11 Jun 1826
Sally 2d and Benjamin Dalton, 3 Dec 1805
Sally and Jonathan Jenness 4th, 28 Mar 1816
Sarah, a.23y, and Wm H. Jenness, a.62y, 23 Feb
   1890
Sarah Ann and Moses Philbrick, 12 Apr 1838
Simon and Elizabeth Brown, 3 Jan 1754
Simon and Widow Rachel Morrison, 20 Dec 1781
Simon and Mary Ann Garland of No. Hampton, 11
   Sep 1825
Simon and Sarah Knowles, 1829

RYE MARRIAGES

GARLAND, Vianna and Horace Brown of No. Hampton, 11 Nov 1868
  William and Charlotte Garland 1827
  William and Almira McDaniel of Nottingham, 1861
  William Cutter and Mary Marden, 1834
GODARD, Elizabeth and Moses Norton, 23 Nov 1775
GODFREY, Jacob, of Hampton, and Nettie Downing, 20 Nov 1869
  James, of Hampton, and Patience _____, 4 Feb 1740
  John, of Hampton, and Abigail Seavey, 25 Nov 1801
  Jonathan, of Hampton, and Elizabeth Lamprey, 3 Oct 1749
  Susannah and Josiah Knowles, 6 Apr 1820
GOODWIN, Mary Charlotte, a.28y, of So. Berwick, ME, and James Henry Perkins, a.23y, Jun 1874
  Sarah and Andrew Herrick of Cape Ann, 20 Oct 1763
  Sarah, of Star Island (Isles of Shoals), and George Randall, Nov 1830
GORDON, John, of Brentwood, and Hannah Clark, 5 Jan 1756
GOSS, Abbie F. and John Wallace of Philadelphia, 3 Nov 1869
  Abigail and Joseph Brown, 27 Nov 1746
  Arthur L., a.41y, and Susie A. Knowlton, a.33y, 10 Mar 1880
  Clarence Albert and Mary Mace, 1876
  Daniel and Hannah Perkins, 6 Apr 1820
  Daniel, of Gilmanton, and Mrs. Sarah Mace of the Isles of Shoals, 25 Jun 1801
  James M. and Lucinda Snow of Orleans, MA, at Orleans, MA, 20 Apr 1834
  Jethro and Polly Wells, 16 Nov 1796
  John and Abigail Rendall, 14 Jun 1790
  John S. and Mrs. Sula A. Foss, 7 Oct 1855
  Jonathan and Salome Lock, 22 May 1735
  Jonathan and Patty Davidson, 10 Jan 1796
  Jonathan Jr. and Elizabeth Brown, 16 Feb 1769
  Jonathan Jr. and Olive Adams, 20 Dec 1812
  Joseph and Sally Seavey, 6 Mar 1791
  Levi and Sarah Rand, 18 Aug 1767
  Levi and Mrs. Mary Sanders, 15 Nov 1796
  Martha and Josiah Webster, 21 Sep 1738
  Mary and Thomas Lang, 16 Sep 1757
  Mary and Joseph Tarlton, 10 Jan 1762
  Michael D. and Sally Trundy, 21 Oct 1799
  Olive A., a.20y, and Jos. Arthur Brown, a.22y,

RYE MARRIAGES

Oct 1878
GOSS, Otis and Ann M. Locke, 12 Nov 1852
  Rachel and Job Chapman of Hampton, 6 Jun 1737
  Richard and Polly Foss, 4 Apr 1811
  Richard and Harriet Locke, 17 Oct 1858
  Sally and John Caryl, 31 Oct 1793
  Sally J. and William B. Randall, 8 Apr 1821
  Sarah Ann and Moses Blake of Hampton, 1836
  Sarah Ann and Ira Rand, 28 Apr 1839
  Sarah Jane and Joseph Pickering of Newington, 20 Dec 1831
  Simon and Sally Berry, 27 Apr 1806
  Susanna and Joseph Rand, 24 May 1764
  Thomas and Mary Hall, 5 Dec 1736
  Thomas (Capt.) and Sarah Marden, 17 Dec 1801
  Thomas and Mrs. Elizabeth Jenness, 28 Jun 1803
  Thomas and Abigail Locke, 2 Jun 1816
  Wallace, a.23y, and Sarah E. Caswell, a.18y, 22 May 1880
  William and Betsey Berry, 14 Sep 1823
GOULD, Ephraim and Molly Towle of Epsom, 20 Oct 1791
  Mary and John Brown, 1796
  Ruth and Ephraim Sufferance, both of Sanbornton, 30 Oct 1785
GOVE, Eben and Mary Varrell, both of Portsmouth, 5 Apr 1812
  Mary, of Portsmouth, and Phillip Bowers, 15 Aug 1828
GRANT, Christopher, of York, ME, and Elsa Locke, 7 Aug 1870
  John and Dorothy Foss, 20 Apr 1775
  Peter and Ruth Seavey, 4 Oct 1744
GREEN, Dorcas and Michael Caswell of the Isles of Shoals, 24 Oct 1816
  Lydia and Hiram Wells of Sandown, 1860
  Margaret V. and James Brown Jr., 1855
  Mary Adelaide and Joseph William Berry, 20 Dec 1872
  Polly and Samuel Caswell of Gosport, 28 Apr 1808
  Richard and Mary Mow, 5 Mar 1778
  Stephen and Dolly Webster, 20 Jul 1806
  Susan N. and Simon L. Chesley, 22 Mar 1859
  Thomas and Lizzie A. Ayers of Portsmouth, 1874
  Woodbury C. and Martha S. Trefethern, 1 Jan 1864
GREY, Mary, of Portsmouth, a.21y, and Hezikiah Lang, a.20y, 26 Apr 1879
GROVER, Charity and Joseph T. Burgin, both of Portsmouth, 4 Apr 1811

RYE MARRIAGES

GROVER, Sally and Samuel Todd, both of Portsmouth, 1 Sep 1804
HAINES (HANES), Abigail and Benjamin Libby, 3 Oct 1765
  Annie and James Catherton, both of Greenland, (no date)
  Celia and Eben H. Dalton, both of No. Hampton, 6 Nov 1864
  David and Lydia Cater of Greenland, 17 Feb 1743
  Joshua, of No. Hampton, and Lucy Moulton, 29 Jan 1777
  Margaret and Daniel Dolbear of Chester, 25 May 1767
  Mercy and Isaac Jenness, 10 Jul 1770
  Nathan, of Greenland, and Hannah Johnson of Portsmouth, 16 Mar 1780
  Richard and Prudence Brackett of Greenland, 25 May 1774
  Sarah and Jonathan Lock, 2 Mar 1727
  Thomas and Deborah Lamprey of Hampton, 8 Aug 1745
HALE, Sarah, of Exeter, and Christopher Rymes, 21 May 1767
HALEY, James M., of Gosport, and Hattie A. Clark of Kittery, ME, 3 Jul 1866
  Love and Samuel Robinson of Gosport, 1829
  Mary (Mrs.) and John Newton, both of Gosport, 23 Jul 1804
  Nancy (Mrs.), of York, ME, and John Rand, 1 Jun 1851
  Samuel Jr., of the Shoals, and Love Randall, 14 Dec 1815
HALL, Abigail (Mrs.) and Simon Brown, 7 Apr 1833
  Charles W. and Emily Trefethern, 24 Feb 1856
  Edward and Sarah Rand, 22 Apr 1784
  Elizabeth and Nathaniel Tucker, 8 Feb 1753
  Ephraim and Nancy Rand, 20 Mar 1817
  Esther and Nathaniel Berry Jr., 26 Jan 1804
  Hartwell, of Lee, and Abigail Elkins of Portsmouth, 1823
  James M. and Ann E. Mathes, 4 Jul 1853
  Joseph, of Gosport, and Esther Tucker, 27 Aug 1751
  Joseph and Mary Rand, 11 Jan 1781
  Joseph and Molly Randall, 28 Nov 1805
  Levi and Lucenna J. Trefethern, 26 Apr 1863
  Luther, of Boston, MA, and Olivia Porter, 16 Aug 1837
  Mary and Thomas Goss, 5 Dec 1736

RYE MARRIAGES

HALL, Sarah Ann and John Holmes, both of Portsmouth, 2 Dec 1844
 William and Margaret Norie, both of Portsmouth, 6 May 1809
 William and Sarah Rand, 10 Jul 1824
HAM, William, of Dover, and Eleanor Locke, 16 Feb 1749
 William and Mary Holbrook, both of Portsmouth, 28 Jan 1809
HANSON, Augusta E., of Portsmouth, and Joseph Ira Brown, 1857
 Sarah and George Ladd, both of Great Falls, 20 Jun 1870
HARDY, Charles and Mary Cochran of Portsmouth, 14 Aug 1802
 Enoch, of Bradford, and Hannah Jenness, 4 Mar 1764
 Joseph, of Bradford, and Elizabeth Marden, 17 Mar 1774
 Nathan, of Bradford, and Dorcas Marden, 10 Mar 1738
 Samuel, of Bradford, and Elizabeth Jenness, 23 Oct 1764
 Timothy, of Bradford, and Mary Marden, 27 Sep 1733
HARIED, Christopher W., of Portsmouth, and Amie E. Philbrick, 27 Jul 1856
HARRIS, Nathan L. and Martha A. Trafton, 1856
HART, Elisha and Phebe Caverly, both of Portsmouth, 4 May 1794
 Jeremiah and Mary Kimball, both of Portsmouth, 20 Jul 1799
HARVEY, Francis and Mehitable Tarlton, both of Newcastle, 24 May 1814
HATCH, Betsey, of Newington, and Daniel Henderson of Dover, 10 Aug 1788
HAVEN, John (Rev.), of York, ME, and Martha C. Morrison, 29 Apr 1839
HAYES, Sarah, of Milton, and John E. Locke, 1862
HAYNES, George F., a.22y, of Exeter, and Nellie G. Trefethern, a.23y, Jul 1879
HEAD, Moses and Catherine Osborne, both of Portsmouth, 19 May 1816
HEATH, Mary and A. Hunt of Manchester, 13 Nov 1851
HENDERSON, Daniel, of Dover, and Betsey Hatch of Newington, 10 Aug 1788
HERN, Robert, a.26y, of Limerick, and Ima Belle Marston, a.18y, 6 Oct 1880
HERRICK, Andrew, of Cape Ann, and Sarah Goodwin,

RYE MARRIAGES

HILL, Charles, of Lowell, MA, and Laura G. Locke, 20 Oct 1763
    12 May 1875
HILLS, Sarah J., of Hudson, and William H. Shapley, 27 Sep 1852
HILTON, Abbie J., of Wells, ME, and Fred E. Holmes of Portsmouth, in Portsmouth, 24 Jan 1879
HOARE, Elizabeth and William Perkins, 5 May 1753
HOBBS, Benjamin and Judith Marden, 15 Nov 1780
  Betsey and Asa Locke, 12 Nov 1799
  James and Mary Towle, 6 Jan 1774
  John A., of No. Hampton, and Ellen A. Jenness, 26 Aug 1865
  Jonathan, of Hampton, and Mary Berry, 28 Mar 1745
  Lucy and Levi Towle, 7 Feb 1782
  Nancy and James L. Bunker of Barnstead, 27 Sep 1820
  Polly and Jacob Holmes of Portsmouth, 1798
HODGDEN, Alexander, of Greenland, and Annie D. Jenness, 13 Jul 1871
  Louise A., of Greenland, and Thomas W. Rand, 1858
HOIG, James and Sally Palmer of Kensington, 20 Jul 1818
HOITE (see Hoyt)
HOLBROOK, Mary and William Ham, both of Portsmouth, 28 Jan 1809
HOLMES, Benjamin and Margaret Holmes of Portsmouth, 6 Jul 1780
  Eliza and Kitteridge Sheldon, both of Portsmouth, 12 Jul 1826
  Elizabeth, of Portsmouth, and Samuel Norris, 30 Oct 1766
  Elvira and Hardison Foss, 16 Jul 1843
  Fred E., of Portsmouth, and Abbie J. Hilton of Wells ME, in Portsmouth, 24 Jan 1879
  Jacob, of Portsmouth, and Polly Hobbs, 1798
  Jacob and Nancy Lang, 22 May 1832
  John and Sarah Ann Hall, both of Portsmouth, 2 Dec 1844
  Joseph R. and Charlotte Seavey, 24 Sep 1859
  Margaret, of Portsmouth, and Benjamin Holmes, 6 Jul 1780
  Mary and John Scadgel, 29 Nov 1753
  Mary, of Portsmouth, and Stephen Marden Jr., 15 Oct 1843
  Olive, of Portsmouth, and Richard Berry, 30 Mar

RYE MARRIAGES

1805
HOLMES, Sally and Samuel Norris, both of Portsmouth, 6 Oct 1808
  Sophia C. and John S. Marden, 5 Aug 1855
  William and Sarah Trefethern, 28 Oct 1860
HONIFORD, John and Margaret Johnson, 22 Sep 1763
HOWE, Emily Frances and Joseph Cornelius, both of Portsmouth, 1859
HOYT (HOITE), Cleavlen B., of Dover, and Sally Robinson, 6 Jun 1824
HUBBARD, Elizabeth Lake, of Wells, ME, and Alva Herman Morril, 3 Dec 1872
HUGGINS, Mehitable of Greenland, and Jacob Locke, 4 Jun 1778
HUNT, A., of Manchester, and Mary Heath, 13 Nov 1851
  Mary and Joseph Marden, 20 Jun 1773
  Zebedee and Mary Rand, 13 Jul 1759
HUNTLEY, Tryphene and Nathan Longfellow, 24 Aug 1769
HUNTRESS, Jeannette and Addison W. Banfield of Wolfborough, 7 Sep 1872
  Margaret, of Portsmouth, and Thomas Moses, 4 Apr 1811
HUTCHINS, Mary and Levi Clark, 2 Jan 1876
  Melvin and Georgianna Locke, 25 Nov 1876
HUTCHINSON, Samuel and Hannah Seavey, 15 Jul 1768
HYDE, Elizabeth Leach and Mendum Janvrain, both of Portsmouth, 21 Sep 1815
JAMES, George Francis, a.19y, and Ida May Marden, a.15y, both of Portsmouth, 4 Nov 1875
  James S. and Ann M. Towle, both of Hampton, (no date)
JANVRAIN, Mendum and Elizabeth Leach Hyde, both of Portsmouth, 21 Sep 1815
JARVIS, Benjamin, of Nova Scotia, and Eliza Ann Drake, 5 Feb 1856
JENKINS, Hiram, of York, and Sally L. Varrell, 14 Jun 1829
JENNESS, Aaron, of Rochester, and Sarah Berry, 17 Oct 1776
  Abby O. and Dearborn Batchelder of Hampton, Mar 1841
  Abigail and Barns Merril of Londonderry, 14 Jul 1785
  Abigail and John Locke Jr., 30 Sep 1787
  Abigail and Jonathan Jenness 3d, 30 Jun 1814
  Abigail and Jonathan Palmer of Kensington, 31 Dec 1826

RYE MARRIAGES

JENNESS, Abigail and Simeon Odiorne of Portsmouth, 7 Feb 1870
Adeline and Moses Garland, 8 Mar 1840
Albert Dana, and Clara J. Garland, 1863
Alfred G. and Martha A. Garland, 7 Jun 1843
Alfred G. and Lucinda R. Garland, 3 Jul 1850
Amos and Mary Jane Locke, 8 Nov 1849
Anna M. and Amos P. Brown, 1857
Anna Y. and Obed Rand of Roxbury, MA, 1 Mar 1835
Annie D. and Alexander Hodgden of Greenland, 13 Jul 1871
Benjamin and Hannah Libbee, 16 Mar 1752
Benjamin and Patty Seavey, 11 Mar 1787
Benjamin Jr. and Sarah Jenness, 2 May 1816
Betsey and Reuben Philbrick Jr., 4 Sep 1794
C. Austin and Annie Eliza Brown, 24 May 1870
Charles A., a.37y, and Hattie B. Weeks, a.24y, of Greenland, 21 Jan 1880
Charles Wilson, a.23y, and Mary Butler Cronee, a.23y, of Lawrence, MA, 8 Feb 1875
Clarissa and Samuel Jenness Jr., 31 Dec 1818
Comfort and John Brown, 25 Oct 1789
Cora Bell, a.29y, and Edwin B. Walker, a.29y, 23 Dec 1886
Cotton W. D., and Alice E. Foss, 10 Feb 1881
David and Emily B. Dalton, 7 Mar 1854
David A. and Sarah Ward Drake, 15 Apr 1841
David W. and Molly Jenness, 19 May 1807
David W. and Elizabeth Locke, 2 May 1811
David W. and Sarah T. Jenness, 24 Jun 1816
David W. and Mrs. Mary Drake, 23 Aug 1827
David W. 2d and Abigail Knowles, 28 Apr 1839
Eliza Perkins, of No. Hampton, and Woodbury J. Philbrick, 12 Mar 1874
Elizabeth and Samuel Hardy of Bradford, 23 Oct 1764
Elizabeth and Ozem Dowrst, 29 Oct 1761
Elizabeth and Nathaniel Drake, 20 Nov 1783
Elizabeth and Enoch Burbank of Deerfield, 5 Oct 1784
Elizabeth (Mrs.) and Thomas Goss, 28 Jun 1803
Elizabeth and James Perkins Jenness, 3 Dec 1843
Elizabeth and William J. Rand, 11 Mar 1844
Elizabeth M. and Frederick Colcord of Brentwood, (int). 6 Oct 1838
Elizabeth W. and William Stackpole, both of Portsmouth, 26 May 1844
Ellen A. and John A. Hobbs of No. Hampton, 26

RYE MARRIAGES

Aug 1865
JENNESS, Emery C. and Ellen A. Rand, 3 Dec 1871
  Emily and Samuel H. Rand, 29 Nov 1835
  George A., a.23y, and Hannah McLaughlin, a.22y, 10 Jun 1890
  George Washington, and Elvira Moulton of No. Hampton, 1873
  Gilman H. and Eliza T. Leavitt, 1863
  H. A. and Sarah Foster, both of Newmarket, 12 Oct 1860
  Hannah and Joseph Locke, 4 Dec 1739
  Hannah and Thomas Rand, 9 Dec 1756
  Hannah and Enoch Hardy of Bradford, 4 Mar 1764
  Henry, of No. Hampton, and Charlotte Lamprey, 5 Aug 1813
  Isaac and Mercy Haines, 10 Jul 1770
  Isaac and Hannah Dow, 20 Aug 1778
  James and Hannah Packren, Jun 1718
  James and Lovina Day of Parsonsfield, ME, 1856
  James Perkins and Elizabeth Jenness, 3 Dec 1843
  Joanna and Samuel Berry, 27 Dec 1750
  Job and Mary Jenness, 12 Sep 1735
  Job R. and Sarah E. Perkins, 10 May 1860
  Job Rienza and Emeret A. Brown, 1866
  John and Hannah Langdon, 16 Sep 1732
  John and Elizabeth Seavey, 30 Nov 1732
  John and Elizabeth Cate, 11 Jul 1774
  John, of Moultonborough, and Hannah Webster, 16 Sep 1813
  John and Harriet Cunningham of Beverly, MA, 1868
  John Jr. and Sarah Randall, 23 Dec 1777
  John Jr. and Hannah Wedgewood, 25 Dec 1816
  John Bean and Olive Berry, 22 Jun 1786
  John H., of No. Hampton, and Grace E. Balch, 29 Nov 1882
  Jonathan and Olive Cate of Portsmouth, 9 Jan 1777
  Jonathan and Nabby Garland, 14 Aug 1785
  Jonathan 3d and Abigail Jenness, 30 Jun 1814
  Jonathan 4th and Sally Garland, 28 Mar 1816
  Joseph and Mary Dow, 25 Dec 1750
  Joseph (Lieut.) and Elizabeth Philbrick, 8 Dec 1809
  Joseph and Anna Knox, Aug 1817
  Joseph Jr. and Sarah Philbrick, 8 Dec 1801
  Joseph Jr. and Mary Garland, 19 Dec 1824
  Joseph Drisco and Mary Elizabeth Foye, 9 Dec 1841

RYE MARRIAGES

JENNESS, Joseph G. and Elvira L. Garland, Apr 1857
  Josiah and Huldah Perkins, 7 Jan 1822
  Lelia and Augustus Caswell, 19 Mar 1868
  Levi and Betsey Wallis, 17 Nov 1785
  Lowell and Ann Folsom of Lowell, MA, 19 Oct 1845
  Martha J. and Martin Sleeper, 2 Nov 1855
  Martha S. and Albion D. Parsons, 23 Jan 1851
  Mary and Job Jenness, 12 Sep 1735
  Mary and Abraham Drake, 23 Jul 1767
  Mary and Samuel Drake of Hampton, 19 Sep 1782
  Mary (Mrs.) and Reuben Philbrick, 4 Feb 1805
  Mary and Abraham Drake, 21 Mar 1811
  Mary and Dearborn Batchelder of Hampton, 1833
  Melissa Hannah and Frank Mosher Philbrick, 1872
  Molly and Nathan Brown, both of North Hill, 11 Apr 1801
  Molly and David W. Jenness, 19 May 1807
  Molly and James Marden, 11 May 1809
  Nancy and John Brown 3d, 28 Apr 1807
  Nancy and Simon Jenness Jr., 23 Jun 1814
  Nathaniel and Mary Tarlton, 28 Mar 1771
  Nathaniel Jr. and Mary Wedgewood, 21 Oct 1781
  Nathaniel Abraham and Sarah A. Cotton of No. Hampton, 15 Apr 1849
  Nathaniel Gilbert and Emeline E. Lang, 11 Apr 1848
  Noah and Widow Randall, 15 Jan 1784
  Olive and Lieut. Amos Garland, 18 Nov 1800
  Olive and Benning Leavitt of No. Hampton, 1812
  Oliver and Sidney L. Seavey, 24 Dec 1842
  Oliver P. and Elizabeth Dow Drake, 21 Jun 1842
  Otis S., a.26y, and Anna P. Marston, a.19y, 30 Mar 1875
  Patty W. and Samuel Chapman Jr. of No. Hampton, 15 Apr 1819
  Peter, of Meredith, and Betsey Leavitt of No. Hampton, 20 Feb 1819
  Polly and Eliphalet Sleeper, 31 Mar 1800
  Reuben and Mary Knowles, 5 Oct 1834
  Richard and Mary Dalton, 4 Jan 1770
  Richard, of Deerfield, and Hannah Seavey, 22 Feb 1774
  Richard and Caroline Rand, 2 Aug 1819
  Richard (tert.) and Molly Page of Hampton, 23 Jul 1778
  Richard Jr. and Mrs. Betsey Brown, 18 Dec 1809
  S. Alba and Estelle M. Wilson, 1860
  Sally and Levi Berry, 13 Nov 1785

RYE MARRIAGES

JENNESS, Samuel and Abigail Garland, 15 Nov 1748
Samuel and Abigail Perkins, 1 Mar 1810
Samuel and Polly J. Edmonds, 19 Jul 1835
Samuel Jr. and Mary Locke, 21 Mar 1775
Samuel Jr. and Clarissa Jenness, 31 Dec 1818
Sarah and Joshua Weeks of Greenland, 24 Oct 1734
Sarah and Benjamin Garland, 5 Dec 1757
Sarah and Richard Brown, 12 Jan 1773
Sarah and Benjamin Jenness Jr., 2 May 1816
Sarah and Richard Locke, 15 Nov 1859
Sarah Ann and William Wait Jr. of Malden, MA, 29 Dec 1842
Sarah E. and Adna Brown of No. Hampton, 1 Jul 1853
Sarah T. and David W. Jenness, 24 Jun 1816
Seth, of New Durham, and Sophronia Smiley of Portsmouth, 27 May 1858
Simon and Olly Shapley, 24 Jun 1773
Simon and Nancy Sleeper, 23 Nov 1815
Simon Jr. and Nancy Jenness, 23 Jun 1814
Susan M. and Horace Sawyer of Bradford, MA, 5 Nov 1868
Thomas, of Deerfield, and Sarah Yeaton, 31 Jan 1775
Thomas and Sally Page of No. Hampton, 16 May 1799
Uri H. and Martha H. Brown, 25 May 1851
Wm H., a.62y, and Sarah Garland, a.23y, 23 Feb 1890
Woodbury Levi, a.22y, and Mary Davis Poole, a.21y, of Gloucester, MA, Jul 1874
JEWELL, Charlotte, of Stratham, and Nat Trefethern, 1 Jul 1807
Eleanor, of Stratham, and Benjamin Moore Jr., 11 Mar 1822
Elizabeth, of Stratham, and Samuel Knowles of No. Hampton, 24 Mar 1840
Irena and David French, 13 Feb 1861
John and Sophia Marston, both of Stratham, 23 Nov 1837
JOHNSON, Comfort and Ichabod Weeks, 1 Nov 1770
Deliverance (Mrs.) and Benjamin Marden, 23 Jan 1817
Ebenezer and Margaret Barns of Portsmouth, 19 Feb 1749
Edmund and Abigail Berry, 9 Aug 1789
Edward and Sarah Allard, 25 Feb 1743
Esther and Samuel Towle, 18 Nov 1762
Hannah, of Portsmouth, and Nathan Haines of

RYE MARRIAGES

   Greenland, 16 Mar 1780
JOHNSON, Jacob, of Portsmouth, and Phebe Ayers of Greenland, 4 Jun 1789
  John G. and Sally B. Mace, 13 Jul 1822
  Margaret and John Honiford, 22 Sep 1763
  Maria L. and William H. Locke, 25 Jun 1852
  Mary C. and Ivory Brown, 8 May 1845
  Pern, of Greenland, and Josiah Lang, 17 Dec 1771
  Peter and Mary Yeaton, 18 Sep 1767
  Peter Jr. and Abigail Dalton Batchelder of No. Hampton, 26 Nov 1801
  Sally (Mrs.) and Ithamar Mace, 8 Feb 1827
  Sally and Samuel Johnson, both of Northwood, 5 Jul 1828
  Samuel and Ann Morrison Boyd, both of Londonderry, 15 Aug 1805
  Samuel and Sally Johnson, both of Northwood, 5 Jul 1828
  Susanna, of Greenland, and Robert Ramsey of Londonderry, 23 Jul 1809
JONES, Charles W. and Abby J. Towle of Hampton, 1863
  Cyrus S., a.47y, and Mary E. Towle, a.38y, of Hampton, 2 Aug 1877
  Frank, of Portsmouth, and Mrs. Martha Jones, 15 Sep 1861
  Hannah and Samuel Whidden, 5 Jul 1774
  John and Ann Webster, 27 Aug 1733
  John and Esther Y. Foss, 12 Nov 1827
  Martha (Mrs.) and Frank Jones of Portsmouth, 15 Sep 1861
  Mary, of Boston, and Rev. Samuel Parsons, 9 Oct 1739
  Samuel and Elizabeth Locke, 17 Sep 1855
  Sarah and John Locke Jr., 29 Sep 1769
  Susannah and Joseph Allen, 8 Nov 1781
  True W., of Portsmouth, and Eliza Locke, 12 Jan 1868
  William and Sally Moulton of No. Hampton, 16 Jun 1796
JULYN, Charles W., of Salem, MA, and Jessie M. Brown, 29 Apr 1877
KALDERWOOD, Margaret and Isaac Libby Jr. of Epsom, 20 Sep 1766
KATE (see CATE)
KEEN, Harriet and Warren Keen of Kittery, ME, 25 Dec 1856
  Warren, of Kittery, ME, and Harriet Keen, 25 Dec 1856

RYE MARRIAGES

KEEN, William, of Portsmouth, and Harriet Rand, 3 Mar 1839
KENNEY, Joshua W., of Newcastle, and Isabella T. Neal of Portsmouth, 1 Sep 1816
KENNISON, Jonathan L. and Maria Aspinall, both of Portsmouth, 19 Apr 1807
  Lucy, of Hampton Falls, and Nathan Robie, 2 May 1821
  Susanna and Joseph Seavey, 2 Oct 1771
KERSEYS, John and Olive Dearborn, both of Greenland, 19 Jul 1812
KIMBALL, Mary and Jeremiah Hart, both of Portsmouth, 20 Jul 1799
KINGMAN, Mary and Ebenezer Berry, 14 Nov 1727
  Mary and Henry Seavey, 18 Sep 1740
  William and Elizabeth Webster, 19 Aug 1747
KINSMAN, John Jr., of Portsmouth, and Elizabeth F. Brown of No. Hampton, 1828
KNIGHT, Lydia, of Ipswich, and John Reith of Marblehead MA, 22 Jun 1741
  Susannah and Andrew Sherburne of Portsmouth, 4 Dec 1760
KNOWLAND, Ann E. and Robert Shapley, 1854
KNOWLES, Abigail and David W. Jenness 2d, 28 Apr 1839
  Amos and Elizabeth Libbee, 11 Oct 1744
  Amos and Sally Perkins of Hampton, 8 Mar 1827
  Charles and Annah Garland of No. Hampton, 2 Feb 1868
  Clarissa D. and Joseph Drake, 12 Oct 1838
  Eleazer, of Candia, and Hannah Knowles, 21 Oct 1810
  Elizabeth and William Locke, 31 Jul 1825
  Hannah and Eleazer Knowles of Candia, 21 Oct 1810
  Hannah and Joseph Locke 4th, 28 Nov 1833
  James and Mary Libbee, 11 Oct 1744
  James and Comfort Wallis, 30 Jun 1748
  John and Tryphena Locke, 31 Dec 1713
  Joseph and Love Brackett, 3 Mar 1748
  Josiah and Susannah Godfrey, 6 Apr 1820
  Lydia and Benjamin Palmer of No. Hampton, 10 Oct 1768
  Mary and John Lane, 10 Mar 1738
  Mary and Reuben Jenness, 5 Oct 1834
  Nancy and John Batchelder of No. Hampton, 12 Mar 1795
  Nancy, of Seabrook, and Samuel Robinson of Gosport, 29 Aug 1824

RYE MARRIAGES

KNOWLES, Patty B. and Joseph Philbrick Jr., 1818
  Samuel and Sarah Marden, 17 Mar 1772
  Samuel, of No. Hampton, and Elizabeth Jewell of Stratham, 24 Mar 1840
  Samuel and Abby Tarlton of No. Hampton, 19 May 1848
  Sarah and Simon Garland, 1829
  Sarah and Daniel Sherburne, both of No. Hampton, 1838
  Sarah E. and Warren Caswell, 26 Jun 1861
  Simon and Esther Yeaton, 8 Feb 1779
  Susannah and Samuel Brown, 18 Jul 1745
KNOWLTON, Susie A., a.33y, and Arthur L. Goss, a.41y, 10 Mar 1880
KNOX, Anna and Joseph Jenness, Aug 1817
LADD, George and Sarah Hanson, both of Great Falls, 20 Jun 1870
LAMPREY, Charlotte and Henry Jenness of No. Hampton, 5 Aug 1813
  Deborah, of Hampton, and Thomas Haines, 8 Aug 1745
  Eli and Hannah Sanborn of Hampton, 12 Oct 1823
  Elizabeth and Jonathan Godfrey of Hampton, 3 Oct 1749
  Hannah and John Lane, 28 Sep 1732
  John, of Kensington, and Comfort Batchelder of No. Hampton, 1811
  Louisa, of Hampton, and Sherburne Locke, 15 Aug 1824
  Molly, of No. Hampton, and Daniel Moulton of Gilmanton, 12 Feb 1789
  Morris and Nancy Locke, (no date)
  Sarah and Israel Dolbear, 11 Nov 1736
LANE, Belle O., a.22y, of Portsmouth, and Daniel Woodbury Dalton, a.27y, Mar 1877
  Eliza, of Hampton, and Carr Leavitt of No. Hampton, 5 Sep 1837
  Elizabeth and James Philbrick, 11 Nov 1736
  Enoch M., of Stratham, and Mary A. Seavey, 13 Jan 1842
  Isaac, of Chester, and Abigail Garland, 8 Jun 1780
  Joel and Mahala Brown of Kensington, 2 Jan 1814
  John and Hannah Lamprey, 28 Sep 1732
  John and Mary Knowles, 10 Mar 1738
  John D. and Margaret Dow, 30 Nov 1843
LANG, Abigail and Peter Barnes, 21 Jun 1759
  Adeline H. and Daniel W. Barber of Methuen, MA, 28 Feb 1847

RYE MARRIAGES

LANG, Anna, of Greenland, and Moses Remick, 3 Mar 1805
 Anne and John Verril, 22 Apr 1784
 Benjamin and Mary Thompson of Portsmouth, 4 Jun 1756
 Betsey and Nathaniel Berry Jr., 9 Feb 1797
 Bickford and Martha Locke, 8 Mar 1764
 Bickford Jr. and Abigail Locke, 2 Jan 1797
 Eben M. and Hannah Trefethern, 1859
 Elizabeth, of Portsmouth, and David Marden, 7 Jun 1813
 Emeline E. and Nathaniel Gilbert Jenness, 11 Apr 1848
 Hannah, of Portsmouth, and Benjamin W. Marden, 23 Sep 1821
 Hezekiah, a.20y, and Mary Grey, a.21y, of Portsmouth, 26 Apr 1879
 Jeffery and Esther Morril of Salem, 5 Dec 1751
 John, of Portsmouth, and Catherine Pope of Kittery, 31 Dec 1747
 Josiah and Pearn Johnson of Greenland, 17 Dec 1771
 Leonard and Data Garland, 1829
 Mark, of Portsmouth, and Hannah Marden, 9 Oct 1792
 Mary, of Portsmouth, and Elias Perkins, 7 Jul 1822
 Mary Ann and Mark Webster, 26 Nov 1829
 Nancy and Jacob Holmes, 22 May 1832
 Patty and Jeremiah Fogg of No. Hampton, 19 Jul 1795
 Richard, of Portsmouth, and Comfort Foss, 28 Sep 1797
 Richard and Nancy Walker, both of Portsmouth, 31 Dec 1798
 Sarah, of Greenland, and Job Foss, 1 Nov 1750
 Sarah and Joseph W. Seavey, 29 May 1829
 Susannah and Joseph Yeaton, 17 Jul 1751
 Thomas and Mary Goss, 16 Sep 1757
 Thomas M., of Portsmouth, and Martha L. Verril, 25 Oct 1840
 William and Elizabeth Rand, 9 Dec 1751
 William and Betsey Walker, both of Portsmouth, 13 Nov 1794
LANGDON, Eliza and Samuel Whidden 3d, both of Portsmouth, 1 Mar 1827
 Elizabeth, of Portsmouth, and Edward Butler, 5 Oct 1759
 Hannah and John Jenness, 16 Sep 1732

RYE MARRIAGES

LANGDON, Hannah, of Portsmouth, and Samuel Whidden of Greenland, 8 Jan 1745
  Mary and Amos Seavey, 25 Oct 1744
  Mary, of Portsmouth, and Amos S. Parsons, 31 Mar 1828
  Temperance, of Portsmouth, and Joseph L. Seavey, 15 Nov 1832
LANGLEY, Ann, of Lee, and James Bunker, 1862
LANGMAID, John, of Chichester, and Patty Wallis, 1 Mar 1796
  William and Deborah Berry, 13 Dec 1739
LASKEY, Henry, of Portsmouth, and Augusta Yeaton, 31 Jul 1870
LAWES, Curtis, of Ft. Constitution, and Olive Mullen of Newcastle, 16 Sep 1811
LAWRY, Clara T. and John A. Mace, 20 Aug 1884
  Mary and John Rand, 8 Dec 1771
LEACH, Emma Giles and Chester W. Eaton, 14 May 1868
LEAR, Benjamin and Polly Morrison, 25 Nov 1790
  Betsey and Joseph Tucker, 23 Jul 1795
  Charles H., a.36y, and Elizabeth Rumesy, a.38y, 16 Dec 1880
  Christa and Frank A. Otis of Portsmouth, 5 Jul 1870
  Deborah B. and James Beck of Portsmouth, 13 Nov 1794
  Elizabeth, of Portsmouth, and Caleb Brewster, 28 Dec 1766
  Elisabeth A. and Joseph Jackson Seavey, 22 Feb 1867
  Harriet N. and John W. Randall of Gosport, 1858
  John and Elizabeth Verril, 21 Mar 1775
  John and Nancy Downs of Gosport, 1827
  John W. and Addie Remick of Elliot, ME, 7 Jan 1871
  Samuel and Sally Salter, 5 Feb 1792
  Sarah and John O. Downs of Gosport, 4 Mar 1863
LEAVITT, Abigail, of No. Hampton, and Samuel Warner, 20 Aug 1833
  Amos T., of Hampton, and Abigail L. Brown of No. Hampton, 14 Jun 1829
  Benning, of No. Hampton, and Olive Jenness, 1812
  Betsey, of No. Hampton, and Peter Jenness of Meredith, 20 Feb 1819
  Carr, of No. Hampton, and Eliza Lane of Hampton, 5 Sep 1837
  Edmund Rand, of Hampton, and Mehitable Edmonds, 19 Oct 1769

RYE MARRIAGES

LEAVITT, Eliza T. and Gilman H. Jenness, 1863
  Esther R. (Mrs.) and Joseph Locke 2d, 3 Apr 1860
  John, of No. Hampton, and Eliza Perkins, 23 Nov 1826
  John Edwin and Addie Philbrick of Kittery, ME, 21 Dec 1873
  Joseph, of No. Hampton, and Esther R. Marden, 1840
  Mary and Nathaniel Rand, 8 Dec 1757
  Samuel Jr. and Abiel Dowrst, 5 Dec 1757
  Sarah and James Locke, 14 Jun 1750
  Sarah Ann, of No. Hampton, and Richard Locke, 20 Jan 1824
  Tappan and Elizabeth Page of No. Hampton, 2 Oct 1814
  Ursula, of No. Hampton, and Morris Dalton, 13 Jan 1827
  Vianna J., a.23y, and Daniel W. Rand, a.32y, 19 Nov 1879
  William, of No. Hampton, and Louisa Dalton, 20 Jun 1837
LEE, Rachel and Jacob Scadgel, 21 Jan 1755
LEWIS, Langley B., of Charlestown, MA, and Abigail Berry, 26 Oct 1847
LIBBY (LIBBEE), Abraham and Abigail Page, 24 Feb 1763
  Arthur and Deborah Smith, 23 Apr 1752
  Benjamin and Abigail Hanes, 3 Oct 1765
  Elizabeth and Amos Knowles, 11 Oct 1744
  Eunice and Benjamin Woodbridge Dean of Exeter, 26 Sep 1765
  Hannah and Benjamin Jenness, 16 Mar 1752
  Isaac and Ann Symms, 5 Feb 1748
  Isaac Jr., of Epsom, and Margaret Kalderwood, 20 Sep 1766
  John and Eleanor Berry, 26 Jun 1743
  Joseph and Deborah Rand, 12 Feb 1789
  Mary and James Knowles, 11 Oct 1744
  Molly, of Hampton, and Nathaniel Bachelder of Deerfield, 10 Jun 1781
  Ruth and Joseph Edmonds, 27 Sep 1753
  Sally and Webster Salter, 14 Dec 1806
  Samuel and Abigail Symes, 4 Dec 1744
  Samuel and Mehitable Seavey, 21 Sep 1780
  Sarah and Samuel Blake, 24 Nov 1743
  Sarah and Pennel Chapman, 17 Jan 1744
LIBERTY, Ceaser and Phoebe Ozel, 2 Aug 1783
LIGHTFORD, Elizabeth and Joseph E. Stoddard, both of Portsmouth, 28 Aug 1864

RYE MARRIAGES

LITTLEFIELD, Dudley, of Greenland, and Abba Drake, 25 Feb 1862
    Edson and Lydia Davis of No. Hampton, 7 Dec 1837
LOCKE, Aaron and Ena Rand, 24 Apr 1871
    Abigail and Robinson Trefethern of Newcastle, 25 Jan 1748
    Abigail and James Perkins, 23 Feb 1758
    Abigail and Joseph Purington of Epping, 27 Dec 1759
    Abigail and Bickford Lang Jr., 2 Jan 1797
    Abigail and Benjamin Berry of Moultonborough, 31 Aug 1815
    Abigail and Thomas Goss, 2 Jun 1816
    Abigail and Asa Locke Jr., 15 Apr 1824
    Adeline P. and Hiram Trefethern of Newcastle, (int.) 19 Oct 1839
    Alice and Nehemiah Berry, 14 Mar 1705
    Ann and John Perkins, 10 Mar 1748
    Ann M. and Otis Goss, 12 Nov 1852
    Annah and Timothy Prescott of Kensington, 2 Jan 1794
    Asa and Betsey Hobbs, 12 Nov 1799
    Asa Jr. and Abigail Locke, 15 Apr 1824
    Charity (Mrs.) and Peter Ackerman of Epsom, 19 Oct 1797
    David and Hannah Lovering, 9 Feb 1758
    David and Mrs. Olive Elkins, 24 May 1809
    Deborah and William Buckinan, 19 Oct 1720
    Eleanor and William Ham of Dover, 16 Feb 1749
    Eleanor D. and Joseph Rand Jr., 21 May 1826
    Elijah and Hulde Perkins, 22 Mar 1739
    Elijah Jr. and Elizabeth Brown, 21 Nov 1776
    Elijah Jr. and Hannah Sanders, 21 Jan 1802
    Elisha and Tryphene Moulton, 13 Jan 1743
    Eliza and True W. Jones of Portsmouth, 12 Jan 1868
    Elizabeth and Christopher Palmer, 24 Jul 1705
    Elizabeth and Jude Allen of Stratham, 6 Jan 1743
    Elizabeth and David W. Jenness, 2 May 1811
    Elizabeth and John Caswell Jr. of the Shoals, 2 Nov 1816
    Elizabeth and Nathaniel Marden, 21 May 1848
    Elizabeth and Samuel Jones, 17 Sep 1855
    Elsa and Christopher Grant of York, ME, 7 Aug 1870
    Elvin and Louisa Berry, 2 Apr 1835
    Emeline and John Gardner, both of Portsmouth, 29 Apr 1849
    Ephraim and Comfort Dowrst, 14 May 1752

RYE MARRIAGES

LOCKE, Francis and Sarah Page of Hampton, 24 Jan 1751
  Gardner T. and Julia A. Garland of No. Hampton, 28 Dec 1844
  Gardner T. and Mrs. Anna Garland, 3 Jan 1876
  Georgianna and Melvin Hutchins, 25 Nov 1876
  Hall J. and Abigail Amazeen, 11 Jan 1809 (Newcastle Record)
  Hamilton C. and Mary Ann Rand, 2 Jan 1825
  Hannah and Jeremiah Berry, 3 Oct 1745
  Hannah and Samuel Mow, 2 Oct 1803
  Hannah and William Randall, 29 Jul 1816
  Hannah E. and Benjamin W. Marden, 9 Aug 1864
  Hannah W. and Joseph J. Berry, 18__
  Harriet and Richard Goss, 17 Oct 1858
  Jacob and Mehitable Huggins of Greenland, 4 Jun 1778
  Isaac M. and Jenny E. Williams of Lynn, MA, 11 Mar 1865
  James and Sarah Leavitt, 14 Jun 1750
  James and Martha Seavey, 29 Sep 1774
  James and Hannah Berry, 17 Apr 1801
  James and Mrs. Sally Allen, 19 Aug 1827
  James, of Seabrook, and Hannah P. Chesley, 11 Jan 1841
  James and Mrs. Hannah Jane Frisbee of Kittery, ME, 4 Mar 1847
  James Jr., of Portsmouth, and Eleanor Berry, 18 Feb 1808
  James H. and Mrs. Sally Allen, 19 Aug 1827
  Janey and Benjamin Brown, 31 Mar 1817
  Jemima and John Blake of Greenland, May 1740
  Jeremiah and Mary Elkins, 15 Feb 1753
  Jeremiah Jr. and Sukey Rand, 21 Nov 1793
  Jeremiah Jr. and Mehitable Rand, 14 Jan 1800
  Jethro and Hannah Rand, 2 Feb 1748
  Jethro and Martha Webster, 26 Apr 1801
  Jethro and Martha Mason, 3 Sep 1826
  Job and Abigail Philbrick, 9 Dec 1806
  Job and Sally Locke, 25 Nov 1810
  John and Thankful Blazo, 18 Aug 1796
  John and Mary Powers, 27 Oct 1816
  John, of Newcastle, and Martha Rand, 7 Jan 1822
  John Jr. and Sarah Jones, 29 Sep 1769
  John Jr. and Abigail Jenness, 30 Sep 1787
  John E. and Sarah Hayes of Milton, 1862
  John Langdon, and Mary Randall, 16 May 1833
  John Oliver and Annie M. Tarlton of Boston, MA, 29 Feb 1864

RYE MARRIAGES

LOCKE, John Oliver and Josephine Trefethern, 19 Feb 1867
  John W. P. and Mary Brown Locke, 19 Nov 1826
  John Wilkes and Sarah Hannah Randall, Oct 1872
  Jonathan and Sarah Haines, 2 Mar 1727
  Jonathan and Mary Vennard, both of Newcastle, 24 Dec 1812
  Jonathan and Almira Brown, 2 Dec 1838
  Jonathan and Martha French of Stratham, 1862
  Jonathan Jr. and Olly Rand, 23 Nov 1785
  Jonathan D. and Caroline Garland, 23 Dec 1838
  Joseph and Hannah Jenness, 4 Dec 1739
  Joseph and Mary Odiorne, 20 Apr 1768
  Joseph and Abigail Marden, 4 Dec 1794
  Joseph and Olly Foss, 16 Jul 1804
  Joseph 2d and Mrs. Esther R. Leavitt, 3 Apr 1860
  Joseph 3d and Lucy Marden, 13 May 1795
  Joseph 3d and Hannah Berry, 11 Sep 1814
  Joseph 4th and Sarah Wedgewood, 29 Nov 1816
  Joseph 4th and Hannah Knowles, 28 Nov 1833
  Joseph Jr. and Martha Dow, 25 Jun 1778
  Joseph Jr. and Mary Brown, 16 Nov 1794
  Joshua and Charity Marden, 18 Jan 1776
  Judith and William Berry, 8 Jul 1678
  Laura G. and Charles Hill of Lowell, MA, 12 May 1875
  Lemuel and Esther Y. Remick, 31 May 1832
  Levi and Hannah Prescott of Hampton Falls, 31 Aug 1796
  Lucretia and Moses L. Garland, 18 Jul 1822
  Margaret and Richard Swan of Portsmouth, 24 Mar 1728
  Martha and Bickford Lang, 8 Mar 1764
  Mary and Solomon White, 25 Jun 1745
  Mary and Robert Saunders Jr., 7 Jul 1765
  Mary and Samuel Jenness Jr., 21 Mar 1775
  Mary and Amos Pain, 28 Dec 1775
  Mary and John A. Trefethern, 20 Nov 1834
  Mary Brown and John W. P. Locke, 19 Nov 1826
  Mary Jane and Amos Jenness, 8 Nov 1849
  Mehitable B., of Chichester, and Elihu Brown, 1856
  Mercy and Samuel Mason, 12 Nov 1801
  Molly and Jonathan Perkins, 1801
  Nancy and Morris Lamprey (no date)
  Olive R. and Thomas H. Philbrick, 28 Feb 1847
  Olive S. and William Berry of Greenland, 12 Feb 1818
  Patience and Noah Moulton, 16 Nov 1749

RYE MARRIAGES

LOCKE, Patty and Reul Garland, 11 Jun 1826
  Permelia A. and Joseph W. Berry, 1854
  Polly and Jonathan Brown Jr., 5 Nov 1805
  Prudence and Israel Marden, 27 Dec 1753
  Rachel and Joseph Brown of Epsom, 15 Mar 1810
  Richard and Sarah Palmer, 2 Nov 1769
  Richard and Sarah Ann Leavitt of No. Hampton, 20 Jan 1824
  Richard and Sarah Jenness, 15 Nov 1859
  Richard 3d and Sarah Woods, 19 Mar 1807
  Richard 3d and Betsey Tucker, 20 Feb 1817
  Sally and Job Locke, 25 Nov 1810
  Salome and Jonathan Goss, 22 May 1735
  Samuel and Polly W. Waldron, 21 Dec 1817
  Samuel J. and Elizabeth Marden, 24 Apr 1834
  Sarah and John Marden, 20 Mar 1746
  Sarah and Joseph Seavey Jr., 24 Dec 1769
  Sarah and Edward Caswell of the Shoals, 13 Jun 1819
  Sarah A., of No. Hampton, and Benjamin W. Dow of Exeter, 8 Apr 1857
  Sarah Palmer, and Lemuel Caswell of Gosport, 4 Apr 1823
  Sherburne and Louisa Lamprey of Hampton, 15 Aug 1824
  Simon and Elizabeth L. Allen, 10 Nov 1803
  Sula Ann and Samuel Wallis Foss, 10 Aug 1845
  Susannah (Mrs.) and Thomas Babb of Barrington, 22 Apr 1810
  Tryphena and John Knowles, 31 Dec 1713
  William and Elizabeth Rand, 5 Jan 1734/5
  William and Abigail Sanders, 28 Oct 1779
  William and Elizabeth Knowles, 31 Jul 1825
  William H. and Maria L. Johnson, 25 Jun 1852
LONGFELLOW, Nathan and Tryphene Huntley, 24 Aug 1769
LORD, Lydia H., of Berwick, ME, and Isaac Carleton of Pelham, ME, 26 Mar 1856
  Mary H., of Berwick, ME, and John Varrell, 11 Aug 1844
  Peter, of Charlestown, and Sarah Ann Philbrick, 6 May 1838
LOUGEE, George, of Exeter, and Semira Brown, 1859
LOVERING, Hannah and David Locke, 9 Feb 1758
  John, of No. Hampton, and Lydia Towle of Hampton, 20 Jun 1776
  Mary, of No. Hampton, and Joseph Taylor, 20 Jun 1776
LUFKINS, Moses, of Ipswich, and Sarah Brown 30 Jun

RYE MARRIAGES

1756
MACE, Abby H. (Mrs.) and David Remick, 15 Nov 1849
  Anna C. and Albert L. Remick, Nov 1876
  Charles I. and Frances O. Mathes, 2 Feb 1864
  Henry, of the Shoals, and Elizabeth H. Tucker, 13 Feb 1820
  Ithamar, of the Shoals, and Rachel Berry, 6 Dec 1764
  Ithamar, of Gosport, and Ruth Seavey, 16 Apr 1785
  Ithamar and Deborah Verril, 6 Nov 1817
  Ithamar and Mrs. Sally Johnson, 8 Feb 1827
  John and Rachel Rendall, 27 Jun 1793
  John and Elizabeth A. Caswell, Jul 1855
  John Jr. and Molly Berry, 18 Oct 1821
  John A. and Clara T. Lawry, 20 Aug 1884
  John W. and Abigail Philbrick, Jan 1841
  Joseph and Elizabeth Rugg, both of Gosport, 11 Mar 1787
  Joseph, of Hampton, and Abigail Fogg of No. Hampton, 15 Nov 1796
  Judith and William Rugg, both of Gosport, 8 Dec 1792
  Mary and John Clark, 19 Jun 1766
  Mary and John Sheafe of Newcastle, 4 Apr 1811
  Mary and Clarence Albert Goss, 1876
  Molly (Mrs.) and Richard Varril, 4 Mar 1824
  Ruth and John Nelson of Portsmouth, 1803
  Sally B. and John G. Johnson, 13 Jul 1822
  Sarah (Mrs.), of the Isles of Shoals, and Daniel Goss of Gilmanton, 25 Jun 1801
  Woodbury N. and Mary E. Randall of Gosport, 25 Dec 1865
MARDEN, Abiel and William Foss, 11 Mar 1790
  Abigail and Samuel Rand, 14 Feb 1774
  Abigail and Joseph Locke, 4 Dec 1794
  Abigail and Nathan Clough of Seabrook, 29 Oct 1837
  Amanda and John O. Foss, 24 May 1866
  Anna B. and Richard G. Caswell, at Greenland, 22 Jun 1828
  Annabelle, dau of Levi, and Edwin R. Phillips of Raymond, 29 Apr 1886
  B. N., of Lewiston, and Louise Chamberlain of Auburn, ME, 1 Jan 1866
  Benjamin and Rebecca Whidden, 12 May 1746
  Benjamin and Rachel Dowrst, 31 Jan 1754
  Benjamin and Hannah Rand, 26 Jan 1772
  Benjamin and Mrs. Deliverance Johnson, 23 Jan

RYE MARRIAGES

1817
MARDEN, Benjamin W. and Hannah Lang of Portsmouth, 23 Sep 1821
Benjamin W. and Mrs. Elizabeth Drake, 28 Dec 1834
Benjamin W. and Hannah E. Locke, 9 Aug 1864
Betsey and Samuel Marden, both of Portsmouth, 6 Aug 1799
Charity and Joshua Locke, 18 Jan 1776
Charles C. and Mary O. Burton of No. Hampton, 12 Dec 1875
Clara A., a.29y, and Charles A. Walker, a.41y, 15 Jan 1879
Daniel and Elizabeth Curtis, both of Portsmouth, 28 Aug 1828
Daniel and Artimissa Brown, 29 May 1842
David and Elizabeth Lang of Portsmouth, 7 Jun 1813
Dorcas and Nathan Hardy of Bradford, 10 Mar 1738
Dorcas and Ephraim Mow, 8 Sep 1754
Ebenezer and Ester Berry, 17 Jan 1735
Ebenezer and Lovey Berry, 26 Jun 1806
Eliza and Samuel Berry, 13 Nov 1780
Elizabeth and Timothy Dalton, 29 Dec 1763
Elizabeth and Joseph Hardy of Bradford, 17 Mar 1774
Elizabeth and Samuel J. Locke, 24 Apr 1834
Esther and Joshua Rand, 4 Nov 1802
Esther R. and Joseph Leavitt of No. Hampton, 1840
George and Sarah Webster, 19 Jan 1769
George, of Portsmouth, and Mary E. Thomas, 24 Sep 1845
George and Mrs. Martha Marden, 29 Mar 1851
Gilman J. and Caroline T. Seavey, 1860
Hannah and Jonathan Dolbear, 21 Dec 1744
Hannah and Samuel Clark, 30 Mar 1758
Hannah and Mark Lang of Portsmouth, 9 Oct 1792
Hannah and Samuel Walker of Portsmouth, 21 Jul 1799
Hannah and William Whidden of Portsmouth, 1 Dec 1811
Hepsibah and William Neil Jr., 6 Feb 1779 (Newcastle Record)
Ida F., a.24y, and Herbert E. Philbrick, a.23y, Dec 1880
Ida May, a.15y, and George Francis James, a.19y, both of Portsmouth, 4 Nov 1875
Israel and Prudence Locke, 27 Dec 1753

RYE MARRIAGES

MARDEN, James and Priscilla Foss, 2 Jan 1751
  James and Sarah Webster, 4 Jan 1803
  James and Molly Jenness, 11 May 1809
  James, of Portsmouth, and Mercy Page of No. Hampton, 22 Dec 1822
  Jenness and Mary A. Garland, 1860
  John and Sarah Locke, 20 Mar 1746
  John and Sarah Saunders, 23 Mar 1769
  John S. and Sophia C. Holmes, 5 Aug 1855
  Joseph and Mary Hunt, 20 Jun 1773
  Josiah and Hannah Berry, 24 Dec 1801
  Judith and Benjamin Hobbs, 15 Nov 1780
  Laura and Adams Drake, 23 Jun 1871
  Louise M., a.31y, and Howard F. Rand, a.37y, May 1879
  Lucy and Joseph Locke 3d, 13 May 1795
  Martha (Mrs.) and George Marden, 29 Mar 1851
  Mary and Timothy Hardy of Bradford, 27 Sep 1733
  Mary and George Foss, 3 Apr 1746
  Mary, of Stratham, and Pelahah Crockett, Dec 1760
  Mary and David Smith Jr., 31 Oct 1765
  Mary and Jonathan Philbrick, 8 Dec 1768
  Mary and William Cutter Garland, 1834
  Molly and Lowell Sanborn of Gilmanton, 13 May 1802
  Nancy T. and Samuel Marden, 2 Mar 1800
  Nathan and Susannah Berry, 7 Oct 1743
  Nathaniel and Hannah Berry, 21 Jul 1768
  Nathaniel and Anna Towle, 29 May 1777
  Nathaniel and Elizabeth Locke, 21 May 1848
  Olivia B. and Joseph P. Trefethern, 1837 or 1839
  Olly and Samuel Elkins, 24 Jun 1773
  Olly and Joseph Rand, 18 Oct 1795
  Prudence, of Portsmouth, and Joseph Cate of Nottingham, 7 May 1789
  Rachel and Joshua Foss, 29 Nov 1762
  Ralph, a.30y, and Eliza A. Parsons (divorcer), a. 26y, 23 Oct 1890
  Reuben and Hannah Moulton, 14 Apr 1810
  Reuben and Mrs. Charlotte Moulton, 1835
  Ruth and Levi Towle, 11 Oct 1753
  Samuel and Margaret Seavey, 22 Oct 1769
  Samuel and Betsey Marden, both of Portsmouth, 6 Aug 1799
  Samuel and Nancy T. Marden, 2 Mar 1800
  Samuel 3d and Cecelia A. Foye, 7 Jun 1842
  Samuel Jr. and Sally Philbrick, 3 Apr 1806
  Sarah, of Bradford, and Wm Atwood, 29 Dec 1743

RYE MARRIAGES

MARDEN, Sarah and Samuel Knowles, 17 Mar 1772
  Sarah and Jonathan Philbrick Jr., 22 Oct 1795
  Sarah and Capt. Thomas Goss, 17 Dec 1801
  Sarah Ann and H. Gates Wentworth of Portsmouth, 23 Jan 1872
  Solomon and Huldah Remick, 15 Jul 1802
  Stephen and Elizabeth Rand, 5 Feb 1757
  Stephen, of Candia, and Anne Stead of Portsmouth, 18 Dec 1777
  Stephen and Mary Smith, 12 Nov 1789
  Stephen Jr. and Elizabeth Webster, 28 Aug 1760
  Stephen Jr. and Mary Holmes of Portsmouth, 15 Oct 1843
  Susan S., of Portsmouth, and Ivory Purrington of Exeter, 28 Mar 1863
  Thomas and Mary Smith, 4 Mar 1729
  Thomas and widow Hannah Fogg, 9 Jun 1761
  William and Hannah Wallis, 29 Apr 1773
  William and Lucy Ann Garland, 1832
MARSH, Dolly, of Hampton, and John Wentworth of Hampton Falls, 5 May 1824
  Sally H. and John Wiggin, both of Greenland, 19 Aug 1827
  Thomas, of Hampton Falls, and Elizabeth Turner of Hampton, 30 Mar 1823
MARSHALL, Gideon, of Hampton Falls, and Abigail Randall, 2 May 1770
MARSTON, Anna P., a.19y, and Otis S. Jenness, a,26y, 30 Mar 1875
  Catherine and William Caswell of Gosport, 1817
  Clarissa, of No. Hampton, and David Marston, 19 May 1825
  Clarissa L. and Andrew Shaw, Jan 1843
  David and Clarissa Marston of No. Hampton, 19 May 1825
  David Jr., of No. Hampton, and Olive Stevens of Stratham, 28 Jul 1839
  Eleanor, of Greenland, and Edward Call of Portsmouth, 9 Oct 1809
  Hannah and William Rendall, 24 Apr 1745
  Ima Belle, a.18y, and Robert Hern, a.26y, of Limerick, 6 Oct 1880
  Jacob, of Greenland, and Sarah Drake, 27 Jan 1851
  Jonathan, of Hampton, and Sarah Weeks, 30 Jun 1743
  Paul Smith and Catherine Elkins, 15 Feb 1763
  Sarah and Joshua Weeks, 4 Sep 1760
  Simon, of Portsmouth, and Eliza Rand, 14 Dec

RYE MARRIAGES

MARSTON, Sophia and John Jewell, both of Stratham, 23 Nov 1834
  Thomas W., of Portsmouth, and Clara D. Garland, 1860
MARTEN, Susan M. and John L. Downs, both of Portsmouth, 25 Apr 1858
MASON, Benjamin, of Stratham, and Sarah Rand, 2 Mar 1797
  Daniel and Eliza Norton of Greenland, 20 Apr 1775
  Daniel Jr. and Mercy Rand, 7 Apr 1807
  Edmond, of Hampton, and Olive Philbrick, 9 Dec 1834
  Elizabeth and John Trefethern, 1 Nov 1840
  Hannah Neal and Stephen Foye, 1 Apr 1804
  Joseph and Patty W. Foss, 25 Jan 1809
  Martha and Jethro Locke, 3 Sep 1826
  Nathaniel and Olive Moulton, both of Stratham, at Stratham, 12 Dec 1840
  Nicholas and Mary M. Rand, 23 Aug 1807
  Nicholas, of Newington, and Sarah Philbrick, 27 Sep 1842
  Patty W. (Mrs.) and Robinson Foss, 12 Nov 1818
  Ruhamah and Aaron Moses of Portsmouth, 10 Feb 1805
  Samuel and Mercy Locke, 12 Nov 1801
MATHES (MATHEWS), Abram and Betsey M. Berry, 23 Oct 1830
  Abram, a.65y, and Adelaide Pollard, a.40y, of Haverhill, MA, Apr 1877
  Abraham and Mary Thomas, 26 Jun 1774
  Ann E. and James M. Hall, 4 Jul 1853
  Betsy and John Downs, 21 Jun 1815
  Clara E. and Henry D. Foss, 5 Oct 1858
  Frances O. and Charles I. Mace, 2 Feb 1864
  Harriet and Samuel P. Mow, 6 Oct 1833
  Hattie and John W. Caswell, 10 Jul 1864
  Minerva H. and Henry A. Ryder of Staten Island, NY, 1 Oct 1865
  Robert and Betsey Randall, 12 Feb 1807
  Mary E. and Jonathan W. Varrell, Jan 1839
  William and Elizabeth Foss, 17 Feb 1812
McDANIEL, Almira, of Nottingham, and William Garland, 1861
McDONALD, Andrew and Susan Welch, both of Portsmouth, 4 Feb 1817
McLAUGHLIN, Hannah, a.22y, and George A. Jenness, a.23y, 10 Jun 1890

RYE MARRIAGES

McLAWLIN, Ellen A., of Georgetown, MA, and William Clancy Walker, 3 Jun 1867
MEAD, John B. and Sarah H. Smith of No. Hampton, 1817
MELOON (MALOON,MELOWN), Alfred A. Jr. and Sarah E. Yeaton, both of Newcastle, 11 Mar 1872
  Ann, of Greenland, and Jonathan Palmer, 9 Oct 1735
  Henry and Susannah Symes of Greenland, 16 Aug 1750
  Joseph and Deliverance Walker of Greenland, 31 Dec 1741
  Joseph and Hannah Philbrick of Greenland, 30 Jan 1755
MERRIAM, George, of New London, and Hannah Rand, 5 Sep 1852
MERRIL, Barns, of Londonderry, and Abigail Jenness, 14 Jul 1785
  Betsey L. and Elisha Chase, both of Stratham, 13 Sep 1809
  Hannah, of So. Hampton, and Benjamin Edmonds of Wolfborough, 1812
  Polly and Moses Wells Jr., both of Hampton Falls, 31 May 1804
MERSERVE, Sarah and Samuel Dearborn Jr., both of Greenland, 7 Jan 1807
MILLER, William and Eliza Ann Dean, 18 Feb 1813
MONTGOMERY, David H., of Strafford, and Abbie G. Perkins, 15 May 1862
MOORE, Benjamin Jr. and Eleanor Jewell of Stratham, 11 Mar 1822
MORAN, Henry W. and Mary P. Remick, both of Portsmouth, 1 Mar 1858
MORRIL, Alva Herman and Elizabeth Lake Hubbard of Wells, ME, 3 Dec 1872
  Esther, of Salem, and Jeffery Lang, 5 Dec 1751
MORGAN, Nathaniel and Mary Bickford of Epsom, 9 Mar 1777
MORRISON, Alexander and Rebecah Rand, 6 Jul 1773
  Martha C. and Rev. John Haven of York, ME, 29 Apr 1839
  Polly and Benjamin Lear, 25 Nov 1790
  Rachel (widow) and Simon Garland, 20 Dec 1781
  Samuel and Mary Billings, 25 Dec 1775
  William and Abigail Trefethern, 14 Nov 1779
MOSES, Aaron, of Portsmouth, and Ruhamah Mason, 10 Feb 1805
  Elizabeth and Michael W. Tucker, both of Portsmouth, 18 Feb 1808

RYE MARRIAGES

MOSES, James, of Portsmouth, and Mary Odiorne, 2 Oct 1803
  Nadab, of Portsmouth, and Abigail Wallis, 13 Jun 1776
  Patty and Billy Rand, 29 May 1800
  Ruth and William Seavey, 23 Jan 1752
  Samuel, of Epsom, and Bridget Weeks of Greenland, 9 Apr 1760
  Thomas and Margaret Huntress of Portsmouth, 4 Apr 1811
MOULTON, Abigail, of Stratham, and Daniel Perrier of Exeter, 30 Dec 1821
  Adeline, of No. Hampton, and George H. Seavey, 9 Dec 1871
  Charlotte (Mrs.) and Reuben Marden, 1835
  Cora Jane, a.21y, of No. Hampton, and George Henry Brown, a.21y, Dec 1876
  Daniel and Ruth Watson, 21 Nov 1744
  Daniel, of Gilmanton, and Molly Lamprey of No. Hampton, 12 Feb 1789
  Daniel and Molly Brown of No. Hampton, 9 Aug 1818
  Daniel G., of No. Hampton, and Hannah J. Verrill, 1855
  Elizabeth and Thomas Rand, 5 Jul 1748
  Ella C., of No. Hampton, and Frank E. Chesley, 27 Nov 1884
  Elvira, of No. Hampton, and George Washington Jenness, 1873
  Hannah and Reuben Marden, 4 Apr 1810
  Jacob A. Jr., of No. Hampton, and Emma R. Philbrick, 3 Jan 1870
  John and Charlotte Towle of Hampton, 7 Mar 1827
  John H., of Center Harbor, and Susan S. Porter, 23 May 1832
  Lucia and Moses Chase of Stratham, 22 Dec 1755
  Lucy and Joshua Haines of No. Hampton, 29 Jan 1777
  Mary and John Quin, 26 Nov 1747
  Morris and Harriet Fogg, both of No. Hampton, 17 Sep 1860
  Nathan, of Hampton Falls, and Charlotte Prescott of Kensington, 1816
  Noah and Patience Locke, 16 Nov 1749
  Olive and Nathaniel Mason, both of Stratham, at Stratham, 12 Dec 1840
  Phebe and Simon Berry, 29 Nov 1757
  Reuben and Hannah Philbrick, 24 Nov 1748

RYE MARRIAGES

MOULTON, Sally and Rev. Huntington Porter, 1796
  Sally, of No. Hampton, and William Jones, 16 Jun 1796
  Simon, of Hampton, and Olive Garland, 23 Jun 1825
  Thomas and Hannah Down of No. Hampton, 1 Aug 1750
  Tryphene and Elisha Locke, 13 Jan 1743
MOW (MOWE), Dorcas and Jude Allen of Stratham, 4 Oct 1776
  Ephraim and Dorcas Marden, 8 Sep 1754
  Mary and Richard Green, 5 Mar 1778
  Sally and Samuel Allen, 8 Apr 1824
  Samuel and Hannah Locke, 2 Oct 1803
  Samuel P. and Harriet Mathes, 6 Oct 1833
MUCHMORE, Deborah, of Portsmouth, and John G. Brewster, 7 Aug 1808
MUDGE, Martha E., of Lynn, MA, and Amos S. Brown, at Lynn, MA, 29 Sep 1869
MULLEN, Olive, of Newcastle, and Curtis Lawes of Ft. Constitution, 16 Sep 1811
MURRAY (MUREY), Samuel and Hannah Dalton, 4 May 1769
NASON, David, of So. Berwick, and Margery T. Foss, 12 Nov 1822
  Levi, of Dover and Elizabeth Philbrick, Dec 1839
NEAL (NEIL), Isabella T., of Portsmouth, and Joshua W. Kenney of Newcastle, 1 Sep 1816
  Robert and Alice Clark of Newcastle, 19 Apr 1750
  William Jr. and Hepsibah Marden, 6 Feb 1779 (Newcastle Record)
NELSON, David and Mary Atwood of Ipswich, 26 Sep 1740
  John and Mrs. Sarah Randall, 3 Jan 1788
  John, of Portsmouth, and Ruth Mace, 1803
  William and Anne Whitton, 24 Jun 1763
  William and Hannah Stiggins of Portsmouth, 25 Sep 1803
NEWMAN, Betsey (Mrs.), of No. Hampton, and John T. Dow, 16 Jun 1822
NEWMARCH, Hannah, of Portsmouth, and Richard Billings, 22 Aug 1777
NEWTON, Isaac and Mrs. Mary Newton, both of the Isles of Shoals, 6 Mar 1827
  James, of Gosport, and Patience Seavey Foss, 1 Nov 1815
  John and Mrs. Mary Haley, both of Gosport, 23 Jul 1804
  Mark and Mary Caswell, both of the Isles of

RYE MARRIAGES

Shoals, 31 Mar 1817
NEWTON, Mary (Mrs.) and Isaac Newton, both of the Isles of Shoals, 6 Mar 1827
NOBLE, Christopher and Martha Rowe of Portsmouth, 26 Dec 1744
NORIE, Margaret and William Hall, both of Portsmouth, 6 May 1809
NORRIS, Martha and Thomas Downing, both of Greenland, 14 Aug 1796
  Samuel and Elizabeth Holmes of Portsmouth, 30 Oct 1766
  Samuel and Sally Holmes, both of Portsmouth, 6 Oct 1808
NORTON, Abigail, of Portsmouth, and Samuel Batchelder of Greenland, 3 Aug 1815
  Benjamin, of Portsmouth, and Mary Webster, 10 May 1840
  Dudley and Hannah Varrel, 6 Mar 1785
  Eleanor, of Portsmouth, and John Varrel, 8 May 1808
  Eliza, of Greenland, and Daniel Mason, 20 Apr 1775
  Eliza and Joseph Odiorne, at No. Hampton, 17 Dec 1818
  Moses and Elizabeth Godard, 23 Nov 1775
  Ruhamah and Levi Ayers, 10 Dec 1778
NOWELL, Eunice, of Portsmouth, and David Webster, 1 Feb 1809
  John and Sarah Randall of Gosport, 8 Sep 1782
NUDD, Ruth and John Perkins, 26 Feb 1789
  Samuel and Hannah Tarlton of Greenland, 17 Jun 1779
NUTTER, Mary Ann and Joseph Bailey, both of Portsmouth, 10 Jul 1816
ODELL, George, of No. Hampton, and Sally Towle of Hampton 15 Oct 1818
ODIORNE, Benjamin and Dolly Yeaton of Newcastle, 1798
  Benjamin and Olive Seavey, 7 Apr 1825
  Benjamin T. and Ambrenetta J.M. Remick, 1858
  Betsey and John Beck, both of Portsmouth, 16 Sep 1798
  Charles B. and Mary Yeaton of Newcastle, 27 Sep 1840
  Clara E. and Howard F. Rand, 1862
  Cynthia A. and Daniel W. Philbrick, 9 Jan 1872
  Eben Lewis and Augusta Stoddard of Portsmouth, 26 Jun 1858
  Ebenezer and Martha Webster, 3 Feb 1822

RYE MARRIAGES

ODIORNE, Ebenezer L. and Mary Brown, 27 Nov 1825
  Elizabeth and Minas Daniels, 26 Mar 1753
  Elzada, a.22y, and Arthur A. Rand, a.27y, 30 Oct 1890
  Hannah M. and John Foss, 10 Dec 1855
  John and Eunice Seavey, 25 Jul 1753
  John E. and Lucy B. Foss of So. Newmarket, 26 Jun 1859
  Joseph and Eliza Norton, at No. Hampton, 17 Dec 1818
  Joseph W. and Martha A. Verril, 15 Dec 1863
  Katherine, of Newcastle, and James Tarlton of Portsmouth 16 Jan 1755
  Lizzie and Harold Foye, both of Portsmouth, 20 Jan 1859
  Martha (Mrs.) and John Foye, 5 Nov 1829
  Mary and Joseph Locke, 20 Apr 1768
  Mary and Nathaniel Rand (tert.), 28 May 1778
  Mary and James Moses of Portsmouth, 2 Oct 1803
  Mary Abby and Oren Drake, 30 Apr 1848
  Samuel Jr. and Hannah Rand, 23 Jun 1830
  Sarah A. and Thomas Sterling of Kittery, 1858
  Simeon, of Portsmouth, and Abigail Jenness, 7 Feb 1870
OLIVER, Robert and Mary Rand, 3 Aug 1793 (Newcastle Record)
ORDWAY, Lemuel and Anna Dearborn, both of Loudon, 14 Nov 1802
OSBORNE, Catherine and Moses Head, both of Portsmouth, 19 May 1816
OTIS, Frank A., of Portsmouth, and Christa Lear, 5 Jul 1870
OZEL, Phebe and Ceaser Liberty, 2 Aug 1783
PACKREN, Hannah and James Jenness, Jun 1718
PAGE, Abigail and Abraham Libby, 24 Feb 1763
  Anna and George Sanders Jr., 24 Nov 1768
  Augusta M., of No. Hampton, and George Walker, 9 Sep 1871
  Benjamin and Mary Fogg of No. Hampton, 30 May 1781
  Betsey and Joseph Philbrick, 1810
  Daniel, of Epsom, and Betsey Saunders, 6 Feb 1810
  Daniel, of No. Hampton, and Jane Foss, 24 Dec 1812
  David C. and Mary F. Clark, 18 Oct 1848
  Elizabeth, of No. Hampton, and Tappan Leavitt, 2 Oct 1814
  Jeremiah, of Hampton, and Lydia Philbrick, 27

RYE MARRIAGES

Feb 1769
PAGE, Mary, of No. Hampton, and Jeremiah Robinson of Exeter, Oct 1784
  Mary and Joses 3d Philbrick, 3 Nov 1803
  Mercy, of No. Hampton, and James Marden of Portsmouth, 22 Dec 1822
  Molly, of Hampton, and Richard Jenness (tert.), 23 Jul 1778
  Nathaniel and Olive Pierce of Portsmouth, 31 Dec 1845
  Sally, of No. Hampton, and Thomas Jenness, 16 May 1799
  Sally, of No. Hampton, and Jeremiah Sanborn of Sanbornton, 29 Nov 1800
  Sarah, of Hampton, and Francis Locke, 24 Jan 1751
  Sarah and Daniel Fogg, 22 Oct 1754
  Stacy, of No. Hampton, and Huldah Berry, 12 Oct 1828
PAIN, Amos and Mary Locke, 28 Dec 1775
PALMER, Arvillon Vincy and Elizabeth Anna Smith of Newmarket, 25 Sep 1875
  Benjamin, of No. Hampton, and Lydia Knowles, 10 Oct 1768
  Christopher and Elizabeth Locke, 24 Jul 1705
  Jeremiah and Lucy Yeaton of Portsmouth, 26 Jun 1819
  Jonathan and Ann Maloon of Greenland, 9 Oct 1735
  Jonathan and Abigail Rowe of Hampton, 21 May 1746
  Jonathan, of Kensington, and Abigail Jenness, 31 Dec 1826
  Joseph and Sarah Willey, 9 Mar 1767
  Mercy and Stephen Rand, 3 Jul 1759
  Nathaniel, of Portsmouth, and Sarah E. Varrell, 3 Nov 1851
  Sally, of Kensington, and James Hoig, 20 Jul 1818
  Sarah and Richard Locke, 2 Nov 1769
  William and Jane Foss, 27 Jun 1736
PARSONS, Albion D. and Martha S. Jenness, 23 Jan 1851
  Almira and Jonathan Brown, 3 Jan 1832
  Amos S. and Mary Langdon of Portsmouth, 31 Mar 1828
  Amos Seavey and Patty Dow, 3 Aug 1796
  Betsey and John Garland, 15 Aug 1799
  Eliza and Lyman Seavey, 4 Apr 1822

RYE MARRIAGES

PARSONS, Eliza A. (divorcer), a.26y, and Ralph Marden, a.30y, 23 Oct 1890
  Elizabeth and Samuel Wallis, 16 Nov 1773
  Ella M., a.20y, and John Fraser, a.26y, of Scotland, 29 Sep 1880
  Emily and Joseph Brown 3d (alias Joseph Ward Brown), 24 Mar 1829
  John W. and Abigail Garland, 11 Aug 1803
  Joseph and Mary Seavey, 31 Jan 1768
  Joseph and Hannah Perkins, 1798
  Lovina and Lewis Perkins, 11 Jun 1839
  Martha and Cotton W. Drake, 14 Jul 1822
  Mary and Rev. John Tuck of Epsom, 4 Mar 1762
  Mary D. and Dr. Joseph Dalton of Brentwood, 9 Jan 1825
  Samuel (Rev.) and Mary Jones of Boston, 9 Oct 1739
  Thomas J. and Eliza Brown, (no date)
  Warren and Sarah Ann Dow, 1 Jan 1845
PATTERSON, Polly and James Ayers, both of Greenland, 12 Mar 1793
PAUL, Olive and William Dennett Jr., both of Portsmouth, 16 Jun 1816
  Sally, of Elliot, ME, and Joseph Remick, 5 Mar 1801
PERKINS, Abbie G. and David H. Montgomery of Strafford, 15 May 1862
  Abigail and John Garland, 18 Oct 1778
  Abigail and Samuel Jenness, 1 Mar 1810
  Abraham and Christina Philbrick, Jan 1839
  Clara H., a.26y, of Memphis, Tenn., and Fred Philbrick, a.24y, Mar 1880
  Eliza and John Leavitt of No. Hampton, 23 Nov 1826
  Elias and Mary Lang of Portsmouth, 7 Jul 1822
  Florence J. and John A. Coe, 16 Apr 1882
  Hannah and Joseph Parsons, 1798
  Hannah and Daniel Goss, 6 Apr 1820
  Huldah and Nathaniel Thurston of Bradford, 8 Sep 1799
  Huldah and Josiah Jenness, 7 Jan 1822
  Hulde and Elijah Lock, 22 Mar 1739
  James and Abigail Locke, 23 Feb 1758
  James (Lieut.) and Mrs. Mehitable Garland, 14 Jun 1812
  James Henry, a.23y, and Mary Charlotte Goodwin, a.28y, of So. Berwick, ME, Jun 1874
  Jane M. and Ira Brown, 6 Sep 1820
  John and Ann Locke, 10 Mar 1748

RYE MARRIAGES

PERKINS, John and Ruth Nudd, 26 Feb 1789
  Jonathan and Molly Locke, 1801
  Josiah and Betsey Batchelder of No. Hampton, Spring 1807
  Lewis and Lovina Parsons, 11 Jun 1839
  Mary and Nathaniel Emery of Hampton, 1 Apr 1777
  Nancy and Jonathan Sherburne of Portsmouth, 4 Mar 1787
  Nancy and David P. Brown of No. Hampton, 2 Aug 1828
  Polly and Levi Garland Jr., 21 Nov 1811
  Sally, of Hampton, and Amos Knowles, 8 Mar 1827
  Sarah E. and Job R. Jenness, 10 May 1860
  William and Elizabeth Hoare, 5 May 1753
PERRIER, Daniel, of Exeter, and Abigail Moulton of Stratham, 30 Dec 1821
PERVIERE, Abigail and James Philbrick, 21 May 1801
PHILBRICK, Abigail and Mark Rendall, 24 Nov 1748
  Abigail, of No. Hampton, and James Chapman, 10 Dec 1801
  Abigail and Job Locke, 9 Dec 1806
  Abigail and Josiah H. Sanborn of Cambridge, MA, Sep 1835
  Abigail and John W. Mace, Jan 1841
  Addie, of Kittery, ME, and John Edwin Leavitt, 21 Dec 1873
  Albion Reuben and Georgia Anna Pressey of Manchester, 1872
  Amie E. and Christopher W. Haried of Portsmouth, 27 Jul 1856
  Benjamin and Angelina E. Batchelder of No. Hampton, 29 Dec 1844
  Benjamin P. and Mrs. Mary Verril, 8 Feb 1807
  Betsey and John Y. Remick, 17 Feb 1825
  Christina and Abraham Perkins, Jan 1839
  Clara A. and Hiram Chase of Stratham, 1859
  Cornelius O. and Mary P. Powers of Hampton, Sep 1876
  Daniel and Betsey Wells, 25 Dec 1794
  Daniel and Sarah Ann Philbrick, 7 Jul 1835
  Daniel W. and Cynthia A. Odiorne, 9 Jan 1872
  Elizabeth, of Hampton, and Isaac Towle, 17 Feb 1754
  Elizabeth and Reuben Rand, 10 Apr 1760
  Elizabeth, of Greenland, and Samuel Philbrick, 15 Apr 1779
  Elizabeth and Lieut. Joseph Jenness, 8 Dec 1809
  Elizabeth and Levi Nason of Dover, Dec 1839
  Ella Frances, a.26y, and Sylvanus W. Foss,

RYE MARRIAGES

 a.34y, 3 Apr 1879
PHILBRICK, Emma A. and Abraham J. Drake, 20 Oct 1870
 Emma R. and Jacob A. Moulton Jr. of No. Hampton, 3 Jan 1870
 Emmons B. and Vienna M. Dalton of No. Hampton, 1859
 Emmons Brown, a.41y, and Mary Charlotte Seavey, a.22y, 14 Oct 1875
 Frank Mosher and Melissa Hannah Jenness, 1872
 Fred, a.24y, and Clara H. Perkins, a.26y, of Memphis, Tenn., Mar 1880
 Hannah and Reuben Moulton, 24 Nov 1748
 Hannah, of Greenland, and Joseph Meloon, 30 Jan 1755
 Hannah and Amos Towle of No. Hampton, 1 Aug 1792
 Herbert E., a.23y, and Ida F. Marden, a.24y, Dec 1880
 Irena and Jesse Philbrick, 26 Oct 1836
 James and Elizabeth Lane, 11 Nov 1736
 James and Abigail Perviere, 21 May 1801
 Jemima, of No. Hampton, and Ebenezer Fogg, 17 May 1824
 Jesse Philbrick and Irena Philbrick, 26 Oct 1836
 John and Sally Brown, 25 Dec 1831
 Jonathan and Mary Marden, 8 Dec 1768
 Jonathan Jr. and Sarah Marden, 22 Oct 1795
 Jonathan Jr. and Sarah Wells, 1 Jun 1797
 Jonathan Jr. and Abigail Brown, 26 Feb 1834
 Joseph and Ann Towle, 2 Dec 1760
 Joseph and Betsey Page, 1810
 Joseph and Mrs. Sally Emery of Bartlett, 9 Mar 1813
 Joseph Jr. and Patty B. Knowles, 1818
 Joses and Susanna Pitman, 7 Jul 1782
 Joses 3d and Mary Page, 3 Nov 1803
 Joses Jr. and Sarah Smith, 12 Jan 1790
 Josiah, of No. Hampton, and Mary Elkins, 10 Dec 1801
 Josiah W. and Sarah Ann Brown, 25 Jun 1833
 Lydia and Jeremiah Page of Hampton, 27 Feb 1769
 Martha Ann and Woodbury Seavey, 1 Feb 1839
 Mary and Joseph William Seavey, 1861
 Mary Ann and John Batchelder Jr. of No. Hampton, 26 Dec 1842
 Mary M. and James Batchelder of No. Hampton, Dec 1828
 Moses and Sarah Ann Garland, 12 Apr 1838
 Nancy and Josiah Weeks of Greenland, 13 Mar 1796

RYE MARRIAGES

PHILBRICK, Nancy and Edmund Batchelder, both of
   No. Hampton, 1810
   Olive and Edmond Mason of Hampton, 9 Dec 1834
   Polly and Samuel H. Rand, 12 May 1808
   Reuben and Mrs. Mary Jenness, 4 Feb 1805
   Reuben and Molly Beck, 9 Sep 1806
   Reuben Jr. and Betsey Jenness, 4 Sep 1794
   Sally and Samuel Marden Jr., 3 Apr 1806
   Sally and Benjamin Akerman of Farming-
      ton, 5 Mar 1821
   Samuel and Elizabeth Philbrick of Greenland, 15
      Apr 1779
   Sarah and Amos Brown, Jun 1784
   Sarah and Joseph Jenness Jr., 8 Dec 1801
   Sarah and Nicholas Mason of Newington, 27 Sep
      1842
   Sarah Ann and Daniel Philbrick, 7 Jul 1835
   Sarah Ann and Peter Lord of Charlestown, 6 May
      1838
   Thomas H. and Olive R. Locke, 28 Feb 1847
   Thomas W. and Jane C. Benson of Portsmouth, 4
      Jul 1852
   Tryphene and John Sanders, 29 Jan 1760
   Woodbury J. and Eliza Perkins Jenness of No.
      Hampton, 12 Mar 1874
PHILLIPS, Edwin R., of Raymond, and Annabelle
   Marden, dau of Levi, 29 Apr 1886
PICOAT, Ellen M., of Kittery, ME, and Elbridge A.
   Thomas, 25 Dec 1865
PICKERING, Joseph, of Newington, and Sarah Jane
   Goss, 20 Dec 1831
   Lydia, of No. Hampton, and Lyford Thing of
      Brentwood, 18 Jan 1826
   Mary and Thomas Adams, both of Portsmouth, 11
      Mar 1812
PIERCE, Olive, of Portsmouth, and Nathaniel Page,
   31 Dec 1845
   William and Widow Randall of the Shoals, 11 Nov
      1780
PIKE, Helen Augusta, of Pembroke, and Joseph
   Jenness Rand, 28 May 1874
   Sewell, of Hampton Falls, and Polly Prescott of
      Kensington, 11 Nov 1813
PIPER, Noah, of Stratham, and Mary Crimble of No.
   Hampton, 12 Apr 1820
   Noah and Hannah Crimble of Stratham, 12 Mar 1837
   Susannah, of Stratham, and William Trefethern, 1
      Feb 1821
PITMAN, Dorcas and John Sanders Jr., 9 Nov 1767

RYE MARRIAGES

PITMAN, Ruth and Henry Shapley, 18 Nov 1772
  Susanna and Joses Philbrick, 7 Jul 1782
PLAISTED, Joseph and Mary Fitzgerald, 13 Nov 1780
POLLARD, Adelaide, a.40y, of Haverhill, MA, and
  Abram Mathes, a.65y, Apr 1877
POOLE (POOL), John, of Kittery, ME, and Angelina
  E. Caswell, 25 Jun 1860
  Mary Davis, a.21y, of Gloucester, MA, and
  Woodbury Levi Jenness, a.22y, Jul 1874
POOR, Robert, of Portsmouth, and Betsey Shapley, 4
  Jul 1788
POPE, Catherine, of Kittery, and John Lang of
  Portsmouth, 31 Dec 1747
PORTER, Allen, of Newcastle, and Anna T. Rand,
  (int.) 25 Aug 1838
  Allen, a.63y, and Mrs. Debra Warren, a.62y, of
  Portsmouth, 22 Jun 1875
  Huntington (Rev.) and Sally Moulton, 1796
  Maria and Asa Robinson of Brentwood, 18 Dec 1821
  Merinda P. and David Remick, 18 May 1873
  Louisa and William Weeks of Greenland, 26 May
  1835
  Olivia and Luther Hall of Boston, MA, 16 Aug
  1837
  Sarah E. and Rev. Charles Adams of Stratham, 31
  Jul 1833
  Susan S. and John H. Moulton of Center Harbor,
  23 May 1832
POWERS, Mary and John Locke, 27 Oct 1816
  Mary P., of Hampton, and Cornelius O. Philbrick,
  Sep 1876
PRAY, Hannah and Thomas Rand, 24 May 1722
PRESCOTT, Charlotte, of Kensington, and Nathan
  Moulton, 1816
  Hannah, of Hampton Falls, and Levi Locke, 31 Aug
  1796
  Josiah D. and Lucy A. Batchelder, 3 Jun 1865
  Polly, of Kensington, and Sewell Pike of Hampton
  Falls, 11 Nov 1813
  Timothy, of Kensington, and Annah Locke, 2 Jan
  1794
PRESSEY, Georgia Anna, of Manchester, and Albion
  Reuben Philbrick, 1872
PURRINGTON, Ivory, of Exeter, and Susan S. Marden
  of Portsmouth, 28 Mar 1863
  Joseph, of Epping, and Abigail Locke, 27 Dec
  1759
QUIN, John and Mary Moulton, 26 Nov 1747
RAMSEY, Robert, of Londonderry, and Susanna John-

RYE MARRIAGES

son of Greenland, 23 Jul 1809
RAND, Aaron and Elizabeth H. Yeaton, 1 Nov 1840
  Abigail and Nathaniel Berry, 21 Apr 1747
  Abigail and James Stevens of Epsom, 22 Apr 1787
  Adeline and Thomas J. Rand, 5 Dec 1839
  Anna T. and Allen Porter of Newcastle, (int.) 25 Aug 1838
  Anne and Thomas Shannon, 31 May 1753
  Arthur A., a.27y, and Elzada Odiorne, a.22y, 30 Oct 1890
  Augustus Yeaton and Amanda Downs, 26 Jun 1870
  Benjamin and Elizabeth Rand, 25 Nov 1773
  Bethiah and Nathaniel Rand (tert.), 22 Jan 1761
  Betsey and Joshua Rand, 29 Mar 1810
  Billy and Patty Moses, 29 May 1800
  Billy Jr. and Charlotte Batchelder of No. Hampton, 28 Feb 1811
  Caroline and Richard Jenness, 2 Aug 1819
  Charles and Sophia Brown, 20 Feb 1848
  Charles M., a.24y, and Augusta M. Drake, a.23y, 19 Nov 1879
  Daniel and Dolly Seavey, 24 Feb 1801
  Daniel W., a.32y, and Vianna J. Leavitt, a.23y, 19 Nov 1879
  David and Polly Salter, 22 Jul 1798
  David L. and Mary Yeaton, 4 Oct 1839
  Deborah and Joseph Libby, 12 Feb 1789
  Eliza and William Wormwood, 19 Apr 1770
  Eliza and Joseph Yeaton Jr., 5 Feb 1776
  Eliza and Simon Marston of Portsmouth, 14 Dec 1834
  Eliza and Jeremy Webster, 24 May 1837
  Elizabeth and William Locke, 5 Jan 1734/5
  Elizabeth and William Lang, 9 Dec 1751
  Elizabeth and Stephen Marden, 5 Feb 1757
  Elizabeth and Benjamin Rand, 25 Nov 1773
  Elizabeth and Reuben Wallis of Greenland, Jan 1785
  Elizabeth, of Hampton, and Benjamin Broughton of Marblehead, 27 Jan 1851
  Ellen A. and Emery C. Jenness, 3 Dec 1871
  Elvin and Martha Ann Willey of Portsmouth, 16 Nov 1839
  Ena and Aaron Locke, 24 Apr 1871
  Ephraim and Mary Smith, 22 Sep 1757
  Esther and John Bond, 17 Aug 1752
  George and Naomi Sherburne, 19 May 1768
  Hannah and Jethro Locke, 2 Feb 1748
  Hannah (widow) and Jonathan Woodman of So.

RYE MARRIAGES

Hampton, 12 Dec 1769
RAND, Hannah and Benjamin Marden, 26 Jan 1772
  Hannah and William Foye, 15 Nov 1804
  Hannah (Mrs.) and John Foye Jr., 1 Dec 1805
  Hannah and Samuel Odiorne Jr., 23 Jun 1830
  Hannah and George Merriam of New London, 5 Sep 1852
  Harriet and William Keen of Portsmouth, 3 Mar 1839
  Henry S. and Mary S. Trefethern, 6 Dec 1863
  Howard F. and Clara E. Odiorne, 1862
  Howard F., a.37y, and Louise M. Marden, a.31y, May 1879
  Ira and Sarah Ann Goss, 28 Apr 1839
  James B. (Capt.) and Abigail Berry of Greenland, (int.) 13 Oct 1838
  John and Mary Lawry, 8 Dec 1771
  John and Mrs. Nancy Haley of York, ME, 1 Jun 1851
  John Jr. and Hannah Seavey, 4 Jun 1772
  John Ira and Mary Jane Garland, 15 Nov 1849
  John O. and Sarah J. Thomas, 9 May 1844
  John T. and Betsey Dow, 4 May 1820
  Joseph and Deborah Seavey, Jul 1758
  Joseph and Susanna Goss, 24 May 1764
  Joseph and Sally Amazeen, 13 Aug 1791
  Joseph and Olly Marden, 18 Oct 1795
  Joseph Jr. and Eleanor D. Locke, 21 May 1826
  Joseph Jenness and Helen Augusta Pike of Pembroke, 28 May 1874
  Joseph Wm and Emily J. Foss, 1884
  Joshua Jr. and Ruth Seavey, 2 Oct 1777
  Joshua and Esther Marden, 4 Nov 1802
  Joshua and Betsey Rand, 29 Mar 1810
  Julia and Henry C. Bickford, 23 May 1868
  Lizzie and Orlando Garland of Gloucester, MA, 19 Oct 1862
  Louisa and Henry Amazeen of Newcastle, Sep 1826
  Martin H. and Florence L. Berry, 25 Nov 1875 (divorced 1886)
  Martha and John Locke of Newcastle, 7 Jan 1822
  Mary and William Chamberlain, 27 Nov 1729
  Mary and John Garland, 14 Feb 1744
  Mary and Benjamin Chandler of Kittery, 16 Mar 1749
  Mary and Zebedee Hunt, 13 Jul 1759
  Mary and William Rand, 21 Oct 1779
  Mary and Joseph Hall, 11 Jan 1781
  Mary and Robert Oliver, 3 Aug 1793 (Newcastle

RYE MARRIAGES

Record)
RAND, Mary and Thomas Foye of Boston, 10 Nov 1808
  Mary and Albert B. Trefethern, Dec 1864
  Mary Ann and Hamilton C. Locke, 2 Jan 1825
  Mary M. and Nicholas Mason, 23 Aug 1807
  Mehitable and Jeremiah Locke Jr., 14 Jan 1800
  Mehitable and James Elkins, 7 Mar 1809
  Mercy and Elijah Saunders, 29 Nov 1792
  Mercy and Daniel Mason Jr., 7 Apr 1807
  Meribah and Thomas Foss of Barrington, 18 Sep 1760
  Moses, of Portsmouth, and Hannah Seavey, 13 Oct 1851
  Nancy and Ebenezer Taylor of No. Hampton, 6 Aug 1802
  Nancy and Ephraim Hall, 20 Mar 1817
  Nathaniel and Mary Leavitt, 8 Dec 1757
  Nathaniel and Sarah Seavey, 22 Nov 1787
  Nathaniel and Abigail Trefethern, 5 Nov 1791
  Nathaniel (tert.) and Bethiah Rand, 22 Jan 1761
  Nathaniel (tert.) and Mary Odiorne, 28 May 1778
  Obed, of Roxbury, MA, and Anna Y. Jenness, 1 Mar 1835
  Olly and Jonathan Locke Jr., 23 Nov 1785
  Patty Lang and Simon Dow Jr. of Hampton, 11 Nov 1813
  Polly and Richard Kate of Barrington, 16 Nov 1790
  Polly and John Brown, 9 Dec 1839
  Rachel and Daniel Seavey, 5 Dec 1783
  Rebecah and Alexander Morrison, 6 Jul 1773
  Reed V. and Hannah Garland, 6 May 1824
  Reuben and Elizabeth Philbrick, 10 Apr 1760
  Ruth and Joseph Bickford, Jul 1760
  Ruthy and Samuel Kate of Barrington, 28 Sep 1801
  Sally and Jonathan Woodman, 12 Apr 1812
  Samuel and Sarah Dowrst, 10 May 1748
  Samuel and Abigail Marden, 14 Feb 1774
  Samuel and Hannah Dolbear, 5 Jan 1784
  Samuel and Sarah J. Rand, 22 Jan 1855
  Samuel H. and Polly Philbrick, 12 May 1808
  Samuel H. and Emily Jenness, 29 Nov 1835
  Sarah and Levi Goss, 18 Aug 1767
  Sarah and William Rand, 2 Dec 1773
  Sarah and Edward Hall, 22 Apr 1784
  Sarah and Benjamin Mason of Stratham, 2 Mar 1797
  Sarah and William Hall, 10 Jul 1824
  Sarah J. and Samuel Rand, 22 Jan 1855
  Stephen and Mercy Palmer, 3 Jul 1759

RYE MARRIAGES

RAND, Stephen and Sarah Fogg, 17 May 1781
  Stephen and Ruth Tarlton, 17 Sep 1807
  Stephen Jr. and Betsey Tarlton of Portsmouth, 8
    Jun 1806
  Sukey and Jeremiah Locke Jr., 21 Nov 1793
  Temperance and Noah Seavey, 6 May 1763
  Thomas and Hannah Pray, 24 May 1722
  Thomas and Elizabeth Moulton, 5 Jul 1748
  Thomas and Hannah Jenness, 9 Dec 1756
  Thomas and Mary Tucke, 4 Apr 1790
  Thomas Jr. and Sarah Ann Brown, 24 Nov 1831
  Thomas J. and Adeline Rand, 5 Dec 1839
  Thomas W. and Louisa A. Hodgden of Greenland,
    1858
  William and Sarah Tucker, 8 Feb 1753
  William and Sarah Rand, 2 Dec 1773
  William and Mary Rand, 21 Oct 1779
  William and Dolly Rollins, 12 Aug 1804
  William J. and Elizabeth Jenness, 11 Mar 1844
RANDALL (RENDALL), Abigail and Gideon Marshall of
    Hampton Falls, 2 May 1770
  Abigail and John Goss, 14 Jun 1790
  Amelia and Samuel Saunders, 29 Nov 1792
  Benjamin and Mary Rugg, both of Gosport, 14 Jan
    1791
  Benjamin, of Gosport, and Sarah Saunders, 27 Aug
    1793
  Betsey and Robert Mathews, 12 Feb 1807
  Betty, of Gosport, and Samuel Caswell, 25 Sep
    1783
  Dolly and James Shapley, 19 Oct 1820
  Elizabeth and Richard Webster, 29 Oct 1778
  George and Sarah Berry, 18 Jul 1751
  George and Elizabeth Berry, 14 Nov 1782
  George and Betsey Downs of Gosport, 15 Nov 1832
  George and Sarah Goodwin of Star Island (Isles
    of Shoals), Nov 1830
  George Jr., of Gosport, and Widow Abigail Whid-
    den, 11 Mar 1824
  Hannah, of Gosport, and Peter Robinson, 16 Jul
    1811
  James and Mary Sherburne, 24 Nov 1748
  Job L. and Louisa Randall of Gosport, at Isles
    of Shoals, 16 Aug 1838
  John and Bathsheba Webber of Gosport, 8 Sep 1782
  John and Hannah Bragg, 6 Jul 1816
  John, of Gosport, and Mary H. Caswell, 19 Feb
    1850
  John W., of Gosport, and Ann M. Verrill, 17 Apr

RYE MARRIAGES

1853
RANDALL, John W., of Gosport, and Harriet N. Lear, 1858
  John Y. and Mrs. Hannah Foye, 19 Oct 1828
  Levi D. and Abigail Webster, Apr 1809
  Louisa, of Gosport, and Job L. Randall, at Isles of Shoals, 16 Aug 1838
  Love and Samuel Haley Jr. of the Shoals, 14 Dec 1815
  Lydia, of Gosport and Henry N. Caswell, 15 Mar 1871
  Mark and Abigail Philbrick, 24 Nov 1748
  Mary and Nicholas Dolbear, 27 May 1773
  Mary, of Portsmouth, and Richard Tucker Varrell, 31 Oct 1803
  Mary and John Langdon Locke, 16 May 1833
  Mary E., of Gosport, and Woodbury N. Mace, 25 Dec 1865
  Mercy, of Portsmouth, and John Reding, 13 Sep 1802
  Molly and Joseph Hall, 28 Nov 1805
  Paul and Hannah Adams, 4 Feb 1752
  Rachel and John Mace, 27 Jun 1793
  Reuben S. and Elizabeth M. Berry, 26 Nov 1818
  Richard and Dorcas Down of Gosport, 20 Sep 1781
  Samuel and Betsey Smith, 26 Jan 1817
  Sarah and John Jenness Jr., 23 Dec 1777
  Sarah, of Gosport, and John Nowell, 8 Sep 1782
  Sarah and William Rendall, both of Gosport, 24 Nov 1785
  Sarah (Mrs.) and John Nelson, 3 Jan 1788
  Sarah Hannah and John Wilkes Locke, Oct 1872
  William and Hannah Marston, 24 Apr 1745
  William and Sarah Rendall, both of Gosport, 24 Nov 1785
  William and Hannah Locke, 29 Jul 1816
  William and Eliza G. Caswell, 11 Dec 1827
  William and Mary C. Downs, Nov 1834
  William B. and Sally J. Goss, 8 Apr 1821
  William Bates and Deborah Yeaton, 26 Feb 1793
  ____ (widow), of the Shoals, and William Pierce, 11 Nov 1780
  ____ (widow) and Noah Jenness, 15 Jan 1784
RAWLINS, John and Esther Abbott of Greenland, 29 Jul 1754
REDING, John and Mercy Randall of Portsmouth, 13 Sep 1802
REID, Betsey and Joseph Tucker, 29 Jan 1806
REITH, John, of Marblehead, MA, and Lydia Knight

RYE MARRIAGES

of Ipswich, 22 Jun 1741
REMICK, Addie, of Elliot, ME, and John W. Lear, 7 Jan 1871
  Albert L. and Anna C. Mace, Nov 1876
  Ambrenetta J.M. and Benjamin T. Odiorne, 1858
  Charles M. and Emily B. Brown, dau of Chas. J. Brown, 24 Dec 1884
  David and Mrs. Abby H. Mace, 15 Nov 1849
  David and Merinda P. Porter, 18 May 1873
  Esther Y. and Lemuel Locke, 31 May 1832
  George O., a.27y, and Clara E. Varrell, a.18y, 30 Oct 1877
  Hannah and Andrew Clark, 23 Nov 1797
  Huldah and Solomon Marden, 15 Jul 1802
  Isaac and Meribah Smith, 23 Jan 1755
  Isaac and Mary Disco, 23 Aug 1759
  Isaac and Jane Foss, 19 Nov 1790
  Isaac and Esther Yeaton, 7 Nov 1793
  Isaac and Lydia Verril, 24 Nov 1808
  Isaac and Hannah Verril, 28 Jan 1827
  John S. and Mary T. Seavey, 22 Jun 1851
  John Y. and Betsey Philbrick, 17 Feb 1825
  Joseph and Sally Paul of Elliot, ME, 5 Mar 1801
  Mary P. and Henry W. Moran, both of Portsmouth, 1 Mar 1858
  Moses and Anna Lang of Greenland, 3 Mar 1805
RICKER, Wentworth and Nancy M. Dorr, both of Portsmouth, 9 Apr 1860
RING, Mary, of Portsmouth, and Thomas Currier, 3 Dec 1772
ROBIE (ROBEY), Eliza, of Hampton, and William Currier of Epping, 31 May 1770
  John, of No. Hampton, and Mary Garland, 13 Dec 1781
  Jeremiah H., of No. Hampton, and Hannah P. Seavey, 20 May 1852
  Nathan and Lucy Kenniston of Hampton Falls, 2 May 1821
ROBINSON, Asa, of Brentwood, and Maria Porter, 18 Dec 1821
  Asa C., of Stratham, and Mary B. Downs, 12 Feb 1824
  James and Mrs. Sally Downs, 27 Feb 1821
  Jeremiah, of Exeter, and Mary Page of No. Hampton, Oct 1784
  John and Mary Shapley, both of Gosport, 27 Apr 1789
  Lovina and Reuben Shapleigh, 21 Apr 1825
  Mary Ann and William J. Walker, 22 Oct 1861

RYE MARRIAGES

ROBINSON, Peter and Hannah Randall of Gosport, 16 Jul 1811
  Robert and Tammy Caswell of Gosport, 18 May 1826
  Sally and Clevlen B. Hoite, 6 Jun 1824
  Samuel, of Gosport, and Nancy Knowles of Seabrook, 29 Aug 1824
  Samuel, of Gosport, and Love Haley, 1829
  Sarah E. and Charles R. Caswell, 16 Sep 1863
ROLLINS, Dolly and William Rand, 12 Aug 1804
  Elizabeth and John Wells, 9 Nov 1769
  Levi, of Stratham, and Mary Ann Tilton, 11 Nov 1824
ROWE, Abigail, of Hampton, and Jonathan Palmer, 21 May 1746
  Frederick and Mary Verril, both of Portsmouth, 31 Oct 1824
  Martha, of Portsmouth, and Christopher Noble, 26 Dec 1744
  Merribah, of Portsmouth, and Samuel Rowe, 10 Jul 1761
  Samuel and Merribah Rowe of Portsmouth, 10 Jul 1761
  ____ and ____ Welch of Portsmouth, 15 Aug 1762
RUGG, Elizabeth and Joseph Mace, both of Gosport, 11 Mar 1787
  Mary and Benjamin Randall, both of Gosport, 14 Jan 1791
  William and Judith Mace, both of Gosport, 8 Dec 1792
RUMESY, Elizabeth, a.38y, and Charles H. Lear, a.36y, 16 Dec 1880
RUSWICK, John and Mary Barker of Hampton, Dec 1739
RYDER, Henry A., of Staten Island, NY, and Minerva H. Mathes, 1 Oct 1865
RYMES, Christopher and Sarah Hale of Exeter, 21 May 1767
SALTER, Alexander and Molly Berry, 18 Mar 1803
  Alexander and Anna Webster, 22 Nov 1810
  Lucy and Levi Garland, 24 Nov 1789
  Martha, of Newcastle, and Ebenezer Sanborn of Hampton, May 1740
  Polly and David Rand, 22 Jul 1798
  Sally and Samuel Lear, 5 Feb 1792
  Webster and Sally Libby, 14 Dec 1806
SANBORN, E.A., a.55y, and Bernard F____, a.60y of Portsmouth, Jan 1879
  Ebenezer, of Hampton, and Martha Salter of Newcastle, May 1740
  Enoch and Hannah Walker of Newbury, 16 Dec 1773

RYE MARRIAGES

SANBORN, Hannah, of Hampton, and Eli Lamprey, 12 Oct 1823
  Huldah, of Chichester, and Constantin Sinclair of Sanbornton, 23 Jul 1776
  Jeremiah, of Sanbornton, and Sally Page of No. Hampton, 29 Nov 1800
  Josiah H., of Cambridge, MA, and Abigail Philbrick, Sep 1835
  Lowell, of Gilmanton, and Molly Marden, 13 May 1802
  Samuel and Mary Barnes, 18 Mar 1767
SARGEANT, Betsey, of Haverhill, MA, and David Tenny Foss of Barrington, 7 Jan 1793
SAUNDERS (SANDERS), Abigail and William Locke, 28 Oct 1779
  Amelia and John Bragg, 7 Jun 1796
  Betsey and Daniel Page of Epsom, 6 Feb 1810
  Elijah and Mercy Rand, 29 Nov 1792
  Elizabeth and Edward Verril, 4 Nov 1773
  Esther and John Yeaton, 24 Aug 1759
  George and Mary Shapley, 29 Jul 1789
  George Jr. and Anna Page, 24 Nov 1768
  Hannah and Elijah Locke Jr., 21 Jan 1802
  Huldah and Philip Yeaton, 1797
  John, of Gosport, and Mary Berry, 17 Apr 1740
  John and Tryphene Philbrick, 29 Jan 1760
  John Jr. and Dorcas Pitman, 9 Nov 1767
  Mary and Elisha Blake, 11 Dec 1766
  Mary and William Thomas, 24 Nov 1763
  Mary (Mrs.) and Levi Goss, 15 Nov 1796
  Mercy (Mrs.) and Nathaniel Coleman, 7 Aug 1796
  Mercy H. and James Shapley of Portsmouth, 13 Sep 1787
  Olive and William Tucker, 13 Mar 1787
  Polly and Reuben Shapleigh, 19 Feb 1796
  Robert 3d and Mary Foss, 12 Apr 1787
  Robert Jr. and Mary Locke, 7 Jul 1765
  Samuel, of the Shoals, and Hannah Foss, 21 Aug 1741
  Samuel and Amelia Rendall, 29 Nov 1792
  Sarah and John Marden, 23 Mar 1769
  Sarah and William Sanders, 6 Mar 1783
  Sarah and Benjamin Randall of Gosport, 27 Aug 1793
  Sarah (Mrs.) and Joseph Varrell of the Shoals, 25 Aug 1794
  Tryphene and Jotham Berry, 16 Apr 1780
  William and Sarah Sanders, 6 Mar 1783
SAWYER, Horace, of Bradford, MA, and Susan M.

RYE MARRIAGES

Jenness, 5 Nov 1868
SAYMORE, Henry and Ann Cutt of Portsmouth, 13 Sep 1750
SCADGEL, Benjamin and Dorcas Barnes, 20 Oct 1747
  Jacob and Rachel Lee, 21 Jan 1755
  John and Mary Holmes, 29 Nov 1753
  Mary and Jeremiah Fuller, 26 Jul 1745
SCAMMON, Elizabeth W., of Stratham, and Michael Dalton 2d, 28 Apr 1839
SCOTT, Sarah and Joseph Seavey, 22 Nov 1744
SEAVEY, Abigail and Abraham Clifford, May 1746
  Abigail and John Godfrey of Hampton, 25 Nov 1801
  Alfred V. and Charlotte A. Garland, 31 Jan 1861
  Alfred V. and Mary J. Drake, 17 Feb 1870
  Amos and Mary Langdon, 25 Oct 1744
  Amos and Sarah Drake, 16 Jun 1807
  Ann E. and Albert Dow, 21 Nov 1847
  Anne and John Seavey, 20 Nov 1791
  Betsey and Joseph Brown Jr. of No. Hampton, 26 Apr 1804
  Calvena E. and Amos P. Brown, 27 Jan 1867
  Caroline T. and Gilman J. Marden, 1860
  Charles E. and Fidelia Garland, 31 Jan 1861
  Charlotte and Joseph R. Holmes, 24 Sep 1859
  Daniel and Rachel Rand, 5 Dec 1783
  Deborah and Joseph Rand, Jul 1758
  Dolly and Daniel Rand, 24 Feb 1801
  Elijah, of Barrington, and Sarah Berry, 4 Sep 1764
  Elizabeth and John Jenness, 30 Nov 1732
  Elizabeth and Isaac Dow, 21 Aug 1777
  Emaline and John N. Frost of Newcastle, 29 Dec 1824
  Ephraim and Betsey Garland, 1823
  Eunice and John Odiorne, 25 Jul 1753
  Fanny and Benjamin Garland, 15 May 1803
  George H. and Adeline Moulton of No. Hampton, 9 Dec 1871
  Hannah and Samuel Seavey, 6 Nov 1734
  Hannah and Jacob Sheafe of Newcastle, 24 Jul 1740
  Hannah and William Seavey, 25 Sep 1748
  Hannah and Samuel Hutchinson, 15 Jul 1768
  Hannah and John Rand Jr., 4 Jun 1772
  Hannah and Richard Jenness of Deerfield, 22 Feb 1774
  Hannah and William Foye, 23 Feb 1795
  Hannah and Jonathan Wedgewood, 23 Mar 1790

RYE MARRIAGES

SEAVEY, Hannah and Stephen Fields, 7 Jul 1799
  Hannah and Moses Rand of Portsmouth, 13 Oct 1851
  Hannah P. and Jeremiah H. Robie of No. Hampton, 20 May 1852
  Harrison and Martha J. Webster, 21 May 1854
  Henry and Mary Kingman, 18 Sep 1740
  Henry and Elizabeth Fuller, 28 Sep 1745
  Isaac and Abigail Gardner of Portsmouth, 6 Apr 1785
  James Jr. and Patience Berry, 23 May 1780
  James E. and Charlotte Foss, 13 Jun 1869
  Joanna and Joseph Fuller, 8 Mar 1733
  John and Anne Seavey, 20 Nov 1791
  Joseph and Sarah Scott, 22 Nov 1744
  Joseph and Susanna Kennison, 2 Oct 1771
  Joseph Jr. and Sarah Locke, 24 Dec 1769
  Joseph Jackson and Elizabeth A. Lear, 22 Feb 1867
  Joseph L. and Temperance Langdon of Portsmouth, 15 Nov 1832
  Joseph Langdon and Elizabeth Garland, 17 Jul 1777
  Joseph W. and Sarah Lang, 29 May 1829
  Joseph William and Mary Philbrick, 1861
  Joshua and Betsey Webster, 16 Apr 1797
  Lettis and Thomas J. Berry of Greenland, 16 Apr 1828
  Lyman and Eliza Parsons, 4 Apr 1822
  Margaret and Samuel Marden, 22 Oct 1769
  Martha and James Locke, 29 Sep 1774
  Martha and Amos S. Garland, 28 Nov 1816
  Martha J. and John Wesley Foye, 22 Feb 1871
  Mary and Joseph Conner, 25 Jan 1738
  Mary and Joseph Parsons, 31 Jan 1768
  Mary and Simon Brown Jr., 4 Jan 1837
  Mary A. and Enoch M. Lane of Stratham, 13 Jan 1842
  Mary Charlotte, a.22y, and Emmons Brown Philbrick, a.41y, 14 Oct 1875
  Mary T. and John S. Remick, 22 Jun 1851
  Mehitable and Joshua Atwood of Bradford, 6 Jan 1745
  Mehitable and Edward Blue, 4 Jan 1753
  Mehitable and Samuel Libby, 21 Sep 1780
  Mehitable and Peter Garland Jr. 30 Sep 1792
  Noah and Temperance Rand, 6 May 1763
  Olive and Benjamin Odiorne, 7 Apr 1825
  Patty and Benjamin Jenness, 11 Mar 1787
  Patty and Samuel Willey of Nottingham, 5 Apr

RYE MARRIAGES

1798
SEAVEY, Paul and Sarah Wallis, 10 May 1764
  Polly and Simon Brown, 16 Mar 1806
  Ruth and Peter Grant, 4 Oct 1744
  Ruth and Joshua Rand Jr., 2 Oct 1777
  Ruth and Ithamar Mace of Gosport, 16 Apr 1785
  Sally and Joseph Goss, 6 Mar 1791
  Samuel and Hannah Seavey, 6 Nov 1734
  Sarah and Nathaniel Rand, 22 Nov 1787
  Sidney L. and Oliver Jenness, 24 Dec 1842
  Solomon and _____ Fuller, 30 Mar 1758
  Susan H. and John A. Brown of Gloucester, MA, 22 Jan 1832
  Theodore J. and Betsy Stevenson of Poplin, 21 Dec 1820
  William and Hannah Seavey, 25 Sep 1748
  William and Ruth Moses, 23 Jan 1752
  Woodbury and Martha Ann Philbrick, 1 Feb 1839
SEWARD, Joanna, of Kittery and Joseph R. Foss, 6 Dec 1826
SHANNON, Elizabeth and Samuel Dowrst, 8 Jan 1754
  Thomas and Anne Rand, 31 May 1753
SHAPLEY (SHAPLEIGH), Betsey and Robert Poor of Portsmouth, 4 Jul 1788
  Dorcas and Benjamin Foss, 17 Feb 1814
  Eliza and Richard Foss, 17 Oct 1819
  Emily A. and Daniel Dalton, 16 Nov 1876
  Henry and Ruth Pitman, 18 Nov 1772
  Henry and Mary Berry, 16 Sep 1790
  Henry C. and Sally Caswell, 22 Sep 1811
  James, of Portsmouth, and Mercy H. Saunders, 13 Sep 1787
  James and Dolly Randall, 19 Oct 1820
  Mary and John Robinson, both of Gosport, 27 Apr 1789
  Mary and George Saunders, 29 Jul 1789
  Olly and Simon Jenness, 24 Jun 1773
  Reuben and Polly Sanders, 19 Feb 1796
  Reuben and Lovina Robinson, 21 Apr 1825
  Robert and Ann E. Knowland, 1854
  Ruth, of the Shoals, and Nathaniel Ayers of Portsmouth, 23 Nov 1750
  Samuel and Eliza Yeaton, 18 Apr 1779
  Samuel and Rachel Foss, 17 Apr 1817
  Sarah A. and John Berry, 11 Aug 1844
  William H. and Sarah J. Hills of Hudson, 27 Sep 1852
SHAW, Abigail, of Hampton, and Josiah Davison, 28 Oct 1794

RYE MARRIAGES

SHAW, Andrew and Clarissa L. Marston, Jan 1843
  Dearborn T. and Clarissa Blake, both of Hampton, 4 May 1828
  Elijah, of Kensington, and Mrs. Sarah Wells of No. Hampton, 26 Mar 1809
  Elizabeth, of Hampton, and Dearborn Blake of Epping, 23 Oct 1777
  John and Betsey Folsom, both of Exeter, 19 Jun 1785
  Josiah Jr. and Rhoda Dow, both of Hampton, 23 Dec 1816
  Moses, of Hampton, and Abigail Dalton, 12 Feb 1799
  Sarah, of Kensington, and Benjamin Carr of Salisbury, MA, 1816
SHEAFE, Jacob, of Newcastle, and Hannah Seavey, 24 Jul 1740
  John, of Newcastle, and Mary Mace, 4 Apr 1811
  Sarah, of Newcastle, and John Simpson, 4 Sep 1748
SHELTON, Kitteridge and Eliza Holmes, both of Portsmouth, 12 Jul 1826
SHERBURNE, Andrew, of Portsmouth, and Susannah Knight, 4 Dec 1760
  Daniel and Sarah Knowles, both of No. Hampton, 1838
  Jonathan, of Portsmouth, and Nancy Perkins, 4 Mar 1787
  Mary and James Rendall, 24 Nov 1748
  Naomi and George Rand, 19 May 1768
SIMPSON, John and Sarah Sheafe of Newcastle, 4 Sep 1748
SINCLAIR, Constantin, of Sanbornton, and Huldah Sanborn of Chichester, 23 Jul 1776
SLEEPER, Eliphalet and Polly Jenness, 31 Mar 1800
  Jane B. and Jesse M. Walker, 2 Mar 1825
  Martin and Martha J. Jenness, 2 Nov 1855
  Mary and David Wedgewood, 2 Mar 1794
  Nancy and Simon Jenness, 23 Nov 1815
  Richard J. and Emily Garland, 6 Jun 1829
  Sally J. and Sergt. Zachariah Chickering of Ft. Constitution, 24 Dec 1826
  Theophilus Wm. and Sarah Jane Boardman of Stratham, (int.) 10 Nov 1838
  Thomas and Sally Berry, 1798
  Tristram and Ruth Tarlton, 18 Dec 1766
  William and Sally Smith of Exeter, 1803
SLOPER, Sarah and Joseph Tucker, 21 Jan 1756
SMILEY, Sophronia, of Portsmouth, and Seth Jenness

RYE MARRIAGES

of New Durham, 27 May 1858
SMITH, Arianna, of Exeter, and Stephen B. Tarlton 1860
  Betsey and Samuel Randall, 26 Jan 1817
  David Jr. and Mary Marden, 31 Oct 1765
  Deborah and Arthur Libby, 23 Apr 1752
  Elizabeth Anna, of Newmarket, and Arvillon Vincy Palmer, 25 Sep 1875
  Joanna and Christopher Flanders of Hawke, 21 Nov 1771
  John (Lieut.), of New Salisbury, now residing at Ft. Constitution, and Caroline Gratia Maria Willard of Newcastle, 3 Jun 1813
  Joseph Jr., of Chester, and Anna Garland, 13 Nov 1798
  Mary and Thomas Marden, 4 Mar 1729
  Mary and Ephraim Rand, 22 Sep 1757
  Mary and Stephen Marden, 12 Nov 1789
  Meribah and Isaac Remick, 23 Jan 1755
  Ruth, of No. Hampton, and James Young of Wakefield, 1816
  Sally, of Exeter, and William Sleeper, 1803
  Sarah and Joses Philbrick, 12 Jan 1790
  Sarah H., of No. Hampton, and John B. Mead, 1817
SNELL, John, of Portsmouth, and Olive Cate of Greenland, 2 Mar 1797
SNOW, Lucinda, of Orleans, MA, and James M. Goss, at Orleans, MA, 20 Apr 1834
SPINNEY, Samuel and Mary E. Waldron, both of Portsmouth, 7 Nov 1852
SPRAGUE, Seth, of Greene ME, and Hannah R. Clark, 27 Nov 1845
STACKPOLE, William and Elizabeth W. Jenness, both of Portsmouth, 26 May 1844
STANTON, Ezekiel and Mary Yeaton of Barrington, 11 Sep 1782
STEAD, Anne, of Portsmouth, and Stephen Marden of Candia, 18 Dec 1777
STERLING, Thomas, of Kittery, and Sarah A. Odiorne, 1858
STEVENS, Harriet, of Newport, RI, and Benjamin Walker, 5 Apr 1849
  James, of Epsom, and Abigail Rand, 22 Apr 1787
  Olive, of Stratham, and David Marston Jr. of No. Hampton, 28 Jul 1839
STEVENSON, Betsy, of Poplin, and Theodore J. Seavey, 21 Dec 1820
STIGGINS, Hannah, of Portsmouth, and William Nelson, 25 Sep 1803

RYE MARRIAGES

STOCKELS, Robert and Elizabeth Tucker, both of
   Portsmouth, 30 Aug 1810
STODDARD, Augusta, of Portsmouth, and Eben Lewis
   Odiorne, 26 Jun 1858
  Joseph E. and Elizabeth Lightford, both of
   Portsmouth, 28 Aug 1864
SUFFERANCE, Ephraim and Ruth Gould, both of San-
   bornton, 30 Oct 1785
SWAN, Ebenezer and Elizabeth Ballard of Boston, 7
   Jul 1753
  Richard, of Portsmouth, and Margaret Locke, 24
   Mar 1728
SYMES (SYMMS), Abigail and Samuel Libby, 4 Dec
   1744
  Ann and Isaac Libby, 5 Feb 1748
  Sarah and John Berry, May 1746
  Susannah, of Greenland, and Henry Maloon, 16 Aug
   1750
TARLTON, Abby, of No. Hampton, and Samuel Knowles,
   19 May 1848
  Annie M., of Boston, MA, and John Oliver Locke,
   29 Feb 1864
  Betsey, of Portsmouth, and Stephen Rand Jr., 8
   Jun 1806
  Betsey, of Portsmouth, and Hunking Wheeler, 6
   Jul 1808
  Hannah, of Greenland, and Samuel Nudd, 17 Jun
   1779
  James, of Portsmouth, and Katherine Odiorne of
   Newcastle, 16 Jan 1755
  James and Harriet Atkins, both of Portsmouth, 20
   Dec 1806
  Joseph and Mary Goss, 10 Jan 1762
  Joseph and Comfort Cotton, both of Portsmouth
   30 Dec 1784
  Margaret, of Newcastle, and Jacob Waldron of
   Portsmouth, 3 Jun 1811
  Mary and Nathaniel Jenness, 28 Mar 1771
  Mehitable and Francis Harvey, both of Newcastle,
   24 May 1814
  Mercy and John Ayers, both of Portsmouth, 18 Mar
   1796
  Richard and Mary Cotton, 2 Nov 1752
  Ruth and Tristram Sleeper, 18 Dec 1766
  Ruth and Stephen Rand, 17 Sep 1807
  Stephen B. and Arianna Smith of Exeter, 1860
TAYLOR, Ebenezer, of No. Hampton, and Nancy Rand,
   6 Aug 1802
  Joseph and Mary Lovering of No. Hampton, 20 Jun

RYE MARRIAGES

TAYLOR, Thomas, of No. Hampton, and Betsey Foss, 1776
THING, Lyford, of Brentwood, and Lydia Pickering of No. Hampton, 18 Jan 1826
THOMAS, Benjamin and Hannah Cushing of Portsmouth, 1803
  Elbridge A. and Ellen M. Picoat of Kittery, ME, 25 Dec 1865
  Mary and Abraham Mathews, 26 Jun 1774
  Mary E. and George Marden of Portsmouth, 24 Sep 1845
  Sarah J. and John O. Rand, 9 May 1844
  William and Mary Saunders, 24 Nov 1763
THOMPSON, Amy and Mark Foss, 28 Nov 1745
  Eliza, of Greenland, and Henry Beck, 20 Jan 1763
  Elizabeth and Samuel Wells, 28 Apr 1763
  Mary, of Portsmouth, and Benjamin Lang, 4 Jun 1756
THURSTON, Nathaniel, of Bradford, and Huldah Perkins, 8 Sep 1799
TILTON, Mary Ann and Levi Rollins of Stratham, 11 Nov 1824
TODD, Samuel and Sally Grover, both of Portsmouth, 1 Sep 1804
TOWLE, Abby J., of Hampton, and Charles W. Jones, 1863
  Amos, of No. Hampton, and Hannah Philbrick, 1 Aug 1792
  Ann and Joseph Philbrick, 2 Dec 1760
  Ann M. and James S. James, both of Hampton, (no date)
  Anna and Nathaniel Marden, 29 May 1777
  Charles W. and Effie A. Downs, 6 Feb 1867
  Charlotte, of Hampton, and John Moulton, 7 Mar 1827
  Darius and Sally Downs of Hampton, 1836
  Hannah and William Yeaton, 17 Sep 1780
  Huldah, of Hampton, and Merrifield Berry, 17 Aug 1756
  Isaac and Elizabeth Philbrick of Hampton, 17 Feb 1754
  Levi and Ruth Marden, 11 Oct 1753
  Levi and Lucy Hobbs, 7 Feb 1782
  Lydia, of Hampton, and John Lovering of No. Hampton, 20 Jun 1776
  Mary and James Hobbs, 6 Jan 1774
  Mary E., a.38y, of Hampton, and Cyrus S. Jones, a.47y, 2 Aug 1877

RYE MARRIAGES

TOWLE, Molly, of Epsom, and Ephraim Gould, 20 Oct 1791
  Sally, of Hampton, and George Odell of No. Hampton, 15 Oct 1818
  Samuel and Rachel Elkins of Hampton, 21 Aug 1760
  Samuel and Esther Johnson, 18 Nov 1762
TRAFTON, Martha A. and Nathan L. Harris, 1856
TREDICK, Edward and Jane Trundy of Newcastle, 13 Oct 1776
  William Jr. and Lucretia Bell, both of Newcastle, 9 Jan 1785
TREFETHERN, Abigail and William Morrison, 14 Nov 1779
  Abigail and Nathaniel Rand, 5 Nov 1791
  Albert B. and Mary Rand, Dec 1864
  Charles Elvin, a.28y, and Martha Ellen Balch, a.27y, Sep 1877
  Daniel H., of Kittery, ME, and Annie Walker, 22 Apr 1863
  Elizabeth and Joseph Yeaton, 9 Oct 1758
  Emily and Charles W. Hall, 24 Feb 1856
  George and Rosette Webster, 16 Oct 1860
  Hannah and Eben M. Lang, 1859
  Hiram, of Newcastle, and Adeline P. Locke, (int.) 19 Oct 1839
  Horace L. and Ann M. Clark, 1 Oct 1856
  Izette, a.44y, and Oren Drake, a.56y, 1 Feb 1880
  John and Elizabeth Mason, 1 Nov 1840
  John A. and Mary Locke, 20 Nov 1834
  Joseph and Hannah Berry, 29 Jan 1810
  Joseph P. and Olivia B. Marden, 1837 or 1839
  Josephine and John Oliver Locke, 19 Feb 1867
  Laura Frances and Morris Abraham Drake, 1872
  Lucenna J. and Levi Hall, 26 Apr 1863
  Lydia M. and John W. Adams, 1858
  Martha S. and Woodbury C. Green, 1 Jan 1864
  Mary S. and Henry S. Rand, 6 Dec 1863
  Nancy and Samuel Ayers, 28 Mar 1819
  Nat and Charlotte Jewell of Stratham, 1 Jul 1807
  Nellie G., a.23y, and George Haynes, a.22y, of Exeter, Jul 1879
  Oliver Winslow and Alveda H. Clough, 27 Oct 1874
  Robinson, of Newcastle, and Abigail Locke, 25 Jan 1748
  Sabrina and David Webster, 7 Apr 1861
  Sarah and William Holmes, 28 Oct 1860
  Supply and Mary E. Clark, 13 Jun 1862
  Temperance and Isaac Berry, 17 Oct 1790 (Record at Great Island, NH)

RYE MARRIAGES

TREFETHERN, William and Elizabeth Tucker, 27 Jan 1774
  William and Susnnah Piper of Stratham, 1 Feb 1821
  William Jr. and Lydia Berry, 20 Jan 1801
  William Jr. and Hannah Garland, 24 Aug 1837
TRUNDY, Jane, of Newcastle, and Edward Tredick, 13 Oct 1776
  Sally and Michael D. Goss, 21 Oct 1799
TUCK (TUCKE), John (Rev.), of Epsom, and Mary Parsons, 4 Mar 1762
  Mary and Thomas Rand, 4 Apr 1790
TUCKER, Betsey (Mrs.) and Samuel Downs, 16 Aug 1814
  Betsey and Richard Locke 3d, 20 Feb 1817
  Elizabeth and William Trefethern, 27 Jan 1774
  Elizabeth and Robert Stockels, both of Portsmouth, 30 Aug 1810
  Elizabeth H. and Henry Mace of the Shoals, 13 Feb 1820
  Esther and Joseph Hall of Gosport, 27 Aug 1751
  Grace and Shadrach Bell, Dec 1739
  Joseph and Sarah Sloper, 21 Jan 1756
  Joseph, of Portsmouth, and Mary Wallis, 25 Dec 1781
  Joseph and Betsey Lear, 23 Jul 1795
  Joseph and Betsey Reid, 29 Jan 1806
  Mary and Nathaniel Foss, 16 Oct 1740
  Mary and Timothy Berry, 19 May 1760
  Michael W. and Elizabeth Moses, both of Portsmouth, 18 Feb 1808
  Nathaniel and Elizabeth Hall, 8 Feb 1753
  Sarah and William Rand, 8 Feb 1753
  Sarah and John Foss, 6 Mar 1783
  Stephen, of Kittery, and Hannah Yeaton, 26 Nov 1787
  Susan A., of Portsmouth, and Moses L. Clark, 1858
  Susannah and Edward Edmonds, 21 Dec 1744
  William and Olive Saunders, 13 Mar 1787
TURNER, Elizabeth, of Hampton, and Thomas Marsh of Hampton Falls, 30 Mar 1823
VARRELL (VERRILL), Abigail and Jonathan C. Batchelder, 1 Mar 1827
  Ann M. and John W. Randall of Gosport, 17 Apr 1853
  Benjamin L. and Mary Caswell, 9 Jan 1850
  Clara E., a.18y, and George O. Remick, a.27y, 30 Oct 1877

RYE MARRIAGES

VARRELL, Deborah and Ithamar Mace, 6 Nov 1817
  Edward and Elizabeth Sanders, 4 Nov 1773
  Edward and Mary Berry, 19 Nov 1784
  Edward, of Salem, and Mary Dearborn of Greenland, 3 Aug 1809
  Elizabeth and John Lear, 21 Mar 1775
  Hannah and Dudley Norton, 6 Mar 1785
  Hannah and Isaac Remick, 28 Jan 1827
  Hannah J. and Daniel G. Moulton of No. Hampton, 1855
  James and Henrietta Chickering of Kittery, ME, 21 Jul 1861
  John and Anne Lang, 22 Apr 1784
  John and Eleanor Norton, of Portsmouth, 8 May 1808
  John and Mary H. Lord of Berwick, ME, 11 Aug 1844
  Jonathan W. and Mary E. Mathes, Jan 1839
  Joseph, of the Shoals, and Mrs. Sarah Sanders 25 Aug 1794
  Lydia and Isaac Remick, 24 Nov 1808
  Martha A. and Joseph W. Odiorne, 15 Dec 1863
  Martha L. and Thomas M. Lang of Portsmouth, 25 Oct 1840
  Mary (Mrs.) and Benjamin P. Philbrick, 8 Feb 1807
  Mary and Eben Gove, both of Portsmouth, 5 Apr 1812
  Mary and Frederick Rowe, both of Portsmouth, 31 Oct 1824
  Mary E. and Charles R. Caswell, 9 Nov 1853
  Mima, and George Boss of Portsmouth, 2 Dec 1882
  Nathaniel Gilman and Sarah A. Caswell, 4 Dec 1856
  Richard and Mrs. Molly Mace, 4 Mar 1824
  Richard Tucker, and Mary Rendall of Portsmouth, 31 Oct 1803
  Robert W. and Eliza Esther Foss, 16 Apr 1848
  Sally L. and Hiram Jenkins of York, 14 Jun 1829
  Samuel and Elizabeth S. Waldron, 26 Nov 1812
  Sarah E. and Nathaniel Palmer of Portsmouth, 3 Nov 1851
  William and Anna J. Berry, 22 May 1825
VENNARD, Mary and Jonathan Locke, both of Newcastle, 24 Dec 1812
WAIT, Sarah, of Amesbury, and Jonathan Dearborn, 24 Apr 1746
  Wilber and Emily Yeaton, 15 Mar 1858
  William Jr., of Malden, MA, and Sarah Ann Jen-

RYE MARRIAGES

ness, 29 Dec 1842
WALDRON, Elizabeth S. and Samuel Varrel, 26 Nov 1812
  Jacob, of Portsmouth, and Margaret Tarlton of Newcastle, 3 Jun 1811
  Jonathan Belcher and Elizabeth Foss, 24 Sep 1789
  Isaac Jr., of Barrington, and Mary Jones Wallis, 8 May 1796
  Mary E. and Samuel Spinney, both of Portsmouth, 7 Nov 1852
  Polly W. and Samuel Locke, 21 Dec 1817
WALKER, Annie and Daniel H. Trefethern of Kittery, ME, 22 Apr 1863
  Benjamin and Harriet Stevens of Newport RI, 5 Apr 1849
  Betsey and William Lang, both of Portsmouth, 13 Nov 1794
  Charles A., a.41y, and Clara A. Marden, a.29y, 15 Jan 1879
  Deliverance, of Greenland, and Joseph Melown, 31 Dec 1741
  Edwin B., a.29y, and Cora Bell Jenness, a.29y, 23 Dec 1886
  George and Augusta M. Page of No. Hampton, 9 Sep 1871
  Hannah, of Newbury, and Enoch Sanborn, 16 Dec 1773
  Jesse M. and Jane B. Sleeper, 2 Mar 1825
  Jonathan and Mary Esther Brown, 12 Jul 1831
  Levi and Harriet A. Dow, 5 Sep 1855
  Lewis Everett and Annie Julia Foss, 13 May 1873
  Nancy and Richard Lang, both of Portsmouth, 31 Dec 1798
  Samuel, of Portsmouth, and Hannah Marden, 21 Jul 1799
  William J. and Anna Cater, both of Portsmouth, 21 Apr 1804
  William and Mary Ann Robinson, 22 Oct 1861
  William Chauncy, and Ellen A. McLawlin of Georgetown, MA, 3 Jun 1867
WALLACE, John, of Philadelphia, and Abbie F. Goss, 3 Nov 1869
WALLIS, Abigail and Nadab Moses of Portsmouth, 13 Jun 1776
  Benjamin and Deborah Fuller, both of Greenland, 18 Mar 1785
  Betsey and Levi Jenness, 17 Nov 1785
  Comfort and James Knowles, 30 Jun 1748
  Hannah and William Marden, 29 Apr 1773

RYE MARRIAGES

WALLIS, Joseph and Margaret Fuller of Greenland, 23 Nov 1769
  Martha, of Greenland, and Weymouth Wallis, 8 Jul 1772
  Mary and Joseph Tucker of Portsmouth, 25 Dec 1781
  Mary Jones and Isaac Waldron Jr. of Barrington, 8 May 1796
  Patty and John Langmaid of Chichester, 1 Mar 1796
  Reuben, of Greenland, and Elizabeth Rand, Jan 1785
  Samuel and Elizabeth Parsons, 16 Nov 1773
  Sarah and Paul Seavey, 10 May 1764
  Weymouth and Martha Wallis of Greenland, 8 Jul 1772
  William and Comfort Cotton of Portsmouth, 15 Aug 1738
WARD, Simon and Abigail Fullington of No. Hampton, 2 Mar 1784
WARNER, John, of No. Hampton, and Estella Garland, 28 Jan 1869
  Samuel and Abigail Leavitt of No. Hampton, 20 Aug 1833
WARREN, Debra (Mrs.), a.62y, of Portsmouth, and Allen Porter, a.63y, 22 Jun 1875
WATSON, John and Alice Clark, 25 Oct 1767
  Mary, of Nottingham and Levi Garland Jr., 29 May 1838
  Ruth and Daniel Moulton, 21 Nov 1744
WEBBER, Bathesheba, of Gosport, and John Rendall, 8 Sep 1782
WEBSTER, Abigail and Samuel B. Berry, Feb 1798
  Abigail and Levi D. Randall, Apr 1809
  Ann and John Jones, 27 Aug 1733
  Anna and Alexander Salter, 22 Nov 1810
  Betsey and Joshua Seavey, 16 Apr 1797
  Charity and Zachariah Berry, 23 Oct 1734
  David and Eunice Nowell of Portsmouth, 1 Feb 1809
  David and Sabrina Trefethern, 7 Apr 1861
  Dolly and Stephen Green, 20 Jul 1806
  Elizabeth and William Kingman, 19 Aug 1747
  Elizabeth and Stephen Marden Jr., 28 Aug 1760
  Hannah and John Jenness of Moultonborough, 16 Sep 1813
  Jeremy and Eliza Rand, 24 May 1837
  John and Elizabeth H. Clark, 20 Sep 1827
  Josiah and Martha Goss, 21 Sep 1738

RYE MARRIAGES

WEBSTER, Mark and Mary Ann Lang, 26 Nov 1829
  Martha and Ozem Dowrst of Deerfield, 3 Nov 1796
  Martha and Jethro Locke, 26 Apr 1801
  Martha and James Brown, 9 Dec 1819
  Martha and Ebenezer Odiorne, 3 Feb 1822
  Martha J. and Harrison Seavey, 21 May 1854
  Mary and Henry Elkins, 1806
  Mary and Noah Wiggin of Stratham, 14 Feb 1816
  Mary and Benjamin Norton of Portsmouth, 10 May 1840
  Mary C. and Charles P. Abbot of Portsmouth, 24 Apr 1862
  Richard and Elizabeth Rendall, 29 Oct 1778
  Richard and Fanny Conner of Portsmouth, 1854
  Rosette and George Trefethern, 16 Oct 1860
  Sarah and George Marden, 19 Jan 1769
  Sarah and James Marden, 4 Jan 1803
WEDGEWOOD, David and Mary Sleeper, 2 Mar 1794
  Eliphalet and Mrs. Hannah Brown, 15 Apr 1861
  Hannah and John Jenness Jr., 25 Dec 1816
  Jonathan and Hannah Seavey, 23 Mar 1790
  Mary and Nathaniel Jenness Jr., 21 Oct 1781
  Sarah and Joseph Locke 4th, 29 Nov 1816
WEEKS, Bridget, of Greenland, and Samuel Moses of Epsom, 9 Apr 1760
  Eunice D. and William L. Foye, 7 Nov 1822
  Hattie B., a.24y, of Greenland, and Charles A. Jenness, a.37y, 21 Jan 1880
  Helen A., of Greenland, and Charles A. Drake, 1859
  Ichabod and Comfort Johnson, 1 Nov 1770
  Joshua, of Greenland, and Sarah Jenness, 24 Oct 1734
  Joshua and Sarah Marston, 4 Sep 1760
  Josiah, of Greenland, and Nancy Philbrick, 13 Mar 1796
  Sarah and Jonathan Marston of Hampton, 30 Jun 1743
  William, of Greenland, and Louisa Porter, 26 May 1835
WELCH, Daniel and Elizabeth Abbot of Greenland, 29 Feb 1744
  Susan and Andrew McDonald, both of Portsmouth, 4 Feb 1817
  _____, of Portsmouth, and ____ Rowe, 15 Aug 1762
WELLS, Betsey and Daniel Philbrick, 25 Dec 1794
  Hiram, of Sandown, and Lydia Green, 1860
  John and Elizabeth Rollins, 9 Nov 1769
  Moses Jr. and Polly Merril, both of Hampton

RYE MARRIAGES

Falls, 31 May 1804
WELLS, Olive and Joseph Batchelder, Feb 1799
  Polly and Jethro Goss, 16 Nov 1796
  Samuel and Elizabeth Thompson, 28 Apr 1763
  Sarah and Jonathan Philbrick Jr., 1 Jun 1797
  Sarah (Mrs.), of No. Hampton, and Elijah Shaw of Kensington, 26 Mar 1809
WENDALL, Abraham and Sukey Gardner, both of Portsmouth, 24 Oct 1809
  Elizabeth and William Berry, 6 Mar 1796
WENTWORTH, H. Gates, of Portsmouth, and Sarah Ann Marden, 23 Jan 1872
  John, of Hampton Falls, and Dolly Marsh of Hampton, 5 May 1824
WETHAM, ___ M. and _____, both of ____, 1829
WHEELER, Hunking and Betsey Tarlton of Portsmouth, 6 Jul 1808
WHIDDEN, Abigail (widow) and George Randall Jr. of Gosport, 11 Mar 1824
  Anna, a.21y, of Portsmouth, and Irving W. Garland, a.27y, 17 Dec 1877
  Nettie R., of Portsmouth, and Horace W. Garland, 27 Dec 1869
  Rebecca and Benjamin Marden, 12 May 1746
  Samuel, of Greenland, and Hannah Langdon of Portsmouth, 8 Jan 1745
  Samuel and Hannah Jones, 5 Jul 1774
  Samuel 3d and Eliza Langdon, both of Portsmouth, 1 Mar 1827
  Samuel, of Portsmouth, and Data Brown, 22 Dec 1842
  Thankful, of Portsmouth, and Reuben H. Critchet of Greenland, 17 Jan 1813
  Thomas, of Portsmouth, and Francis P. Foss, 3 Jan 1830
  William, of Portsmouth, and Hannah Marden, 1 Dec 1811
WHITE, Albert A., of Newcastle, and Sarah G. Foss, 21 Oct 1841
  Solomon and Mary Locke, 25 Jun 1745
WHITTON, Anne and William Nelson, 24 Jun 1763
WIGGIN, Hannah, of Stratham, and Stephen Wiggin, 5 Oct 1809
  John and Sally H. Marsh, both of Greenland, 19 Aug 1827
  Lovey, of Greenland, and Levi Clark of Stratham, 6 Jun 1790
  Noah, of Stratham, and Mary Webster, 14 Feb 1816
  Sarah A. and John Emery, both of Stratham, 30

RYE MARRIAGES

Jun 1861
WIGGIN, Stephen and Hannah Wiggin of Stratham, 5 Oct 1809
WILLARD, Caroline Gratia Maria, of Newcastle, and Lieut. John Smith of New Salisbury, now residing at Ft. Constitution, 3 Jun 1813
WILLEY (WILLEE), Clarissa and Thomas Foye, 28 Nov 1822
  Martha Ann, of Portsmouth, and Elvin Rand, 16 Nov 1839
  Samuel, of Nottingham, and Patty Seavey, 5 Apr 1798
  Sarah and Joseph Palmer, 9 Mar 1767
WILLIAMS, Jenny E., of Lynn, MA, and Isaac M. Locke, 11 Mar 1865
  John F. and Peggy Appleton, 4 Jul 1790
WILSON, Estelle M. and S. Alba Jenness, 1860
WOODMAN, Betsey and Jonathan Garland, 14 May 1797
  Elizabeth of Greenland, and John Crosby, 15 Oct 1778
  Emery and Mary Bickford of Deerfield, 1860
  Jonathan, of So. Hampton, and Widow Hannah Rand, 12 Dec 1769
  Jonathan and Sally Rand, 12 Apr 1812
WOODS, Sarah and Richard Locke 3d, 19 Mar 1807
WORMWOOD, William and Love Fuller, 26 Oct 1747
  William and Eliza Rand, 19 Apr 1770
YEATON, Abba L. and John Brown, both of Portsmouth, 14 Aug 1863
  Augusta and Henry Laskey of Portsmouth, 31 Jul 1870
  Betty and John Berry, 27 Jul 1757
  Deborah and William Bates Randall, 26 Feb 1793
  Dolly, of Newcastle, and Benjamin Odiorne, 1798
  Eliza and Samuel Shapley, 18 Apr 1779
  Elizabeth H. and Aaron Rand, 1 Nov 1840
  Emily and Wilber Wait, 15 Mar 1858
  Esther and Simon Knowles, 8 Feb 1779
  Esther and Isaac Remick, 7 Nov 1793
  Hannah and Stephen Tucker of Kittery, 26 Nov 1787
  Hopley and Lydia Foye, 7 Nov 1813
  John and Esther Saunders, 24 Aug 1759
  John A., of Portsmouth, and Margaret E. Foss, 10 Jul 1864
  Joseph and Susanna Lang, 17 Jul 1751
  Joseph and Elizabeth Trefethern, 9 Oct 1758 (Newcastle Record)
  Joseph Jr. and Eliza Rand, 5 Feb 1776

RYE MARRIAGES

YEATON, Lucy, of Portsmouth, and Jeremiah Palmer, 26 Jun 1819
  Mary and Peter Johnson, 18 Sep 1767
  Mary, of Barrington, and Ezekiel Stanton, 11 Sep 1782
  Mary and David L. Rand, 4 Oct 1839
  Mary, of Newcastle, and Charles B. Odiorne, 27 Sep 1840
  Philip and Huldah Saunders, 1797
  Sarah and Thomas Jenness of Deerfield, 31 Jan 1775
  Sarah E. and Alfred A. Meloon Jr., both of Newcastle, 11 Mar 1872
  William and Hannah Towle, 17 Sep 1780
YOUNG, David and Mary Durgins of Portsmouth, Jun 1834
  James, of Wakefield, and Ruth Smith of No. Hampton, 1816

SURNAMES MISSING

_____, Patience and James Godfrey, 4 Feb 1740
_____, ___ and ___ M. Wetham, both of _____, 1829
_____, Bernard F., a.60y, of Portsmouth, and E.A. Sanborn, a.55y, Jan 1879

NEGROES

Benjamin and Martha of Newcastle, 26 Jun 1777

RYE DEATHS

ADAMS, Deborah, 1 Jun 1803
  Margaret A., widow of Joseph B. Adams of Portsmouth, 23 Jun 1875, a.52y 4mo
  Rebecca, wife of Rev. J.W., 1 Dec 1857, a.29y
AIKEN, _____, child of Mr. Aiken of Andover, MA, at the Union House, 13 Aug 1854, a.12y
ALLEN, Dorcas, widow of Jude, 31 Oct 1817, a.83y
  Osborn, son of Samuel, 18 Feb 1848, a.24y
  Samuel, son of Elizabeth, (killed by blasting rocks), at Newburyport, MA, 23 Oct 1826
AYERS, Ruhamah, 24 Aug 1831, a.74y
BABB, Suky, 24 Jun 1841, a.73y or 74y
BACON, Charles, son of _____ of Portsmouth, 14 Feb 1872, a.22y
BALCH, Julia H., wife of Nathl., in Portsmouth, 23 Nov 1884, a.36y 8mo
BATCHELDER, Abigail, widow of Jonathan, at Portsmouth, 11 Feb 1867, a.68y
  Jonathan, son of Josiah, at the Navy Yard, 23 Oct 1865, a.64y 9mo
  Josiah, 3 Nov 1833, a.56y
  Martha Ann, dau of Jonathan, 21 Oct 1858, a.20y
  Sarah Adelaide, dau of Jonathan, 10 Oct 1838, a.6y
BEAN, John W., (Lung Fever), 31 Jan 1825, a.50y
BECK, George, 15 Dec 1814
BERRY, Abigail, wife of Samuel, 19 Jun 1750, a.75y
  Abigail, wife of Oliver, of & at Greenland, 7 May 1855, a.30y 10mo
  Abigail, widow of Samuel Brackett, 4 Sep 1860, a.83y
  Alfred, son of Jeremiah, at Savannah, 15 May 1828 a.19y
  Alvina, child of Gilman, 11 Aug 1853, a.1y 5mo
  Benjamin, son of Ebenezer & Keziah, 20 Sep 1735
  Betsey, dau of Ebenezer & Polly, 4 Jan 1803, a.13y
  Betsey, widow of Joseph, 23 Feb 1859, a.62y
  Betsey W., wife of Joseph J., 1 Apr 1817, a.22y
  Brackett, child of Gilman, 25 Jul 1845, a.2y
  Brackett M., son of Jeremiah, 29 Jul 1826, a.10y
  Charles W., son of Joseph J., at Seattle, Washington Territory, 10 Sep 1879, a.48y
  Clara Marilla, dau of Samuel F., 29 Sep 1857, a.2y 11mo
  Dolly, dau of William, (disease of the brain), 12 Jul 1822, a.24y

RYE DEATHS

BERRY, Ebenezer, son of Ebenezer & Keziah, 3 Nov 1735
    Ebenezer, son of Ebenezer, at sea, 16 Nov 1810, a.22y
    Elizabeth, widow of Jotham, 16 Dec 1828, a.84y
    Elizabeth J., wife of Gilman, 15 Feb 1887, a.62y 8mo
    Esther, widow of Nathaniel, 1 Oct 1876, a.95y 13ds
    Gilman Woodbury, son of Gilman, 3 Oct 1875, a.30y
    Hannah, wife of Jeremiah, 1 Jul 1770, a.46y
    Hannah, widow of James, 4 May 1826, a.69y
    Horace A., son of Gilman, 1 Jun 1861, a.2y 6mo
    Huldah, wife of Merrifield, 9 Nov 1809
    Ira, child of Jeremiah, 28 Oct 1826, a.15y
    J. Albert, son of Capt. Levi, of & at Greenland, 30 Jul 1861, a.36y
    James Jr., 14 Jul 1812, a.33y
    James Towle, son of Merrifield & Huldah, 29 Oct 1818, a.60y
    Jeremiah, son of William, 24 Aug 1809, a.87y
    Jeremiah, son of William, (Consumption), 23 Mar 1820, a.36y
    John W.P., son of Nathaniel, at Portsmouth, 19 Nov 1855, a.32y
    Joseph, son of James, (Consumption from drinking), 29 Jul 1824, a.37y
    Joseph (Lt.), son of Levi & Sarah, 2 Jun 1868, a.79y
    Keziah, dau of Ebenezer & Keziah, 23 Sep 1735
    Levi, son of Jeremiah, 1 Apr 1833, a.74y
    Levi, son of Levi, 27 Sep 1873, a.69y 8ds
    Levinia, wife of Samuel F., 20 Aug 1871, a.50y
    Lilia, child of John O., 11 Sep 1879, a.3y
    Love, wife of William, 17 Jan 1795
    Lyndan Otis, child of Joseph W. Berry & Mary A. Green, 10 Feb 1875, a.1y
    Maribla, dau of Samuel, 4 Oct 1849, a.2y
    Mary Abby, dau of Gilman, 25 Aug 1866, a.24y
    Merrifield, son of Ebenezer & Mary, 20 May 1817, a.84y
    Nathaniel, son of Nehemiah, 16 Dec 1815, a.72y
    Nathaniel, son of Samuel, 15 Apr 1834, a.58y
    Olive, relict of Richard, Jan 1858, a.75y
    Oliver, child of Joseph J., 30 Jun 1842, a.5y
    Parmelia Ann, wife of Joseph W., 21 Feb 1886, a.58y 3mo
    Polly, relict of Ebenezer, 26 Apr 1857, a.87y

RYE DEATHS

BERRY, Rachel, widow of Jacob, 10 Dec 1811, a.66y
  Richard, son of Jacob & Rachel, 23 Jun 1816, a.43y
  Robinson Foss, son of Jeremiah (formerly of Rye), 29 Jun 1864
  Ruth, dau of Ebenezer & Mary, 10 Sep 1735
  Sally, relict of Levi, 6 Sep 1851, a.87y
  Sally Goss, (blind) at the County Farm in Brentwood, 8 Nov 1874, a.50y
  Samuel, son of Nathaniel, 30 Oct 1805, a.1y 2mo
  Samuel B., son of Gilman, 5 Aug 1853, a.5y
  Samuel B. Jr., 10 May 1828
  Samuel Brackett, son of William & Love, 1 Feb 1823, a.46y
  Sarah, wife of William, 3 Jan 1776, a.88y
  Sarah (widow), 2 Oct 1821, a.31y
  Thomas, son of Lydia, at the Alms House, 17 Jun 1850, a.abt 22y
  Thomas G., son of Ebenezer, 21 Oct 1870, a.83y 11mo 11ds
  Thomas J., son of Thomas, in & of Greenland, 23 Jan 1880
  William, 8 Oct 1786, a.93y
  William, son of Jeremiah, 16 Dec 1827, a.75y
  William, son of Samuel B., (hung himself), 20 Mar 1877, a.73y 7mo 1d
  Willie E., son of Woodbury & wife Locke, 22 May 1871, a.5mo
  _____, child of Molly, 2 Apr 1816
  _____, child of Nancy, 14 Nov 1823, a.1y 8mo
  _____, child of Samuel B., 12 Nov 1815, a.abt 15y
  _____, child of Samuel, 2 Sep 1841
  _____, child of William B., 10 Oct 1816, a.14y
BLASDELL, John, formerly of Portsmouth & Lexington, MA, 17 Aug 1873, a.65y
BLODGETT, Clara Josephine, dau of L.D., 6 Apr 1848, a.10mo
BOYCE, Maudana, wife of Jeremiah & dau of John Foye, at Boscawen, 2 Jan 1866, a.38y
BRACKETT, Samuel, 25 Oct 1766
BRAGG, John, died on Hampton Flats in a boat after clams, 14 Feb 1814, a.68y
  Molly, widow of John, 10 Dec 1816, a.abt 69y
BROWN, Abby Ann, dau of Joseph & Emily, 28 Aug 1858, a.14y
  Abigail, widow of Lt. Simon, 5 Feb 1877, a.90y 9mo 18ds

RYE DEATHS

BROWN, Albertine, boy child of William, 22 Feb 1864, a.2mo
Almira Parsons, wife of Jonathan, 15 Apr 1871, a.62y 3mo
Anzolette, dau of Simon, of & at Lynn, MA, Sep 1857, a.10y 4mo
Augusta, widow of Langdon, 8 Feb 1872, a.38y 8mo
Benjamin, of North Hampton, (drowned), 19 Dec 1850, a.35y
Comfort, widow of John, 30 Oct 1846, a.85y
David, formerly of No. Hampton, 17 Aug 1854, a.83y
Elihu, son of James, 12 Feb 1859, a.36y 10mo
Eliza, widow of David (late of No. Hampton), 16 Aug 1860, a.54y
Eliza Ann, dau of Ira, 25 Oct 1843, a.16y
Elizabeth, child of James, (scalded with hot water), 27 Oct 1842, a.18mo
Elizabeth, wife of Langdon, 9 Oct 1848, a.31y
Emeline, child of James, 23 Sep 1838, a.11y
Emily, dau of Ira, 24 May 1841, a.20y
Emily, wife of Simon, in & of No. Hampton, 22 Sep 1880
Emily Parsons, wife of Joseph Ward, 15 Feb 1879, a.72y 9mo
Esther, wife of Simon, 25 May 1805, a.32y 10mo
Goodman, of & at Hampton, NH, 23 Mar 1689, a.90y
Hannah, widow of Jonathan & dau of J. Drake, 23 Nov 1864, a.81y
Henry, son of Simon, 30 Oct 1805, a.2y 9mo
Ira, son of Simon, in Portsmouth, 10 Jul 1845, a.50y
Ira, son of John, 20 Apr 1848, a.37y
Ira Arvin, son of Ira, at Chelsea, 19 Oct 1856, a.18y
Ivory, son of John Brown & Nancy Jenness, 7 Feb 1853, a.45y 2mo
James (Capt.), son of John, 8 Mar 1875
James, son of James & Martha, 11 Jul 1880, a.56y 5mo 26ds
Jane M., wife of Ira, 3 Mar 1841, a.42y
John, of & at Hampton, NH, 28 Feb 1686, a.98y
John, son of Jonathan, 21 Jan 1807, a.47y
John, 5 Sep 1822, a.62y
John, son of John, 24 May 1863, a.88y
John, son of James & Martha, 21 Jan 1887, a.56y
John Jr., son of John, 10 Dec 1854, a.75y
John S.J., son of John & Comfort, 3 Sep 1815, a.17y

RYE DEATHS

BROWN, John Shirley, son of Langdon, 22 Dec 1859, a.1y 3mo
Jonathan, 27 Jan 1798
Jonathan, son of Joseph, 31 Jan 1843, a.62y
Jonathan, son of Jonathan, 30 Oct 1872, a.65y 8mo 3ds
Jonathan Jr., son of John & Salome, 18 Sep 1831, a.49y
Jonathan A. 3d, son of Jonathan, 12 Aug 1838, a.8y
Joseph, one of the Selectmen, 1771
Joseph, son of Joseph, (drowned out fishing), 9 Sep 1806, a.24y
Joseph, son of Jonathan, 7 Mar 1841, a.86y
Joseph, son of John (called Gould), 28 Oct 1871, a.69y 3mo
Joseph W., son of Jonathan & Hannah, 29 Mar 1883
Langdon, son of Simon, 23 Jan 1867, a.52y 7mo
Lucetta, dau of Simon, 20 Oct 1850, a.26y
Margaret A., wife of Amos P., 18 Nov 1862, a.24y
Martha, widow of Joseph, 19 May 1842, a.85y
Martha, wife of James, 25 Oct 1846, a.51y
Mary, 12 Nov 1736
Mary, Jun 1803
Mary, wife of Simon, 1 Mar 1832, a.52y
Mary, wife of John, 24 Jan 1839, a.63y
Mary, wife of Joseph, 23 Apr 1843, a.45y
Mary (widow), 2d wife of Jo Gould, 15 Aug 1885, a.73y 11mo
Mary, widow of Simon of Lynn (formerly of Rye), at sea, 10 Aug 1886, a.70y 11mo
Mary Esther, dau of Gen. Ira, 29 Dec 1848, a.19y
Mehitable, widow of Elihu, at Portsmouth, 17 Jan 1888, a.58y
Nancy, widow of John (late of Rye), at Boston, Dec 1864
Otis Simon, child of Langdon, 25 Dec 1848, a.9mo
Polly, relict of Jonathan, 6 Dec 1853, a.65y
Polly, wife of Ivory, 18 Aug 1850, a.38y
Polly, wife of John, 20 Jul 1868, a.82y
Polly, dau of John, 27 Mar 1873, a.72y 11mo
Rhoda, dau of Jonathan Jr., 16 Nov 1839, a.22y
Robert W., child of Joseph Ira, 26 Oct 1864, a.2mo
Rosilla, dau of James, 20 Dec 1887, a.68y
Sally, dau of John Jr., 31 Jan 1833, a.17y
Sarah, dau of James, 2 Jul 1848, a.13y
Sarah Ann, wife of Daniel, 3 May 1884, a.71y 2ds
Simon, son of Simon of No. Hampton, 24 Mar 1846,

RYE DEATHS

a.79y
BROWN, Simon, of Lynn, MA (formerly of Rye), 2 Mar 1882, a.70y 5mo
  William, son of James, 29 Jun 1887, a.61y 7mo
  Willie M., son of William, 5 May 1875, a.15y 10mo
  Willy M., son of Ira of Barrington, 16 Sep 1858, a.4mo
  _____, child of Ira, 27 Mar 1831, a.5y
  _____, child of John, Apr 1803
  _____, child of John, 23 Dec 1805
  _____, child of John 3d, 29 Sep 1811, a.1y
  _____, child of John 3d, 13 Nov 1811, a.1y
  _____, child of Jonathan, 18 Sep 1810, a.2mo
  _____, child of Jonathan, 6 Oct 1813
  _____, child of Joseph, 13 Sep 1804
  _____, child of Polly, 23 Dec 1826, a.5y
BUCK, Rebeccah, of Boston, MA, 18 Jul 1870, a.57y
BUNKER, Belinda, dau of James, 4 Oct 1884, a.57y
  Christy A., dau of Lemuel, 15 Aug 1876, a.21y
  Izette, wife of Lemuel, 8 Mar 1850, a.26y
  Izette, dau of Lemuel J., 15 Oct 1878, a.19y 6mo 24ds
  James, formerly of Barnstead, 3 Nov 1879, a.77y
  Mary Ann, dau of James, 9 Oct 1878, a.57y 9mo 15ds
  Nancy, wife of James, 7 Dec 1853, a.62y
CARTER, Mary, 22 Jun 1819, a.29y
CASWELL, Alfred, son of Richard, 6 Feb 1847, a.14y
  Ann M., wife of John William, of & at the Shoals, 4 Jun 1855, a.28y
  Charles R., son of Richard G., (drowned), 11 Nov 1865, a.30y
  Charlotte B., wife of Joseph, 12 Feb 1884, a.78y 2ds
  Dorcas, widow of Michael, 18 Apr 1887, a.93y 5mo
  Eliza, 14 Sep 1836
  Elizabeth, 6 Apr 1836, a.16y
  James, child of William, 4 Sep 1824, a.7y
  Louisa B., 19 Jul 1831, a.13y
  Mary O., wife of Charles Reuben, 31 Mar 1863, a.31y 10mo
  Michael, son of Samuel of Gosport, 11 Sep 1861, a.72y
  Polly, child of William, 20 Feb 1822, a.10ds
  Polly, wife of William, 6 Feb 1868, a.76y 6mo
  Richard, son of Samuel, 2 Nov 1862, a.54y
  Sally, wife of Edward, 29 Sep 1868, a.78y
  Samuel, formerly of Gosport, 19 Aug 1846, a.

RYE DEATHS

abt 85y
CASWELL, Samuel, son of Samuel & Mary, 3 Mar 1882, a. 67y 2mo
  Sarah Angelette, dau of Richard & Anna, 6 Feb 1847
  Sarah E., wife of Warren, 2 Aug 1866, a.32y
  Sarah Elizabeth, widow of Charles R., 20 May 1878, a.51y
  Sarah F., wife of Edmond, 16 Dec 1832, a.36y
  Ursula, dau of William, at Newburyport, 8 Mar 1849, a.20y
  William, son of Michael, 7 Jun 1867, a.33y 6mo
  William, son of Samuel (formerly of Gosport), 20 Nov 1884, a.84y 4mo
  _____, child of Edward, 24 Dec 1827
  _____, child of Edward, 22 Oct 1831
  _____, child of Edward, 27 Aug 1832
  _____, child of John, at Portsmouth, Jul 1872
  _____, child of Michael, 18 Jan 1832
  _____, child of Samuel, 5 Jan 1814
  _____, child of William, 21 Jan 1828, a.2mo
CATE, John, 9 Jan 1887, a.55y 8mo
CHASE, Lucy, wife of Moses, 17 Mar 1757
CHESLEY, Adriannah Clemin, dau of Samuel, 3 Sep 1847, a.4y
  Olive, widow of Simon, 6 Oct 1872, a.89y 3ds
  Samuel E., son of Simon & Olive, 14 Jun 1880, a.72y 11mo
  Simon, son of Simon, 23 Jul 1851, a.68y
  William E., son of Simon, 12 Nov 1887, a.71y 5mo
CHURCHILL, _____, infant son of Robert J., 2 Feb 1881
CLARK, Andrew, formerly of Rye, at Kittery, 12 Feb 1860, a.86y
  Charles, son of Moses, 13 Jan 1888, a.18y
  Daniel, son of Andrew, 2 May 1831, a.23y
  Emily, dau of Andrew, 8 Jun 1831, a.19y
  Etla (Miss), 23 Jan 1887, a.20y 4mo
  Hannah, dau of Andrew, 3 Oct 1831, a.21y
  Hannah, wife of Andrew, 8 Apr 1844, a.70y
  John, son of Andrew, 8 Aug 1847, a.43y
  Mary, wife of John, 9 Sep 1831, a.29y
  Mary Ann, dau of Andrew, 2 Jul 1831, a.23y
  _____, child of Andrew, 4 Jul 1819, a.2y
CLOUGH, Nathan, formerly of Seabrook & Weare, 14 Jan 1872, a.59y 3mo
  Zelina, dau of Nathan, 21 Feb 1878, a.35y
COFFIN, Ovid G., son of Nathaniel, 21 Aug 1867, a.2y 5mo

COGSWELL, Elliot, of Northwood, at Foss Beach, 7 Sep 1887, a.73y
COLDEN, Frances Wilkes (Mrs.), of New York, at the Farragut House, 12 Aug 1877, a.83y
COLEMAN, John, 19 Jul 1829, a.19y
  Nathaniel, Apr 1803
CUMMINGS, Mary P.(Mrs.), 1 Jul 1885, a.43y 10mo
CURRIER, Emma, dau of Joseph J. Jenness, 23 Jan 1887, a.35y 5mo
CURTIS, Mary (widow), of Goffstown, Jun 1878
DALTON, Benjamin, son of Michael, 10 Sep 1861, a.81y
  Charles Emery, child of Joseph B., 26 Jul 1850, a.2y
  Daniel, 13 Jul 1888, a.73y
  Daniel Curtis, child of Joseph B., 26 Apr 1848, a.8y
  Daniel P., son of Michael, 13 Sep 1842, a.58y
  Ebenezer, at North Hampton, 12 Nov 1846, a.78y
  Eliza A., dau of Daniel, 8 Oct 1865, a.21y 8mo
  Eliza J., wife of Daniel, 4 Sep 1875, a.46y 5mo
  Hannah, wife of Joseph B., 9 Oct 1850, a.35y
  Joseph (MD), of & at Brentwood, 25 or 15 Dec 1856, a.66y
  Martha, child of Anna, 27 Jul 1839, a.6mo
  Martha, wife of Daniel, 4 Feb 1866, a.46y
  Mary, 20 Feb 1829, a.23y
  Mercy, 28 Feb 1829, a.21y
  Mercy, widow of Michael, 19 Nov 1846, a.83y 6mo
  Michael, 6 Oct 1846, a.abt 93y
  Michael, son of Daniel (late of Rye), at No. Hampton, 16 Nov 1869, a.57y 8mo
  Patty, relict of Daniel, 8 Jul 1854, a.68y 3mo
  Polly Parsons, in Chicago, Ill., 25 Dec 1874
  Sally, wife of Benjamin, 8 Jun 1844, a.64y
  _____, child of Benjamin, 8 Mar 1811, a.4mo
DANA, _____, (widow), of Boston, 18 Sep 1854, a.40y
DANNEY, John, 30 Apr 1833, a.60y
DAVIDSON, Abigail (widow), 20 Jan 1817, a.77y
  Elias, child of Josiah, 14 Mar 1823, a.14y
  Josiah, 14 Jun 1806
  William, 21 Mar 1807
DAVIS, Edmund, formerly of Greenland, 31 Jan 1867, a.64y
DEARBORN, Adeline, 3 Apr 1816, a.abt 20y
DECATUR, Maria S., at Orange, NJ, 2 Aug 1879
DELANY, Anna G., dau of Charles, 15 Feb 1886, a.18y 5mo

RYE DEATHS

DOLBEE (DOLBER), Jonathan, 18 Mar 1761
DORR, Jennie A., of Scottsville, NY, 29 Jul 1884, a.43y
_____, child, at Rufus W. Philbrick's, 4 Jul 1880, a.1y 5mo
DOW, Albert, son of James & Data, 10 Apr 1886, a. 67y 2mo
  Angeline, widow of James Henry (late of Rye), at Portsmouth, 9 Apr 1871, a.45y 3mo 6ds
  Ann E., wife of Albert, 3 Jun 1854, a.28y
  Cazendana, dau of James & Data, 2 Apr 1847, a.17y
  Charity, widow of Isaac, 22 Jun 1772, a.69y
  Charles H., son of James, at Portsmouth, 18 Mar 1869, a.15y 1mo
  Data, wife of James & dau of Jonathan Drake, 24 Apr 1848, a.56y
  Eli, son of James, 30 Aug 1858, a.30y
  Eli, son of James Henry, 20 May 1860, a.2y 9mo
  Elizabeth, widow of Isaac, 17 Dec 1823, a.67y
  Ella F., child of James H., 28 Feb 1864, a.5mo
  Harriet, dau of James H., 5 Sep 1853, a.1y 1mo
  Henry, 4 Oct 1769, a.43y
  Isaac, 29 Nov 1793, a.39y
  James, son of Henry & Martha, 8 Aug 1838, a.73y
  James, son of Isaac, 19 May 1853, a.68y
  James H., son of James, 20 Jan 1864, a.38y 2mo 27ds
  James W., son of Albert, 13 Nov 1861, a.10y
  John, 27 Nov 1756
  John H., son of Albert, 29 Jul 1865, a.16y 6mo
  Martha Adalaide, child of Albert, 28 Oct 1855, a.2y 1mo
  Martha Ann, dau of James, 11 Apr 1845, a.21y
  Mary Parsons, wife of James, 7 Dec 1842, a.72y
  Simon, 23 Oct 1815, a.29y
  _____, child of James, 16 Jun 1850, a.10wks
DOWNING, Samuel, formerly of Newington, son of Samuel, 6 Nov 1867, a.72y
  William C., 28 May 1887, a.70y 6mo
DOWNS (DOWNE), Abner, 7 Apr 1818
  Abner, son of Abner, (drowned), 30 Dec 1844, a.26y
  Betsey, widow of John, at the Alms house, 27 Apr 1863, a.75y
  Betsey, widow of Samuel, (she was first the widow of Jo. Tucker), 26 Sep 1870, a.82y 8mo
  Edward, child of Abner, 27 Sep 1816, a.7y
  Edward, son of John, 10 Jun 1870, a.52y

RYE DEATHS

DOWNS, Eliza, of the Shoals, (county pauper), dau of Ben, 26 Sep 1883, a.57y
  Elizabeth A., at Lowell, MA, Sep 1883
  Elizabeth P., widow of Henry & of Abner, 24 Mar 1882, a.72y
  Henry, 2 Oct 1839, a.37y
  John Henry, formerly of Rye, of Portsmouth, son of Mary, at sea (Small Pox), 30 Nov 1864, a.30y 10mo
  Lovey, dau of Abner & Sarah, 21 Mar 1835, a.21y
  Mary Abby, wife of Edward, 27 Dec 1866, a.38y
  Samuel, 1797
  Samuel, died while fishing, Dec 1850
  Samuel Washington, child of Samuel, 3 Dec 1831, a.8y
  _____, child of John, 17 Jan 1822, a.1y
  _____, child of Henry, 24 Mar 1838, a.2y
DOWRST (DOUST), Abial, dau of Solomon & Elizabeth, 24 Aug 1735
  Elizabeth, dau of Ozem & Elizabeth, 6 Sep 1730
  Elizabeth, dau of Solomon & Elizabeth, 19 Nov 1735
  John, son of Ozem & Elizabeth, 13 Sep 1730
  Samuel, son of Solomon & Elizabeth, 19 Aug 1735
  Simeon, son of Samuel & Rachel, 26 Oct 1734
  Solomon, son of Solomon & Elizabeth, 13 Nov 1735
  Thomas, son of Solomon & Elizabeth, 27 Aug 1735
  _____, 30 Aug 1787
DRAKE, A. Mary, wife of Oren, 2 Jan 1877, a.51y 7mo
  Abraham, son of Jonathan, 10 Jun 1825, a.39y
  Abraham, son of Abraham & Mary, 1 Sep 1826
  Anna, dau of Abraham, 9 Jul 1826, a.14y
  Cotton Ward, son of Jonathan & Martha, 10 Nov 1880, a.79y 5mo 13ds
  George Weston, son of Morris A., 20 Feb 1877, a.4y 2mo
  James Buchanan, son of Joseph J., 5 Oct 1874, a.18y 4mo
  John (Capt.), son of Jonathan & Sarah, 29 Oct 1882, a.78y 11mo
  John Haven, son of Joseph & Clarissa, 11 Feb 1848, a.6 1/2mo
  Jonathan, formerly of No. Hampton, son of Abraham, 21 Mar 1848, a.90y
  Jonathan Jr., son of Jonathan, 21 Jan 1833, a.36y
  Joseph, child of John O., Dec 1877
  Linden A., son of Adams E., 21 May 1881, a.3mo

RYE DEATHS

DRAKE, Maria Martha, dau of Cotton W., 26 Oct 1870, a.40y 9mo 12ds
  Nathan D., child of Joseph J., 11 Feb 1840, a.1y
  Oliver, son of Jonathan, 14 Jun 1843, a.23y
  Sarah, wife of Jonathan, 31 Dec 1822, a.61y
  _____, child of Abraham, 28 Jan 1816, a.2wks
  _____, child of Abraham (deceased), 3 Sep 1826, a.6y
DREW, Betsey, 28 Dec 1807
DROWN, Isabella, relict of Henry of Rochester, 23 Mar 1858, a.92y
DUTTON, Tamah, widow of Manasiah, 7 Jan 1852, a.64y
EATON, Mary A., 2 Aug 1890, a.55y 8mo
EDMONDS, Jonathan, 26 Jun 1829, a.54y
  _____, child of Jonathan, 15 Apr 1809
ELKINS, Albertine, child of Levi W., 5 Jun 1864, a.1y 9mo
  Henry, 16 Nov 1834, a.95y 2mo
  Hipsey, 16 Nov 1824, a.77y
  Mary, dau of Henry & Catherine, 4 Jan 1733
  Samuel, son of Henry, 21 Feb 1807, a.62y
  Samuel, formerly of Rye, at Portsmouth, 11 Aug 1836
  Samuel, son of Henry & Mary, 8 Jun 1868, a.59y 2mo
FISHER, John, Feb 1803
FITZ, Stephen, keeper of Sagamons House, Little Harbor, 1 Sep 1860, a.36y
FOLSOM, Samuel Gilman, formerly of Portsmouth, son of Nat, 9 May 1879, a.60y
FOGG, Fannie, dau of Richard of No. Hampton, 8 Sep 1884, a.15y 11mo
FOSS, Abigail, widow of William, 12 Jul 1856, a.89y 5mo
  Adeline L., wife of Joel N., at Florence MN, 13 Aug 1870, a.47y
  Alexander, son of Job, 30 Jul 1860, a.46y 11mo
  Benjamin, son of William, 4 Aug 1850, a.56y
  Charles, son of John O., 23 Jun 1861, a.5y 7mo
  Charles E., son of Robert, at Little Rock, AR, 18 Jul 1888, a.abt 34y
  Charles Osmond, son of John O. & Sarah Amanda, (drowned in Parsons' Creek), 4 Jul 1881, a.13y 10mo
  Charlotte, wife of Robinson & dau of Henry & Eliza Drown, 29 Feb 1868, a.72y
  Charlotte D., dau of Robinson & Charlotte, 14 Nov 1837

RYE DEATHS

FOSS, Eliza, wife of John H., 18 Dec 1862
  Eliza S., widow of Richard, 20 Jun 1886, a.87y 14ds
  Elizabeth, (supported by the town), 11 Apr 1804
  Ezra, son of Hardison, 28 Jan 1868,, a.17y 6mo
  Ezra Drown, son of Hardison, 28 Feb 1848, a.11mo
  Hardison, son of Robinson & Patty, 15 Dec 1882, a.61y 10mo
  Henry Hermin, son of Henry D., 31 Jul 1862
  Isaac, son of Jas. R., 12 May 1840, a.14y
  Jane, relict of Solomon, 27 May 1847, a.67y
  Joanna, widow of Joseph R., 21 Jan 1860, a.50y
  Job, son of John, 15 Apr 1827, a.42y
  John, son of Joshua, 15 Feb 1731, a.24y
  John, son of Job & Sarah, 1 Jan 1819, a.62y
  John Henry, son of Richard & Eliza, 7 Sep 1825
  Joseph R., son of Solomon, 19 Nov 1857, a.57y
  Mable Jane, dau of John O., 23 Jan 1876, a.14y 8mo
  Martha, wife of Job, 11 Sep 1826, a.34y 2mo
  Mary Jane, wife of John O., 11 May 1864, a.32y 3mo
  Mary P., dau of Joshua M. (formerly of Rye), at Haverhill, MA, 9 Aug 1860, a.15y
  Mehitable, widow of Nat, 11 Apr 1837, a.77y
  Minnie, wife of Alby H., 22 Jul 1887, a.30y 5mo
  Nathaniel, 4 Jan 1804, a.91y
  Nathaniel, son of Nathaniel, 31 Mar 1817, a.22y
  Nathaniel, son of Nathaniel & Mary, 11 Dec 1821, a.65y
  Orin, son of Richard & Eliza, 13 Sep 1825
  Patty W., wife of Robinson, 1 Apr 1828, a.40y
  Rachel, widow of Joshua, 23 Mar 1818, a.abt 75y
  Richard, son of John, 4 May 1842, a.48y
  Rieusa, son of Joseph, 5 Jun 1861, a.5y
  Robinson T., son of John & Sarah, 1 Jan 1878, a.90y 4mo
  Robinson T. Jr., son of Robinson T., 8 Dec 1865, a.28y
  Sally, dau of William, 13 May 1810, a.19y
  Sally (widow), 15 Jun 1833, a.77y
  Salome, relict of Samuel, 10 Apr 1851, a.87y
  Samuel, son of Nathaniel, 8 Apr 1867, a.68y 11mo
  Samuel Wallis, son of Solomon, 13 Apr 1849, a.31y
  Solomon, 13 Nov 1824, a.46y or 55y
  William, son of Joshua & Rachel, 7 Dec 1815, a.46y
  _____, child of Job, 6 Apr 1822, a.1y 5mo

RYE DEATHS

FOSS, _____, child of Joseph R., 11 Aug 1840
  _____, child of Richard & Eliza, 7 Sep 1825, a.6y
  _____, child of Richard & Eliza, 17 Sep 1825, a.2y
  _____, child of Robinson, 5 Apr 1827, a.1wk
  _____, child of Robinson T., 14 Nov 1837, a.2y
  _____, child of Solomon, 16 Mar 1804, a.3wks
FOYE, Aaron L., son of William, 11 or 12 Mar 1824, a.7y
  Amos, son of John Jr., in Boston, 5 Apr 1847, a.24y
  Ann Mary, dau of John Jr., 29 Oct 1851, a.20y
  Anna T., dau of John, 26 Nov 1804, a.2y
  Betsey, wife of John, 10 Feb 1805
  Eliza, dau of Nathaniel, 22 Jun 1843, a.16y
  Elizabeth, dau of John, 16 Apr 1826, a.30y
  Eunice, wife of William, 26 May 1830, a.29y
  Fidelia, dau of Nathaniel, 26 May 1861, a.30y
  Hannah, wife of William, 14 Nov 1803, a.27y
  Hannah, wife of John, 7 Feb 1829, a.67y
  Hannah B., widow of John Jr., 27 Aug 1886, a.84y 5mo 26ds
  John, 17 Jan 1818, a.82y
  John (Lt.), son of John, 16 Dec 1859, a.90y 1mo 1d
  John, son of John, 25 Sep 1884, a.84y 1mo 28ds
  Lydia, widow of John, 17 Jun 1830, a.94y
  Maria, 10 Feb 1840, a.21y
  Martha, widow of John, at Portsmouth, 13 Oct 1865, a.84y
  Martha A., dau of Nathaniel, 15 Jul 1844, a.15y
  Martha L., widow of Nathaniel G., 18 Sep 1885, a.86y 4mo 6ds
  Nathaniel, son of John, 27 Jan 1873, a.74y 3mo
  Stephen, 25 Dec 1802, a.45y
  William, son of John, 28 Aug 1824, a.49y or 50y
  _____, child of Nathaniel G., 31 Aug 1838, a.1y
  _____, child of Stephen, 10 Sep 1808
  _____, child of William, 6 Aug 1829, a.6y
FROST, Henry, of Newcastle, 30 Apr 1863, a.79y
FULLER, Anna D., wife of Hiram & dau of Cotton W. Drake, 6 Mar 1872, a.44y 9mo 9ds
GAGE, Emma F., dau of Capt. John Bragg, 16 Aug 1886, a.31y 5mo
GARLAND, Abby, twin child of Calvin, in No. Hampton, 12 Feb 1848
  Abigail, dau of John, 23 Dec 1828, a.19y
  Abigail, relict of John, 23 Jun 1844, a.83y

RYE DEATHS

8mo
GARLAND, Abigail, relict of John, 13 Mar 1851, a.88y
  Abigail Perkins, dau of Reul, 22 Dec 1865, a.33y 10mo
  Adeline S., wife of Moses, 18 Aug 1884, a.63y 9mo 2ds
  Albert W., son of Moses, 8 Mar 1862, a.19y 9mo
  Alfred Curtis, son of Joseph, 5 Dec 1869, a.20y 8mo
  Amos, son of Benjamin & Sarah, 21 Feb 1833, a.65y
  Amos S., son of John, 21 Feb 1843, a.53y
  Amos R., son of William, 31 Aug 1869, a.20y
  Angenette, dau of David, 29 Jul 1858, a.16y
  Benjamin, son of John, 2 May 1802, a.67y
  Benjamin, son of Benjamin & Sarah, 14 Jan 1835, a.70y
  Benjamin, son of John & Abigail, (drowned probably at Newcastle, suppose by going suddenly from a heated atmosphere to bath into the sea), 5 Jul 1847, a.56y
  Benjamin Jr., 4 Jun 1831, a.58y
  Betsey, 23 Jan 1838, a.64y
  Betsey, of No. Hampton, wife of John, 20 Feb 1843, a.66y
  Betsey, dau of Peter, 16 Jan 1847, a.74y
  Betsey, dau of Joseph, 14 Dec 1866, a.79y
  Caroline, wife of Calvin of No. Hampton, 31 Aug 1857, a.38y
  Charlotte, wife of William S., 11 May 1845, a.42y
  David, son of John of No. Hampton, in Boston, 30 Oct 1846, a.30y
  David Howe, son of William & Elizabeth, 11 Dec 1838, a.28y
  Edward L., son of Levi, 7 Jul 1872, a.49y
  Edwina A., dau of Joseph, 31 Aug 1875, a.37y 2mo 9ds
  Elvira, wife of William C., 2 Jul 1884, a.73y 9mo
  Elvira J., dau of Joseph Wm., 18 Aug 1872, a.3y 9mo
  Eliza J., wife of Orlando, 15 Oct 1868, a.33y 1mo 22ds
  Elizabeth, wife of Peter, of & at Hampton, NH, 19 Feb 1687/8, a.88y
  Elizabeth, wife of Calvin of No. Hampton, 11 Oct 1851, a.37y

RYE DEATHS

GARLAND, Elizabeth, widow of William, 5 Sep 1866, a.81y
  Elmira A., dau of Joseph, 31 Aug 1875, a.37y 2mo 9ds
  Emeline A., dau of Joseph, 7 Jan 1875, a.19y 8mo 2ds
  Fanny, relict of Benjamin Jr., 15 Jun 1857, a.69y 8mo
  Frances, wife of Oliver Perry, 9 Oct 1876, a.42y
  Frank Pierce, infant of Calvin, 10 Sep 1855, a.4mo
  Gideon, son of William, 9 Mar 1858, a.28y
  Gilman, 4 Nov 1805
  Ivory Cilley, son of Joseph, 22 Aug 1847, a.5y
  James, son of John & Abigail Perkins, 21 Jul 1850, a.66y
  James Abner, child of Calvin of No. Hampton, 5 Nov 1857, a.4mo
  John, son of Benjamin & Sarah, 24 Mar 1844, a.85y
  John, son of Joseph, 28 Oct 1854, a.69y 10mo
  John, of No. Hampton (formerly of Rye), 31 Oct 1865, a.88y 11mo
  John 3d, 28 Nov 1820, a.54y
  John 6th, 10 Dec 1805
  John Jr., son of Peter & Mary, 23 Apr 1837, a.75y
  Jonathan, son of Peter & Mary, 23 Oct 1826, a.62y
  Joseph, son of Simon, 8 Mar 1846, a.86y
  Joseph, son of Joseph, (hung himself), 9 May 1857, a.52y
  Levi, son of Peter, 4 Feb 1857, a.90y
  Levi Jr., son of Levi, 17 Dec 1863, a.70y 6mo
  Lizzie J., dau of Oliver Perry, 15 Dec 1876, a.3y
  Lucretia, wife of Moses, 22 Dec 1869, a.66y 6mo 14ds
  Lucy, wife of Levi, 2 Jan 1814, a.45y
  Maria, dau of Moses, 17 Apr 1856, a.2y
  Marshall W., son of Calvin, in Confederate Army, at Lake City FL, 20 Feb 1864, a.21y 11mo
  Martha, wife of Gilman, 25 Feb 1854 a.25y
  Martha, widow of Amos, at Portsmouth, 23 Jun 1866, a.72y
  Martha H., dau of Samuel P. & Eliza D., 21 Mar 1882, a.30y 4mo
  Mary, widow of Peter, 12 May 1826, a.90y
  Mary, dau of Peter, 17 Mar 1843, a.85y

RYE DEATHS

GARLAND, Mary, wife of William Cutter, 14 Feb 1856, a.41y
  Mary Ann, wife of Simon, 13 Oct 1826, a.26y
  Mary Ann, widow of David & of Charles Marden, 23 Jan 1887, a.63y 10mo
  Mary Jane, child of Levi Jr., 18 Nov 1826, a.12y
  Mary L. (widow), formerly of Newmarket, at Newmarket, 8 Apr 1860, a.78y
  Mehitable, dau of Joseph, 26 Apr 1873, a.80y 10mo 14ds
  Millard Fillmore, son of Gilman, 15 Jan 1854
  Moses, son of Benjamin, 12 Mar 1885, a.66y 2mo
  Moses L., in Portsmouth, 24 Aug 1890, a.89y 5mo
  Nabby, wife of William, 26 Jan 1852, a.47y 8mo
  Nancy, _____ of Levi, 7 May 1846, a.64y
  Nathan W., son of Simon, 3 Feb 1836, a.11mo
  Olive, wife of Amos, 16 Dec 1830, a.56y
  Patience, wife of Joseph, 9 Sep 1844, a.83y
  Patty, wife of Reul, 17 Feb 1866, a.64y
  Peter, son of John & Sarah, 26 Apr 1816, a.84y
  Peter Jr., 24 Jul 1804, a.abt 33y
  Polly Perkins, wife of Levi, 26 Jan 1829, a.35y
  Rachel, relict of Simon, 2 Apr 1803
  Reul, son of John, 28 Aug 1869, a.70y 7mo 29ds
  Reul W., son of Joseph Wm & Ann, 25 Dec 1877, a.15ds
  Sally, wife of Benjamin 3rd, 2 Apr 1829, a.34y
  Samuel Patten, son of Amos S., 3 Sep 1878, a.57y 7mo
  Sarah, widow of Col. Benjamin, 18 Feb 1803, a.66y
  Sarah, dau of Benjamin, 4 Jul 1846, a.73y
  Sarah, wife of Simon, 22 Apr 1876 a.69y
  Sarah Ann, child of Amos, 11 Oct 1812
  Sarah Ann, child of Amos, 27 Jun 1815, a.11ds
  Semira, dau of Amos S., 22 Nov 1884, a.55y 11mo 29ds
  Semira P., wife of Rufus, 22 Dec 1884, a.58y 4mo 16ds
  Simon, of N. Hampton, 26 May 1842
  Simon, son of John & Abigail, 15 Nov 1878, a.85y 9mo
  Sophia P., wife of Charles, 3 Nov 1858, a.32y
  Thomas Reul, son of Reul, (killed by the accidental discharge of his gun), 9 Oct 1854, a.15y 6mo
  Walter, son of Charles, 22 Dec 1860, a.2y 8mo
  Wesley, son of Calvin, 9 Apr 1850, a.13y
  William, son of Benjamin, 31 Jul 1820, a.46y

RYE DEATHS

GARLAND, William, son of Peter, 14 Mar 1862, a.66y 6mo
  William Seavey, son of John, 11 Aug 1871, a.70y 10mo
  _____, child of Benjamin, 9 Nov 1810, a.7mo
  _____, child of Calvin, 2 Apr 1836
  _____, (son) of Peter Jr., 22 Mar 1813
  _____, wife of Emmons, at Portsmouth, Mar 1875
GODFREY, John, at sea (fast rope broke while handling jib), 1 Jan 1820
  Nabby, wife of John (who was drowned in 1820), 9 Dec 1818
  Nabby, child of John, 9 Jan 1819, a.10y
  ____, child of John & Abigail, 29 Dec 1817, a.1y
GORDON, Lydia, wife of William, 5 Oct 1855, a.32y
GOSS, Abigail, widow of Genl. Thomas, 26 Feb 1881, a.88y 3mo
  Ann M., wife of Otis, 9 Feb 1867, a.36y 9mo
  Betsey, dau of Thomas, 15 Oct 1827, a.74y
  Betsey, dau of Betsey, 5 Dec 1870, a.76y 7mo 28ds
  Betsey, wife of William, 1 Jan 1880, a.75y 7mo
  Charles Carrol, son of William, 25 Jan 1859, a.24y
  Daniel, formerly of Rye, of & at Portsmouth, 2 Mar 1840
  Eliza M.L., wife of Joseph, 9 Feb 1857, a.53y
  Elizabeth, widow of Thomas Jr., 7 Jul 1824, a.70y
  Ester, dau of Jethro & Ester, 18 Aug 1735
  Esther, dau of Jethro, 31 Dec 1822
  J. Grenville, son of Jas. Madison, (drowned at Exeter), 16 Jul 1854, a.17y 7mo
  James, child of Michael D., 27 Aug 1806, a.1y 5mo
  James, son of Michael D., 17 Aug 1811, a.7y
  James, son of Thomas, 11 Apr 1825, a.79y
  James M., son of Michael D., 21 Feb 1870, a.60y 5mo 16ds
  James W., son of William, at Lynn, MA, 24 Jan 1888, a.62y 1mo
  Jonathan, son of Jonathan Goss Jr. & Elizabeth Brown, 29 Aug 1851, a.80y
  Joseph, son of Esther, 26 Apr 1795
  Joseph, son of Hannah Berry by Joseph Goss, 8 Apr 1872, a.76y 10mo
  Josiah Snow, son of James M., 29 Jan 1870, a.23y 10mo
  Levi, son of Jethro & Ester, 18 Aug 1735

RYE DEATHS

GOSS, Levi, formerly of Rye, at Portsmouth, 23 Jul 1836, a.88y
  Lucinda, widow of James Madison Goss & wife of Josiah Seavey, (she was a Snow), 3 Jul 1874, a.61y 5mo
  Mary, widow of Thomas, 17 Aug 1802, a.93y
  Michael D., son of Betsey, 18 Mar 1851, a.74y
  Nathan, son of Thomas & Mary, 23 Apr 1819, a.77y
  Nathan, son of Richard, 27 Feb 1845, a.33y
  Patty, wife of Jonathan, 21 May 1843, a.66y
  Polly, widow of Richard, 10 Mar 1867, a.76y 5mo
  Richard, killed in the Rev. War, 17 Oct 1777
  Richard, son of Nathan & Sarah, 6 Feb 1814, a.36y
  Sally, wife of Daniel, 27 Nov 1819, a.68y
  Sally, dau of Esther, 29 Oct 1845, a.80y
  Sally, relict of Michael D., 10 Nov 1851, a.73y 9mo
  Samuel, son of Jethro & Ester, 22 Aug 1735
  Sarah, wife of Nathan, 24 Dec 1810, a.66y
  Sarah, wife of Thomas, 26 May 1815, a.36y
  Sarah, wife of Levi, 10 Apr 1821, a.72y
  Sarah B., wife of Simon, 16 May 1822, a.35y
  Sheridan, son of Thomas & Sarah, 23 Dec 1813, a.5y
  Simon, son of Nathan, 13 Aug 1828, a.57y
  Thomas, son of Thomas & Mary, 17 Feb 1823, a.76y
  Thomas (Genl.), son of Nathan, 7 Oct 1857, a.89y 1mo
  Tobias Trundy, son of Michael, 17 Aug 1824, a.23y 5mo
  _____, child of Jonathan Jr., 5 Feb 1816, a.1y
  _____, child of Joseph, 21 Oct 1805
  _____, child of William, 24 Aug 1825, a.2y
GOULD (GOULDE), _____, (widow), supported by the town, 25 Dec 1805
GRANT, Christopher, formerly of York, ME, 21 Apr 1880, a.34y
  Ella J., dau of Christopher, 1 Dec 1875, a.3y
  Elsie C., widow of Christopher, 28 Aug 1880, a.28y 3mo 10ds
GREEN (GREENE), Alexander Foss, son of Thomas, 19 Jan 1870, a.26y 10mo
  Brackett B., son of Thomas, at Portsmouth, 7 Jan 1874, a.38y 9mo 25ds
  Charles, son of Thomas, 16 Dec 1854, a.4y
  Charles, son of Richard & Mary, 22 Apr 1884, a.89y 1mo
  Cyrus Fayette, son of Charles & Mary, 5 May 1836

RYE DEATHS

GREEN, Elizabeth, wife of Thomas, 1 Jun 1868, a.57y
  Ella F., dau of Thomas, 5 Nov 1859, a.5y
  Mary, relict of Richard, 14 May 1854, a.96y 4mo 28ds
  Mary, wife of Charles, 21 Mar 1858, a.55y
  Richard, son of Richard, in West Indies, 29 Mar 1806, a.27y
  Richard, an Englishman & Rev. soldier, 4 Mar 1832, a.94y
  Sarah W., dau of Thomas, 2 Jan 1874, a.21y 11mo
  Woodbury C., son of Charles, 20 Sep 1864, a.27y 11mo
  _____, child of Charles, 5 May 1836, a.2y
GROVES (GROVE), Nathaniel, 15 Feb 1810, a.39y
  _____, of Concord, (burnt at Straw's Point), 4 Aug 1877, a.23y
HAINES, Reuben, 24 Mar 1806
HALEY, Samuel, of Gosport, 24 Oct 1823
HALL, Ann, wife of James, 12 May 1856, a.26y 3mo
  Charles Wm., son of William, 24 Mar 1873, a.42y
  Edward, son of Edward, at sea on return trip from Demerara, 10 Apr 1806, a.20y
  Edward, son of Joseph, (drowned), 6 Jun 1827, a.62y
  Ephraim R., at the County Farm, 25 Nov 1870, a.76y 11mo
  George, son of William, 13 Aug 1854, a.8y
  Hannah, dau of Joseph, 17 May 1839, a.58y
  Joseph, Mar 1801
  Joseph, son of Edward, at sea on return trip from Demerara, 1 Apr 1806, a.22y
  Joseph, son of Joseph & Mary, 26 Mar 1828, a.22y
  Joseph, son of Ephraim R., 15 Jun 1855 a.29y
  Mary, widow, 19 Mar 1808
  Nancy, wife of Ephraim of Portsmouth, 7 Dec 1842, a.48y
  Rachel, widow of Joseph, 9 Nov 1806
  Sarah, dau of Joseph, Jun 1803
  Sarah, relict of Edward, 15 Nov 1851, a.87y.
  Sarah Rand, widow of William, 14 Dec 1885, a.84y 8mo 2ds
  William, son of Edward, 29 Jan 1864, a.68y 1mo 3ds
  _____, child (girl) of Levi, 26 Sep 1871, a.3mo
HAM, John, formerly of Portsmouth, (choked by meat), 25 Dec 1855, a.65y
  Mary, widow of John, 29 Aug 1874, a.89y 7mo 2ds
HARDY, George E., at W. Harvey Locke's, 18 Mar

RYE DEATHS

1887, a.11y 7mo
HARGRAVES, Olive Jarvice, 12 Sep 1836, a.82y
HEATH, Abel, at Nashua, 22 Jun 1852, a.55y
HILL, Joseph, of Portsmouth, 4 Jan 1859, a.60y
HOBBS, James, son of Jonathan, Feb 1803
  John P., of No. Hampton, (drowned at Porter's Point in Rye Harbor while bathing), 28 Jul 1873, a.18y
  Jonathan, son of James, 20 Dec 1810, a.32y
  Jonathan, son of Jonathan & Molly, 5 Oct 1815, a.65y
  Lucy, dau of James, 19 Mar 1776
  Lucy, 11 Dec 1783
  Mary, widow of James, 17 Dec 1825, a.70y
  Nathaniel, 21 Jan 1788
  Perney, dau of James, 26 Mar 1809, a.16y
HOLLIS, Josephine, dau of Edward of Newton, MA, at Woodbury Dalton's, 19 Aug 1880, a.1y 6mo
HOLMES, Earnest, son of William Ira, 18 Feb 1881, a.8y 9mo
  Eliza, wife of Jacob, 3 May 1842, a.31y
  Jacob, son of Jacob, 30 Dec 1870, a.70y 9mo 21ds
  Mary, wife of William, 24 Mar 1863, a.55y
  Mary A., child of William, 27 Jul 1864, a.9mo 17ds
  Nancy, wife of Jacob, 25 Mar 1834, a.30y
  Olivette Davis, child of William, 14 May 1864, a.2y 9mo
  Polly, widow of Jacob, 28 Sep 1843, a.60y
  Sarah Ann, wife of John, at Portsmouth, 22 Jan 1850, a.28y
  Sylvanus, child at Robinson Foss's (by wife's 1st husband) 16 Dec 1837, a.14y
  _____, child of Jacob, 1 Sep 1842, a.6mo
JACKSON, Isabella Nevins, formerly of Portsmouth, 14 Nov 1848, a.8y
JENNESS, Abbot C., child of Amos J., 18 Jun 1863, a.2y
  Abigail, wife of Richard, 2 Jan 1755, a.37y
  Abigail, wife of Richard, 27 Sep 1780
  Abigail (Nabby), wife of Jonathan 3d, 17 Nov 1818, a.27y
  Abigail, wife of Samuel, 14 Mar 1833, a.41y
  Abigail, 23 Apr 1840, a.78y
  Abigail, widow of _____, 24 May 1844, a.79y
  Abigail, widow of David W., 9 Feb 1888, a.71y
  Alvira, wife of George W., 23 Oct 1880, a.36y 10mo 15ds
  Amos Seavey, son of Benjamin & Martha, 30 Mar

RYE DEATHS

1886, a.84y 5mo 17ds
JENNESS, Andrew J., son of Mrs. Caroline, 11 Feb 1882, a.67y
Ann Eliza, wife of Charles Austin, 11 Jun 1877, a.31y 6mo
Anna, wife of Joseph, 8 Mar 1801, a.abt 30y
Anna, relict of Joseph, 23 Jun 1816, a.75y
Anna, dau of Job & Mary, 26 Feb 1825, a.75y-78y
Anna, widow of Joseph, 15 Sep 1862, a.82y
Anna Elizabeth, dau of Oliver, 26 Apr 1858, a.5y 2mo
Benjamin, 1769
Benjamin, son of Richard, 8 Feb 1824, a.60y
Betsey, dau of Simon, (after suffering 17 days with St. Vitus Dance), 22 Jul 1799, a.16y
Betsey, dau of Noah, 22 Aug 1811, a.17y
Betsey, wife of David W., 27 Aug 1812, a.25y
Betsey, wife of Joseph, 29 Jan 1816, a.32y
Betsey, wife of Richard, 11 Jun 1835, a.53y
Betsey, wife of Richard, 17 Dec 1859, a.69y
Caroline, widow of Richard, 5 Mar 1886, a.89y 4mo
Charlotte, wife of Henry, 3 Sep 1867 a.74y 1mo
Clarissa, wife of Samuel Jr., 14 Aug 1842, a.42y
Clarissa, wife of James, 29 Jul 1854, a.32y
David A., son of Simon, 28 Mar 1869, a.54y 7mo
David W., son of Nathaniel, 22 Jan 1843, a.61y
David W., son of John, at Boston, 4 Jun 1872, a.55y
Eliza True, wife of G. Harrison, 6 Oct 1884, a.39y 4mo
Elizabeth, wife of Levi, 9 Feb 1821, a.59y
Elizabeth, wife of Joseph T., 15 Mar 1837, a.24y
Elizabeth Drake, wife of Oliver P., May 1888, a.64y 4mo
Elmer M., son of Albert Dana, in Portsmouth, 15 Nov 1878, a.12y 4mo
Elvira, wife of Joseph G., 13 Oct 1864, a.37y
Emeline, child of Jonathan 4th, 1 May 1824, a.1y 6mo
Emeline, wife of Dana, 27 Nov 1858, a.22y
Emeline, wife of Rienza, 27 Feb 1864
George M., son of Joseph G. & Elvira, 16 Jul 1884, a.20y 5mo 18ds
George W., 15 Feb 1887, a.59y 9mo
Gracia, wife of John H. & dau of Edward H. Balch, 23 Nov 1887, a.23y 4mo
Hannah W., wife of John, 26 Oct 1870, a.76y 7mo

RYE DEATHS

JENNESS, Henry, son of Isaac, 11 Mar 1869, a.82y 11mo 4ds
Howard Le Trobe, child of Austin, 29 Feb 1876, a.1y 8mo
Huldah, widow of Josiah, 23 Aug 1880, a.76y 6mo
James, son of Nathaniel, (drowned while out fishing), 9 Sep 1806, a.abt 24y
Job, died in the Rev. War, 15 Nov 1777
Job, 25 Apr 1806
Job, son of Richard, at Exeter, Mar 1855, a.68y
Job, son of John, 29 Feb 1888, a.76y 7mo
Job Rienza, son of Job of Rye, at Washington, 4 Feb 1872, a.33y
John, son of Hezekiah, 14 Feb 1744/5, a.35y
John, son of Richard, 28 Jan 1855, a.73y 9mo
John, son of John Bean, 31 Aug 1874, a.84y 5mo 2ds
John B., 21 Aug 1840, a.77y 1mo 10ds
Jonathan, son of Joseph, 29 Dec 1836, a.76y
Jonathan, son of John, 17 Apr 1852, a.30y
Jonathan, son of Nathaniel, 2 Feb 1870, a.77y 3mo
Jonathan, son of Jonathan & Abigail, 12 Jul 1870, a.79y 3mo 13ds
Jonathan 2d, son of Ruth Tarlton, 11 Feb 1836, a.56y
Joseph, son of Richard & Mary, 23 Feb 1815, a.89y
Joseph (Lieut), son of Joseph, 13 Sep 1845, a.74y 6mo 23ds
Joseph, son of Jonathan & Abigail, 16 Mar 1873, a.77y 9mo
Joseph, son of Isaac, at No. Hampton, 10 Feb 1875, a.84y
Joseph T., son of Thomas, (hung himself), in Hampton, 5 Aug 1885, a.81y
Joseph Tarlton, 7 Jan 1804
Josephine, dau of Joseph, at Exeter, 6 Jan 1851
Josiah, son of Levi, 12 Apr 1876, a.78y 7mo
Keziah, wife of Job, 19 Jan 1879, a.65y
Langdon, son of Richard, 2 Aug 1873, a.57y 8mo 9ds
Levi, son of Samuel, 29 Feb 1824, a.67y
Lucinda, wife of Alfred G., 11 Aug 1861, a.43y
Lydia, relict of John, 18 Apr 1857, a.66y
Martha, wife of Benjamin, 27 May 1830, a.72y
Martha, wife of Joseph Jerome, 19 Apr 1875
Martha A., wife of Alfred, 17 Jun 1849, a.24y
Mary, widow of Nathaniel, 30 Jun 1814, a.71y

RYE DEATHS

JENNESS, Mary, 12 Jan 1833, a.68y
  Mary, 21 Apr 1840, a.87y
  Mary, widow of David W. & of Abraham Drake, 28 Oct 1885, a.92y 4mo 9ds
  Mary B., wife of Charles W., at Fall River, MA, 26 Sep 1885, a.33y 3mo
  Mary E., wife of Jos. Disco, 29 Aug 1880, a.59y 6mo 4ds
  Nabby, dau of Benjamin & Martha, 28 Jan 1816, a.19y
  Nancy, dau of Joseph, 6 Jun 1808
  Nancy, widow of Simon, 3 Jun 1866, a.75y
  Nancy, widow of Col. Simon, 19 Feb 1876, a.80y
  Nathaniel, son of John, 7 Feb 1812, a.86y
  Nathaniel, 8 Oct 1824, a.64y or 68y
  Nathaniel Abraham, son of David W., 10 Mar 1851, a.22y
  Noah, son of Nathaniel, 17 Oct 1801, a.39y 7mo
  Olive, wife of John B., 7 Jun 1823, a.60y
  Olive, widow of Simon, 27 May 1845, a.90y
  Oliver Peter, child of Jonathan 3d & Abigail, 3 Oct 1818, a.3y
  Peter, son of Samuel, 30 Sep 1836, a.81y
  Polly, dau of Benjamin & Martha, 24 Jan 1803, a.12y 3mo
  Polly, dau of Nathaniel, 27 Jul 1805, a.19y 11mo
  Polly, wife of David, 29 Nov 1807
  Polly, dau of Noah, 9 Jun 1824, a.16y
  Polly, wife of Samuel, 17 Aug 1841, a.36y
  Polly, widow of Joseph, 13 Aug 1877, a.77y 8mo
  Reuben P., son of Lt. Joseph, 1 Jun 1862, a.54y 6mo
  Richard, (Tanner Richard so called), 1 Sep 1785, a.70y
  Richard, son of Job, (killed by lightening), 20 or 27 Jul 1809, a.56y
  Richard, 8 Jul 1843, a.63y
  Richard, son of John B., 28 Feb 1870, a.83y 1mo 9ds
  Richard, formerly of Deerfield, at Portsmouth, 2 Feb 1872, a.71y
  Richard, son of Richard & Betsey, 5 Dec 1885, a.60y 4mo
  Rufus, son of Richard, 24 May 1847, a.24y
  Ruth W., wife of Capt. Samuel Jr., 20 Jul 1858, a.59y
  Sally, wife of Joseph, 1 Nov 1808
  Sally, wife of Benjamin, 16 Mar 1826, a.33y
  Samuel, son of Levi, 2 Mar 1875, a.87y

RYE DEATHS

JENNESS, Samuel Jr., son of Peter, 11 Jan 1875,
   a.80y 3mo 28ds
  Sarah E., dau of R.R. Locke, 1 Feb 1890, a.63y
   3mo
  Sarah Eliza, dau of Alfred, 5 Jan 1866, a.22y
  Sarah S., wife of Samuel, 1 Mar 1875, a.84y
  Sarah T., wife of D.W., 23 Jun 1825, a.29y
  Sarah Ward, widow of David A., 12 May 1881,
   a.62y 3mo
  Sheridan, Dec 1888
  Simon, 27 Apr 1798
  Simon, son of Noah, 17 Dec 1846, a.61y
  Simon (Col.), son of Simon, 3 Dec 1870, a.78y
  Susan Ladd, dau of Joseph D., 15 Sep 1847, a.4y
  Thomas, son of Nathaniel, 28 Nov 1850, a.78y
  Wallis Avery, son of Woodbury, 15 Feb 1856, a.6y
  William, son of Richard (grandson of Job), 22
   Oct 1851, a.69y
  Woodbury, son of Col. Simon, 9 Jan 1852, a.27y
   8mo
  _____, child of Benjamin, 22 Jan 1826, a.1y
  _____, child of David, 13 Nov 1807
  _____, child of James, 20 Dec 1827, a.1y
  _____, child of John, 20 Dec 1821
  _____, child of Jonathan, 28 Jun 1825, a.1wk
  _____, child of Joseph, 27 Nov 1807
  _____, child of Joseph, 8 Jun 1817, a.2y
  _____, child of Joseph 3d, 10 May 1836, a.7mo
  _____, child of Joseph T. Jr., 14 May 1833,
   a.3mo
  _____, child of Joseph T., 7 Jun 1834
  _____, child of Josiah, 10 Jun 1833, a.2y
  _____, child of Loel, formerly of Rye, at Portsmouth, 27 Mar 1850, a.3y 6mo
  _____, child of Richard & Elizabeth, 22 Jun
   1825, a.1wk
  _____, child of Samuel, 1 Nov 1821, a.2y
  _____, child of Simon, 18 Aug 1826, a.6y
  _____, child (dau) of Sheridan, 13 May 1858,
   a.7mo
JOHNSON, Abigail, child of Peter, 5 Feb 1816
  Edmond, at sea, (U.S. Navy), 10 Nov 1810
  Edmund, son of Edmund, 18 Jan 1826, a.34y
  Greenleaf, at Bay Port, FL, (whose father went
   there from Rye), 17 Aug 1880, a.31y
  John, son of Greenleaf (formerly of Rye), at Bay
   Port FL, drowned with his son John, 5 Jun
   1859, a.36y
  John B., 11 Nov 1890, a.84y 3mo

RYE DEATHS

JOHNSON, John Greenleaf, son of Edmund, 2 Aug 1824, a.22y
  Giles (Capt), Mar 1801
  Mary, widow of Peter, 20 Aug 1831, a.84y
  Mary F., wife of John B., 16 Dec 1883, a.73y
  Mary W., wife of Gilman, in Portsmouth, 5 Dec 1885, a.47y 10mo
  Nabby, wife of Edmond, 28 Feb 1808
  Nabby, wife of Peter, 4 Feb 1816
  Peter, son of Peter, 12 Oct 1816, a.75y
  Peter, 4 May 1832, a.54y
  Polly, wife of Jacob, 25 Feb 1830, a.62y
  Sally, 2 May 1794, a.22y
  Simon, 15 Jul 1813, a.68y
  _____, child of Simon, 26 Feb 1808
  _____, child, on Sheafe farm, Nov or Dec 1858, a.8y
JONES, Anna, dau of John & Anna, (supported by the town), 28 Nov 1806, a.65y
  Elizaette, wife of True W. & dau of Jos. Locke, 10 Mar 1872, a.28y
  Esther (Mrs.), 21 Jan 1887, a.78y 10mo
  Hiram, formerly of Barrington, (by suicide, cut his throat), 2 Jul 1859, a.31y 5mo
  John, son of William, 17 Sep 1835, a.28y
  Joseph, son of Wm., (drowned) at sea, 3 May 1831, a.21y
  Sally, widow of William, 25 Jan 1850, a.80y
  William, son of William, 29 Aug 1835, a.64y
JUDKINS, Betsey, 23 Mar 1817, a.21y
KEEN, Addie P., child of Warren W., 16 Apr 1871, a.5y 6mo
  George W., child of Warren W., 28 Jan 1875, a.1y 5mo
  William, formerly of Kittery, ME, 22 Aug 1874, a.81y
KEITH, _____, of Kentucky, 2 Dec 1879
KNOWLES, Hannah, wife of Nathan, 8 Nov 1819, a.75y
  John, son of Nathan, 29 Mar 1862, a.51y
  John Clifford, son of Nathan, 7 Nov 1837, a.70y
  John Langdon, son of Nathan, 24 Jan 1806
  Nathan, son of Amos, 19 Jan 1820, a.75y
  Nathan, son of Nathan, 17 Oct 1863, a.88y
  Samuel, died in the Rev. War, 16 Jun 1778
  Sarah H., wife of Nathan, 22 Dec 1859, a.81y
  Simon, son of Joseph & Love, 7 Nov 1823, a.75y 5mo
KNOWLTON, Susan R., wife of Timothy, 18 Jul 1842, a.25y

RYE DEATHS

KNOX, Drisco, 5 Dec 1835, a.87y
  Margaret, wife of Drisco, 2 Aug 1832, a.80y
  Ruth (Miss), of So. Newmarket, 5 Jun 1870, a.75y 11mo
LAMPREY, Hunt, 19 Feb 1809
  Margaret, widow of Simon, 22 Jul 1846, a.80y
  Martha, widow of Simon, 17 Oct 1825, a.94y
  Simon, son of Simon, 29 Jan 1847, a.81y 8mo
LANG, Aaron, son of Mark & Hannah, 11 Apr 1803
  Annaniah, dau of Mark & Hannah, 30 Apr 1803
  Betsey, 18 Feb 1803
  Comfort, relict of Richard, 4 Apr 1854, a.83y
  Daniel, son of Mark & Hannah, May 1861, a.64y
  Elizabeth, dau of Mark, 14 Jan 1804, a.51y
  Elizabeth, wife of William, 2 Jan 1862, a.61y
  Fanny, 30 Mar 1803
  Fanny (maiden lady), dau of Richard, 27 Dec 1870, a.71y 8mo
  George, at Greenland, NH, 6 Oct 1789, a.44y
  Hannah, widow of Mark, of & at Portsmouth, 29 Mar 1855, a.83y
 John Langdon, son of Mark & Hannah, 27 Aug 1833, a.24y
  Mark, 25 Jul 1808
  Mark, in Portsmouth, 3 Aug 1845, a.78y
  Mark, son of Mark & Hannah, 23 Feb 1862, a.63y
  Mark, son of Mark, in Portsmouth, 21 Feb 1863, a.63y
  Nancy, widow of Richard (late of Rye), at Salem, MA, 12 Apr 1860, a.82y
  Polly, dau of Mark & Hannah, 14 Jan 1797
  Richard, son of Thomas, 24 Jan 1823, a.52y
  Richard, son of Mark, 6 May 1854, a.76y
  Sarah, 1801, a.96y 6mo
  Sarah, widow of Mark, 14 or 23 Mar 1810, a.68y
  Sarah, 9 Jan 1819, a.73y
  Stephen, died in the Rev. War, 6 Jul 1778
  William, son of Mark, 3 May 1831, a.58y
  William, son of Richard, 3 Apr 1869, a.66y 4mo
  _____, child of Ebenezer W., 28 Nov 1829, a.3mo
  _____, child of Eliza, 8 Dec 1831
  _____, child of Mark of Portsmouth, 14 Apr 1822
  _____, child of William, 26 Feb 1809
  _____, child of Eben M., 18 Oct 1865
  _____, wife of Richard (formerly of Rye), in Boston, 20 Jun 1851, a.37y
LANGDON, Ann, dau of Samuel, 20 Jan 1725, a.6mo
  Joseph, 27 Aug 1767, a.73y
  Mark, of Portsmouth, NH, 25 Jun 1808

RYE DEATHS

LANGDON, Mary, wife of Capt. Jos.?, 10 Aug 1753, a.49y
  Patience, widow of Rev. Joseph, 8 Apr 1846, a.88y
  Samuel, 2 Dec 1725, a.25y
  Samuel, 14 Nov 1779, a.58y
LEACH, Elizabeth T., wife of Rev. Giles (Pastor of Congregational Church), 15 Jun 1868, a.59y
  John, 1749
LEAR, Alexander, son of Benjamin, 10 Oct 1813
  Benjamin, 27 Oct 1838, a.75y
  Daniel, son Benjamin, 22 Mar 1813, a.6y
  John, son of Benjamin, at the Shoals, 19 Oct 1865, a.60y 10mo
  Mary, wife of Benjamin, 13 Jun 1834, a.60y
  Nancy, widow of John, 23 Apr 1867, a.57y
  William, died in Rev. War, 4 Jul 1778
  _____, child of John, 25 Nov 1831, a.1y
LEAVITT, Abigail, of No. Hampton, 13 Mar 1842, a.28y
  Benjamin, of No. Hampton, 14 Mar 1801, a.63y
  Benjamin (Capt.), of No. Hampton, 8 Nov 1835, a.69y
  Benjamin, of No. Hampton, 20 Mar 1836, a.32y
  Betsey, of No. Hampton, 10 Oct 1842, a.42y
  Carr, son of Ebenezer L., 8 Sep 1863, a.56y 10mo
  Eben True, child of Carr, (drowned), 21 Apr 1843, a.3y
  Ebenezer, of No. Hampton, 13 Dec 1843, a.73y
  Eliza J., of No. Hampton, 2 Feb 1845, a.38y
  John, of No. Hampton, 22 Jun 1848, a.44y
  Joseph, of No. Hampton, 4 Jul 1844, a.33y
  Levina, of No. Hampton, 6 May 1838, a.23y
  Luther, of No. Hampton, 30 Apr 1837, a.38y
  Mary, of No. Hampton, 16 Jun 1850
  Mirriam, of No. Hampton, 3 Jun 1820
  Olive, of No. Hampton, 16 Jun 1847, a.52y
  Philip, of No. Hampton, 1 Sep 1829, a.38y
  Ruth, of No. Hampton, Jun 1820, a.82y
  Sally J., of No. Hampton, 18 May 1851, a.77y
  Tappan, of No. Hampton, Dec 1818, a.23y
  _____, child of Carr, 24 Aug 1854, a.8mo
  _____, child of Carr, 30 Aug 1855, a.3mo
LEWIS, Abby, widow of Langley, 20 Sep 1878, a.56y 4mo
  Abby Frances, dau of Langley B., 26 Jul 1871, a.14y
  Fanny B., dau of Charles Mace, 4 Jul 1890, a.24y 10mo

RYE DEATHS

LEWIS, Joseph, off Sandy Beach, (drowned when boat capsized), 31 Aug 1855, a.54y
  Langley B., at Valledgio near San Francisco, CA, 19 Mar 1873, a.47y
LIBBY, Aaron S., son of Samuel, in West Indies, 26 Mar 1806, a.24y 7mo
  Abigail, wife of Abraham, 2 Jun 1764
  Daniel, child of Samuel, 26 Sep 1804, a.4y
  Joseph, 1764
LOCKE (LOCK), Aaron, son of James J., 12 Jan 1888, a.40y 4mo
  Abby, dau of Jonathan & Elmira, 2 Oct 1877, a.21y
  Abby A., dau Elvin, 15 Nov 1861, a.10y 8mo
  Abigail, wife of John, 4 Jul 1812, a.43y
  Abigail, widow of Jonathan, 22 Mar 1817, a.81y
  Abigail, child of Samuel J., 20 Jan 1824, a.1mo
  Abigail, relict of Joseph, 25 Mar 1848, a.72y
  Abigail M., wife of Lemuel, 15 Jun 1882, a.76y 8mo
  Abner, son of John & Sarah, 11 Aug 1736
  Abner, son of Jonathan, in Rev. War, 16 Aug 1778
  Abner, son of Richard & Elizabeth, 15 Apr 1825, a.71y
  Adna Parsons, son of Joseph & Hannah, 26 May 1877, a.28y
  Almira, wife of Jonathan, 29 Oct 1860, a.45y
  Anna, wife of John Oliver, 16 Mar 1865, a.20y
  Arthur, son of Richard, 11 Mar 1887, a.18y 5mo
  Asa, son of Richard, 23 May 1857, a.81y 9mo
  Asa, son of Asa, 1 Nov 1863, a.62y
  Belinda, wife of Lemuel, 25 Aug 1863, a.54y
  Betsey, wife of Simon, (hung herself), 29 Nov 1838, a.62y
  Betsey, wife of Asa, 1 Dec 1845, a.65y
  Calvin K., son of John, at Boston, 30 Jun 1866, a.36y
  Charles, son of Joseph L. Jr., 28 Aug 1846, a.27y
  Charles A., son of Elvin, at Portsmouth, 6 Sep 1872, a.28y 6mo
  Clarissa Amanda, wife of Robert P., of & in No. Hampton, 16 Oct 1881, a.51y 10mo
  Daniel, son of Jonathan, 1 Jan 1840, a.68y
  Daniel A., son of Miss Sally, 5 Apr 1852, a.39y
  David, son of Jonathan & Sarah, 7 Jun 1810, a.75y
  David, son of Simon, shot in the War at Petersburg, VA, 29 Sep 1864, a.42y

RYE DEATHS

LOCKE, Elbridge G., son of Jos. L., in Portsmouth,
  24 Mar 1839, a.14y
 Elizabeth, wife of William, 8 Jun 1851, a.55y
 Elizabeth Marden (Mrs.), widow of Samuel J., 20
  Sep 1877, a.83y 10mo 14ds
 Elleanor, wife of James, 25 Jun 1849, a.70y
 Ellen, dau of Job, at Boston, May 1855
 Elvin (Lieut.), son of John & Abigail, 23 Jun
  1882, a.73y 2mo
 Emmeline, child of John, 7 May 1810, a.12y
 Esther Y., wife of Lemuel, 1 Aug 1838, a.27y
 Greensville, son of Job Jr., at Boston, 25 Dec
  1854, a.19y
 Hannah (widow), 12 Sep 1769, a.92y
 Hannah, 20 Feb 1805
 Hannah, wife of Job, 29 Jan 1806
 Hannah, wife of David, 23 Sep 1807, a.abt 70y
 Hannah, widow of James, 10 Jan 1810, a.36y
 Hannah, wife of Joseph, 18 Dec 1851, a.69y
 Hannah, widow of Job Jr., 24 Dec 1855, a.55y
 Hannah Knowles, wife of Joseph 2d, 18 Oct 1858,
  a.50y
 Harvey, 23 Jan 1887, a.56y 10mo
 Horace Wm., child of Joseph 4th, 3 Jan 1839,
  a.1y 7mo
 Ida G., dau of James J., 13 Jun 1876, a.17y
 Ira, son of Jeremiah, 14 Oct 1824, a.23y
 Isaac Hill, son of Joseph L., 13 Jun 1848, a.10y
 Isaac Moses, son of Lemuel, 22 Jul 1867, a.33y
  1mo
 Jacob, son of John & Sarah, 1736
 James, son of James of Deerfield & Portsmouth,
  13 Nov 1858, a.81y
 James H., son of Richard, 8 Jan 1808, a.34y
 James H., son of Asa, 24 Oct 1886, a.87y 10mo
  7ds
 James J., son of James, 10 Feb 1871, a.49y
 James W., son of Joseph, at Portsmouth, 25 Mar
  1871, a.54y 5mo 24ds
 Jennie or Jane, widow of Isaac M., 6 Feb 1869,
  a.31y
 Jeremiah, 28 Jan 1795
 Jeremiah, son of John, 21 Oct 1804, a.33y
 Jesse, son of Joseph, 23 Jun 1860, a.53y
 Jethro, son of Jonathan & Abigail, 3 Apr 1821,
  a.46y
 Jethro, formerly of Rye, at Portsmouth, 23 Sep
  1848, a.51y
 Job, son of Richard, 20 Jul 1849, a.87y or 88y

RYE DEATHS

LOCKE, Job, son of Job Locke & wife Hannah Lang, 1 Jul 1852, a.53y
John, son of John & Sarah, 23 Jun 1730
John, son of Jonathan & Abigail, 27 Mar 1814, a.47y
John, son of Joseph, 20 Jun 1843, a.48y
John, son of Jeremiah Jr. & Susan, 10 Jan 1868, a.71y 6mo
John, child of John Oliver, at Newmarket, 23 Sep 1875, a.7mo
John O., child of Asa, 16 Aug 1822
John Quincy, in Mexican War, Jun 1848, a.abt 22y
John Rings, son of John & Mary Ann, 10 Feb 1837, a.19y
John W., child of Samuel J., 19 May 1819
John W., son of Job Locke Jr. & Hannah Randall, 14 May 1848, a.4y 6mo
John W.P., son of Job, 25 Apr 1841, a.38y
Jonathan, son of Jonathan & Sarah, 17 Sep 1813, a.82y
Jonathan, son of John, 14 Jun 1826, a.26y
Jonathan Dearborn, son of Asa, 16 Oct 1885, a.74y 6mo
Jonathan Hobbs, son of Jas., 16 Feb 1847, a.44y
Joseph (Capt), Mar 1768, a.68y
Joseph, 22 Apr 1790
Joseph, son of Samuel, 17 Sep 1806
Joseph, son of Jonathan & Abigail, 27 Jan 1816, a.45y
Joseph, son of Joseph, 3 Mar 1841, a.73y
Joseph, son of Richard, 2 Nov 1853, a.75y 5mo
Joseph, son of Jonathan of New Castle, at Portsmouth, 6 Sep 1858, a.66y
Joseph, son of Joseph, 19 Jun 1864, a.11y 1mo 15ds
Joseph, son of Joseph & Abigail M., 23 May 1886, a.79y 5mo 23ds
Julia Ann, wife of Gardiner T., 14 Jul 1873, a.51y 7mo
Levi, child of Joseph 3d, 6 Feb 1832
Louisa, wife of Elvin, 5 Oct 1861, a.48y 4mo
Lucy, wife of Joseph, 19 May 1813, a.37y
Lucy Ann, child of Joseph Jr., 7 Sep 1820, a.2mo
Martha, widow of Joseph & dau of Henry Dow, 31 Jan 1792, a.34y
Martha, widow of Jethro, 2 May 1856, a.75y
Martin V.B., son of Joseph L., at Insane Asylum, 21 Aug 1871, a.38y
Mary, dau of John & Sarah, Jul 1736

RYE DEATHS

LOCKE, Mary, wife of Joseph, Nov 1803, a.37y
  Mary, widow of Joseph, 28 Jan 1825, a.81y or 91y
  Mary, widow of John, 18 Jan 1869, a.71y or 72y
  Mary, widow of William, 29 Jun 1873, a.72y 3mo
  Mary Ann, wife of John, 10 Jan 1840, a.39y
  Mary B., wife of Jesse & relict of John W.P. Locke, 10 Mar 1852, a.45y 5mo
  Mary Eliza, dau of John James, 19 Aug 1875, a.8y 5mo
  Mary Elizabeth, child of Asa, 5 Dec 1809, a.2y
  Mary Elizabeth, dau of Asa Jr., 25 Feb 1825, a.1y
  Mary Jane, dau of James H., (suicide), at Portsmouth, 18 Feb 1867, a.28y
  Mary Olive, child of Samuel J., 5 Aug 1828, a.3mo
  Nabby, wife of Simon, 8 Feb 1803
  Nabby Philbrick, wife of Job, 11 Mar 1810, a.41y
  Nancy, dau of Job, 14 Sep 1826, a.19y
  Olive, wife of Joseph, 5 Mar 1825, a.46y
  Olive (who was a Marden), 4 Dec 1835, a.88y
  Olive, wife of Joseph, 13 Mar 1859, a.66y
  Oliver Luther, son of John, (Small Pox), 17 Mar 1876, a.43y
  Patience, 11 May 1755, a.45y
  Perna, dau of Asa, 3 Oct 1829, a.16y
  Perna T., dau of Asa & Betsey, 5 Dec 1809
  Polly W., wife of Samuel J., 22 Aug 1831, a.39y
  Rhoda B., child of Jonathan, 9 Mar 1842, a.2y
  Richard, 22 May 1804, a.82y
  Richard, formerly of Rye, at Northwood, 23 Oct 1823, a.79y
  Richard, son of Richard, 26 Dec 1827, a.77y
  Richard, of Epsom, son of Richard, 10 Jul 1840, a.63y
  Richard, son of Jeremiah & Susan, 20 Jan 1877, a.82y 6mo
  Robert W., son of Samuel J., 31 Aug 1825, a.4y
  Sally, 31 Dec 1831, a.40y
  Sally H., dau of Asa, 12 Aug 1825, a.25y
  Samuel J., son of John, 29 Mar 1861, a.71y 1mo
  Sarah, dau of Jonathan & Sarah, 26 Sep 1742
  Sarah, dau of Jonathan Locke & S. Haines, 31 Dec 1796
  Sarah, wife of Richard, 8 Feb 1803, a.abt 53y
  Sarah, wife of Richard, 22 Oct 1815, a.26y
  Sarah, relict of Job, 29 Aug 1852, a.80y 6mo
  Sarah, wife of James, 6 Feb 1857, a.50y
  Sarah, dau of Hannah Locke (now wife of W.

RYE DEATHS

Marden), 23 Aug 1879, a.23y 11mo
LOCKE, Sarah Abby, dau of Joseph 2d, 22 Mar 1858, a.18y
  Sarah Ann, wife of Richard, 14 May 1870, a.70y 4mo
  Sarah Hannah, wife of John W., 12 Aug 1876, a.29y
  Sarah W., widow of Joseph L., 30 Nov 1879, a.82y 2mo 6ds
  Simon, son of Richard L. & E. Garland, 31 Jul 1863, a.92y 11mo 14ds
  Simon Jr., son of Simon, 1 Aug 1819, a.22y
  Thomas, son of Simon, 16 Sep 1824, a.17y
  Thomas B., child of Job Jr., 11 Jan 1839, a.2y
  Thomas L., son of Asa Jr., (drowned at sea), 3 Jun 1848, a.22y
  Trepenna, dau of John & Sarah, 13 Feb 1736
  Triphena, dau of Richard & Elizabeth, 3 Aug 1830, a.71y
  William (Deacon), 22 Jan 1768, a.91y
  William, child of Joseph, 26 Jan 1816, a.2y
  William, 19 Apr 1828, a.75y
  William, son of Joseph of Portsmouth, killed at Bangor, Jul 1853, a.19y
  William, son of Trefenna, 24 Jan 1873, a.72y 5mo
  Willie L., son of Isaac, 20 Aug 1870, a.5y 5mo
  Willis E., son of Wm. Harvey, 22 Sep 1863, a.7y 11mo
  Woodbury B., son of John, at Meredith, 25 Feb 1852, a.25y
  ____, child of James, 16 Sep 1825, a.11y
  ____, child (dau) of Job, 1 May 1819
  ____, child of Job, 26 Sep 1830, a.2y
  ____, child of John & Mary Ann, 8 Sep 1825, a.2y
  ____, child of Joseph, 21 Dec 1805
  ____, child of Joseph 3rd, 25 May 1823, a.4mo
  ____, child of Joseph 4th, 22 Jan 1812
  ____, child of Samuel & Polly, 14 Sep 1830
  ____, child of Simon, 24 Aug 1811
  ____, child of Simon, 28 Aug 1812
  ____, child of Simon, 10 Nov 1813
  ____, child of Simon, 2 May 1819
  ____, child of Simon, 16 Jul 1819, a.2y
  ____, child of Trepenna, 2 Oct 1798
LORD, Daniel (Capt.), 13 Dec 1882, a.85y 2mo
  Sarah, wife of Daniel, 26 Nov 1880, a.83y 2mo
LOUD, Harrie, son of William H., 22 Sep 1869, a.3mo
LOUGEE, John, at Exeter, 5 Feb 1866, a.74y

RYE DEATHS

LOUGEE, Josephine M., 3d wife of George, 24 Oct 1885
  Semira, wife of George & dau of Ira Brown, at Exeter, 27 Oct 1863, a.30y 8mo 5ds
  _____, child of George, 28 Sep 1874, a.17ds
MACE, Addie M., wife of Horace S., 14 Nov 1881, a.22y 2mo
  Deborah, wife of Ithamar, 18 Nov 1824, a.28y
  Elizabeth Angelina, widow of John, 1 Nov 1863, a.28y
  Evrett Ann, dau of Ithamar, 11 Mar 1864, a.25y 7mo
  Frances O., wife of Chas.I., 29 Jan 1876, a.43y 6mo
  Frederick, son of Charles, 22 Dec 1873, a.1y 7mo 10ds
  Ithamar, son of John, 20 Jan 1858, a.62y
  James E., son of Ithamar, 3 Jul 1864, a.22y 8mo
  John, 7 Jun 1834
  John Jr., lost overboard at sea, 6 Jun 1822, a.25y
  John A., son of John, 24 Feb 1862, a.40y
  Levi, 1 Apr 1814
  Lizzie A., child of Mary, 20 Jan 1875, a.2mo 25ds
  Lizzie M., child of Woodbury, 28 Sep 1862, a.5mo
  Mary E., wife of Woodbury, 14 Jul 1862, a.22y 5mo
  Mary J., dau of Ithamar, 15 Oct 1838, a.8y
  Nathaniel, son of Ithamar, 19 Jun 1849, a.29y
  Rachel, wife of John, 17 Feb 1830, a.66y
  Sally, widow of Ithamar, 18 Sep 1870, a.66y 6mo
  Sarah, dau of John, 3 May 1846, a.81y
  _____, child of Ithamar, 5 Mar 1824, a.1y 3mo
  _____, child of Ithamar, 20 Nov 1824, a.1wk
  _____, child of John, 16 Sep 1805
MARDEN, Abigail, dau of James, 17 Jul 1736
  Abigail or Moses, child of Solomon, 20 Nov 1810, a.1y 8mo
  Abigail, dau of Ebenezer & Esther, 28 Mar 1820, a.81y
  Almira, dau of Solomon & Huldah, in Portsmouth, 5 Mar 1881, a.64y
  Artemissa R., dau of Daniel, 14 Aug 1858, a.9mo
  Artemissa, widow of Daniel, 5 Aug 1860, a.40y
  Benjamin, son of Benjamin & Rachel, 24 Jun 1769
  Benjamin, 1 Jan 1805, a.80y
  Benjamin, son of Benjamin, 26 Feb 1826, a.75y
  Benjamin, son of Solomon, 11 Feb 1876, a.68y 5mo

RYE DEATHS

MARDEN, Benjamin W. (Capt.), son of Samuel, 27 Oct 1882, a.82y
 Betsey, dau of Solomon, 29 Oct 1828, a.26y
 Betsey, wife of David S., 19 Jun 1848, a.55y
 Betty, dau of Nathaniel & Anna, 17 Dec 1781
 Charles (twin), son of Reuben, 19 Jul 1851, a.7y
 Charles A., son of Daniel & Artimesa, 4 Feb 1848, a.4y
 Charles C., son of Thomas, in Portsmouth, 11 Jul 1878
 Charles E., son of Daniel, 16 May 1867, a.12y
 Charley, child of Samuel 2d, 23 Mar 1828, a.1y 11mo
 Daniel, son of Samuel, 4 Mar 1860, a.47y 8mo
 David, son of David, 15 Mar 1869, a.41y
 David L., son of Stephen, 20 Dec 1860, a.70y
 David L., son of Josiah, 8 Mar 1864, a.53y
 Deliverance (Dilly), wife of Benjamin, 17 Oct 1821, a.70y
 Ebenezer, son of Nathaniel, 5 Dec 1862, a.83y 10mo
 Ebenezer, son of Ebenezer, in Boston, 24 Jul 1880, a.62y
 Eliza J., wife of Benjamin W., 28 Aug 1861, a.60y 1mo
 Elizabeth, dau of Nathaniel, 12 Jul 1788, a.3y
 Elizabeth, widow of Nat, 1 Nov 1831, a.79y
 Elizabeth, dau of David, 13 Nov 1853, a.34y
 Elizabeth M., Aug 1887, a.76y 4mo
 Ella Grace, dau of Benjamin W., 21 Mar 1866
 Ellen, child of Ebenezer, 3 Apr 1824, a.2wks
 Emery B., son of William, 6 Aug 1854, a.4y 10mo
 Eva Augusta, dau of David, 6 Mar 1872, a.17y 6mo
 Fannie Bell, dau of Charles, 24 Sep 1877, a.3mo 12ds
 Francis I., son of Ebenezer & Lovey, 2 Apr 1824
 Frank D., son of John, 21 Aug 1858, a.10mo
 Frank M., son of William B., in Portsmouth, 25 Nov 1890, a.53y
 George, child of John, 23 Sep 1865
 George, son of Josiah, 28 Feb 1888, a.84y
 Gilman, son of Thomas, 30 Mar 1861, a.23y 6mo
 Hannah, wife of Nathaniel, 11 Apr 1773, a.25y
 Hannah, wife of Benjamin, 1 Sep 1812, a.59y
 Hannah (Anna), widow of Nathaniel, 5 Jul 1813, a.54y
 Hannah, wife of Reuben, 26 Jan 1822, a.40y
 Hannah, wife of Benjamin, 9 or 16 Oct 1827, a.27y

RYE DEATHS

MARDEN, Hannah, widow of William, 21 Sep 1830
  Hannah, dau of Samuel, 14 Sep 1835, a.29y
  Hannah, wife of Josiah, 27 Aug 1850, a.69y
  Hepsebeth, dau of Samuel & Sarah, in the 7th year of her age
  Huldah, wife of Solomon, 30 Jan 1841, a.63y
  James, son of Ebenr & Ester, 14 Feb 1749/50
  James, Jul 1777, a.80y
  James, of & at Portsmouth, 16 Jun 1832, a.51y
  James, son of William, 5 Nov 1851, a.67y 8mo
  James, formerly of Portsmouth, son of Francis, 10 May 1854, a.69y
  James L., son of William & Lucy Ann, 6 Jul 1837
  Jenness, son of William & Lucy, 11 Sep 1880, a.43y 2mo 2ds
  John, son of James, 3 Jul 1756, a.32y
  Jonathan, son of Nathaniel, 8 Apr 1853, a.83y
  Jonathan T., son of Nathaniel, (fell from a tree), Mar 1803, a.8y
  Josiah, son of George of Chester, 11 Jan 1861, a.81y
  Judith, 31 Jul 1796
  Julia, wife of Eben W., at Boston, 6 Mar 1855, a.35y
  Laura A., dau of Lowell, 13 Aug 1853, a.10mo
  Laura Ann, child of Lowell, 14 Jan 1849, a.4y
  Leavitt Worcester, son of Ebenezer W., at Boston, 11 Oct 1847, a.1y 3mo
  Lizzie F., wife of William Jackson, 3 Apr 1886, a.46y
  Lovey, widow of Ebenezer, 21 Jul 1876, a.88y 2mo
  Lowell, son of Samuel (formerly of Rye), at Boston, MA, 2 Jan 1866, a.46y
  Lucy A., wife of William, 24 Aug 1870, a.58y 7mo 16ds
  Lucy Ann, dau of David, 27 Feb 1851, a.22y
  Margaret, widow of Benjamin, 17 Jun 1880, a.77y 3mo
  Martha Mason, wife of George, 8 Dec 1867, a.58y
  Mary, dau of Samuel & Sarah, in the 2d year of her age
  Mary, widow of Stephen, 4 Dec 1849, a.80y
  Mary B., dau of Ebenezer & Love, 29 Mar 1882, a.68y 7mo
  Mary Loel, dau of Lowell, at Boston, 30 Dec 1859, a.8mo
  Moses or Abigail, child of Solomon, 7 Aug 1810, a.4mo
  Moses R., son of Solomon & Huldah, 25 Jan 1884,

RYE DEATHS

a.72y 5mo
MARDEN, Nancy, wife of Samuel, 22 Jul 1832, a.54y
   Nat Dearborn, child of Benjamin, 16 Sep 1827,
      a.4y 5mo
   Nathaniel, son of Jonathan & Hepzebeth, 7 Dec
      1735
   Nathaniel, son of Jonathan, 21 Nov 1804, a.59y
   Nathaniel (Deacon), son of Ebenezer, 30 Mar
      1823, a.77y
   Otis Daniel, son of Daniel, 31 Dec 1874, a.25y
      7mo 29ds
   Phebe, dau of Samuel & Sarah, in the 5th year of
      her age
   Polly, relict of James, 1 Oct 1853, a.68y
   Rachel, dau of Benjamin & Rachel, 28 Jan 1766
   Rachel, widow of Benjamin, 11 Dec 1812, a.77y
   Rebeccah, dau of Benjamin, 22 Nov 1845, a.73y
   Reuben, son of Nathaniel, 22 Oct 1851 a.69y
   Sally, 7 Nov 1845, a.41y
   Sally, widow of Samuel 2d, 23 Mar 1860, a.71y
      6mo
   Samuel, formerly of Rye, at Boston, 6 Feb 1856,
      a.80y 6mo
   Samuel Jr., son of Benjamin, 11 May 1853, a.74y
      8mo
   Samuel Berry, son of Josiah, 28 Dec 1846, a.38y
   Sarah, dau of Samuel, 10 Jun 1839, a.28y
   Sarah, dau of Daniel, 29 Mar 1864, a.19y 5mo
   Sarah A., dau of David, 17 Oct 1851, a.37y
   Solomon, son of Benjamin, 10 Dec 1843, a.71y
   Sophia C., wife of John Salter, 11 Feb 1885,
      a.56y 5mo
   Stephen, son of Benjamin, 21 Sep 1844, a.80y
   Thomas, child of Solomon Marden, 26 Apr 1804
   Thomas, son of Stephen, 11 May 1846, a.46y
   William, son of James, 18 Jul 1736
   William, son of James, 14 Nov 1816, a.72y
   William, son of Josiah, 29 Apr 1848, a.46y
   William, son of James & Polly, 15 Jan 1883,
      a.72y 2ds
   William H., son of Thomas, 8 Aug 1865, a.24y
   Willie P., son of Nathaniel, 3 Mar 1869, a.7y
   _____, child of Thomas, 15 Jul 1831, a.7y
   _____, child of William, 6 Jul 1837, a.4y
   _____, child of Widow Eliza, 28 Jun 1846, a.9wks
MARSTON, Clara Garland, late wife of Thomas,
      (divorced), 21 Oct 1866, a.26y
   Ella Parsons, dau of John Drake, 24 Jun 1885,
      a.6y 7mo

207

RYE DEATHS

MARSTON, Hannah, relict of John, 6 Sep 1825, a.55y
  Ida Bell, child of Thomas W., 21 Mar 1862, a.1y 1mo
  John, son of John, 19 Jul 1815, a.44y
  Williard, son of John, 25 Oct 1872, a.70y 3mo
  _____, child of John, 23 Aug 1809
MASON, Betsey, 20 Nov 1820
  Daniel, 30 Oct 1834 a.92y
  Daniel, in Portsmouth, 8 Dec 1849
  Elizabeth, wife of Daniel, 5 Apr 1829, a.75y
  Joseph, of Hampton, at sea, 10 Mar 1811, a.28y
  Nicholas, son of Daniel (formerly of Rye), at Portsmouth, 28 Jul 1866, a.83y
  Samuel, at Portsmouth, 10 Sep 1837
  _____, child of Nicholas, 21 Jun 1821
MATHES (MATTHEWS), Betsey M. wife of Abraham, 23 Dec 1863, a.54y
  Edward, child of Betsey Downs, 11 Jan 1817, a.10y
  Elizabeth, widow of William T., 22 Jul 1873, a.80y
  Joseph Wm., son of Abraham, 16 Apr 1838, a.3y
  Mary, widow of Abraham, 10 Apr 1816, a.72y
  Mary Esther, child of Abraham, 8 Aug 1834, a.1y 3mo
  Oscar A., son of William, 9 Sep 1862, a.32y 7mo
  Robert, 27 Sep 1813, a.abt 45y
  Sally Ann, dau of William, 27 Aug 1874, a.50y
  William T., son of Wm., shot in the War, Jun 1864, a.45y
  William Thomas, son of Abraham, 5 Jun 1873, a.82y 6mo 22ds
  _____, son, of widow Mathes, 28 Aug 1814
McCANNON, Mary, mother of Benjamin Odiorne's wife, 22 Feb 1888, a.71y 3mo
McGREGORY, William, 13 Jan 1812, a.abt 38y
MILLER, Emily, relict of John, 25 Sep 1847, a.26y
  John, of Portsmouth, 26 Dec 1846, a.23y
MINER, George, a child belonging to Boston, 2 Dec 1847
MITCHELL, Charles, of Kittery, (drowned in a whale boat), 31 Aug 1855, a.43y
MORRILL, Benjamin, son of Joseph & Tabitha, 20 Feb 1728
MOSHER, Martha F., wife of Samuel, 4 Feb 1862, a.62y
MOSHER, Samuel, 9 Nov 1878, a.81y
MOULTON, Hannah, 15 Nov 1824, a.64y
  Jonathan, 22 May 1735

RYE DEATHS

MOULTON, Jonathan, son of Ruben & Hannah, 24 Mar 1767
  Margaret (widow), 26 Jul 1813, a.80y
  Mary, dau of Nehemiah, 31 Dec 1858, a.94y
  Mary Olive, dau of Daniel, 10 Mar 1864, a.5y 7mo
  Nehemiah, 15 Aug 1816, a.abt 75y
  Reuben, 30 Mar 1803
MOW, Elizabeth, dau of Ephraim & Olive, 30 Apr 1850, a.24y
  Hannah, relict of Samuel, 19 Dec 1851, a.78y 9mo
  Harriet, widow of Samuel P., 11 Oct 1875, a.63y 4mo 4ds
  Mary Ann, at No. Hampton, 8 Apr 1884, a.60y
  Samuel, son of Ephraim, 2 Mar 1841, a.68y
MURRAY, Elizabeth, wife of Samuel, 27 Dec 1750
NASON, ____, child of Widow Ann, 17 Apr 1838, a.8y
NAY, Martha Ann, wife of George & dau of Jos. Philbrick, at East Boston, 15 Feb 1852, a.25y
NELSON, Sarah, Mar 1803
NORRIS, Sarah, widow of Samuel (late of Portsmouth), 25 Jul 1853, a.102y
NORTON, Lucy, 22 Sep 1835, a.74y
ODIORNE, Abby, child of Ebenezer, 8 May 1805, a.3y
  Adelaide, dau of Chas. B. (suicide by drowning), 27 Sep 1859, a.16y
  Ambronetta Jane, wife of Benjamin T., 3 Oct 1865, a.23y
  Benjamin, 6 Jul 1804, a.57y
  Ebenezer, son of Benjamin, 19 Jan 1826, a.52y
  Ebenezer J., son of Ebenezer L., 28 Oct 1864, a.30y 8mo
  Ebenezer L., son of Ebenezer, suddenly in Portsmouth, 11 Nov 1865, a.65y 6mo
  Eliza, widow of Joseph, 9 May 1881, a.80y 11mo
  George, (drowned), 14 May 1828
  George E., child of Benjamin, 27 Mar 1867, a.2y 8mo
  Georgianna, dau of William (formerly of Rye), at Chelsea, 26 Jan 1869, a.31y 3mo
  Georgie, child of _____, Jul 1888
  Hannah, dau of Samuel, 25 Jan 1830, a.25y
  John J., (hung himself), 1 Jul 1886, a.45y
  John S., son of Ebenezer, 2 Nov 1847, a.40y
  Jonathan, of Portsmouth, 1749
  Jonathan B., son of Ebenezer L., 24 May 1859, a.33y
  Joseph, son of Benjamin Odiorne & Mary Beck, 20 Feb 1863, a.74y
  Joseph, son of Samuel, at Pembroke, 2 Sep 1854,

RYE DEATHS

 a.18y
ODIORNE, Joseph Jr., son of Samuel, 6 Jan 1821, a.16y
 Lizzie, child of John E., 22 Sep 1862, a.2y 6mo
 Lydia (Hitty), 4 Oct 1810
 Mary, wife of Ebenezer, 19 Oct 1820, a.49y
 Mary, wife of Ebenezer L., 19 Dec 1859, a.54y
 Mary A., 20 Jun 1890, a.46y 8mo
 Mary Abby, dau of Ebenezer L., 6 Oct 1857, a.29y
 Mary T., wife of William, 7 Apr 1867, a.66y 2mo
 Morris E., child of Benjamin, 16 Mar 1863, a.1y
 Olive, widow of Samuel, 26 Jul 1870, a.89y 8mo
 Samuel, 2 Jun 1840, a.64y
 Samuel Almond, child of Charles, 17 Sep 1852, a.9mo
 Trueman S., son of William S., 3 Dec 1881, a.57y 2mo 9ds
 William, son of Ebenezer, 4 Nov 1869, a.72y 1mo 9ds
 _____, child of Samuel & Hannah, 27 Feb 1835
 _____, child of Ebenezer, 1 Aug 1838, a.6y
 _____, child of Ebenezer, 20 Oct 1839, a.1y 6mo
 _____, (widow), 14 Dec 1822, a.77y
OTIS, John T., child of Rev. J.T., 3 May 1848, a.4y 6mo
OZEL, Pheobe, 26 Nov 1820, a.87y or 90y
PADDEFORD, Jonathan, of Marlborough or Sandwich, 13 Jan 1816, a.50-60y
PAGE, Daniel, formerly of No. Hampton, 21 Jan 1852, a.61y 5mo
 Jane, widow of Daniel, at Boston, Apr 1864
 _____, child of Daniel, 15 May 1813
 _____, child of Daniel Jr., at Boston, Apr 1864
PALMER, D. (Mrs), 24 Oct 1825
 Dodipher, 23 Oct 1824, a.30y or 39y
 _____, child of Dodipher, 30 Oct 1824, a.3y
 _____, 3 children of William, 30 Oct 1825, a.3y,2y,6y
PARKER, Elisha (Capt.) of Hopkinton, (one of 17 of Washington's Life Guards, so said), 6 Oct 1830, a.71y
PARSONS, Abigail, child of John W., 21 Mar 1816, a.5y
 Abigail, wife of Samuel, in Portsmouth, 27 Jan 1848, a.42y
 Abigail, relict of Dr. John W., 22 Sep 1857, a.75y
 Albion D., son of Thomas J., 15 Sep 1890, a.61y 6mo

RYE DEATHS

PARSONS, Amos (Col), son of Dr. Joseph, 7 Nov 1850, a.82y
  Charles G., son of John Wilkes, 9 Sep 1844, a.36y
  Charles H., of Cedar Kayo, FL, son of Thomas, 13 Sep 1867, a.31y 8mo
  Charles Wm., son of Thomas Jr., 1 Feb 1834, a.3y
  Eliza B., wife of Thomas J., 20 Dec 1888, a.83y 11mo
  Eliza Esther, dau of Thomas, 27 Sep 1839, a.15mo
  Elizabeth R., widow of Isaac D., at Portsmouth, 12 Dec 1860, a.67y
  Eveline, infant of Albion D., 5 Nov 1856, a.1d
  Hannah, wife of Joseph Jr., 17 Mar 1801, a.20y 10mo
  Hannah, dau of Rev. Samuel, 25 Jun 1840, a.82y
  Isaac D., of Portsmouth, son of A.S., at sea, 9 Aug 1850, a.52y
  John (Maj.), at Bay Port, FL, 28 May 1888, a.72y 4mo
  John Decatur, son of Maj. John of Bay Port, FL, in New York, 29 Sep 1884, a.22y 3mo
  John W. (Dr.), son of Dr. Joseph, 18 Sep 1849, a.70y 9mo
  Joseph (Dr.), son of Rev. Samuel & Mary, 8 Feb 1832, a.85y
  Mary, widow of Rev. Samuel, 15 Oct 1796
  Mary, relict of Joseph, 29 Sep 1836, a.90y
  Patty, wife of Amos S., 6 Jul 1819, a.40y
  Samuel, son of Amos S. (formerly of Rye), 7 Aug 1875, a.71y 5mo 11ds
  Sarah A., wife of Dr. Warren, 2 Nov 1850, a.29y
  Semira, child of Dr. J.W., 15 Sep 1829, a.7y
  Susan Decatur, wife of Maj. John (formerly of Rye), in New York, 20 Mar 1873, a.52y
  Thomas H., son of Thomas, at Bay Port, FL, 1 Apr 1857, a.32y 6mo
  Thomas J., son of John W., 4 Mar 1890, a.86y 2mo
  William Irving, son of Dr. Warren, 30 Mar 1851, a.2y 9mo
  William (Capt), son of Dr. J.W., at Hambourg, Germany, 3 Sep 1867, a.54y
  ____, child of Amos S., 5 Jul 1819
  ____, child of Samuel & Abigail, 14 Feb 1825, a.1y
PAUL, Susan, of Elliot, ME, 17 Apr 1852, a.68y
PEMBERTON, Helen (Mrs.), of Quebec, Canada, 14 Jul 1868, a.55y
PERKINS, Abigail, ____ of James, Feb 1803, a.66y

RYE DEATHS

PERKINS, Ada, dau of James, Mar 1888
  Betsey,, widow of Josiah, 22 Jan 1859, a.74y
  Christiana R., wife of Abraham, 23 Jul 1886, a.64y
  Eliza J., child of Abraham, 12 Mar 1850, a.3y
  Esther, dau of Elias & Mary, 14 Jul 1838
  Horace W., son of Abraham, 1 Jan 1861, a.5y
  Huldah, widow of James, 7 May 1774, a.81y
  James, 18 Apr 1774, a.79y
  James, son of James of Hampton, 2 Nov 1805, a.72-73y
  James, child of James & Mehitable, 3 Nov 1816, a.2y
  James (Lieut), son of James Perkins & wife Abigail Locke, 2 May 1852, a.83y
  James Jr., son of James, 26 Sep 1806, a.5y 6mo
  James Jr., son of Josiah, 20 Jun 1838, a.28y
  John, son of James & Mehitable, 3 Feb 1816, a.7y
  John, son of Elias, in Portsmouth, 21 Feb 1863, a.37y 10mo
  Jonathan, son of James, 13 Aug 1809, a.37y
  Josiah, son of James, 5 Dec 1848, a.74y
  Lewis L., son of Josiah, at Rowley, MA, 15 Jun 1884, a.67y 5mo
  Lovina, wife of Lewis L., 1 Jun 1880, a.66y 11mo 20ds
  Mary, wife of James, 7 Jan 1810, a.40y
  Mary, dau of Elias, at Portsmouth, 1 Jan 1859, a.31y
  Mehitable, wife of Lieut. James & widow of Peter Garland, 2 May 1850, a.75y
  William of & at New Market, 1732, a.116y
  _____, child of Abraham, 3 May 1845, a.3y
PERRY, Abigail, dau of Samuel B. Berry, 2 May 1890,, a.80y 4mo
PHILBRICK, Abigail, widow of James, 8 Feb 1862, a.82y
  Abigail, widow of Jonathan, 8 Apr 1873, a.71y
  Adeline, child of James, 18 Mar 1816, a.4y
  Angeline, 17 Apr 1885, a.60y
  Ann Matilda, dau of John, 3 Aug 1851, a.18y
  Anna, relict of Joseph, 5 Jan 1824
  Benjamin, son of Joses, (Consumption), 11 Mar 1820, a.34y
  Benjamin, son of Benjamin, 21 Jan 1857, a.37y 1mo
  Bertha L., dau of J. Curtis, 7 Mar 1883, a.12y
  Betsey (widow), 1 Sep 1840
  Betsey, wife of Joseph, 6 Apr 1871, a.82y 2mo

RYE DEATHS

PHILBRICK, Bickford, son of Jose, at Brentwood, Apr 1888
Caroline, dau of John, 15 Nov 1855, a.18y
Charlotte Addie, dau of Thomas H., 10 Aug 1863, a.14y
Clarissa, wife of Thomas, 22 Jul 1850, a.45y
Daniel, son of Joses, at Portsmouth, 20 Jul 1868, a.78y 3mo
Daniel, son of Jonathan & Sarah, 11 Mar 1882, a.76y 9mo
Daniel D., son of Thomas (late of Rye), at Boston, 28 Aug 1864, a.24y 2mo
Data, child of Jonathan, 24 Dec 1843, a.8y
David, son of Thomas, 23 Oct 1827, a.2y 6mo
Eliza, child of Bickford, 15 Mar 1864, a.2y 4mo
Elizabeth (widow), 14 Nov 1834
Emerson, child of James, 22 Mar 1816, a.3y
Emily, dau of Daniel, 25 Feb 1858, a.20y
Ephraim (Elder), son of Jonathan, 25 Jan 1860, a.79y 4mo
Florence M., dau of Fred & _____ Perkins of Boston, 18 Mar 1882, a.1y
Freddie B., son of Emmons B., 16 Mar 1875
Hannah, 10 Sep 1831
Harriet, dau of James, 16 Aug 1821, a.19y
Horace, son of Josiah Webster, 19 May 1852, a.14y
Ira, son of Daniel, 14 Apr 1867, a.20y
James, son of Joseph & Anna, 25 Oct 1855, a.75y 3mo
John, son of Joses & Sarah, 12 Sep 1877, a.73y 8mo 7ds
John, son of Samuel Bickford, 30 Apr 1881, a.26y 6mo
John C., son of Ephraim, 15 Jan 1869, a.50y 9mo 6ds
John E., son of J. Curtis, 10 Nov 1874, a.1y 7mo
John Ira, son of Joseph Jr. & Patty, 26 Feb 1838
John Tyler, son of Jonathan, 28 Feb 1866, a.24y
John William, son of John, 9 Aug 1866, a.19y
Jonathan, son of Joses & Abigail, 1 Apr 1822, a.76y
Jonathan, son of Joseph & Anna, 26 Apr 1843, a.70y
Jonathan, son of Jonathan, 28 Aug 1865, a.63y 3mo
Joseph, son of Jonathan & Mary, 12 Apr 1879, a.90y 11mo
Joseph 3d, son of Jonathan, 9 Dec 1873, a.76y

RYE DEATHS

27ds
PHILBRICK, Joseph 5th, in West Indies, 5 May 1826
Joses, son of Joseph & Anna, 27 Sep 1811, a.50y
Joses, 21 Jul 1835, a.68y
Joses, 18 Jun 1838, a.57y
Josiah Webster, son of Ephraim, 17 Oct 1870, a.63y 15ds
Julia Ann, 17 Dec 1831, a.22y
Langdon, son of James, 30 Jun 1824, a.19y
Louisa A., child of John, 25 Feb 1842, a.14mo
Martha, child of Bickford, 7 Mar 1864, a.5y
Martha B., widow of Joseph Jr., 16 Sep 1874, a.74y 1mo
Mary, 4 Jan 1803
Mary, 24 Mar 1813
Mary, wife of R., 25 Dec 1805
Mary, child of James, 26 Sep 1820, a.9mo
Mary (Beck), widow of Reuben, 30 Jun 1826, a.65y or 66y
Mary, dau of Samuel Bickford, 1 Nov 1877, a.18y 8mo
Mary F., 24 Nov 1839, a.16y
Moses C., son of Ephraim, 8 Apr 1875, a.62y
Nancy, widow of Joses, (fell down cellar), 2 May 1860, a.85y
Oliver B., son of Benjamin & Polly, 21 Apr 1884, a.71y 1mo 2ds
Polly, widow of Benjamin, 18 Jan 1842, a.56y
Reuben, son of Joses & Abigail, 26 Jun 1819, a.83y
Reuben, son of Reuben, 12 Jun 1831, a.59y
Reuben 3d Jr., son of Reuben & Betsey, in West Indies, 23 Feb 1819, a.24y
Sarah, wife of Joses, 22 Dec 1842, a.71y
Sarah, relict of Jonathan, 27 Apr 1854, a.83y
Sarah, widow of Ephraim, 20 Mar 1863,, a.77y
Sarah Ann, wife of Josiah Webster, 22 Sep 1870, a.60y 6mo
Sheridan, son of Jonathan, 30 Jun 1824, a.11y
Susannah, relict of Joses, 15 Apr 1843, a.78y
Thomas, son of Joses, 15 Mar 1858, a.58y
Thomas H., son of James, 13 Oct 1879, a.56y
Vienna, wife of Emmons B., 4 Nov 1769. a.29y 4mo
William, son of Joses (formerly of Rye), 1 Nov 1839, a.27y
____, child of Ephraim & Sarah, 3 Apr 1816
____, child of Jonathan, 15 Mar 1816, a.9y
____, child of Joseph, 8 Jun 1826, a.1y
____, child of Joseph Jr., 29 Jan 1833

RYE DEATHS

PHILBRICK, ____, child of Joseph Jr., 26 Feb 1838, a.3y
   ____, child of Joses, 30 Oct 1824, a.1y 2mo
   ____, child of Josiah, 27 Feb 1837, a.3wks
   ____, child of Rufus W., Jun 1861, a.1d
   ____, child (dau) of Samuel Bickford, 8 Jan 1875, a.4y
PIERCE, Hannah, widow of Andrew C., 6 Jan 1789, a.82y
PLACE, Caroline (Mrs.), 29 Dec 1872, a.38y 8mo
PLAYLE, Frederick Scheen, son of John, 21 Jul 1855, a.3mo 8ds
POOR (POWERS), Eliza, dau of Robert, 26 Dec 1871, a.77y 5mo
  Elizabeth, relict of Robert, 10 Jun 1850, a.84y
  Robert, 29 Apr 1807
  Robert, son of Robert, at sea, 25 Dec 1810
  Sarah, dau of Robert, 21 May 1867, a.75y 10mo
PORTER, Anna T., wife of Allen, 14 Nov 1871, a.59y 4mo 14ds
  Charles H., child of Huntington, 1 Sep 1816, a.3wks
  Eliphalet, at sea, 31 Jan 1824, a.25y
  Huntington, at Lynn, 7 Mar 1844, a.89y
  Huntington Jr., son of Rev. Huntington, 7 Jun 1836, a.23y 6mo
  John, son of Rev. Huntington, 29 Mar 1825, a.34y
  Nathaniel, son of Rev. Huntington, 20 Sep 1827
  Sarah, wife of Rev. Huntington, 2 Jan 1835, a.56y
  Susannah, wife of Rev. Huntington, 24 Feb 1794, a.29y
POWERS (see POOR)
PUSLEY, Willie, son of Wm A. of Boston, MA, 28 Jul 1869, a.5y
RAND, Aaron, 3 Nov 1890, a.74y 7mo
  Abby, dau of Levi & Hannah Warner, 29 Apr 1847, a.11y
  Addie P., dau of Samuel, 4 Aug 1862, a.6y
  Adeline, wife of William of Kittery (formerly of Rye), at Bangor, Aug 1854
  Amanda, child of Levi, 1 Nov 1843, a.5y
  Angolette, child of Thomas Jr., 6 Jan 1838, a.2y
  Atwell Y., son of Aaron, 7 Apr 1865, a.22y
  Betsey, wife of William, 16 Jan 1806
  Betsey, wife of John T., 18 Mar 1834, a.42y
  Betsey, relict of Joshua, 15 Aug 1857, a.84y
  Betsey, wife of Stephen, 3 Sep 1869, a.85y 26ds
  Billy, son of Samuel & Sarah, 2 Apr 1819, a.52y

RYE DEATHS

RAND, Billy, son of Dowrst, 26 Dec 1846, a.58y
  Charles Edward, of Boston, son of Thomas (formerly of Rye), shot in the Army, May 1863, a.30y 2mo
  Charles Elvin, son of Elvin, 3 Apr 1875, a.22y
  Charlotte, widow of Billey, 15 Sep 1873, a.80y 6mo
  Clara E., wife of Howard, 3 Oct 1875, a.32y
  Cyrus, son of Joseph Jr., 16 Mar 1848, a.3y
  Daniel, son of Joshua, 10 Oct 1851, a.73y 9mo
  David, formerly of Rye, in Portsmouth, 14 Oct 1851, a.75y
  David Jr., in schooner "Cadimus" at sea, 10 Jan 1820, a.20y
  David L., son of John, (after laying in bed 11 years & speechless), 20 Aug 1854, a.38y
  Dorothy, widow of Daniel, 16 Oct 1865, a.84y
  Dorothy M., widow of Samuel, at Portsmouth, 3 Jan 1888, a.84y
  Dowrst, husband of Hannah, 12 Jan 1847, a.82y
  Edward, son of Thomas, at Portsmouth, 18 Nov 1868, a.62y 10 mo
  Eliza J., wife of Jedediah, 2 Jun 1865, a.54y
  Emily, wife of Samuel, 5 Aug 1866, a.59y
  Emma Julia, dau of John Ira, 1 May 1861, a.1y
  Emma M., child of Samuel, 3 Oct 1862, a.3y 9mo
  Estella May, child of Henry S., 1 Jul 1874, a.8mo 18ds
  Esther, wife of Joshua, 2 Oct 1809, a.24y
  Fannie, dau of Charles H., 25 Aug 1884, a.15y 3mo
  Florinda, dau of Thomas, 25 Aug 1866, a.65y
  Francis, son of David L., in the War, 20 Jan 1864, a.24y
  George, 1802
  George, Mar 1803, a.59y
  Hannah, relict of John, 13 May 1812, a.62y
  Hannah, 30 Dec 1836
  Hannah, widow of Dowrst of Rye, at Portsmouth, 16 May 1860, a.90y
  Harry, son of Joshua, at Portsmouth, 5 Feb 1868, a.64y 8mo
  Horace, son of Ira, 14 May 1870, a.16y 7mo
  Ira, son of Joseph & Olive, 17 Jan 1880, a.65y 3mo 20ds
  James, son of Joshua, knocked overboard at sea, 23 Nov 1807
  James B., son of Billy, in Greenland, 28 Mar 1880, a.68y 6mo

RYE DEATHS

RAND, John, son of Joshua, 17 Sep 1808, a.67y
  John, son of John, 5 Aug 1861, a.83y
  John Tuck, son of Thomas, 29 May 1867, a.75y 10mo
  Joseph, son of Joshua & Mary, 25 Dec 1813, a.66y
  Joseph, son of Joseph, 18 Aug 1855, a.86y
  Joseph P., child of Henry S., 3 Jul 1874, a.3y
  Joshua, 13 Mar 1791
  Joshua, child of Samuel H., 24 Dec 1836, a.12y
  Joshua, son of Joseph, 20 Sep 1852, a.73y
  Joshua, (single) son of John, 22 Jan 1867, a.82y 10mo
  Lebedee, child of Joseph, Mar 1803, a.3y
  Levi M., son of Billey, 11 Mar 1874, a.62y 5mo
  Mary, dau of John & Hannah, 26 Jan 1825, a.50y
  Mary, wife of Thomas, 19 Mar 1835, a.72y
  Mary, relict of Samuel, 11 Jul 1854, a.71y
  Mary, dau of Samuel, 22 May 1858, a.50y
  Mary Abby, wife of James, 7 Feb 1866, a.22y
  Mary Tuck, dau of Thomas, 5 Mar 1851, a.52y
  Maryetta Josephine, dau of William J., 8 Apr 1852, a.3mo
  Mercy, 5 Apr 1825
  Moses, son of Joshua Jr., (Small Pox), at Portsmouth, NH 10 Jun 1811, a.23y
  Nabby, 2 Apr 1803
  Nahum, son of Joshua of Rye, at Philadelphia, 4 Jan 1884, a.70y
  Nancy, 2d wife of John, 13 Aug 1852, a.65y
  Nancy, wife of Nathaniel M., at Portsmouth, 20 Jan 1862, a.47y
  Nathaniel, Jun 1803
  Nathaniel Marden, in Portsmouth, 25 Dec 1887, a.81y 3mo
  Olive, dau of John & Hannah, 24 Feb 1836, a.47y
  Olive, relict of Joseph, 15 Dec 1859, a.85y
  Patty, relict of William, 9 Oct 1848, a.71y
  Polly, child of Joseph, (Throat Distemper), Mar 1803, a.5y
  Polly, widow of David (formerly of Rye), at Portsmouth, 21 Jun 1866, a.89y
  Reid V., son of Samuel, at Portsmouth, 28 Dec 1879, a.82y 2mo
  Richard, Apr or May 1769, a.abt 65y
  Rosilla Green, wife of James M., 1 May 1879, a.41y 2mo
  Rosamond, wife of Charles H., 13 Jun 1884, a.52y 3mo
  Ruth, wife of Joshua, 13 Dec 1752 (buried 15 Dec

RYE DEATHS

1752)
RAND, Ruth, widow of Joshua, 2 Jul 1829, a.73y
  Ruth, widow of Stephen, 1 Nov 1837, a.75y
  Sally, dau of Joseph, 9 Aug 1825, a.40y
  Samuel, Mar 1803, a.abt 50y
  Samuel, son of Ephraim, 2 Mar 1825, a.68y 3mo
  Samuel, son of Joseph, 25 Jun 1846, a.69y
  Samuel, son of Thomas, in Newcastle, 10 Mar 1875, a.80y
  Samuel, son of S.H., in No. Hampton, 24 Jan 1880
  Samuel Hunt, son of Jos., 5 Jan 1876, a.72y 8mo
  Samuel M., son of Billy, 17 Oct 1864, a.61y 3mo
  Samuel M., child of James M., 11 Sep 1874, a.1y
  Sarah, dau of Stephen, 9 Sep 1802, a.3y
  Sarah, wife of Stephen, 19 Jun 1803, a.38y
  Sarah (widow), 8 Sep 1807
  Sarah J., wife of John, at Allenstown, 22 Sep 1873, a.60y
  Sidney, wife of John, 31 Jul 1850, a.62y
  Sophia, wife of Charles, 30 May 1850, a.27y
  Stephen, son of Stephen, (fell in a clay pit), 31 Mar 1826, a.66y
  Stephen, formerly of Rye, at Boston, 4 Jan 1871, a.87y 7mo 23ds
  Susan, dau of Joseph, (suicide), 1 Feb 1859, a.49y 6mo
  Sylvannus, son of Ira, at West Tisbury, MA, 1 Aug 1862, a.19y
  Sylvia, dau of Joseph Jr. & Eleanor, 23 Sep 1831
  Thomas, son of Samuel & Sarah, 27 Feb 1839, a.79y
  Thomas Jefferson, son of John, 30 Apr 1875, a.61y
  Veranus, child of John T., 14 Mar 1837, a.10y
  William, son of Joshua, at the Alms House, 22 Jun 1854, a.73y
  _____, child of Daniel, 24 Nov 1821, a.6mo
  _____, child of Daniel Jr., 20 Feb 1833
  _____, child of John T., premature birth, 2 Feb 1821
  _____, child of Joseph, 23 Sep 1831
  _____, child of Oliver P., 25 Dec 1830, a.7y
  _____, child of Samuel H., 10 Mar 1809
  _____, child of William, 31 Aug 1816, a.9y
RANDALL, Arthur G., son of Gilbert & Mary, 10 Jun 1879, a.18y 4mo
  Benjamin, formerly of Rye, at Portsmouth, 22 Nov 1853, a.85y
  Benjamin Jr., son of Benjamin, at sea, Jun 1851,

RYE DEATHS

a.34y
RANDALL, Benjamin Franklin Waldron, son of Wm. S., 3 Jan 1876, a.40y 3mo
Betsey, widow of George, 28 Jun 1842, a.77y
Betsey, widow of George, 1 Jul 1872, a.68y
Betsey, widow of Samuel B., at Portsmouth, 14 Sep 1873, a.78y 3mo 2ds
Daniel, son of Mark & Abigail, 4 Jan 1808
Deborah, wife of William B., 21 Dec 1807, a.38y
Edward, on return trip from Demerara, 18 Apr 1806
George, 24 Dec 1820, a.55y
George, son of George, at Portsmouth, Jul 1852, a.55y
George, son of Benjamin & Sarah, at the County Farm, 23 Apr 1872, a.72y 5mo 17ds
Hannah, wife of William, 15 Oct 1833, a.40y
Hannah, 21 May 1837, a.81y
Hannah, wife of John Y. & widow of William Foye, 14 Apr 1850, a.abt 68y
Hannah Olive, wife John W. of Gosport, 30 Jul 1858, a.30y
Harriet, wife of John Wm., at the Shoals, 19 Aug 1861
Ira Gilbert, son of Wm. S., 29 Sep 1876, a.46y 2mo
James, in Rev. War, 22 Jul 1778
John, son of Mark & Abigail, 19 Oct 1781
John Y., son of William B., 4 Jul 1855, a.64y
Joseph Smith, son of Samuel B., 30 Jun 1824, a.8y
Joses, 16 Oct 1781
Levi D., in Kittery, ME, 15 Apr 1851
Mary, widow of Wm. of Gosport, dau of Abner Downs, 26 May 1864, a.53y
Mary H., wife of John C. of Gosport, 27 Sep 1856, a.27y 9mo
Reuben, son of Benjamin, at Portsmouth, Sep 1862, a.68y
Samuel B., son of George, 9 Jan 1861, a.72y
Sarah (widow), 27 Feb 1812, a.80y
Sarah, widow of Benjamin, 17 Apr 1846, a.73y
William, son of George, 17 Sep 1827
William B., son of George & Sarah, at sea, 10 Jun 1811, a.50y
_____, child of Benjamin, 6 Dec 1810
_____, child of George, 11 Jan 1808
_____, child of John, 10 Dec 1816
_____, child of Reuben, 1 Nov 1820, a.7mo

RYE DEATHS

RANDALL, _____, child of William, 4 Nov 1833, a.8y
_____, child of William B., 3 May 1807
_____, child of William B., 24 Dec 1807
REMICK, Abby S., wife of David & dau of G. Johnson, 21 Feb 1865, a.40y
  Abby S., child of George O., May 1878, a.1mo
  Amos, child of Joseph, (Measles), 15 Nov 1821, a.5y
  Amos, child of David, 5 Apr 1851, a.1y
  Betsey, widow of John Y., 27 Aug 1878, a.82y 6mo 20ds
  Caroline, wife of William, 28 Jul 1869, a.58y
  Charles, son of John Y., 14 Nov 1851, a.21y
  Daniel L., son of William, 16 Sep 1860, a.7y 10mo
  Eliza, dau of Joseph, 29 May 1871, a.58y 8mo
  Esther Y., wife of Isaac, 18 Jan 1808
  George Wm., son of William, at Calcutta, Sep 1854, a.20y
  Hannah, wife of Isaac, 31 Jul 1831, a.41y
  Isaac, son of Isaac, 3 Feb 1834, a.66y
  James Francis, child of William, 12 Nov 1841, a.1y
  John S., son of John Y., 5 Sep 1885, a.58y 11mo 1d
  John Y., son of Isaac, 13 Apr 1860, a.65y
  Joseph, son of Isaac, 14 Jul 1827, a.63y
  Joseph, child of Isaac, 12 Mar 1832
  Joseph, son of William, 19 Oct 1852, a.16y
  Lydia, wife of Isaac, 27 May 1826, a.44y
  Mary, dau of Isaac, 23 Feb 1829, a.64y
  Mary F., wife of John, 2 Mar 1861, a.31y 1mo
  Moses, son of Isaac, 23 Jun 1808, a.27mo
  Moses, formerly of Rye, at Kittery, 22 May 1837
  Nancy (Anna), wife of Moses, 29 Jan 1808
  Nancy, dau of Joseph, 27 Jan 1869, a.65y 7mo
  Sally, widow of Joseph, 13 Dec 1860, a.82y
  Sarah (widow), 23 Dec 1811, a.76y
  William, son of Isaac, 15 May 1875, a.61y
  _____, child (dau) of David, 24 Oct 1853, a.1y 7mo
  _____, child of George S., 10 Jul 1880
  _____, child of Isaac, Apr 1803
  _____, child of Isaac, 9 Jun 1831, a.4mo
  _____, child of Joseph, 5 Oct 1808
RIDDLE, Ursula (Mrs.), of Portsmouth, 19 Jun 1876, a.61y
RIGGS, Martha S., in Concord, 22 Nov 1890, a.81y
ROBBINS, _____, a boarder at Ira Marden's, 19

RYE DEATHS

Aug 1883
ROBIE, Henry, of & at Hampton, 27 Apr 1688
   John, of No. Hampton, 19 Sep 1842, a.84y
ROBINSON, Hitty, dau of Robert, 9 Sep 1867, a.58y
   James, formerly of Isles of Shoals, 1 Sep 1840, a.53y
   James M., son of James, (drowned), 30 Dec 1844, a.20y
   Mary, 21 Aug 1815, a.82y
   Sally, wife of Robert, 21 Dec 1825
   Sarah, widow of James, 26 Aug 1865, a.77y
   _____, child of James, 1 Dec 1823, a.2y
   _____, child of James, 16 Feb 1824
   _____, child of James, 30 Dec 1825
   _____, (2 infants), of James, 3 Oct 1818
SADDLER, _____, child of Ward of Mass., 15 Jun 1849, a.2wks
SALTER, Abiah, widow of Alexander, 10 May 1811, a.69y
   Alexander, Mar 1801, a.58y
   John, 22 May 1804
   Mary, wife of Alexander, 13 May 1810, a.25y
   _____, child of Alexander, 13 May 1810
SANBORN, Warren Daniel, son of Levi Thomas, 6 Apr 1879, a.2y 2mo
SARGENT, Edward, of Portsmouth, 24 Mar 1820, old age
SAUNDERS (SANDERS), George, 1786
   Henry Shapley, son of George, at sea, 12 Mar 1811, a.21y
   John, son of William & Sarah, 26 Feb 1868, a.78y 11mo
   Molly, dau of Samuel, 10 Jul 1850, a.abt 57y
   Patience L., dau of Elijah, at the Alms House, 4 Nov 1847, a.53y
   Robert, 7 Mar 1807, a.92y
   Sarah (widow), 5 May 1813, a.78y
   William, 25 Dec 1805
SCHAGLEUBERG, Nina, of NY City, dau of William & Cornelia, at Lampre's boarding house, 16 Jun 1888
SCHUTZ, Augustus, of Concord, 5 Sep 1879, a.52y
SEATON, Emily (Miss), of New York, 24 Sep 1868, a.31y
SEAVEY (SEAVY), Albert, son of Eben L., 11 Jul 1864, a.1y 6mo
   Alfred, 29 Oct 1821, a.16y 8mo
   Amos, son of William, 19 Feb 1807, a.87y or 89y
   Amos (Lieut), formerly of Rye, in Greenland, 5

221

RYE DEATHS

 Sep 1852, a.74y
SEAVEY, Anna, wife of Wm, 17 Nov 1826, a.78y
 Anna, wife of John, 26 Jan 1827, a.72y
 Anna Maria, dau of Joseph Wm., 6 Dec 1874, a.6y
  2mo 15ds
 Betsey, wife of Theodore, 12 Jun 1835, a.38y
 Betsey B., wife of Ephraim, 16 Aug 1865, a.73y
  10mo
 Caroline T., dau of John L., 10 Oct 1840,
  a.23y
 Cato (colored), 4 Apr 1829, a.98y to 108y
 Ceasar Wallis (a black man), 18 Nov 1821, a.81y
 Charlotte Ann, wife of Alfred V., 10 Mar 1869,
  a.28y 8mo
 Charlotte M., widow of James E., 11 Mar 1878,
  a.34y 6mo
 Dorothy, dau of Amos, 7 Jan 1827, a.66y
 Ebenezer Leavitt, son of Joseph & Mary, 20 Mar
  1886, a.67y 1mo 20ds
 Edward, son of Joseph, 23 Oct 1873, a.63y 3mo
  3ds
 Eliza Ann, dau of Capt. William, 28 Mar 1877,
  a.70y 8mo 14ds
 Eliza Jane, dau of Theodore, 29 Jul 1850, a.15y
 Eliza W., 10 Jan 1890, a.72y 5mo
 Elizabeth, widow of James, 14 Jul 1804, a.71y
 Elizabeth, 16 Aug 1817
 Elizabeth, relict of Capt. William, 28 Oct 1856,
  a.75y
 Elizabeth A., wife of Joseph Jackson, 25 May
  1887, a.55y 7mo
 Elizabeth G., wife of Joseph L., 19 Nov 1786,
  a.26y
 Emily, widow of John W., 28 Dec 1855, a.23y
 Ephraim, 17 Feb 1735/6, a.10y or 12y
 Ephraim, son of Joseph L., 15 Sep 1870, a.78y
  4mo 2ds
 Everett, son of Eben L., 11 Jan 1862, a.11y
 George H., son of Edward, 31 Oct 1886, a.45y
 Hannah (widow), 31 Jan 1749, a.abt 85y
 Hannah, 3 Oct 1781
 Hannah M., widow of William Warren, 4 May 1882,
  a.73y 1mo
 Harrison, son of Wm., (committed suicide), 8 Oct
  1858, a.36y
 Henry, Feb 1803
 James (Cornet), 19 Oct 1801
 James, 1 Apr 1829, a.75y
 James E., son of Edward, 12 Aug 1873

RYE DEATHS

SEAVEY, James Jr., son of James, 15 Jul 1811, a.54y
John, 24 Jul 1741, a.24y 9mo 14ds
John, 9 Feb 1821, a.61y
John L., son of William, 26 Aug 1845, a.52y
John William, son of John L., 23 Dec 1855, a.27y 2mo
John William, child of Joseph W., 10 Aug 1865, a.7mo
Joseph, father of Nabby Godfrey, buried at the expense of the town, 15 Mar 1818
Joseph, son of James, 8 Nov 1849, a.82y
Joseph L., son of Amos, 4 Mar 1803, a.52y
Joseph L., son of Joseph L., 2 Mar 1860, a.61y
Joseph Whidden, son of Joseph & Mary, 8 Aug 1877, a.69y 6mo
Lydia, probably at Portsmouth, 30 Jun 1778, a.31y
Martha, relict of Joseph L., 20 Oct 1850, a.88y
Mary, relict of Amos, 23 Feb 1807, a.83y
Mary, widow of Joseph, 7 Aug 1853, a.77y
Mary, wife of Edward, 28 Mar 1863, a.54y
Mary Abigail, dau of Ephraim, 9 Oct 1878, a.50y 8mo 14ds
Mary J., wife of Alfred V., 3 Sep 1875, a.32y
Mary S., 4 Nov 1842, a.30y
Moses, son of Samuel & Abigail, 4 Sep 1730
Nancy Johnson, widow of John D., of Portland, ME, 29 Mar 1877
Patience, wife of James, 13 Aug 1826, a.64y
Sally, dau of Joseph L., 1797, a.20y
Sarah, 31 Oct 1804, a.84y
Sarah, widow of Amos formerly of Rye, at Greenland, 3 Apr 1874, a.84y 8mo 9ds
Sarah H., dau of Joseph W. 5 Aug 1860, a.22y
Sarah L., widow of Joseph W., 18 May 1886, a.76y 8mo
Sarah Lang, child of Joseph, 23 Feb 1818, a.1y
Sidney, relict of John L., 8 Mar 1858, a.62y
Susannah, wife of Joseph, 12 Sep 1808
Theodore, son of Joseph L., 15 Jul 1857, a.71y 8mo
Thomas, 12 Feb 1794, a.74y
William, 24 Sep 1744, a.30y
William, 30 Oct 1752, a.70y
William, son of John L., 13 Mar 1824
William, son of Amos, 15 Mar 1829,, a.84y
William (Capt), son of William, 19 Sep 1854, a.80y 3mo

RYE DEATHS

SEAVEY, William L., son of Wm., 26 Sep 1802, a.1y 2mo
  William W., son of Wm., 3 Jan 1861, a.53y
  _____, child of Amos, 30 Dec 1811
  _____, child of Amos, 27 Oct 1812
  _____, child of Amos, 29 May 1813
  _____, child of Amos & Sarah, 29 Mar 1817
  _____, child of William, Oct 1788
  _____, the mother of ? William, 20 Sep 1744, a.50-52y
  _____, 30 Oct 1752, a.70y
SEWALL, Samuel (Rev.), 16 Mar 1826, a.63y
SHAPLEY (SHAPLEIGH), Abbie, wife of Reuel, 2 Oct 1881, a.40y 9mo
  Benjamin, son of James Jr., 8 May 1828, a.35y
  Betsey, wife of Henry, 3 Feb 1808
  Dolly, widow of James, 1 Jul 1830, a.27y
  George, son of James, (drowned), 4 Oct 1851, a.30y
  Henry, son of Henry C., 13 Jul 1845, a.78y
  Henry C., son of Henry, 17 Mar 1830, a.87y
  James, son of Henry, (found dead in pasture), 4 Aug 1821, a.62y
  James, son of James, (drowned), 6 Oct 1827, a.29y
  John, son of Reuben, killed in the War at Waynesborough, VA, 28 Sep 1864, a.26y
  Jotham, 30 Apr 1845
  Jotham B., son of Reuben & Lovina, 1 Sep 1850, a.20y
  Lovina, widow of Reuben, 27 Jun 1880, a.74y
  Margaret, child of Reuben, 20 Apr 1843, a.14y
  Mary, wife of Henry, 8 Mar 1843, a.76y
  Mercy H., relict of James of Gosport, 18 Nov 1847, a.80y
  Rachel, widow of Samuel, 3 Apr 1863, a.68y
  Reuben, son of Henry & Mary, 10 Jun 1868, a.61y 10mo
  Reuben Jr., son of James, 11 May 1846, a.21y
  Robert P., son of Reuben, at Darnstown in the War, (Small Pox), 2 Jun 1865, a.29y
  Sally, relict of Henry C., 2 Oct 1853, a.74y
  Sally, dau of James, 4 Dec 1875, a.84y 1mo 22ds
  Samuel, son of Henry, 7 Feb 1862, a.71y
  Semira P., dau of Reuben, 9 Jun 1869, a.26y 5mo
  _____, child of Henry, 21 Sep 1805
  _____, child of Henry, 23 Oct 1820
  _____, child of James, 30 Jun 1829, a.9y
  _____, child of Samuel, 6 Aug 1817, a.4ds

RYE DEATHS

SHEAFE, Daniel, son of Jacob, 22 Feb 1854, a.70y
SHERBURNE, James Henny, child of Jonathan, 7 Mar 1810, a.7y
  John, 1749
  Martha, dau of Andrew & Susanah, 14 Mar 1763
  Nancy, wife of Jonathan, 4 Apr 1811, a.44y
  Samuel, killed by the Indians at Casco, 4 Aug 1691
SIMES, William, in & of Portsmouth, 15 May 1880, a.74y
SIMMONDS, Alice (Miss), of Warner, (seized with cramps while bathing), 24 Jul 1862
SLEEPER, Edward, son of Richard, 16 Feb 1832, a.1y 4mo
  Eliphalet, son of Tristram, 17 Mar 1843, a.73y
  Emily, wife of Richard J., 12 Feb 1859, a.48y 5mo
  Mary, widow of Eliphalet, 30 Jun 1847, a.69y
  Ruth (widow), 23 Feb 1832
  Sally, wife of Thomas, 29 Jul 1813, a.34y
  Sarah, widow of William, 8 Jan 1861, a.85y 6mo
  Tristram, son of Benjamin & Abigail, 26 Jan 1811, a.67y
  William, son of Tristram, 2 Jan 1861, a.85y 8mo
SMITH, Anna, of No. Hampton, Sep 1819
  David, 1 Jun 1804, a.70y
  Elizabeth, relict of Samuel, 11 Sep 1847, a.87y
  Joseph, son of Samuel & Elizabeth, 20 Jan 1816, a.19y
  Mary, widow of David, 22 Nov 1810, a.75y
  Samuel, 4 Jan 1824, a.71y
  Sarah, wife of James W., 5 Nov 1884, a.38y
SPEAR, Lizzie R., wife of Charles, 10 Nov 1886, a.34y 1mo 16ds
  Mary Frances, child of Charles & Lizzie, 20 Mar 1886, a.1y 2mo
STEVENS, Alexander, (killed by lightening), 21 Jul 1856, a.36y
  Hannah, dau of Edward of Brentwood, 12 Jul 1848, a.56y
  Theodore L., child of Alexander, 5 Feb 1856, a.5mo
TARLTON, Comfort, wife of Joseph, 2 Mar 1824, a.61y
  Joseph, formerly of Portsmouth, 6 Apr 1852, a.89y 6mo
  _____, child of Comfort, 19 May 1812
THAYER, ____ (Mrs.), (convulsions), 20 Jul 1874, a.23y

RYE DEATHS

THOMAS, James, at Portsmouth, 11 Jan 1865, a.86y
  Lois, wife of James, 6 Mar 1859, a.83y
  _____, child of James, 6 Nov 1819
  _____, child of James, 24 Mar 1834
  _____, child of James, 25 Aug 1840
THURSTON, John, drowned from schooner "Rachel & Nancy" which was driven ashore at Little Neck, 23 Dec 1850
TREADWELL, Hitty (widow), a deranged woman who lived at John Webster's, 28 Dec 1819, a.80y
  Thomas, boarding in Rye, at Portsmouth, 5 Nov 1878, a.73y
TREFETHERN, Benjamin B., at Lynn, MA, 8 Mar 1872, a.66y 6mo
  Charlotte, widow of Nathaniel, 19 Dec 1868, a.84y 3mo
  Daniel, 6 May 1887, a.47y 4mo
  Daniel J., son of Nathaniel, 8 Jun 1841, a.29y
  Eliza, wife of Sebastian (formerly of Rye), at _____stick, Ill., 29 Dec 1854, a.45y
  Elizabeth, relict of William, 12 Feb 1837, a.83y
  Franklin P., son of Samuel, 2 Aug 1853, a.2y
  Hannah J., child of Thomas, 7 Feb 1842, a.14mo
  Hannah L., widow of Joseph, 29 Aug 1863, a.72y
  Hanson Hoit, son of William, 12 Oct 1853, a.31y
  Henry, son of Wm., 8 Sep 1828, a.33y
  Henry, son of Simon, 11 Jun 1853, a.14y
  John A., son of William & Elizabeth, 4 Oct 1870, a.71y 2mo
  Joseph, son of Samuel, 4 Aug 1853, a.4y
  Joseph, son of William, 10 Feb 1859, a.71y 5mo
  Levi, son of Jos., (lived in Boston), at Portsmouth, 15 Jul 1848, a.29y
  Levi B., formerly of Rye, at Kittery, 5 Oct 1858, a.50y
  Louisa, widow of Simon, at Portsmouth, 5 Mar 1865, a.50y
  Lydia, 1st wife of William, 9 Jun 1820, a.43y
  Mary, widow of John A., Sep 1888, a.79y
  Mary Eliza, child of George LeRoy, 30 Aug 1865, a.1y 7mo
  Nat, son of William, 18 Mar 1856, a.71y
  Olive B., wife of Joseph P., 14 Apr 1889, a.73y 3mo 20ds
  Sabrina, wife of Daniel, 6 Jan 1842, a.28y
  Samuel, son of Joseph, 10 Apr 1869, a.47y 7ds
  Samuel H., son of Samuel, (fell 55 feet from a building & lived 8 days), at Boston, 22 Dec 1873

RYE DEATHS

TREFETHERN, Sarah P., wife of Oliver, 13 Sep 1875, a.39y
  Simon, son of Jos., 8 Sep 1861, a.50y
  Susannah, widow of Wm., 14 Aug 1864, a.83y
  Susie E., dau of Charles E., 7 Jan 1880, a.1y 3mo
  Walter, son of Simon, 2 Mar 1850, a.14y
  William, son of Robinson, 17 Jun 1825, a.74y
  William, son of William, 5 Oct 1853, a.78y 5mo
  William, son of William, 11 Aug 1890, a.80y
  William Henry, child of Joseph, 7 May 1838, a.7y
  _____, child of Charles, 23 Sep 1854, a.10mo
  _____, child of Joseph, 21 Jul 1836
  _____, child of Nat, 18 Apr 1838, a.2y
  _____, child of Sebastian J., 24 Oct 1844, a.14ds
TUCKE (TUCKEY), Betsey (widow), of Boston, 30 Jul 1851, a.64y
  Mary, dau of Rev. Samuel Parsons, 24 Apr 1804
TUCKER, Ann, child of James, 3 Mar 1852, a.3ds
  Betsey, wife of Joseph, Mar 1803, a.26y
  Elizabeth, widow of Nathaniel, 18 Jul 1807, a.75y
  Elizabeth, dau of Nathaniel & Elizabeth, 12 Feb 1837, a.83y
  Hall, Mar 1803
  James, son of Joseph, 12 Sep 1855, a.45y
  John, (see Upham, Jay W.)
  Joseph, son of William, 6 Mar 1807
  Joseph, son of Nathaniel & Elizabeth, 14 Mar 1811, a.38y
  Joseph, son of Joseph, 8 Sep 1834, a.37y
  Olive, wife of William, 4 Nov 1816, a.50y
  Sarah (Mrs.), Feb 1803, aged said to be over 100y
  William, 9 Aug 1820, a.60y to 70y
  _____, child of William, 16 Mar 1807
  _____, child of William, 24 Aug 1886, a.3mo
TULLEY, George, 20 Jan 1877, a.35y
TURNER, Henry, supported by the Town & County, 10 Jul 1878, a.66y 8mo 23ds
UPHAM, Jay W. (alias John Tucker), in G. Falls, 14 May 1880
VARRELL (Verrill), Albert J., son of Jonathan, 5 May 1855, a.6mo
  Almar G., son of Gilman N., 16 Mar 1870, a.10mo 14ds
  Ann M., dau of Benjamin, 3 Jul 1855, a.2mo 5ds
  Anna, wife of John, 26 Jul 1807, a.44y

RYE DEATHS

VARRELL, Anna, child of William, 18 Sep 1807
Anna, relict of William, 13 Jul 1836, a.77y
Benjamin, son of Washington, 16 Apr 1857, a.36y
Betsey, dau of John, 26 Jan 1811, a.19y
Carrietta, infant of Gilman, 3 Apr 1859, a.3 1/2 mo
Cordelia, child of Richard, 18 Aug 1837, a.13y
Edward, 13 Nov 1818, a.abt 75y
Edwin H., son of Gilman, in Portsmouth, 25 Dec 1890, a.18y
Eleanor, relict of John, 6 Mar 1847, a.87y
Elizabeth, child of Benjamin, 25 Jul 1851, a.3mo
Elizabeth, relict of Samuel, 1 Nov 1857, a.67y
Ellen Maxwell, adopted dau of John, 19 Sep 1853, a.3y 9mo
Frank Otis, son of Robert W., 11 Apr 1853, a.5ds
Gilman, child of Richard, 29 Mar 1831, a.abt 3y
Hannah, relict of John, 1 Feb 1839, a.66y
Henry P., child of John, 1 Sep 1870, a.4mo
Herman, son of Gilman, 12 Oct 1868, a.1y 8mo
John, son of Solomon & Deborah, 10 Sep 1811, a.52y
John, son of Washington, 17 May 1881
John C.F., child of Gilman, 1 Jan 1857, a.14ds
Jonathan W., son of Samuel, 24 Jan 1873, a.58y 2mo 24ds
Laura A., child of William, 20 Feb 1840, a.3y
Lydia, dau of Nathaniel, 28 Jun 1845, a.34y
Lydia C., dau of Wm., drowned at the Shoals, 10 Sep 1864, a.17y
Maria, dau of R. Tucker & Polly, 9 Jun 1829, a.26y
Martha, of Saco, Me, 31 May 1844, a.25y
Martha Olive, child of John, 16 Apr 1845, a.9ds
Mary, relict of Edward, 23 Feb 1849, a.81y
Mary, wife of Richard, 1 May 1856, a.58y
Mary, widow of Washington, 12 Sep 1861, a.66y
Mary Maria, wife of John, at Portsmouth, 21 Dec 1864, a.40y
Mary Eliza, child of James T., 30 Jan 1864, a.6ds
Nancy J., wife of William, 19 Feb 1881, a.79y 11mo
Nathaniel, son of John, 18 Jan 1856, a.70y
Richard, son of Edward, at Town Farm, (found hanging in the barn), 21 Mar 1861, a.55y
Richard Harvey, son of Jonathan, 12 Apr 1855, a.11y 2mo
S. Harvey, son of Samuel, in Boston, 13 Sep

RYE DEATHS

1836, a.18y
VARRELL, Samuel, son of Edward, 29 Oct 1857, a.70y 10mo
  Sarah Anzeletta, wife of Gilman N., 28 May 1877, a.40y 8mo
Washington, son of John, 28 Dec 1857, a.58y 10mo
William, son of Solomon & Deborah, 20 Mar 1813, a.51y
William, son of Jonathan, 16 Sep 1862
William, son of William, 3 Dec 1884, a.83y 6mo
_____, child of Abigail, 21 Oct 1820, a.2mo
_____, child (dau) of Gilman N., 18 Sep 1877, a.4mo
_____, child of James, at the Shoals, 11 Jan 1867
_____, child of Robert W., 10 Aug 1864, a.5mo
_____, child of Washington, 18 Sep 1828
_____, child of Washington, 24 Mar 1831, a.4y
_____, child of William, 2 Sep 1804, a.1y
WALDRON, Elizabeth, relict of Jonathan B., 5 Jan 1835, a.72y
Jonathan Belcher, (came from Portsmouth Plains to live with old Robert Saunders), 25 Oct 1813, a.52y
Joshua, formerly of Rye, at Portsmouth, Jun 1855
Lydia, widow of Richard H., at Portsmouth, 21 Dec 1864, a.61y 9mo
Martha, wife of Robert S., 25 Dec 1831, a.42y
Richard H., son of Jonathan, at Portsmouth, May 1864, a.64y
Robert S., son of Jonathan B., 25 Jul 1835, a.42y
Sarah, wife of Richard H., 5 May 1846, a.31y
_____, child of Richard H., 20 Jul 1846
WALKER, Adeline H., wife of Levi T., 1 Sep 1858, a.26y
Augusta M., wife of George, 7 Mar 1886, a.31y 10mo 28ds
George Storer, son of Jesse M. & Jane Sleeper, 11 Mar 1848, a.4y
Hannah, wife of Samuel, 8 Dec 1858, a.78y 5mo
Helen, dau of Levi, 28 Nov 1858, a.1y 8mo
Jenness, son of Albert M., 24 Aug 1865, a.2y
Jesse M., son of Samuel, at the Navy Yard, 8 Oct 1867, a.68y
Jonathan Towle, son of Samuel, 29 Dec 1884, a.80y 3mo
Levi Henry, child of Jonathan T., 30 Oct 1845, a.6y

WALKER, Levi Towle, son of Samuel, 12 Aug 1874, a.65y
  Mary E., wife of Jonathan T., 11 Apr 1858, a.51y 3mo
  Nathaniel, son of Samuel, at Georgetown, DC, 24 Feb 1854, a.36y
  Samuel, 2 Apr 1862, a.86y 2mo
  William, son of Samuel, drowned at sea, 3 May 1831, a.24y
  _____, child of George, 12 Dec 1872, a.4ds
  _____, child of Capt. William of Concord, 12 Aug 1874, a.1mo
WALLIS, Dorothy, wife of Ebenezer, 20 Oct 1813, a.89y
  Ebenezer, son of William, 30 Mar 1812, a.90y
  Elizabeth, wife of Samuel, 9 Jun 1827, a.73y
  Phillis (a negro woman), 17 Mar 1821, a.80y
  Samuel (Lieut.), son of Samuel, 25 Feb 1832, a.85y
WATERS, Esther (Goulde), 18 Mar 1832 a.75y
  Mary, 11 Apr 1793
WATSON, Moody, of Nottingham, 21 May 1875, a.73y 8mo
WEBSTER, Abby, dau of Mark R., 19 Sep 1862, a.21y
  Betsey, wife of Richard, 14 Mar 1826, a.70y
  Daniel, son of Richard Jr., 21 Nov 1865, a.51y
  Daniel C., son of John H. & Elizabeth, 7 May 1880, a.47y
  Dorothy, widow of John, 9 Aug 1837, a.84y
  Eliza, widow of Jeremy, 10 Sep 1865, a.60y 10mo
  Elizabeth H., widow of John H., 11 Oct 1880, a.78y 10mo 28ds
  Fanny, dau of Josiah, at Boston, 25 Dec 1805, a.15y
  Jeremy, son of John, 4 Mar 1842, a.50y
  John, son of Josiah, 22 Sep 1823, a.72y
  John H., son of John, 2 Aug 1866, a.71y
  Josiah, (found dead in the barn), 1764, a.40y
  Josiah, son of Josiah, 16 May 1805, a.48y
  Mark R., son of Richard, 17 Jul 1865, a.71y 2mo
  Martha, 18 Nov 1798
  Olive R., dau of Richard, 15 Aug 1802, a.5y 9mo
  Patty, wife of Josiah, 1798, a.84y
  Polly, widow of Richard, at Portsmouth, 14 Apr 1867, a.75y
  Richard, son of Josiah, 16 Jan 1836, a.83y
  Richard, son of Richard & Elizabeth, at Portsmouth, 1 Nov 1856
  Sabrina, wife of Daniel, at Portsmouth, 21 Sep

RYE DEATHS

1863
WEBSTER, _____, child of Elizabeth (widow of Jeremy), 8 Jun 1842, a.2y
WEDGEWOOD, Abby, dau of David & Polly, (insane), 29 Nov 1882, a.61y 1mo
 Charles, son of David, 27 Dec 1862, a.43y 6mo
 David, 23 Aug 1814, a.44y
 David, son of David & Polly, 23 Jun 1837, a.6y
 David, son of Jonathan, 31 Aug 1878, a.86y 3mo
 Eliphalet, son of David, 28 Aug 1865, a.67y
 Gilman, son of Eliphalet, at Chicago, 19 Nov 1855, a.28y
 Hannah, relict of Jonathan, 2 Nov 1848, a.80y
 Hannah, wife of Eliphalet, 15 Jan 1855, a.56y
 Jonathan, 10 Aug 1841, a.75y
 Polly, widow of David Jr., 19 Jun 1841, a.68y
 Polly, widow of David, 27 Dec 1882, a.86y
 Sally, dau of David & Polly, 22 Jan 1838, a.7y
WELLY, Ellen, dau of William, 9 Feb 1840
WHIDDEN, Hannah, 21 Apr 1801, a.74y
WHITE, Elvin, son of George & Polly, 9 Jun 1886, a.2y 5mo 28ds
WILLEY, Martha, wife of Samuel, 7 Jun 1855, a.74y
WILLIAMS, _____, child of Charles, 15 Jun 1859, a.5ds
WOODBURY, Betsey (Patty), 2 Nov 1820, a.43y
 Charles, (drowned himself), 5 Jul 1881, a.abt 50y
WOODMAN, Jonathan, 9 Dec 1805
 Jonathan, (fell in the barn on the 10th), 11 Aug 1859, a.66y
 Mary G., wife of Emery, 20 Jan 1886, a.48y 8mo
 Sarah, widow of Jonathan, (fell in the well), 15 Mar 1860, a.74y
 _____, child of Emery, 3 Apr 1862, a.3ds
 _____, child of Emery, 18 May 1863, a.5ds
 _____, child of Jonathan, 6 Jul 1821, a.4y
YEATON, Hopeley, son of Ebenezer of Newcastle, 30 Jan 1875, a.83y
 Lavinia, wife of William F., 28 Aug 1870, a.51y 6mo 6ds
 Lydia S., widow of Hopley, at Newcastle, 15 Jun 1879, a.84y
 William F., son of Hopley & Lydia, 8 Aug 1880, a.66y 4mo 23ds
YOUNG, Annah E., wife of William P., 12 Nov 1860, a.22y
 Willie, son of William P. of Portsmouth, 12 Oct 1860, a.1y 4mo

RYE DEATHS

SURNAME MISSING

_____, child of Richard, 23 Dec 1804
_____, a nurse? child at John Locke's, 24 Mar 1832
_____, Five persons perished from a vessel which came ashore at the Wallis farm where Hopley Yeaton lived, 30 Nov 1842
_____, a seaman from schooner "Clio" of Salem, off Dow's Beach, 18 Dec 1859, a.18y

1790 CENSUS OF RYE, NH

Berry, Ebenezer   82b   1-2-1-0-0
    Rye Town, Rockingham CO., NH

EBENEZER BERRY, bpt Rye, NH 23 Mar 1766 son of
Merrifield & Huldah (Towle) Berry (VR Rye): m Rye,
NH 10 Nov 1786 Polly Garland (VR Rye), bpt Rye, NH
22 Apr 1770 dau of Benjamin & Sarah (Jenness)
Garland (VR Rye): d Rye, NH 26 Apr 1857 aged 87y
(VR Rye).

Children: bpt Rye, NH (VR Rye)
  1. Thomas Garland, bpt 11 Oct 1789: d Rye, NH 21
     Oct 1870 (VR Rye)
  2. Ebenezer, bpt 11 Oct 1789: d at sea, 16 Nov
     1810 (VR Rye)
  3. Betsey Garland, bpt 15 Aug 1790: d Rye, NH 4
     Jan 1803 aged 13y (VR Rye)
  4. Charles, b 1792 (HR p.300)

Berry, Jacob   82b   1-0-2-0-0
    Rye Town, Rockingham Co., NH

JACOB BERRY, b Rye, NH 7 Jul 1738 son of Nehemiah
& Sarah Berry (VR Rye): m Rachel Rand (HR p.298),
bpt Rye, NH 1 Dec 1745 dau of John Rand (VR Rye),
d Rye, NH 10 Dec 1811 aged 66y (VR Rye).

Children: born Rye, NH (VR Rye)
  1. Isaac, b 20 Apr 1767: d Newcastle, NH (HR
     p.298): m Rye, NH 17 Oct 1790 Temperance
     Trefethern (VR Rye)
  2. Richard, bpt 26 Apr 1772: d Rye, NH 23 Jun
     1816 aged 43y (VR Rye): m Rye, NH 30 Mar
     1805 Olive Holmes of Portsmouth (VR Rye)
  3. Sarah, bpt 30 Nov 1777: d Rye, NH 29 Jul
     1813 aged 34y (VR Rye): m Rye, NH 1798
     Thomas Sleeper (VR Rye)

Berry, Jeremiah   82b   1-0-3-0-0
    Rye Town, Rockingham Co., NH

JEREMIAH BERRY, b 1721 son of William & Sarah
(Lane) Berry (HR p.298): d Rye, NH 24 Aug 1809
aged 87y (VR Rye): m(1) Rye, NH 3 Oct 1745 Hannah
Locke (VR Rye), b Rye, NH 1 Jul 1724 dau of Wil-

1790 CENSUS OF RYE, NH

liam & Hannah (Knowles) Locke (LG p.30), d Rye, NH 1 Jul 1770 (VR Rye): m(2) Rye, NH 8 Sep 1771 Widow Eleanor Brackett (VR Rye), b Rye, NH 8 Dec 1733 dau of Isaac & Charity (Berry) Dow (DG p.74). Jeremiah was a Corporal in Capt. Parsons' Co. in the Rev. War.

Children: bpt Rye, NH (VR Rye)
(by 1st wife)
1. Sarah, bpt 20 Apr 1746
2. Hannah, bpt 28 Jun 1747: d Rye, NH 11 Apr 1773 (VR Rye): m Rye, NH 21 Jul 1768 Nathaniel Marden (VR Rye)
3. Sarah, bpt 16 Jul 1749: m Rye, NH 17 Oct 1776 Aaron Jenness (VR Rye)
4. Mary, bpt 24 Mar 1751: m Rye, NH 13 Jan 1774 Samuel Dowrst Foss (VR Rye)
5. William, bpt 15 Apr 1753: d Rye, NH 16 Dec 1827 aged 75y (VR Rye): m(1) Rye, NH 10 Nov 1774 Love Brackett (VR Rye): m(2) Rye, NH 6 Mar 1796 Elizabeth Wendell (VR Rye)
6. Jeremiah, bpt 13 Apr 1755: d 20 May 1817: m Tamsin Hayes (Straff p.25)
7. Joses, bpt 9 Oct 1757
8. Levi, bpt 4 Mar 1760: d Rye, NH 1 Apr 1833 aged 74y (VR Rye): m Rye, NH 13 Nov 1785 Sarah Jenness (VR Rye)
9. Patience, bpt 14 Feb 1762: d Rye, NH 13 Aug 1826 aged 64y (VR Rye): m Rye, NH 23 May 1780 James Seavey (VR Rye)
10. Solomon, bpt 17 Nov 1765: m Rye, NH 5 Oct 1794 Martha Kate (VR Rye)

(by 2nd wife)
11. Hannah, bpt 22 Aug 1773: d Rye, NH 10 Jan 1810 aged 36y (VR Rye): m Rye, NH 17 Apr 1801 James Locke (VR Rye)
12. Lydia, bpt 1 Dec 1776: d Rye, NH 9 Jun 1820 aged 43y (VR Rye): m Rye, NH 20 Jan 1801 William Trefethern, Jr.(VR Rye)

Berry, Jotham   82b   1-0-3-0-0
    Rye Town, Rockingham Co., NH

JOTHAM BERRY, b abt 1711 son of Samuel & Abigail (Webster) Berry: d aft 1790 (DAR I p.56): m(1) Rye, NH 11 Nov 1731 Mary Bates (VR Rye), dau of William Bates: m(2) Rye, NH 16 Apr 1780 widow Tryphene Sanders (VR Rye), b 24 Apr 1729 dau of

1790 CENSUS OF RYE, NH

Joses & Abigail (Locke) Philbrick (HR p.490).

Children: born Rye, NH
1. Sarah, b abt 1733: m Rye, NH 18 Jul 1751 George Randall (VR Rye)
2. Timothy, b abt 1735: d aft 1800: m Rye, NH 19 May 1760 Mary Tucker (VR Rye)
3. Samuel, bpt 20 Apr 1741: d aft 1790 (DAR I p.56): m(1) Rye, NH 26 Aug 1762 Molly Foss (VR Rye): m(2) Rye, NH 13 Nov 1780 Eliza Marden (VR Rye)
4. Rachel, bpt 3 Jul 1743: d Rye NH 9 Nov 1806 (VR Rye): m(1) Rye, NH 6 Dec 1764 Ithamar Mace (VR Rye): m(2) Joseph Hall
5. Judith, bpt Jun 1745: m abt 1766 Jacob Tibbets
6. Mary, d unmd (HR p.299)

Berry, Levi   82b 1-1-3-0-0
Rye Town, Rockingham Co., NH

LEVI BERRY, bpt Rye, NH 4 Mar 1760 son of Jeremiah & Hannah (Locke) Berry (VR Rye): d Rye, NH 1 Apr 1833 aged 74y (VR Rye): m Rye, NH 13 Nov 1785 Sarah Jenness (VR Rye), b Rye, NH 11 May 1764 dau of Joseph & Mary (Dow) Jenness (VR Rye), d Rye NH 6 Sep 1851 aged 87y (VR Rye).

Children: born Rye, NH (VR Rye)
1. Mary, bpt 21 May 1786: d Rye, NH 13 May 1810 aged 25y (VR Rye): m Rye, NH 18 Mar 1803 Alexander Salter (VR Rye)
2. Sally, bpt 20 May 1787: d Rye, NH 16 May 1822 aged 35y (VR Rye): m Rye, NH 27 Apr 1806 Simon Goss (VR Rye)
3. Joseph Jenness, b 17 May 1789; bpt 11 Jul 1789: d Rye, NH 2 Jun 1868 aged 79y (VR Rye): m(1) 1812 Betsey Wedgewood m(2) Rye, NH 1818 Hannah W. Locke (LG p.65)
4. Hannah Locke, b 19 Jun 1791; bpt 4 Sep 1791: d Rye, NH 29 Aug 1863 aged 72y (VR Rye): m Rye, NH 29 Jan 1810 Joseph Trefethern (VR Rye)
5. Olive, b 24 Jun 1793; bpt 16 Mar 1794: d Rye, NH 13 Mar 1859 aged 66y (VR Rye): m 4 Aug 1811 Joseph Locke (LG p.144)
6. Betsey, bpt 7 Oct 1798: d Rye, NH 23 Feb 1859 aged 62y (VR Rye): m Rye, NH 3 Oct 1821

1790 CENSUS OF RYE, NH

    Joseph Berry (VR Rye)
7. Nancy (Anna) Jenness, bpt 8 May 1803: d Rye, NH 19 Feb 1881 (VR Rye): m Rye, NH 22 May 1825 William Varrell (VR Rye)
8. Levi, b 19 Sep 1804 (HR p. 299): d Rye, NH 27 Sep 1873 aged 69y (VR Rye)

Berry, Merryfield   82b   2-0-3-0-0
    Rye Town, Rockingham Co., NH

MERRYFIELD BERRY, b Rye, NH 15 Aug 1733 son of Ebenezer & Mary (Kingman) Berry (VR Rye); d Rye, NH 20 May 1817 aged 84y (VR Rye): m Rye, NH 17 Aug 1756 Huldah Towle (VR Rye), bpt Hampton, NH 14 Dec 1735 dau of James & Kezia (Perkins) Towle (HH p.1002), d Rye, NH 9 Nov 1809 (VR Rye).

Children: born Rye, NH (VR Rye)
1. James Towle, b 15 Mar 1758: d Rye, NH 29 Oct 1818 aged 60y (VR Rye): m Greenland, NH 10 Dec 1778 Hannah Randall (VR Green p.7)
2. Huldah, b 26 Oct 1760: d abt 1776
3. Olly, b 19 Sep 1763: d Rye, NH 7 Jun 1823 aged 60y (VR Rye): m Rye, NH 22 Jun 1786 John Bean Jenness (VR Rye)
4. Ebenezer, b 15 Mar 1766: m Rye, NH 10 Nov 1786 Polly Garland (VR Rye)
5. Abigail, b 26 Dec 1769: d Rye, NH 28 Feb 1808 (VR Rye): m Rye, NH 9 Aug 1789 Edmond Johnson (VR Rye)

Berry, Samuel   82b   1-1-3-0-0
    Rye Town, Rockingham Co., NH

SAMUEL BERRY, bpt Rye, NH 20 Apr 1741 son of Jotham & Mary (Bates) Berry (VR Rye): d aft 1790 (DAR I p.56): m(1) Rye, NH 26 Aug 1762 Molly Foss (VR Rye), bpt Feb 1745 dau of Nathaniel & Mary (Tucker) Foss (VR Rye): m(2) Rye, NH 13 Nov 1780 Eliza Marden (VR Rye). Samuel served under Capt. Parsons in the Rev. War.

Children: bpt Rye, NH (VR Rye)
1. Elizabeth, bpt 4 Mar 1764: d Rye, NH 28 Jun 1842 aged 77y (VR Rye): m Rye, NH 14 Nov 1782 George Randall (VR Rye)
2. Molly, bpt 24 Nov 1765

1790 CENSUS OF RYE, NH

   3. Molly, bpt 13 Sep 1767: d Rye, NH 8 Mar 1843 aged 76y (VR Rye): m Rye, NH 16 Sep 1790 Henry Shapley (VR Rye)
   4. Jotham, bpt 5 Oct 1769
   5. Timothy, bpt 13 Mar 1773
   6. Nathaniel, bpt 13 Aug 1775: d Rye, NH 15 Apr 1834 aged 58y (VR Rye): m(1) Rye, NH 9 Feb 1797 Betsey Lang (VR Rye): m(2) Rye, NH 26 Jan 1804 Esther Hall (VR Rye)

Berry, Timothy   82b   1-1-3-0-0
   Rye Town, Rockingham Co., NH

TIMOTHY BERRY, b abt 1735 son of Jotham & Mary (Bates) Berry (HR p.300): d (of Chichester, NH in 1800): m Rye, NH 19 May 1760 Mary Tucker (VR Rye), b Rye, NH 25 Oct 1740 dau of William & Mary (Archer) Tucker (VR Rye), d. bef 1800. Timothy was a Sargeant in Capt. Joseph Parsons co. in the Rev. War.

Children: bpt Rye, NH (VR Rye)
   1. Sarah, bpt. 3 May 1761: m(1) Joseph Dow of Seabrook, NH, m(2) _____ Lake of Pittsfield, NH
   2. Susannah, bpt 10 Apr 1763: m Rye, NH 21 Apr 1811 Richard Fitzgerald of Portsmouth, NH (VR Rye)
   3. Mary, bpt 12 May 1765: d Rye, NH 23 Feb 1849 (VR Rye): m Rye, NH 19 Nov 1784 Edward Varrell (VR Rye)
   4. Jotham, bpt 24 Jul 1767
   5. Samuel, bpt Sep 1769: d at sea
   6. Mehitable, bpt 6 Sep 1772
   7. Mehitable, bpt 9 Sep 1775: m James Lake of Loudon, NH
   8. Joseph, bpt 21 Sep 1777: d unmd
   9. (dau), killed at school by a thrown rock (HR p.300)

Berry, William   82b   1-2-4-0-0
   Rye Town, Rockingham Co., NH

WILLIAM BERRY, bpt Rye, NH 15 Apr 1753 son of Jeremiah & Hannah (Locke) Berry (VR Rye): d Rye, NH 16 Dec 1827 aged 75y (VR Rye): m(1) Rye, NH 10 Nov 1774 Love Brackett (VR Rye), b Rye, NH 9 Aug

1790 CENSUS OF RYE, NH

1758 dau of Samuel & Eleanor (Dow) Brackett (VR Rye), d Rye, NH 17 Jan 1795 (VR Rye): m(2) Rye, NH 6 Mar 1796 Elizabeth Wendell (VR Rye).

Children: born Rye, NH (VR Rye)
(by 1st wife)
  1. Lydia, bpt 24 Sep 1775: d Rye, NH 9 Jun 1820 aged 43y (VR Rye): m Rye, NH 20 Jan 1801 William Trefethern (VR Rye)
  2. Samuel Brackett, b 14 Apr 1777: d Rye, NH 1 Feb 1823 aged 46y (VR Rye): m Rye, NH Feb 1798 Abigail Webster (VR Rye)
  3. Hannah, b 25 Mar 1781: d Rye, NH 27 Aug 1850 aged 69y (VR Rye): m Rye, NH 24 Dec 1801 Josiah Marden (VR Rye)
  4. Jeremiah, b 16 Dec 1783: d Rye, NH 23 Mar 1820 aged 36y (VR Rye): m Rye, NH 22 Jun 1808 Sally Foss (VR Rye)
  5. Eleanor, b 25 Apr 1786: m Rye, NH 18 Feb 1808 James Locke Jr. (VR Rye)
  6. Love, b 17 May 1788; bpt 26 Jul 1789: d Rye, NH 21 Jul 1876 aged 88y (VR Rye): m Rye, NH 26 Jun 1806 Ebenezer Marden (VR Rye)
  7. William, b 10 Nov 1790
  8. Patty, bpt 28 Oct 1792: d Rye, NH 11 Sep 1826 aged 34y (VR Rye): m Rye, NH 22 Mar 1809 Job Foss (VR Rye)
(by 2nd wife)
  9. Sarah Wentworth, bpt 2 Jan 1797
  10. Dolly, b May 1798 (HR p.299): d Rye, NH 12 Jul 1822 aged 24y (VR Rye)
  11. Sarah Sargent, b 3 Sep 1799: d 13 May 1877: m 17 Feb 1823 Gilman Dearborn. Lived in Portsmouth, NH (HR p.299)
  12. Eliza, b Dec 1806: m A.K. Warren (HR p.299)

Brackett, Phebe   82b   0-0-2-0-0
    Rye Town, Rockingham Co., NH

PHEBE BRACKETT, probably the Phebe born in Newcastle, NH 7 Dec 1718 dau of Samuel & Lydia (Marston) Brackett (NEHGR v50 p.458): d Rye, NH abt 1796 unmd (HR p.308)

Brown, Jeremiah   82b   1-1-3-0-0
    Rye Town, Rockingham Co., NH

1790 CENSUS OF RYE, NH

JEREMIAH BROWN, b 3 Apr 1762 son of Jonathan & Hannah (Gove) Brown: d No. Hampton, NH 28 Dec 1840 (DAR I p.92): m Rye, NH 20 Mar 1785 Sarah Dalton (VR Rye), bpt Hampton, NH 19 Aug 1764 dau of Benjamin & Mary (May) Dalton (HH p.656). Jeremiah served as a private in Capt. Daniel Jewell's Co. for the defense of West Point (DAR Lineage Book v.38 p.119).

Children:
1. Benjamin, m Hannah Parish Perkins (DAR Line-Book v.38 p.118)

Brown, John   82b   1-4-2-0-0
     Rye Town, Rockingham Co., NH

JOHN BROWN, b Rye, NH 13 Nov 1759 son of Jonathan & Mary (Garland) Brown (VR Rye): d Rye, NH 21 Jan 1807 aged 47y (VR Rye): m Rye, NH 4 Feb 1779 Salome Allen (VR Rye), bpt Rye, NH 9 Aug 1761 dau of Jude & Elizabeth (Locke) Allen (VR Rye), d 1852 (LG p.32).

Children: born Rye, NH (HR p.313)
1. John, b 14 Aug (1779): d Rye, NH 10 Dec 1854 aged 75y (VR Rye): m(1) Rye, NH 29 Jul 1802 Sally Foss (VR Rye): m(2) Rye, NH 28 Apr 1807 Nancy Jenness (VR Rye)
2. Jonathan, b 1 Jun 1782: d Rye, NH 18 Sep 1831 aged 49y (VR Rye): m Rye, NH 5 Nov 1805 Mary Locke (VR Rye)
3. Joseph, b 22 Feb 1784: m Rye, NH 15 Mar 1810 Rachel Locke (VR Rye)
4. Elizabeth, m Joseph Yeaton
5. Mary, m Charles Mills. Lived in Concord, NH
6. Jeremiah, m Mary Ball. Lived in Hampton Falls, NH
7. Sarah, m _____ Burnham. Lived in Epsom, NH
8. James, b Nov 1789: m Rye, NH 9 Dec 1819 Martha Webster (VR Rye)
9. William, b 14 Aug 1796: m Lucretta Gray
10. Benjamin, d bef 1819: m Rye, NH 31 Mar 1817 Jane Locke (VR Rye)
11. Abigail, b 12 Mar 1802: d Rye, NH 8 Apr 1873 aged 71y (VR Rye): m Rye, NH 26 Feb 1834 Jonathan Philbrick Jr. (VR Rye)
12. Josiah, m Mary Garland. Lived in Concord, NH

1790 CENSUS OF RYE, NH

Brown, John Junr   82b   1-0-3-2-0
    Rye Town, Rockingham Co., NH

JOHN BROWN JR., b 20 Nov 1760 son of Samuel & Susannah (Knowles) Brown (HR p.313): d Rye, NH 5 Sep 1822 aged 62y (VR Rye): m Rye, NH 25 Oct 1789 Comfort Jenness (VR Rye), b 1760 dau of Job & Mary (Jenness) Jenness (HR p.383), d Rye, NH 30 Oct 1846 aged 85y (VR Rye). John was 1st cousin to John Brown above, so may have been known as John Brown Jr.

Children: born Rye, NH (VR Rye)
  1. Job Jenness, bpt 28 Aug 1791
  2. John Sam Jenness, b 10 May 1798: d Rye, NH 3 Sep 1815 aged 17y (VR Rye)

Brown, Jonathan   82b   1-1-3-0-0
    Rye Town, Rockingham Co., NH

JONATHAN BROWN, b Hampton, NH 20 Dec 1724 son of Joseph & Elizabeth (Moulton) Brown (HH p.620): d Rye, NH 27 Jan 1798 (VR Rye): m Rye, NH 3 Jan 1753 Mary Garland (VR Rye), b Hampton, NH 27 Apr 1728 dau. of John & Elizabeth (Dearborn) Garland (HH p.722).

Children: born Rye, NH (VR Rye)
  1. Elizabeth, b 21 Jun 1755: m Rye, NH 21 Nov 1776 Elijah Locke Jr (VR Rye)
  2. Joseph, b 27 Apr 1757: d Rye, NH 7 Mar 1841 (VR Rye): m 4 Dec 1777 Martha Coffin. Lived in No. Hampton.
  3. John, b 13 Nov 1759: d Rye, NH 21 Jan 1807 aged 47y (VR Rye): m Rye, NH 4 Feb 1779 Salome Allen (VR Rye)
  4. Jonathan, b 13 Apr 1762: d 15 Apr 1782 of Smallpox
  5. Mary, b 24 Aug 1766: d Rye, NH Nov 1803 aged 37y (VR Rye): m Rye, NH 16 Nov 1794 Joseph Locke Jr. (VR Rye)
  6. Abigail, b 29 Jul 1769: d Hampton, NH 29 Mar 1832 (HH p.641): m Hampton, NH Nov 1792 Theodore Coffin (HH p.641)

Dalton, Michael   82c   3-2-2-0-0
    Rye Town, Rockingham Co., NH

1790 CENSUS OF RYE, NH

MICHAEL DALTON, b Hampton, NH 13 Nov 1753 son of Benjamin & Mary (May) Dalton (HH p.656): d Rye, NH 6 Oct 1846 (VR Rye): m Mercy Philbrick (DAR I p.174), b Rye, NH 8 Jan 1763 dau of Daniel & Abigail (Marden) Philbrick (VR Rye): d Rye, NH 19 Nov 1846 aged 83y (VR Rye). Michael was placed on the pension roll of Rockingham Co., 1833 at the age of 82 years for service as a private in the New Hampshire Continental Line (DAR Lineage Book v.18 p.139).

Children: bpt Rye, NH (VR Rye)
1. Benjamin, bpt 12 Aug 1781: d Rye, NH 10 Sep 1861 aged 81y (VR Rye): m Rye, NH 3 Dec 1805 Sarah Garland (VR Rye)
2. Abigail, bpt 16 Jun 1782: d Hampton, NH 1 Mar 1869 (HH p.656): m Rye, NH 12 Feb 1799 Moses Shaw (VR Rye)
3. Daniel Philbrick, bpt 10 Jul 1785: d Rye, NH 13 Sep 1842 aged 58y (VR Rye): m Rye, NH 2 Oct 1809 Patty Brown (VR Rye)
4. Mary (Polly), bpt 15 Jul 1792: m Rye, NH 2 Sep 1813 Alexander Brown of Epsom (VR Rye)

Davison, William   82c   3-0-1-0-0
   Rye Town, Rockingham Co., NH

WILLIAM DAVIDSON, d Rye, NH 21 Mar 1807 (VR Rye): m (1) _____ Roberts: m(2) Abigail Marden (widow of Daniel Philbrick), b 22 Jul 1739 dau of Stephen & Charity (Lang) Marden (LF p.65): d Rye, NH 20 Jan 1817 aged 77y (VR Rye).

Children:
1. William, m Sarah Blake (LG p.139)
2. Josiah, d Rye, NH 14 Jun 1806 (VR Rye): m Rye, NH 28 Oct 1794 Abigail Shaw (VR Rye)
3. John, d (non compos mentis)

Dolbeare, Nicholas   82c   2-3-3-0-0
   Rye Town, Rockingham Co., NH

NICHOLAS DOLBER, b Rye, NH 8 May 1748 son of Jonathan & Hannah (Marden) Dolber (VR Rye): d Epsom, NH 24 Feb 1796 (DAR I p.197): m Rye, NH 27 May 1773 Mary Randall (VR Rye). Nicholas served in the defense of Piscataqua Harbor under Capt. Henry

1790 CENSUS OF RYE, NH

Elkins in the Rev War (DAR Lineage Book v27 p.45).

Children: bpt Rye, NH (VR Rye)
1. Jonathan, bpt 13 Mar 1774
2. Aster, b 9 Nov 1776 Epsom, NH (IGI)
3. John, bpt 23 Aug 1778: m Sally Sherburne of Portsmouth, NH
4. Patty (Martha), bpt 15 Apr 1781: m Epsom,NH 4 Oct 1804 David Libby (LIB p.138 & IGI)
5. Stephen, bpt 1783
6. Molly, bpt 13 Aug 1786
7. Billy, bpt 13 Dec 1789: m Haverhill, NH 16 Nov 1815 Hannah Kimball(IGI & DAR Lineage Book v.27 p.45)
8. Nicholas, b 31 Mar 1792 Epsom, NH (IGI): buried Epsom NH

Dow, Isaac   82c   1-4-4-0-0
     Rye Town, Rockingham Co., NH

ISAAC DOW, b Rye, NH 13 Dec 1754 son of Henry & Martha (Perkins) Dow (VR Rye): d Rye, NH 29 Nov 1793 aged 39y (VR Rye): m Rye, NH 21 Aug 1777 Elizabeth Seavey (VR Rye), b 19 Jun 1753 dau of Amos & Mary (Langdon) Seavey (CG p.121): d Rye, NH 17 Dec 1823 (VR Rye).

Children: born Rye, NH (VR Rye)
1. Patty, bpt 23 May 1779: d Rye, NH 6 Jul 1819 aged 40y (VR Rye): m Rye, NH 3 Aug 1796 Amos Parsons (VR Rye)
2. Amos, bpt 9 Jun 1781: d Newington, NH 1 Oct 1855: m Lydia Fabens (DB p.75)
3. Isaac, bpt 21 Sep 1788: d Newington, NH 25 Feb 1869: m Rye, NH 25 Feb 1809 Lydia Pickering (DB p.75)
4. Henry, bpt 1783: d Portsmouth, NH 22 Oct 1865: m(1) 22 Jan 1811 Elizabeth Fabens (DB p.76): m(2) 1 Jun 1828 Mrs. Elizabeth Briggs (Straff p.128)
5. James, bpt 13 Nov 1785: d Rye, NH 19 May 1853 aged 68y (VR Rye): m Rye, NH 6 Feb 1812 Data Drake (VR Rye)
6. Betsey, bpt 17 Jul 1791: d Rye, NH 18 Mar 1834 aged 42y (VR Rye): m Rye, NH 4 May 1820 John T. Rand (VR Rye)

1790 CENSUS OF RYE, NH

Dow, James   82c   1-0-1-0-0
   Rye Town, Rockingham Co., NH

JAMES DOW, b Rye, NH 18 Jan 1765 son of Henry & Martha (Perkins) Dow (VR Rye): d Rye, NH 8 Aug 1838 aged 73y (VR Rye): m Greenland, NH 19 Jan 1790 Mary Parsons (DB p.77), bpt Rye, NH 2 Sep 1770 dau of Joseph & Mary (Seavey) Parsons (VR Rye), d Rye, NH 7 Dec 1842 aged 72y (VR Rye).

Children:
1. Martha Locke, bpt Rye, NH 8 Sep 1799 (VR Rye): d Rye, NH 18 Sep 1885 (VR Rye): m Rye, NH 10 Aug 1820 Nathaniel G. Foye (VR Rye)

Elkins, Henry   82c   2-0-3-0-0
   Rye Town, Rockingham Co., NH

HENRY ELKINS, probably the Henry Elkins b Rye, NH 21 Sep 1739 son of Henry & Catherine (Marston) Elkins (VR Rye): d Rye, NH 16 Nov 1834 aged 95y (VR Rye): m ? Hipsey who died Rye, NH 16 Nov 1824 aged 77y (VR Rye).

Elkins, Samuel   82c   1-3-5-0-0
   Rye Town, Rockingham Co., NH

SAMUEL ELKINS, b Rye, NH 30 Jan 1744 son of Henry & Catherine (Marston) Elkins (VR Rye): d Rye, NH 21 Feb 1807 aged 62y (VR Rye): m Rye, NH 24 Jun 1773 Olive Marden (VR Rye), b Rye, NH 6 Jan 1747 dau of James & Judith (Bates) Marden (VR Rye), d Rye, NH 4 Dec 1835 aged 88y (VR Rye). Olive m(2) Rye, NH 24 May 1809 David Locke (VR Rye).

Children: born Rye, NH (VR Rye)
1. Henry, b 23 Apr 1775: m Rye, NH 1806 Mary Webster (VR Rye)
2. James, b 3 May 1777: m Rye, NH 7 Mar 1809 Mehitable Rand (VR Rye)
3. Samuel, b 14 May 1779: d Portsmouth, NH 11 Aug 1836 (VR Rye)
4. Mary, b 25 Jun 1781: m Rye, NH 10 Dec 1801 Josiah Philbrick of No. Hampton (VR Rye)
5. Olive, b 3 Oct 1783: d Rye, NH 6 Oct 1872 aged 89y (VR Rye): m Rye, NH 29 Apr 1807 Simon Chesley (VR Rye)

1790 CENSUS OF RYE, NH

6. Abigail, b 18 Apr 1786: d Rye, NH 5 Feb 1877 aged 90y (VR Rye): m(1) Rye, NH May 1823 Hartwell Hall (VR Rye): m(2) Rye, NH 7 Apr 1833 Simon Brown (VR Rye)
7. William, b 21 Dec 1788: d 3 Oct 1789 (HR p.344)

Fitzgerald, Daniel   82c   1-2-3-0-0
   Rye Town, Rockingham Co., NH

DANIEL FITZGERALD, signed a petition in Rye, Dec 1789, to raise money by lottery to build a bridge. (HR p.205).

Children: bpt Rye, NH (VR Rye)
1. Molly, bpt 21 Sep 1794
2. Nancy, bpt 21 Sep 1794

Foss, Job   82c   2-1-3-0-0
   Rye Town, Rockingham Co., NH

JOB FOSS, b abt 1725 son of Joshua & Sarah (Wallis) Foss: d (w) 1790 (LF p.54): m Rye, NH 1 Nov 1750 Sarah Lang (VR Rye), b 7 Dec 1730 (CG p.132) dau of John & Sarah (Bickford) Lang, d Strafford, NH 19 Apr 1818 (CG p.132).

Children: bpt Rye, NH (VR Rye)
1. Sarah, bpt 4 Aug 1751: m Rye, NH 6 Jun 1776 Mark Foss (VR Rye). Lived in Barrington
2. Dorothy, bpt 19 Aug 1753: d 1843 (LF p.54): m Rye, NH 20 Apr 1775 John Grant of Epsom, NH (VR Rye)
3. Hannah, bpt 17 Aug 1755: m 1798 Simon Chapman of Epsom, NH (LF p.54)
4. John, bpt Jun 1757: d Rye, NH 1 Jan 1819 (VR Rye): m Rye, NH 6 Mar 1783 Sarah Tucker (VR Rye)
5. Job, bpt 8 Jul 1759: (Rev. Soldier)
6. Joshua, bpt 30 Aug 1761: d Strafford, NH 30 Jun 1831 (CG p.132): m 1785 Elizabeth Hunt (LF p.54)
7. Mary, bpt 11 Feb 1764: d 12 Jul 1833 (Family Record): m Rye, NH 12 Apr 1787 Robert Saunders Jr (VR Rye)
8. Ebenezer, bpt 20 Sep 1767: m Rye, NH 26 Nov 1789 Mary Foss (VR Rye)

1790 CENSUS OF RYE, NH

9. Comfort, bpt 17 May 1772: d Rye, NH 4 Apr 1854 (VR Rye): m Rye, NH 28 Sep 1797 Richard Lang (VR Rye)

Foss, John   82c   1-2-1-0-0
    Rye Town, Rockingham Co., NH

JOHN FOSS, bpt Rye, NH Jun 1757 son of Job & Sarah (Lang) Foss (VR Rye): d Rye, NH 1 Jan 1819 aged 62y (VR Rye): m Rye, NH 6 Mar 1783 Sarah Tucker (VR Rye), b Rye, NH 31 May 1756 dau of Nathaniel & Elizabeth (Hall) Tucker (VR Rye), d Rye, NH 15 Jun 1833 aged 77y (VR Rye). John served under Capt. Joseph Parsons in the Rev. War.

Children: born Rye, NH (VR Rye)
1. Job, bpt 23 Jul 1786: d Rye, NH 15 Apr 1827 aged 42y (VR Rye): m Rye, NH 22 Mar 1809 Patty Berry (VR Rye)
2. Robinson, bpt 23 Nov 1788: d Rye, NH 1 Jan 1878 (VR Rye): m(1) Rye, NH 12 Nov 1818 widow Patty W. (Foss) Mason (VR Rye): m(2) Rochester, NH 17 Jan 1830 Charlotte Holmes (Straff p.176)
3. Betsey (twin), bpt 14 Jul 1793: d Rye, NH 22 Jul 1873 (VR Rye): m Rye, NH 17 Feb 1812 William Matthews (VR Rye)
4. Olive (twin), bpt 14 Jul 1793: m Hampton, NH 14 May 1815 Joseph Shephard (IGI)
5. Sarah, b (HR p.347): m Rye, NH 22 Jun 1808 Jeremiah Berry Jr. (VR Rye)
6. Richard, b 4 May 1795 (HR p.347): d Rye, NH 4 May 1842 (VR Rye): m Rye, NH 17 Oct 1819 Eliza Shapley (VR Rye)
7. Anna Partridge, bpt 8 Oct 1797: m Rye, NH 3 Jan 1830 Thomas Whidden (VR Rye)

Foss, Mary   82c   0-0-1-0-0
    Rye Town, Rockingham Co., NH

MARY FOSS (probably the widow of Wallis), b Rye, NH 8 May 1723 dau of Samuel & Rachel Dowrst (VR Rye): m Rye, NH 25 Jan 1739 Wallis Foss (VR Rye), son of Joshua & Sarah (Wallis) Foss (LND p.240).

Children: born Rye, NH (VR Rye)
1. Samuel, bpt 28 Oct 1739

1790 CENSUS OF RYE, NH

2. John, bpt 13 Jul 1746: d abt aged 30y: Lived at Rochester, NH
3. Elizabeth, bpt 26 Jun 1748
4. Rachel, bpt 10 Jun 1750: m Rye, NH 28 Nov 1779 Peter Ackerman (VR Rye)
5. Abigail, bpt 24 May 1752: d.y.
6. Samuel Dowrst, bpt 4 Aug 1754: m Rye, NH 13 Jan 1774 Mary Berry (VR Rye)
7. Abigail, bpt 30 Jan 1757: d Gray, ME abt 1815: m ? Portsmouth, NH 31 Mar 1773 Reuben Libby (LIB p.70)
8. Phineas, bpt 16 Sep 1759
9. Mary, bpt 12 Apr 1761
10. Solomon, b abt 1769: d Rye, NH 13 Nov 1824 aged 55y (VR Rye): m Jane Remick

Foss, Nathaniel   82c   2-0-4-0-0
   Rye Town, Rockingham Co., NH

NATHANIEL FOSS, b abt 1713 son of Joshua & Sarah (Wallis) Foss (LND p.240): d Rye, NH 4 Jan 1804 aged 91y (VR Rye): m Rye, NH 16 Oct 1740 Mary Tucker (VR Rye), b Rye, NH 11 Feb 1725 dau of William & Mary (Archer) Tucker (VR Rye).

Children: born Rye, NH (VR Rye)
1. Joshua, b abt 1741: m Rye, NH 29 Nov 1762 Rachel Marden (VR Rye)
2. Mary, bpt Feb 1745: m Rye, NH 26 Aug 1762 Samuel Berry (VR Rye)
3. Sarah, bpt 20 Feb 1746/7
4. William, bpt 17 Apr 1748
5. Olive Rand, bpt 5 Sep 1751
6. Jane, bpt 9 Dec 1753: m Rye, NH 19 Nov 1790 Isaac Remick (VR Rye)
7. Nathaniel, bpt 13 Jun 1756: d Rye, NH 11 Dec 1821 aged 65y (VR Rye): m Portsmouth, NH 30 Jun 1787 Mehitable Jackson (IGI)
8. Job, bpt 13 May 1759: d at sea
9. Samuel, bpt 3 Jul 1762: m 22 Nov 1789 Salome Trefethern (Straff p.174)

Foss, Rachel   82c   0-0-1-0-0
   Rye Town, Rockingham Co., NH

RACHEL FOSS, (widow of Joshua), bpt Rye, NH 27 Sep 1741 dau of William & Rachel Marden (VR Rye): d

1790 CENSUS OF RYE, NH

Rye, NH 23 Mar 1818 (VR Rye): m Rye, NH 29 Nov 1762 Joshua Foss (VR Rye), b abt 1741 son of Nathaniel & Mary (Tucker) Foss.

Children: born Rye, NH (HR p.346)
1. Elizabeth, b 1763: d Rye, NH 5 Jan 1835 aged 82y (VR Rye): m Rye, NH 24 Sep 1789 Jonathan B. Waldron (VR Rye)
2. Mary, b 1766: m Rye, NH 26 Nov 1789 Ebenezer Foss (VR Rye). Lived at Epsom, NH
3. William, b 12 Jul 1769 (VR Rye): d Rye, NH 7 Dec 1815 aged 46y (VR Rye): m Rye, NH 11 Mar 1790 Abiel Marden (VR Rye)

Foss, Samuel Dowse   82c   1-4-3-0-0
    Rye Town, Rockingham Co., NH

SAMUEL DOWRST FOSS, bpt Rye, NH 4 Aug 1754 son of Wallis & Mary (Dowrst) Foss (VR Rye): d abt1790 (DAR II p.75): m Rye, NH 13 Jan 1774 Mary Berry (VR Rye), b Rye, NH 24 Mar 1751 dau of Jeremiah & Hannah (Locke) Berry (VR Rye).

Children: born Rye, NH (VR Rye)
1. Wallis, bpt 24 Sep 1775: m Mary Libby
2. Samuel, bpt 31 Aug 1777: m Abigail Reid
3. Hannah, bpt 15 Jul 1779: d.y
4. Jeremiah Berry, bpt 23 Jul 1780: d 1794 (HR p.347)
5. Polly, bpt 22 Jun 1783: d.y.
6. Mary, bpt 10 Jul 1785: d Rye, NH 29 Aug 1874 aged 89y (VR Rye): m John Ham
7. James Seavey, bpt 22 Jun 1788: d 1860: m 1 Sep 1816 Sally Hodgdon (Straff p.175) Lived in Rochester, NH
8. Patience, b 1789 (HR p.347): m(1) Rye, NH 1 Nov 1815 James Newton (VR Rye): m(2) Joseph Butler: m(3) John Smith.
9. Sarah, bpt 3 Jul 1791 (VR Rye) m Rochester, NH 3 Dec 1812 Samuel Rand (NHGR v.5 p.147)

Foy, John   82c   3-1-2-0-0
    Rye Town, Rockingham Co., NH

JOHN FOYE, possibly the John Foye bpt Kittery, ME 20 Oct 1732 son of Charles & Hepsibah (Seavey) Foye (Old Kit p.412-3 & 811): d Rye, NH 17 Jan

1790 CENSUS OF RYE, NH

1818 aged 82y (VR Rye): m(1) Hannah Fernald: m(2) Kittery, ME 16 Apr 1767 Lydia Stevens (VR Kit p. 152), b abt 1736, d Rye, NH 17 Jun 1830 aged 94y (VR Rye).

Children:
1. William, d Rye, NH 28 Aug 1824 (VR Rye): m(1) Rye, NH 23 Feb 1795 Hannah Seavey (VR Rye): m(2) Rye, NH 15 Nov 1804 Hannah Rand (VR Rye)
2. Stephen, b abt 1757: d Rye, NH 25 Dec 1802 aged 45y (VR Rye): m Rye, NH 1 Apr 1804 Hannah Neal Mason (VR Rye)
3. Eunice, m Kittery, ME 15 Jan 1785 Benjamin Grace (VR Kit p.241)
4. John, b 6 Nov 1769: d Rye, NH 16 Dec 1859 aged 90y (VR Rye): m(1) Elizabeth Seavey: m(2) Rye, NH 1 Dec 1805 widow Hannah Rand (VR Rye): m(3) Rye, NH 5 Nov 1829 widow Martha Odiorne (VR Rye)

Garland, Benjamin   82c   3-1-3-0-0
    Rye Town, Rockingham Co., NH

BENJAMIN GARLAND, b Hampton, NH 29 Oct 1734 son of John & Elizabeth (Dearborn) Garland (HH p.722): d Rye, NH 2 May 1802 aged 67y (VR Rye): m Rye, NH 5 Dec 1757 Sarah Jenness (VR Rye), b Rye, NH 28 Apr 1736 dau of John & Elizabeth (Seavey) Jenness (VR Rye), d Rye, NH 18 Feb 1803 aged 66y (VR Rye). Benjamin was a minuteman in the Rev. War.

Children: bpt Rye, NH (VR Rye)
1. John, bpt 8 Oct 1758: d Rye, NH 24 Mar 1844 (VR Rye): m Rye, NH 18 Oct 1778 Abigail Perkins (VR Rye)
2. Elizabeth, bpt 12 Oct 1760: d Rye, NH 19 Nov 1786 aged 26y (VR Rye): m Rye, NH 17 Jul 1777 Joseph L. Seavey (VR Rye)
3. Abigail, bpt 6 Mar 1763: d Rye, NH 23 Apr 1840 (VR Rye): m Rye, NH 14 Aug 1785 Jonathan Jenness (VR Rye)
4. Sally, bpt 28 Oct 1764: d.y.
5. Benjamin, bpt 22 Mar 1767: d Rye, NH 14 Jan 1835 aged 70y (VR Rye)
6. Amos, bpt 17 Jul 1768: d Rye, NH 21 Feb 1833 aged 65y (VR Rye): m Rye, NH 18 Nov 1800 Olive Jenness (VR Rye)

1790 CENSUS OF RYE, NH

7. Mary (Polly), bpt 22 Apr 1770: d Rye, NH 26 Apr 1857 aged 87y (VR Rye): m Rye, NH 10 Nov 1786 Ebenezer Berry (VR Rye)
8. Sarah, bpt 19 Jul 1772: d Rye, NH 4 Jul 1846 aged 73y (VR Rye)
9. William, bpt 25 Jun 1775: d Rye, NH 31 Jul 1820 aged 46y (VR Rye): m Haverhill, MA 8 Jul 1808 Elizabeth Howe (VR Hav p.130)
10. Thomas, bpt 21 Sep 1777: d.y.

Garland, John 82c 1-3-3-0-0
    Rye Town, Rockingham Co., NH

JOHN GARLAND, bpt Rye, NH 8 Oct 1758 son of Benjamin & Sarah (Jenness) Garland (VR Rye): d Rye, NH 24 Mar 1844 (VR Rye): m Rye, NH 18 Oct 1778 Abigail Perkins (VR Rye), bpt Rye, NH 12 Oct 1760 dau of James & Abigail (Locke) Perkins (VR Rye), d Rye, NH 23 Jun 1844 (VR Rye). John was a soldier in Capt. Parsons' Co. in the Rev. War.

Children: born Rye, NH (VR Rye)
1. John, b 23 Nov 1776: d Rye, NH 31 Oct 1865 of No. Hampton (VR Rye): m Rye, NH 15 Aug 1799 Elizabeth Parsons (VR Rye)
2. Thomas, b 3 Mar 1779: d 1795
3. Abigail, b 14 Aug 1782: d Rye, NH 22 Sep 1857 (VR Rye): m Rye, NH 11 Aug 1803 John W. Parsons (VR Rye)
4. James, bpt 13 Aug 1786: d Rye, NH 21 Jul 1850 (VR Rye)
5. Benjamin, bpt 6 Nov 1791: d Rye, NH 5 Jul 1847 (VR Rye): m Sarah Philbrick
6. Reul, bpt 24 Feb 1799: d Rye, NH 28 Aug 1869 (VR Rye): m Rye, NH 11 Jun 1826 Patty Locke (VR Rye)

Garland, Joseph 82c 1-1-2-0-0
    Rye Town, Rockingham Co., NH

JOSEPH GARLAND, bpt Rye, NH 11 May 1760 son of Simon & Elizabeth (Brown) Garland (VR Rye); d Rye, NH 8 Mar 1846 (VR Rye): m Hampton, NH 5 Mar 1783 Patience Marston (IGI), b abt 1761; d Rye, NH 9 Sep 1844 aged 83y (VR Rye).

Children: bpt Rye, NH (VR Rye)

1790 CENSUS OF RYE, NH

1. John, bpt 21 Aug 1785: d Rye, NH 28 Oct 1854 aged 69y (VR Rye)
2. Betsey Godfrey, bpt 2 Dec 1787: d Rye, NH 14 Dec 1866 aged 79y (VR Rye)
3. Mehitable, bpt 14 Aug 1791
4. Mehitable Godfrey, bpt 20 Jul 1794: d Rye, NH 26 Apr 1873 aged 80y (VR Rye)
5. Joseph, bpt 11 Aug 1805: d Rye, NH 9 May 1857 aged 52y (VR Rye): m 6 Sep 1836 Elizabeth H. Garland (Straff p.189)

Garland, Levi   82c   2-0-1-0-0
    Rye Town, Rockingham Co., NH

LEVI GARLAND, bpt Rye, NH 16 Nov 1766 son of Peter & Mary (Leavitt) Garland (VR Rye): d Rye, NH 4 Feb 1857 aged 90y (VR Rye): m(1) Rye, NH 24 Nov 1789 Lucy Salter (VR Rye), bpt Rye, NH 5 Nov 1769 dau of John & Abiah (Webster) Salter (VR Rye), d Rye, NH 2 Jan 1814 (VR Rye): m(2) 1814 Nancy Leavitt, d Rye, NH 7 May 1846 aged 63y 11mo 24 days. Levi was a member of Capt. Coleman's cavalry in the War of 1812.

Children: bpt Rye, NH (VR Rye)
1. Levi, bpt 4 Aug 1793: d Rye, NH 17 Dec 1863 (VR Rye): m Rye, NH 21 Nov 1811 Polly Perkins (VR Rye)
2. John Sanborn, bpt 3 Apr 1796

Garland, Peter   82c   5-0-5-0-0
    Rye Town, Rockingham Co., NH

PETER GARLAND, b Hampton, NH 24 Jul 1732 son of John & Elizabeth (Dearborn) Garland (HH p.722): d Rye, NH 26 Apr 1816 aged 84y (VR Rye): m Hampton, NH 15 Sep 1757 Mary Leavitt (HH p.814), b Hampton, NH 20 Oct 1736 dau of Jonathan & Mary (Rand) Leavitt (HH p.814), d Rye, NH 12 May 1826 aged 90y (VR Rye).

Children: bpt Rye, NH (VR Rye)
1. Mary, b abt 1758: d Rye, NH 17 Mar 1843 aged 85y (VR Rye): unmd
2. Abigail, bpt 27 Apr 1760: m Rye, NH 8 Jun 1780 Isaac Lane of Chester, NH (VR Rye)
3. John, bpt 2 May 1762: d Rye, NH 23 Apr 1837

1790 CENSUS OF RYE, NH

    (VR Rye)
4. Jonathan, bpt 14 Oct 1764: d Rye, NH 23 Oct 1826 aged 62y (VR Rye): m Rye, NH 14 May 1797 Betsey Woodman (VR Rye)
5. Levi, bpt 16 Nov 1766: d Rye, NH 4 Feb 1857 (VR Rye): m(1) Rye, NH 24 Nov 1789 Lucy Salter (VR Rye): m(2) 1814 Nancy Leavitt
6. Peter, bpt 30 Oct 1768: d Rye, NH 24 Jul 1804 (VR Rye): m Rye, NH 30 Sep 1792 Mehitable Seavey (VR Rye)
7. Anna or Nancy, bpt 27 Jan 1771: d Chester, NH 2 Oct 1842: m Rye, NH 13 Nov 1798 Joseph Smith Jr of Chester, NH (VR Rye)
8. Benjamin, bpt 14 Nov 1772: d Rye, NH 4 Jun 1831 aged 58y (VR Rye): m Rye, NH 15 May 1803 Fanny Seavey (VR Rye)
9. Elizabeth, bpt Feb 1776: d Rye, NH 16 Jan 1847 aged 74y (VR Rye): unmd
10. Sarah, bpt 21 Feb 1779: d Rye, NH 8 Jun 1844 aged 64y (VR Rye): m Rye, NH 3 Dec 1805 Benjamin Dalton (VR Rye)

Garland, Simon   82c 2-0-2-0-0
    Rye Town, Rockingham Co., NH

SIMON GARLAND, b Hampton, NH 16 Jan 1726 son of John & Elizabeth (Dearborn) Garland (HH p.722): d bef 1803: m(1) Rye, NH 3 Jan 1754 Elizabeth Brown (VR Rye), b Hampton, NH 6 Aug 1727 dau of Joseph & Elizabeth (Moulton) Brown (HH p.722): possibly m(2) Rye, NH 20 Dec 1781 widow Rachel Morrison (VR Rye) who died Rye, NH 2 Apr 1803 (VR Rye).

Children: bpt Rye, NH (VR Rye)
1. Mary, bpt Mar 1756: d Hampton, NH 28 Oct 1829 (HH p.937): m Rye, NH 13 Dec 1781 John Robie (VR Rye)
2. Simon, bpt Jul 1758: m Abigail Norton
3. Joseph, bpt 11 May 1760: d Rye, NH 8 Mar 1846 (VR Rye): m Hampton, NH 5 Mar 1787 Patience Marston (IGI)
4. Elizabeth, bpt 6 Nov 1763
5. John, bpt 21 Jun 1767: d Rye, NH 28 Nov 1820 (VR Rye): m Rye, NH 28 Jan 1790 Abigail Seavey (IGI)

1790 CENSUS OF RYE, NH

Goss, James   82c 1-1-2-0-0
    Rye Town, Rockingham Co., NH

JAMES GOSS, bpt Rye, NH 8 Sep 1745 son of Thomas & Mary (Hall) Goss (VR Rye): d Rye, NH 11 Apr 1825 aged 79y (VR Rye). Probably his mother who d Rye, NH 17 Aug 1802 (VR Rye) & his sister Elizabeth Goss lived with him. Elizabeth was bpt Rye, NH 10 Dec 1752 (VR Rye) & died Rye, NH 15 Oct 1827 aged 74y (VR Rye). She had two children:

Children of Elizabeth GOSS: born Rye, NH (VR Rye)
    1. Michael D., b 20 Mar 1777: d Rye, NH 18 Mar 1851 aged 74y (VR Rye): m Rye, NH 21 Oct 1799 Sally Trundy (VR Rye)
    2. Betsey, b 7 Apr 1794: d Rye, NH 5 Dec 1870 aged 76y (VR Rye)

Goss, Levi   82c   3-2-1-0-0
    Rye Town, Rockingham Co., NH

LEVI GOSS, bpt Rye, NH 11 Jan 1747 son of Jethro & Esther (Rand) Goss: d Portsmouth, NH 23 Jul 1836 aged 88y (VR Rye): m Rye, NH 18 Aug 1767 Sarah Rand (VR Rye), bpt Rye, NH 15 Jan 1749 dau of Joshua & Mary (Moses) Rand (VR Rye), d Rye, NH 10 Apr 1821 aged 72y (VR Rye).

Children: bpt Rye, NH (VR Rye)
    1. Levi, bpt 22 Apr 1770: m Rye, NH 15 Nov 1796 Mary Saunders (VR Rye)
    2. John, bpt 2 Sep 1770: m Rye, NH 14 Jun 1790 Abigail Randall (VR Rye)
    3. Jethro, bpt 2 May 1773: m Rye, NH 16 Nov 1796 Polly Wells (VR Rye)
    4. Joshua, bpt Nov 1775
    5. Daniel, d Portsmouth, NH 2 Mar 1840 (VR Rye): m(1) Rye, NH 25 Jun 1801 Sarah Mace (VR Rye): m(2) Rye, NH 6 Apr 1820 Hannah Perkins (VR Rye)

Goss, Nathan   82c   3-1-2-0-0
    Rye Town, Rockingham Co., NH

NATHAN GOSS, bpt Rye, NH 27 Sep 1741 son of Thomas & Mary (Hall) Goss (VR Rye): d Rye, NH 23 Apr 1819 aged 77y (VR Rye): m Sarah Johnson (HR p.369), bpt

1790 CENSUS OF RYE, NH

Hampton, NH 29 Apr 1744 dau of Peter & Sarah (Dow) Johnson (HH p.772): d Rye, NH 24 Dec 1810 aged 66y (VR Rye). Nathan was a 2nd Lieutenant in Capt. Parsons Co. in the Rev. War.

Children: born Rye, NH (VR Rye)
1. Thomas, b 16 Sep 1768 (HR p.369): d Rye, NH 7 Oct 1857 (VR Rye): m(1) Rye, NH 17 Dec 1801 Sarah Marden (VR Rye): m(2) Rye, NH 2 Jun 1816 Abigail Locke (VR Rye)
2. Simon, bpt 9 Aug 1771: d Rye, NH 13 Aug 1828 aged 57y (VR Rye): m Rye, NH 27 Apr 1806 Sarah Berry (VR Rye)
3. Sally (twin), bpt 27 Aug 1775: m Rye, NH 31 Oct 1793 John Caryl (VR Rye)
4. Molly (twin), bpt 27 Aug 1775: d.y.
5. Richard, bpt Nov 1777: d Rye, NH 6 Feb 1814 aged 36y (VR Rye): m Rye, NH 4 Apr 1811 Polly Foss (VR Rye)

Gould, Mary   82c   0-0-3-0-0
    Rye Town, Rockingham Co., NH

MARY GOULD, possibly the dau of Christopher Gould who was a schoolmaster in Rye & died in the Rev. War. A widow Gould died Rye, NH 25 Dec 1805 (VR Rye). A Christopher Gould married Elizabeth Waters 31 Dec 1756, both of Durham, NH (Straff p.205).

Children of Christopher Gould: (HR p.373)
1. Ruth, (poss) m Rye, NH 30 Oct 1785 Ephraim Sufferance (VR Rye)
2. Ephraim, m Rye, NH 20 Oct 1791 Mary Towle of Epsom, NH (VR Rye)
3. Mary (Polly), b abt 1776: d Rye, NH 24 Jan 1839 aged 63y (VR Rye): m Rye, NH 1796 John Brown (VR Rye)
4. Hannah, m _____ Rundlet

Green, Richard   82c   1-4-3-0-0
    Rye Town, Rockingham Co., NH

RICHARD GREEN, b abt 1738; an Englishman & Revolutionary War soldier: d Rye, NH 4 Mar 1832 aged 94y (VR Rye): m Rye, NH 5 Mar 1778 Mary Mow (VR Rye), b Rye, NH 16 Dec 1757 dau of Ephraim & Dorcas (Marden) Mow (VR Rye), d Rye, NH 14 May 1854 aged

1790 CENSUS OF RYE, NH

96y (VR Rye).

Children: born Rye, NH (VR Rye)
1. Richard, b 13 Mar 1779: d West Indies 29 Mar 1806 (VR Rye)
2. John, b 2 Apr 1784: m Abigail Nutter. Lived at Portsmouth, NH
3. Ephraim, b 2 Jun 1786: d No. Hampton, NH
4. Thomas, b 15 May 1788: d in War of 1812
5. Mary, bpt 17 Jul 1791: d Rye, NH 6 Feb 1868 aged 76y (VR Rye): m(1) Rye, NH 28 Apr 1808 Samuel Caswell (VR Rye): m(2) Rye, NH 15 Aug 1819 William Caswell (VR Rye)
6. Dorcas Marden, b 19 Nov 1793: d Rye, NH 18 Apr 1887 aged 93y (VR Rye): m Rye, NH 24 Oct 1816 Michael Caswell (VR Rye)
7. Charles, bpt 7 Mar 1795: d Rye, NH 22 Apr 1884 (VR Rye): m 23 Mar 1826 Mary Smith Lamprey (HR p.374)
8. Joseph, bpt 6 Aug 1798
9. Samuel Marden, bpt 11 Aug 1799

Hall, Edward 82c 1-2-1-0-0
    Rye Town, Rockingham Co., NH

EDWARD HALL, bpt Rye, NH 19 Aug 1764 son of Joseph & Esther (Tucker) Hall (VR Rye): d Rye, NH 6 Jun 1827 aged 62y (VR Rye): m Rye, NH 22 Apr 1784 Sarah Rand (VR Rye), b Rye, NH 2 Nov 1764 dau of Ephraim & Mary (Smith) Rand (VR Rye), d Rye, NH 15 Nov 1851 (VR Rye).

Children: born Rye, NH (HR p.376)
1. Joseph, b Jun 1787: d at sea, 1 Apr 1806 (VR Rye): m Rye, NH 28 Nov 1805 Mary Randall (VR Rye)
2. Edward, b May 1789: d at sea, 10 Apr 1806 (VR Rye)
3. Ephraim R., b 19 Jan 1793: d at County Farm 25 Nov 1870 (VR Rye): m Rye, NH 20 Mar 1817 Nancy Rand (VR Rye)
4. William, b 26 Dec 1795: d Rye, NH 29 Jan 1864 (VR Rye): m Rye, NH 10 Jul 1824 Sarah Rand (VR Rye)

Hall, Joseph 82c 1-0-3-0-0
    Rye Town, Rockingham Co., NH

1790 CENSUS OF RYE, NH

JOSEPH HALL, b Gosport, NH abt 1730 son of Joseph & Mary (Merrifield) Hall: d Rye, NH Mar 1801 (VR Rye): m(1) Rye, NH 27 Aug 1751 Esther Tucker (VR Rye), bpt Gosport, NH 11 May 1735 dau of William & Mary (Archer) Tucker (NEHGR v66 p.255):m(2) Rye, NH 11 Jan 1781 Mary (Smith) Rand (VR Rye), b Rye, NH 25 Sep 1736 dau of David & Sarah Smith (VR Rye): m(3) widow Rachel (Berry) Mace, bpt Rye, NH 3 Jul 1743 dau of Jotham & Mary (Bates) Berry (VR Rye), d Rye, NH 9 Nov 1806 (VR Rye).

Children: bpt Rye, NH (VR Rye)
(by 1st wife)
1. Mary Tucker, bpt 6 Nov 1752
2. Joseph, bpt Jun 1754: d.y.
3. Joseph, bpt 30 Nov 1755: d in Rev. War
4. William Tucker, bpt Nov 1757: d in Rev. War
5. Sarah, bpt 16 Sep 1759: d Rye, NH Jun 1803 aged 44y (VR Rye)
6. Elizabeth, bpt 9 Aug 1761: d Rye, NH 11 Sep 1847 aged 87y (VR Rye): m Mar 1786 Samuel Smith (HR p.543)
7. Edward, bpt 19 Aug 1764: d Rye, NH 6 Jun 1827 aged 62y (VR Rye): m Rye, NH 22 Apr 1784 Sarah Rand (VR Rye)
8. Hannah, b 19 May 1780: d Rye, NH 17 May 1839 (VR Rye): unmd
(by 2nd wife)
9. Esther, bpt 7 Oct 1781: d Rye, NH 1 Oct 1876 (VR Rye): m Rye, NH 26 Jan 1804 Nathaniel Berry (VR Rye)

Hobbs, James   82c   1-1-4-0-0
    Rye Town, Rockingham Co., NH

JAMES HOBBS, b 18 Sep 1748 son of Jonathan & Mary (Berry) Hobbs (HH p.751): d Rye, NH Feb 1803 (VR Rye): m Rye, NH 6 Jan 1774 Mary Towle (VR Rye), bpt Rye, NH Apr 1755 dau of Jonathan & Elizabeth (Jenness) Towle (VR Rye), d Rye, NH 17 Dec 1825 aged 70y (VR Rye).

Children: born Rye, NH (VR Rye)
1. Lucy, b 8 Nov 1774: d Rye, NH 19 Mar 1776 (VR Rye)
2. Jonathan, bpt 22 Nov 1778: d Rye, NH 20 Dec 1810 aged 32y (VR Rye)
3. Lucy, b 2 Sep 1782: d Rye, NH 11 Dec 1783

1790 CENSUS OF RYE, NH

(VR Rye)
4. Nathaniel, bpt 13 Aug 1786: d Rye, NH 21 Jan 1788 (VR Rye)
5. Nancy (Anne), bpt 26 Jul 1789: d Rye, NH 7 Dec 1853 (VR Rye): m Rye, NH 27 Sep 1820 James Bunker (VR Rye)
6. Sally, bpt 12 May 1793
7. Perna Judkins, bpt 17 Nov 1799: d Rye, NH 26 Mar 1809 aged 16y (VR Rye)

Hobbs, Jonathan   82c   1-1-1-0-0
    Rye Town, Rockingham Co., NH

JONATHAN HOBBS, possibly the Jonathan Hobbs b 11 Oct 1754 son of Jonathan & Mary (Berry) Hobbs (HH p.751): d Rye, NH 5 Oct 1815 aged 65y (VR Rye).

Children: bapt Rye, NH (VR Rye)
1. Molly, bpt 10 Nov 1776 (original record reads dau of Jonathan with the name James written underneath & a line drawn to the last name): d 21 Jan 1788 (HR p.379)
2. Elizabeth Jenness, bpt 10 Sep 1780: d Rye, NH 1 Dec 1845 aged 65y (VR Rye): m Rye, NH 12 Nov 1799 Asa Locke (VR Rye)

Jenness, Benjamin   82c   2-0-2-0-0
    Rye Town, Rockingham Co., NH

BENJAMIN JENNESS, bpt Rye, NH 19 Jun 1763 son of Richard & Abigail (Coffin) Jenness (VR Rye): d Rye, NH 8 Feb 1824 aged 60y (VR Rye): m Rye, NH 11 Mar 1787 Martha Seavey (VR Rye), bpt Rye, NH Jun 1758 dau of Amos & Mary (Langdon) Seavey (VR Rye), d Rye, NH 27 May 1830 aged 72y (VR Rye).

Children: bpt Rye, NH (VR Rye)
1. Polly, b 9 Oct 1788: d 15 Jun 1789 (HR p.388)
2. Polly Seavey, bpt 24 Oct 1790: d Rye, NH 24 Jan 1803 aged 12y 3mo (VR Rye)
3. Richard, b 4 Sep 1794: d 25 Sep 1794 (HR p.388)
4. Abigail Coffin, bpt 19 Feb 1797: d Rye NH 28 Jan 1816 aged 19y (VR Rye)
5. Amos Seavey, bpt 3 Oct 1801: d Rye, NH 30 Mar 1886 (VR Rye): m Rye, NH Feb 1819 Sarah

1790 CENSUS OF RYE, NH

Ann Locke (LG p.238 & IGI)

Jenness, Francis   82c   1-1-6-1-0
    Rye Town, Rockingham Co., NH

FRANCIS JENNESS, bpt Rye, NH 4 Mar 1753 son of
Francis & Sarah (Garland) Jenness (VR Rye): d
(Lived at Newmarket): m abt 1778 _____ Batchelder
(HR p.387).

Children: bpt Rye, NH (VR Rye)
  1. Data, bpt 1 Jul 1781
  2. Nancy, bpt 18 Nov 1781
  3. Sally, bpt Jun 1783
  4. Polly, bpt 1 Feb 1787
  5. Hall Jackson, bpt 6 Sep 1788: m Newmarket,
     NH 24 Feb 1824 Mercy Tarlton (NHGR v6 p.160)
  6. Francis, bpt 18 Mar 1791

Jenness, Job   82c   3-0-3-2-0
    Rye Town, Rockingham Co., NH

JOB JENNESS, b Rye, NH 15 Oct 1708 son of John &
Hannah (Foss) Jenness (VR Rye): m Rye, NH 12 Sep
1735 Mary Jenness (VR Rye), b Rye, NH 25 Jan 1718
dau of Hezekiah & Ann (Folsom) Jenness (VR Rye).

Children: born Rye, NH (VR Rye)
  1. Hezekiah, b 26 Aug 1736
  2. Hannah, b 10 Oct 1738: m(1) Rye, NH 9 Dec
     1756 Thomas Rand (VR Rye): m(2) Rye, NH 12
     Dec 1769 Jonathan Woodman (VR Rye)
  3. Job, d 15 Nov 1777 in Rev. War (VR Rye)
  4. Anna, b 1750: d Rye, NH 26 Feb 1825 aged 75y
     (VR Rye)
  5. Richard, b 8 Dec 1751: d Rye, NH 20 or 27
     Jul 1809 (VR Rye): m Rye, NH 23 Jul 1778
     Mary Page (VR Rye)
  6. John, d in the Rev. War
  7. Samuel, b (HR p.383)
  8. Comfort, b 1760 (HR p.383): d Rye, NH 30 Oct
     1846 aged 85y (VR Rye): m Rye, NH 25 Oct
     1789 John Brown (VR Rye)

Jenness, John   82c   1-3-4-0-0
    Rye Town, Rockingham Co., NH

1790 CENSUS OF RYE, NH

JOHN JENNESS, bpt Rye, NH 26 Apr 1752 son of Nathaniel & Hannah (Dow) Jenness (VR Rye): m Rye, NH 23 Dec 1777 Sarah Randall (VR Rye), b Rye, NH 28 Oct 1752 dau of Mark & Abigail (Philbrick) Randall (VR Rye).

Children: bpt Rye, NH (VR Rye)
1. Sarah, bpt 20 Jul 1777
2. Olive, bpt 21 Jun 1778
3. Hannah, bpt Jul 1780
4. John, d.y.
5. Abigail, bpt 23 Jul 1786: m Abraham Clemens
6. Peter Mitchell, bpt 7 Dec 1788
7. John, bpt 12 May 1793: d 1823: m Rye, NH 16 Sep 1813 Hannah Webster (VR Rye)

Jenness, John Bean   82c   1-2-1-0-0
    Rye Town, Rockingham Co., NH

JOHN BEAN JENNESS, b abt 1763 son of Francis & Sarah (Locke) Jenness: d Rye, NH 21 Aug 1840 aged 77y (VR Rye): m Rye, NH 22 Jun 1786 Olive Berry (VR Rye), b Rye, NH 19 Sep 1763 dau of Merrifield & Huldah (Towle) Berry (VR Rye), d Rye, NH 7 Jun 1823 aged 60y (VR Rye).

Children: bpt Rye, NH (VR Rye)
1. Richard, bpt 11 Nov 1787: d Rye, NH 28 Feb 1870 (VR Rye): m Rye, NH 18 Dec 1809 Elizabeth (Seavey) Brown (VR Rye)
2. John, bpt 11 Jul 1790: d Rye, NH 31 Aug 1874 (VR Rye): m Rye, NH 25 Dec 1816 Hannah Wedgewood (VR Rye)
3. Olive, bpt 28 Jun 1795: d Rye, NH 16 Jun 1847 (VR Rye): m Rye, NH 1812 Benning Leavitt (VR Rye)

Jenness, Jonathan   82c   1-1-3-0-0
    Rye Town, Rockingham Co., NH

JONATHAN JENNESS, bpt Rye, NH 11 Oct 1761 son of Richard & Abigail (Coffin) Jenness (VR Rye): d (Lived at Deerfield, NH): m Rye, NH 14 Aug 1785 Abigail Garland (VR Rye), bpt Rye, NH 6 Mar 1763 dau of Benjamin & Sarah (Jenness) Garland (VR Rye), d Rye, NH 23 Apr 1840 aged 78y (VR Rye)

1790 CENSUS OF RYE, NH

Children: (HR p.387)
1. Elizabeth, b 1786: d 11 Sep 1866 aged 80y: m Nathaniel White
2. Benjamin Garland, bpt 12 Oct 1788 (VR Rye)
3. Polly, b 1790: m 1816 David Wedgewood
4. Jonathan, bpt 1 May 1791 (VR Rye): d Rye, NH 12 Jul 1870 aged 79y (VR Rye)
5. William, m Mary J. Saunders

Jenness, Joseph   82c   3-0-2-1-0
    Rye Town, Rockingham Co., NH

JOSEPH JENNESS, b Hampton, NH 28 Feb 1727 son of Richard & Mary (Dow) Jenness (HH p.768): d Rye, NH 23 Feb 1815 aged 89y (VR Rye): m(1) Rye, NH 25 Dec 1750 Mary Dow (VR Rye), b 6 Sep 1730 dau of Isaac & Charity (Berry) Dow (DB p.74): m(2) widow Anna Parker (HR p.385), b abt 1739, d Rye, NH 23 Jun 1816 aged 75y (VR Rye).

Children: bpt Rye, NH (VR Rye)
1. Mary, bpt 19 Jan 1752
2. Isaac, bpt 26 May 1754
3. Isaac, bpt Oct 1755: d 6 Dec 1841 (HR p. 388): m Rye, NH 20 Aug 1778 Hannah Dow (VR Rye)
4. Richard, bpt Jan 1758: m Mary Coffin
5. Jonathan, bpt 27 Jul 1760: d Rye, NH 29 Dec 1836 aged 76y (VR Rye): m 18 Mar 1785 Abigail Locke (LG p.106)
6. Sarah, bpt 13 May 1764: d Rye, NH 6 Sep 1851 aged 87y (VR Rye): m Rye, NH 13 Nov 1785 Levi Berry (VR Rye)
7. Joseph, bpt 26 Feb 1771: d Rye, NH 13 Sep 1845 (VR Rye): m(1) 22 Feb 1791 Anna Yeaton (HR p.389): m(2) Rye, NH 8 Dec 1801 Sarah Philbrick (VR Rye): m(3) Rye, NH 8 Dec 1809 Elizabeth Philbrick (VR Rye): m(4) Rye, NH Aug 1817 Anna Knox (VR Rye)

Jenness, Levi   82c   1-2-2-0-0
    Rye Town, Rockingham Co.,

LEVI JENNESS, bpt Rye, NH 22 May 1757 son of Samuel & Abigail (Garland) Jenness (VR Rye): d Rye, NH 29 Feb 1824 aged 67y (VR Rye): m(1) No. Hampton, NH 3 Mar 1782 Sarah Dearborn (IGI): m(2)

1790 CENSUS OF RYE, NH

Rye, NH 17 Nov 1785 Elizabeth Wallis (VR Rye), bpt Rye, NH Mar 1762 dau of Samuel Wallis (VR Rye), d Rye, NH 9 Feb 1821 aged 59y (VR Rye).

Children: bpt Rye, NH (VR Rye)
1. Samuel Wallis, bpt 9 Sep 1787: d Rye, NH 2 Mar 1875 aged 87y (VR Rye): m(1) Rye, NH 1 Mar 1810 Abigail Perkins (VR Rye): m(2) Rye, NH 19 Jul 1835 Polly Edmonds (VR Rye): m(3) Feb 1861 Sarah S. Randall
2. Levi, bpt 16 Jan 1791: d 1813 unmd (HR p.388)
3. Sarah Dearborn, bpt 28 Jul 1793: d Rye, NH 16 Mar 1826 aged 33y (VR Rye): m Rye, NH 2 May 1816 Benjamin Jenness (VR Rye)
4. Martha Wallis, bpt 25 Oct 1795: m Rye, NH 15 Apr 1819 Samuel Chapman (VR Rye)
5. Josiah, bpt 24 Sep 1797: d Rye, NH 12 Apr 1876 aged 78y (VR Rye): m Rye, NH 7 Jan 1822 Huldah Perkins (VR Rye)

Jenness, Nathaniel   82c   2-3-5-0-0
    Rye Town, Rockingham Co., NH

NATHANIEL JENNESS, b Rye, NH 22 Aug 1725 son of John & Mary (Mason) Jenness (VR Rye): d Rye, NH 7 Feb 1812 (VR Rye): m(1) 27 Dec 1749 Hannah Dow, b Hampton, NH 23 May 1726 dau of Simon & Mary(Lancaster) Dow (HH p.683): m(2) Rye, NH 28 Mar 1771 Mary (Goss) Tarlton (VR Rye), bpt Rye, NH 24 Jul 1743 dau of Thomas & Mary (Hall) Goss (VR Rye), d Rye, NH 30 Jun 1814 aged 71y (VR Rye).

Children: bpt Rye, NH (VR Rye)
(by 1st wife)
1. Simon, (HR p.384)
2. Mary, bpt Nov 1750:
3. Jonathan, d Boston, MA (HR p.384)
4. John, bpt 26 Apr 1752: m Rye, NH 23 Dec 1777 Sarah Randall (VR Rye)
5. Noah, bpt 13 Apr 1755: d Rye, NH 17 Oct 1801 aged 39y (VR Rye): m Rye, NH 15 Jan 1784 Elizabeth (Galloway) Randall (VR Rye)
6. Hannah, bpt Feb 1757: d.y.
7. Nathaniel, bpt 11 Oct 1760: d Rye, NH 8 Oct 1824 aged 64y (VR Rye): m Rye, NH 21 Oct 1781 Mary Wedgewood (VR Rye)
8. Patty, b (HR p.384)

1790 CENSUS OF RYE, NH

9. Hannah, bpt 29 Apr 1765: m Sep 1799 Theodore Fuller (HR p.384)

(by 2nd wife)
10. Joseph Tarlton, bpt 15 Jan 1772: d Rye, NH 7 Jan 1804 (VR Rye)
11. Thomas, bpt 30 Jan 1774: d Rye, NH 28 Nov 1850 (VR Rye): m Rye, NH 16 May 1799 Sarah Page (VR Rye)
12. Richard, bpt 18 Jun 1775: m Rye, NH 2 Aug 1819 Caroline Rand (VR Rye)
13. Betsey, bpt 23 Mar 1777: m Rye, NH 4 Sep 1794 Reuben Philbrick Jr (VR Rye)
14. Molly, bpt 9 Aug 1778: d Rye, NH 30 Jun 1847 aged 69y (VR Rye): m Rye, NH 31 Mar 1800 Eliphalet Sleeper (VR Rye)
15. James, b abt 1782: d Rye, NH 9 Sep 1806 aged abt 24y (VR Rye)

Jenness, Nathaniel Jr.   82c   1-1-2-0-0
   Rye Town, Rockingham Co., NH

NATHANIEL JENNESS JR., bpt Rye, NH 11 Oct 1760 son of Nathaniel & Hannah (Dow) Jenness (VR Rye): d Rye, NH 8 Oct 1824 aged 64y (VR Rye): m Rye, NH 21 Oct 1781 Mary Wedgewood (VR Rye), dau of David & Mary (Marston) Wedgewood.

Children: born Rye, NH (VR Rye)
1. David Wedgewood, b 12 Jan 1782 (HR p.386): d Rye, NH 22 Jan 1843 aged 61y (VR Rye): m(1) Rye, NH 19 May 1807 Molly Jenness (VR Rye): m(2) Rye, NH 2 May 1811 Elizabeth Locke (VR Rye): m(3) Rye, NH 24 Jun 1816 Sarah T. Jenness (VR Rye): m(4) Rye, NH 23 Aug 1827 Mary (Jenness) Drake (VR Rye)
2. Polly, bpt 26 Jul 1789: d Rye, NH 27 Jul 1805 aged 19y (VR Rye)
3. Jonathan, bpt 25 Aug 1793: d Rye, NH 2 Feb 1870 aged 77y (VR Rye): m Rye, NH 28 Mar 1816 Sarah Garland (VR Rye)
4. Nancy, bpt 28 Jun 1795: d Rye, NH 19 Feb 1876 (VR Rye): m Rye, NH 23 Jun 1814 Simon Jenness (VR Rye)
5. Clarissa, bpt 16 May 1801: d Rye, NH 14 Aug 1842 (VR Rye): m Rye, NH 31 Dec 1818 Samuel Jenness (VR Rye)

1790 CENSUS OF RYE, NH

Jenness, Noah   82c   1-2-2-0-0
    Rye Town, Rockingham Co., NH

NOAH JENNESS, bpt Rye, NH 13 Apr 1755 son of Nathaniel & Hannah (Dow) Jenness (VR Rye): d Rye, NH 17 Oct 1801 aged 39y (VR Rye): m Rye, NH 15 Jan 1784 Elizabeth (Galloway) Randall (VR Rye). Elizabeth m(1) Hampton, NH 22 Mar 1778 Jesse Randall (HH p.1053). She m(3) Rye, NH 28 Jun 1803 Thomas Goss (VR Rye) & d Rye, NH 7 Jul 1824 aged 70y (VR Rye).

Children: born Rye, NH (VR Rye)
1. Simon, bpt 3 Sep 1786: d Rye, NH 17 Dec 1846 (VR Rye): m Rye, NH 23 Nov 1815 Nancy Sleeper (VR Rye)
2. Joses, bpt 11 Nov 1787
3. Betsey, bpt 31 Aug 1794: d Rye, NH 22 Aug 1811 aged 17y (VR Rye)
4. Polly, b 27 Mar 1797: d Rye, NH 9 Jun 1824 aged 16y (VR Rye)

Jenness, Richard   82c   1-2-1-0-0
    Rye Town, Rockingham Co., NH

RICHARD JENNESS, bpt Rye, NH Jan 1758 son of Joseph & Mary (Dow) Jenness (VR Rye): m Mary Coffin (HR p.388), b ? Hampton, NH 31 Jan 1760 dau of Amos & Sarah (Hook) Coffin (HH p.641).

Children: born Rye, NH (VR Rye)
1. Sarah, b 24 Aug 1782
2. Joseph, bpt 18 Jun 1786
3. Amos Coffin, bpt 14 Nov 1790

Jenness, Samuel   82c   3-1-5-0-0
    Rye Town, Rockingham Co., NH

SAMUEL JENNESS, b Rye, NH 19 May 1724 son of Richard & Mary (Dow) Jenness (VR Rye): m(1) Rye, NH 15 Nov 1748 Abigail Garland (VR Rye), b 11 Jan 1723 dau of John & Elizabeth (Dearborn) Garland (HH p.722): m(2) Kittery, ME 2 Aug 1765 Elizabeth (Goodwin) Shapley (VR Kit p.227), bpt 6 Sep 1730 dau of Thomas & Elizabeth (Plaisted) Goodwin (NEHGR v95 p.268).

1790 CENSUS OF RYE, NH

Children: bpt Rye, NH (VR Rye)
1. Mary, bpt 6 Nov 1749
2. Samuel, bpt 29 Oct 1752: m Rye, NH 21 Mar 1775 Mary Locke (VR Rye)
3. Peter, bpt 11 Jan 1756: d Rye, NH 30 Sep 1836 aged 81y (VR Rye): m No. Hampton, NH 26 Dec 1782 Abigail Drake (DG p.61)
4. Levi, bpt 22 May 1757: d Rye, NH 29 Feb 1824 aged 67y (VR Rye): m(1) No. Hampton, NH 3 Mar 1782 Sarah Dearborn (IGI): m(2) Rye, NH 17 Nov 1785 Elizabeth Wallis (VR Rye)
5. Mary, bpt Feb 1759: d Hampton, NH 30 Jan 1822 (HH p.692): m Rye, NH 19 Sep 1782 Samuel Drake (VR Rye)
6. Elizabeth, bpt 3 May 1761: d 8 Jan 1853 (DG p.61): m Rye, NH 20 Nov 1783 Nathaniel Drake (VR Rye)
7. John, bpt 10 Apr 1763: m 8 Mar 1787 Abigail Drake (DG p.64)
8. Abigail, bpt 9 Jul 1769: d Rye, NH 4 Jul 1812 aged 43y (VR Rye): m Rye, NH 30 Sep 1787 John Locke (VR Rye)

Jenness, Simon   82c   2-1-4-0-0
    Rye Town, Rockingham Co., NH

SIMON JENNESS, bpt Rye, NH 12 May 1751 son of Richard & Anna Jenness (VR Rye): d Rye, NH 27 Apr 1798 (VR Rye): m Rye, NH 24 Jun 1773 Olive Shapley (VR Rye), bpt 13 Apr 1755 dau of Alexander & Elizabeth (Goodwin) Shapley (NEHGR v95 p.268), d Rye, NH 27 May 1845 (VR Rye).

Children: bpt Rye, NH (VR Rye)
1. Olive, bpt 2 Jun 1776: d Rye, NH 16 Dec 1830 aged 56y (VR Rye): m Rye, NH 18 Nov 1800 Amos Garland (VR Rye)
2. Alexander Shapley, bpt 17 May 1778: d Mar 1799 (JG p.9)
3. Nancy or Anna, bpt 5 Oct 1780: m Rye, NH 28 Apr 1807 John Brown (VR Rye)
4. Betsey, bpt Sep 1783: d Rye, NH 22 Jul 1799 aged 16y (VR Rye)
5. Abigail, bpt 13 Nov 1785
6. Simon, bpt 15 Mar 1787: d.y.
7. Simon, bpt 18 Nov 1792: d Rye, NH 3 Dec 1870 (VR Rye): m Rye, NH 23 Jun 1814 Nancy Jenness (VR Rye)

1790 CENSUS OF RYE, NH

Johnson, Peter   82c   2-0-2-0-0
    Rye Town, Rockingham Co., NH

PETER JOHNSON, b Hampton, NH 11 Jul 1714 son of Peter & Esther (Hobbs) Johnson (HH p.771): m Hampton, NH 19 Apr 1737 Sarah Dow (HH p.771), b Hampton, NH 15 Feb 1714 dau of Simon & Mary (Lancaster) Dow (HH p.682).

Children: bpt Hampton, NH (HH p.771)
1. Esther, bpt 13 May 1739: m Rye, NH 18 Nov 1762 Samuel Towle (VR Rye)
2. Ruth, bpt 7 Oct 1739
3. Peter, bpt 28 Feb 1742: d Rye, NH 12 Oct 1816 (VR Rye): m Rye, NH 18 Sep 1767 Mary Yeaton (VR Rye)
4. Sarah, bpt 29 Apr 1744: d Rye, NH 24 Dec 1810 aged 66y (VR Rye): m Nathan Goss (HR p.398)
5. Simon, bpt 22 Dec 1745: d Rye, NH 15 Jul 1813 aged 68y (VR Rye): m Deliverance Knowles (HR p.398)
6. Mary, bpt 24 Jul 1748

Johnson, Peter Junr   82c   2-1-2-0-0
    Rye Town, Rockingham Co., NH

PETER JOHNSON JR., bpt Hampton, NH 28 Feb 1742 son of Peter & Sarah (Dow) Johnson (HH p.771): d Rye, NH 12 Oct 1816 aged 75y (VR Rye): m Rye, NH 18 Sep 1767 Mary Yeaton (VR Rye), b abt 1747 dau of Joseph & (1st wife) Yeaton, d Rye, NH 20 Aug 1831 aged 84y (VR Rye). Peter served as a drummer in Capt. Parsons' Co., in the Rev. War.

Children: born Rye, NH
1. Edmond, d at sea 10 Nov 1810 (VR Rye): m Rye, NH 9 Aug 1789 Abigail Berry (VR Rye)
2. Peter, b 6 Aug 1778 (VR Rye): d Rye, NH 4 May 1832 aged 54y (VR Rye): m Rye, NH 26 Nov 1801 Abigail D. Batchelder (VR Rye)
3. Sally, b abt 1772: d Rye, NH 2 May 1794 aged 22y (VR Rye)

Knowles, Nathan   82c   2-1-2-0-0
    Rye Town, Rockingham, Co., NH

1790 CENSUS OF RYE, NH

NATHAN KNOWLES, bpt Rye, NH 25 Aug 1745 son of Amos & Elizabeth (Libby) Knowles (VR Rye): d Rye, NH 19 Jan 1820 aged 75y (VR Rye): m Hannah Clifford (HR p.402), b abt 1744, d Rye, NH 8 Nov 1819 aged 75y (VR Rye).

Children: bpt Rye, NH (VR Rye)
1. John Clifford, bpt 23 Oct 1768: d Rye, NH 7 Nov 1837 aged 70y (VR Rye)
2. Nathan, bpt 10 Sep 1775: d Rye, NH 17 Oct 1863 (VR Rye): m 10 Nov 1799 Sarah Hook Brown (HR p.402)
3. Ezekiel, bpt 4 Jan 1778
4. Hannah, bpt 15 Sep 1782: m Theodore Coffin (HR p.402)

Knowles, Samuel 82c 1-0-1-0-0
    Rye Town, Rockingham Co., NH

SAMUEL KNOWLES, bpt Rye, NH 29 Oct 1749 son of Joseph & Love (Brackett) Knowles (VR Rye): d 16 Jun 1778 in Rev. War (VR Rye): m Rye, NH 17 Mar 1772 Sarah Marden (VR Rye), dau of John & Sarah (Locke) Marden (LG p.65-6). Samuel was a Sargeant in Capt. Parsons' Co. in Rev. War.

Children: bpt Rye, NH (VR Rye)
1. Anna Brackett, bpt Dec 1773
2. Samuel, bpt 24 Jul 1774
3. Deliverance, bpt 19 Nov 1775
4. Sarah, bpt 21 Sep 1777

Knowles, Simon 82c 1-0-4-0-0
    Rye Town, Rockingham Co., NH

SIMON KNOWLES, b Rye, NH 16 May 1748 son of Joseph & Love (Brackett) Knowles (VR Rye): d Rye, NH 7 Nov 1823 aged 75y (VR Rye): m Rye, NH 8 Feb 1779 Esther (Saunders) Yeaton (VR Rye), bpt Rye, NH 27 Sep 1741 dau of John & Mary (Berry) Saunders (VR Rye). Esther m(1) Rye, NH 24 Aug 1759 John Yeaton (VR Rye) and had daughters that were unmd in 1790.

Children: of John & Esther YEATON, bpt Rye, NH (VR Rye)
1. John, bpt 17 Aug 1760: m ____ Hayes
2. Mary, bpt 22 Aug 1762

1790 CENSUS OF RYE, NH

3. Mary, bpt 18 Nov 1764
4. Elizabeth, bpt 12 Oct 1766: m John Stanton
5. Esther, bpt 9 Jul 1769: d Rye, NH 18 Jan 1808 (VR Rye): m Rye, NH 7 Nov 1793 Isaac Remick (VR Rye). She had bef marriage a dau Betsey Drew

Lang, Bickford   82c   2-2-5-0-0
    Rye Town, Rockingham Co., NH

BICKFORD LANG, b Greenland, NH 1738 son of John & Sarah (Bickford) Lang: d Effingham, NH 1804 (ME Soldiers, Sailors & Pat p.453): m Rye, NH 8 Mar 1764 Martha Locke (VR Rye), bpt Rye, NH 3 Jan 1742 dau of Elijah & Huldah (Perkins) Locke (VR Rye).

Children: born Rye, NH (VR Rye)
1. John, bpt 12 Apr 1767: d Limerick, ME 31 Aug 1843: m 3 Aug 1787 Mercy Drake (DG p.86)
2. Hannah, bpt Oct 1769: d Portsmouth NH 16 May 1860 aged 90y (VR Rye): m Dowrst Rand (LF p.56)
3. Martha, bpt 16 Feb 1772: m(1) Rye, NH 19 Jul 1795 Jeremiah Fogg (VR Rye): m(2) Rye, NH 30 Apr 1815 John Batchelder (VR Rye)
4. Bickford, bpt 13 Nov 1774: d Huntington, Ohio 5 Apr 1861 (LG p.115): m Rye, NH 2 Jan 1797 Abigail Locke (VR Rye)
5. Sarah, bpt 6 Oct 1776: m(1) Jonathan Crockett: m(2) Josiah Tuck of Effingham, NH (LF p.56)
6. William, bpt 14 Apr 1782: d 1783 (LF p.56)

Lang, Mary   82c   0-2-1-0-0
    Rye Town, Rockingham Co., NH

MARY LANG (widow of Thomas), b Rye, NH 16 Aug 1738 dau of Jethro & Esther (Rand) Goss (VR Rye): d aft 1790: m Rye, NH 16 Sep 1757 Thomas Lang (VR Rye), b Portsmouth, NH abt 1735 son of William & Susanna (Savage) Lang (LF p.79), d bef 1790 (DAR I p.401). Thomas was in Parsons's Vol. Co. in defense of Newcastle in Rev. War.

Children: born Rye, NH (VR Rye)
1. Susannah, bpt Aug 1758
2. William, bpt Feb 1761: d 1815: m 1784 Marga-

      ret Rhimes (LF p.79)
3. Levi, bpt Nov 1763: d (of Deerfield, NH): m Mary Critchett (LF p.80)
4. Anna, bpt Oct 1767
5. Richard, bpt 30 Sep 1770: d Rye, NH 24 Jan 1823 aged 52y (VR Rye): m Rye, NH 28 Sep 1797 Comfort Foss (VR Rye)
6. Sarah, bpt 3 May 1774: m Ebenezer Collins of New Gloucester, ME.
7. Betsey, b abt 1777: d bef 1804: m Rye, NH 9 Feb 1797 Nathaniel Berry (VR Rye)
8. Samuel, b 1781: d Candia, NH 1847: m 1807 Elizabeth Smith (LF p.80)

Lear, Alexander   82c   5-0-6-0-0
    Rye Town, Rockingham Co., NH

ALEXANDER LEAR, one of the signers of a petition from Rye to raise money by lottery to build a bridge, Dec 1789. He m Sarah _____ .

Children: last 3 born Rye, NH (VR Rye)
1. ? Samuel, b 1762: d 20 Nov 1842 (DAR I p.406): m Rye, NH 5 Feb 1792 Sally Salter (VR Rye)
2. ? Benjamin, b abt 1763: d Rye, NH 27 Oct 1838 aged 75y (VR Rye): m Rye, NH 25 Nov 1790 Mary Morrison (VR Rye)
3. Elizabeth, b 18 Jul 1771
4. Molly, bpt 6 Apr 1777
5. Mehitable Odiorne, bpt 28 Jun 1778

Libbey, Joseph   82c   1-0-2-0-0
    Rye Town, Rockingham Co., NH

JOSEPH LIBBY, b Rye, NH 10 Nov 1765 son of Abraham & Mary (Tarlton) Libby (VR Rye): d Guilford, NH 21 Oct 1837 (LIB p.142): m Rye, NH 12 Feb 1789 Deborah Rand (VR Rye), b Rye, NH 3 Sep 1765 dau of Joseph & Deborah (Seavey) Rand (VR Rye), d Holderness, NH 17 Mar 1849 (LIB p.142).

Children:
1. Mary, bpt Rye, NH 11 Apr 1790 (VR Rye): d 12 May 1865: m(1) Meredith, NH 12 Apr 1806 Abraham Folsom (IGI); m(2) Bradstreet Gilman (LIB p.143)

1790 CENSUS OF RYE, NH

2. Joseph, bpt Rye, NH 6 Nov 1791 (VR Rye): m(1) 2 Mar 1815 Mehitable C. Rand: m(2) 26 Nov 1835 Olive Haines (LIB p.307)
3. Benjamin, b Newcastle, NH 27 Jul 1796: d Guilford, NH 5 Nov 1862: m 31 Dec 1818 Ruenna Robinson (LIB p.307)
4. Elias, b Chester, NH 17 Mar 1802: m(1) 10 Feb 1826 Jemima Rand: m(2) 10 May 1835 Clarissa F. Davis (LIB p.308)
5. Sally, b Guilford, NH 30 Jul 1805 (LIB p. 143)
6. Abram, b Guilford, NH 17 Apr 1809: m(1) 16 Feb 1832 Dorcas Hibbard: m(2) 20 May 1858 Betsey G. Hoyt (LIB p.308)

Libbey, Samuel   82c   1-3-3-0-0
    Rye Town, Rockingham Co., NH

SAMUEL LIBBY, bpt Rye, NH Jul 1757 son of Reuben & Sarah (Goss) Libby (VR Rye): d Epsom, NH 27 Feb 1843 (LIB p.137): m Rye, NH 21 Sep 1780 Mehitable Seavey (VR Rye), bpt Rye, NH 12 Feb 1758 dau of William & Ruth (Moses) Seavey (VR Rye), d 9 Apr 1851 (LIB p.137).

Children: born Rye, NH (VR Rye)
1. Aaron Seavey, bpt Jun 1782: d West Indies 26 Mar 1806 aged 24y 6mo (VR Rye)
2. Samuel, b 14 Mar 1783: d Epsom, NH 23 Jan 1857 (LIB p.138)
3. Sarah, bpt 2 Oct 1785: m Rye, NH 14 Dec 1806 Webster Salter (VR Rye)
4. William Seavey, b 26 Feb 1787: d Staten Island, NY 28 Apr 1869: m(1) Salem, MA 23 Sep 1809 Sarah Farrington: m(2) 25 Jan 1827 Elizabeth Winfield (LIB p.298)
5. Nancy Griffith, bpt 15 Nov 1789: m Amos Davis
6. Hitty, bpt 3 Sep 1792: d.y.
7. Mehitable, bpt 10 May 1795: m Caleb Pearson of Schenectady, NY (LIB p.138)
8. Ruth Moses, bpt 4 Jun 1797: d 1804 (HR p.418)
9. Daniel Rand, bpt 27 Jul 1800: d Rye, NH 26 Sep 1804 aged 4y (VR Rye)
10. Richard, bpt 1 Oct 1804: m Sarah Sanborn
11. Maria, bpt 21 Oct 1804: m(1) Amasa Seavey: m(2) Jonathan Brown (LIB p.138)

1790 CENSUS OF RYE, NH

Locke, David   82c   1-2-5-0-0
Rye Town, Rockingham Co., NH

DAVID LOCKE, b Rye, NH 24 Aug 1735 son of Jonathan & Sarah (Haines) Locke (VR Rye): d Rye, NH 7 Jun 1810 aged 75y (VR Rye): m(1) Rye, NH 9 Feb 1758 Hannah Lovering (VR Rye), b 11 March 1739 dau of John Lovering (LG p.51), d Rye, NH 23 Sep 1807 (VR Rye): m(2) Rye, NH 24 May 1809 Olive (Marden) Elkins (VR Rye), b Rye, NH 6 Jan 1747 dau of James & Judith (Bates) Marden (VR Rye), d Rye, NH 4 Dec 1835 aged 88y (VR Rye).

Children: born Rye, NH (VR Rye)
1. Reuben, b 26 Apr 1758: d Corinth, VT 14 Aug 1824: m Epsom, NH 27 Mar 1791 Phebe Chapman (LG p.109)
2. Simeon, b 31 Mar 1760: d East Concord, NH 12 Aug 1839 (LG p.110): m Epsom, NH 29 Jan 1784 Abigail Blake (LG p.109)
3. Sarah, b 21 Nov 1761: m(1) Portsmouth, NH 15 Nov 1780 Joshua Webster (LG p.111): m(2) Solomon Waterhouse
4. Mary, b 7 May 1764: m Hampton, NH 3 Nov 1785 Josiah B. Sanborn (LG p.111)
5. David, b 24 Nov 1765: d Epsom, NH 2 Apr 1856 (LG p.112): m Hampton, NH 31 May 1789 Anna Towle (HH p.1005 & IGI))
6. Jonathan, b 19 Feb 1768: d Freedom, NH Jun 1841: m(1) 23 Dec 1790 Lydia Hall: m(2) 11 Dec 1825 Hannah (Tarlton) Beals (Straff p.337)
7. Levi, b 7 Feb 1770: d Epsom, NH 23 Sep 1850 (LG p.113): m Rye, NH 31 Aug 1796 Hannah Prescott (VR Rye)
8. John, b 22 May 1772: d Chelsea, MA 5 Sep 1846 (LG p.113): m Portsmouth, NH Sep 1800 Abigail Dearborn (Straff p.336)
9. Annah, b 27 Mar 1774: d Gilmanton, NH 23 Nov 1857 (LG p.114): m Rye, NH 2 Jan 1794 Timothy Prescott (VR Rye)
10. William, b 9 Apr 1776: d Irasburg, VT 3 Mar 1841: m 23 Oct 1800 Esther Knowles (LG p.115)
11. Abigail D., b 20 Nov 1778: d Huntington, Ohio 5 Feb 1862 (LG p.116): m Rye, NH 2 Jan 1797 Bickford Lang (VR Rye)
12. Benjamin, b 28 Dec 1780: d Portsmouth, NH Jan or Jul 1816: m 18 Oct 1801 Pamelia

1790 CENSUS OF RYE, NH

Conner of Portsmouth, NH (LG p.116)
13. Nancy, b 9 Mar 1785: d No. Hampton, NH 17 Oct 1853: m Greenland, NH 2 Apr 1801 Morris Lamprey (LG p.117)

Locke, David Junr   82c   1-1-1-0-0
   Rye Town Rockingham Co., NH

DAVID LOCKE JR., b Rye, NH 24 Nov 1765 son of David & Hannah (Lovering) Locke (VR Rye): d Epsom, NH 2 Apr 1856 (LG p.112): m 31 May 1789 Anna Towle (HH p.1005), bpt Hampton, NH 24 Apr 1768 dau of Abraham & Abigail (Moulton) Towle (HH p.1005), d 8 Jul 1839 (LG p.112).

Children: born Epsom, NH (LG p.112)
1. David, b 23 May 1790: bpt 2 Oct 1790 (VR Rye): d Epsom, NH 29 Jan 1872: m Canaan, NH 28 Nov 1819 Polly Carleton (LG p.252)
2. Abigail, b 26 Apr 1796: m Jonathan Green (LG p.252)
3. Nancy, b 9 Aug 1801: d 1 Jan 1858: m Hampton, NH 15 Feb 1826 Ebenezer Gove (LG 252 & IGI)
4. John, b 23 Jun 1807: d 30 Dec 1807 (LG p.112)

Locke, Elijah   82c   1-0-2-0-0
   Rye Town, Rockingham Co., NH

ELIJAH LOCKE, b Rye, NH abt 1714 son of William & Hannah (Knowles) Locke (HR p.424): d 1782 (DAR I p.420: m Rye, NH 22 Mar 1739 Huldah Perkins (VR Rye), b Hampton, NH 28 Sep 1718 dau of James & Huldah (Robie) Perkins (HH p.911).

Children: born Rye, NH (VR Rye)
1. Huldah, b 2 Oct 1739: m Moses Seavey (LG p.59)
2. Martha, bpt 3 Jan 1742: m Rye, NH 8 Mar 1764 Bickford Lang (VR Rye)
3. Mary, bpt 23 Nov 1744: d 1840 aged 96y (LG p.60): m Rye, NH 7 Jul 1765 Robert Saunders Jr (VR Rye)
4. Elijah, bpt 29 Sep 1746: d 1 Nov 1753 (LG p.29)
5. Elizabeth, bpt 15 Jan 1749: d 3 Aug 1753 (LG

1790 CENSUS OF RYE, NH

6. Levi, bpt 9 Dec 1750: d 14 Nov 1753 (LG p.29)
7. William, bpt 8 Apr 1753: d Dec 1753 (LG p.29)
8. Elijah, bpt Dec 1754: d Chichester, NH 1 Aug 1838 (LG p.60): m(1) Rye, NH 21 Nov 1776 Elizabeth Brown (VR Rye) m(2) Nancy (Watts) Fisher (LG p.60)
9. William, bpt Jun 1758: d Alexandria, NH 9 Apr 1828 (LG p.61): m Rye, NH 28 Oct 1779 Abigail Saunders (VR Rye)
10. Hannah, b 2 Feb 1761 (LG p.29)

Locke, Elijah Junr   82c   1-2-2-0-0
    Rye Town, Rockingham Co., NH

ELIJAH LOCKE JR., bpt Rye, NH Dec 1754 son of Elijah & Huldah (Perkins) Locke (VR Rye): d Chichester, NH 1 Aug 1838 (LG p.60): m Rye, NH 21 Nov 1776 Elizabeth Brown (VR Rye), b Rye, NH 21 Jun 1755 dau of Jonathan & Mary (Garland) Brown (VR Rye), m(2) Mrs. Nancy (Watts) Fisher (LG p.60).

Children: born Rye, NH (VR Rye)
1. Elijah, bpt 1 Jul 1781: d Alexandria, NH 12 Aug 1864 (LG p.130): m Rye, NH 21 Jan 1802 Hannah Saunders (VR Rye)
2. Mary, bpt Mar 1784: d 25 Apr 1856: m 12 Apr 1804 John Wallis (LG p.130)
3. Levi, b 20 Mar 1786 (LG p.130): d Chichester, NH 14 Aug 1838: m 15 Aug 1805 Rachel Towle (LG p.130)

Locke, Jeremiah   82c   2-2-6-0-0
    Rye Town, Rockingham Co., NH

JEREMIAH LOCKE, b Hampton, NH 4 Aug 1728 son of Joseph & Salome (White) Locke (HH p.824): d Rye, NH 28 Jan 1795 (VR Rye): m(1) Rye, NH 15 Feb 1753 Mary Elkins (VR Rye), b Rye, NH 16 Feb 1731 dau of Henry & Catherine (Marston) Elkins (VR Rye): m(2) Greenland, NH 28 May 1761 Mary (Berry) Haines (LG p.33). Jeremiah brought up his grandchildren after his son Joseph died.

Children: bpt Rye, NH (VR Rye)

1790 CENSUS OF RYE, NH

1. Joseph, bpt 28 Apr 1754: d Rye, NH 22 Apr 1790 (VR Rye): m Rye, NH 25 Jun 1778 Martha Dow (VR Rye)
2. Mary, bpt Jul 1755: m Rye, NH 21 Mar 1775 Samuel Jenness (VR Rye)

Locke, Job   82c   1-0-3-0-0
   Rye Town, Rockingham Co., NH

JOB LOCKE, bpt Rye, NH 26 Sep 1762 son of Richard & Elizabeth (Garland) Locke (VR Rye): d Rye, NH 20 Jul 1849 (VR Rye): m(1) 10 Nov 1785 Hannah Lang (HH p.430), bpt Rye, NH 10 Nov 1765 dau of Mark & Salome (Goss) Lang (VR Rye), d Rye, NH 29 Jan 1806 (VR Rye): m(2) Rye, NH 9 Dec 1806 Abigail Philbrick (VR Rye), bpt 9 Oct 1768 dau of Joseph & Ann (Towle) Philbrick (VR Rye), d Rye, NH 11 Mar 1810 aged 41y (VR Rye): m(3) Rye, NH 25 Nov 1810 Sarah Locke (VR Rye), bpt 17 Mar 1771 dau of Richard & Huldah (Hobbs) Locke (VR Rye), d Rye, NH 29 Aug 1852 (VR Rye).

Children: bpt Rye, NH (VR Rye)
(by 1st wife)
1. Daniel, bpt 15 Apr 1787: d.y.
2. Sally, bpt 29 May 1791: d Rye, NH 31 Dec 1831 aged 40y (VR Rye)
3. Polly W., b 1793 (HR p.430): m Hampton, NH 7 Nov 1815 James Bowley (LG p.71)
4. Elizabeth Garland, bpt 24 Sep 1797: d Star Island 14 Sep 1836 (LG p.148): m(1) Rye, NH 2 Nov 1816 John Caswell (VR Rye): m(2) Rye, NH 11 Dec 1827 William S. Randall (VR Rye)
5. Job, bpt 5 May 1799: d Rye, NH 1 Jul 1852 aged 53y (VR Rye): m Hannah Randall (HR p.436)
6. John Wilkes Parsons, bpt 10 Apr 1803: d Rye, NH 25 Apr 1841 (VR Rye): m Rye, NH 19 Nov 1826 Mary B. Locke (VR Rye)
(by 2nd wife)
7. Anna, bpt 25 Oct 1807: d.y.
(by 3rd wife)
8. Hannah, bpt 21 Jul 1813: m William Randall (HR p.431)
9. Sally Wood, bpt 21 Jul 1813

Locke, John   82c   2-1-2-0-0

1790 CENSUS OF RYE, NH

Rye Town, Rockingham Co., NH

JOHN LOCKE, bpt Rye, NH 19 Oct 1746 son of Richard & Elizabeth (Garland) Locke (VR Rye): d Rye, NH 5 May 1801 (LG p.70): m(1) Rye, NH 29 Sep 1769 Sarah Jones (VR Rye), d 29 Apr 1795 (LG p.70): m(2) Rye, NH 18 Aug 1796 Thankful Blazo (VR Rye).

Children: bpt Rye, NH (VR Rye)
1. John, bpt 1 Apr 1770: d 1786
2. Jeremiah, bpt 14 Jul 1771: d Rye, NH 21 Oct 1804 aged 33y (VR Rye): m Rye, NH 21 Nov 1793 Susan Rand (VR Rye)
3. Richard, bpt 8 Aug 1773
4. Molly, bpt 8 Aug 1773
5. George Washington, bpt 2 Mar 1777

Locke, Jonathan   82c   3-1-2-0-0
    Rye Town, Rockingham Co., NH

JONATHAN LOCKE, b Rye, NH 29 Jan 1732 son of Jonathan & Sarah (Haines) Locke (VR Rye): d Rye, NH 17 Sep 1813 aged 82y (VR Rye): m 8 Jun 1757 Abigail Towle (HR p.427), b abt 1736, d Rye, NH 22 Mar 1817 aged 81y (VR Rye).

Children: born Rye, NH (VR Rye)
1. Jonathan, b 1 Jan 1759: d Newcastle, NH 1842 (LG p.106): m Rye, NH 23 Nov 1785 Olive Rand (VR Rye)
2. Abner, b 30 Oct 1760: d 16 Aug 1778 in Rev. War (VR Rye)
3. Mary, bpt 12 Jun 1763: d 1763 (HR p.428)
4. Abigail, b 21 Jul 1764: d 24 May 1844 (LG p.107): m 18 Mar 1785 Jonathan Jenness (LG p.106)
5. John, b 15 Jul 1767: d Rye, NH 27 Mar 1814 aged 47y (VR Rye): m Rye, NH 30 Sep 1787 Abigail Jenness (VR Rye)
6. Joseph, b 21 Mar 1770: d Rye, NH 27 Jan 1816 aged 45y (VR Rye): m Rye, NH 4 Dec 1794 Abigail Marden (VR Rye)
7. Daniel, b 26 Oct 1772: d Rye, NH 1 Jan 1840 aged 68y (VR Rye)
8. Jethro, b 29 Jun 1775: d Rye, NH 3 Apr 1821 aged 46y (VR Rye): m Rye, NH 26 Apr 1801 Martha Webster (VR Rye)
9. Hall Jackson, bpt 14 Dec 1777: d 25 May 1836

1790 CENSUS OF RYE, NH

(LG p.108): m(1) Newcastle, NH 11 Jan 1809 Abigail (Underwood) Amazeen (VR Rye): m(2) Kittery, ME 25 Apr 1834 Margery Manson (VR Kit p.291)
10. Elvin (HR p.428)

Locke, Jonathan Junr   1-2-2-0-0
   Rye Town, Rockingham Co., NH

JONATHAN LOCKE JR., b Rye, NH 1 Jan 1759 son of Jonathan & Abigail (Towle) Locke (VR Rye): d Newcastle, NH 1842 (LG p.106): m Rye, NH 23 Nov 1785 Olive Rand (VR Rye), bpt Rye, NH 15 Apr 1762 dau of Nathaniel & Mary (Leavitt) Rand (VR Rye).

Children: born Newcastle, NH (LG p.106)
 1. Jonathan, bpt Rye, NH 18 Nov 1787 (VR Rye): d Newcastle, NH 15 Mar 1853 (LG p.106): m(1) Rye, NH 24 Dec 1812 Mary Vennard (VR Rye): m(2) 10 Oct 1842 Eunice Quincy (LG p.233)
 2. William, b 10 Feb 1788: d 5 Feb 1869
 3. Nabby, b 27 Dec 1789: d Newcastle, NH 15 May 1849 (LG p.233): m Newcastle, NH 21 Feb 1808 William Neal (NHGR v2 p.37)
 4. Joseph L., b Mar 1792: d Portsmouth, NH 6 Sep 1858 (VR Rye): m Rye, NH 29 Nov 1816 Sallie Wedgewood (VR Rye)
 5. Michael, b 1794: d age 20y
 6. Mary Olive, b 25 Dec 1796: d Portsmouth, NH 4 May 1880: m Portsmouth, NH 25 Nov 1821 Asa Watson (LG p.234)
 7. Sarah Ann, b 1799: d.y.
 8. John, b 10 Aug 1800: d New Castle, NH 20 Feb 1864 (LG p.234): m(1) Rye, NH 7 Jan 1822 Martha Rand (VR Rye): m(2) 13 Oct 1847 Almira (Shaw) Lear (LG p.234)

Locke, Joseph 82c 2-0-3-0-0
   Rye Town, Rockingham Co., NH

JOSEPH LOCKE, b Hampton, NH 27 Apr 1716 son of Joseph & Salome (White) Locke (HH p.824): d Rye, NH 22 Apr 1790 (VR Rye): m(1) Rye, NH 4 Dec 1739 Hannah Jenness (VR Rye), b Hampton, NH 4 Jul 1714 dau of Richard & Mary (Dow) Jenness (HH p.768): m(2) Rye, NH 20 Apr 1768 Mary (Yeaton) Odiorne (VR Rye), d Rye, NH 28 Jan 1825 (VR Rye).

274

1790 CENSUS OF RYE, NH

Children: born Rye, NH (VR Rye)
1. Hannah, b 3 Jun 1740: bpt 22 Feb 1741
2. Joseph, bpt 4 Apr 1742: d.y.
3. Richard, bpt 9 Sep 1744: d Northwood, NH 23 Oct 1823 (VR Rye): m Mar 1767 Huldah Hobbs (LG p.67)
4. Joseph, bpt 21 Jul 1751: d.y.
5. Joshua, bpt 28 Apr 1754: d bef 1797: m Rye, NH 18 Jan 1776 Charity Marden (VR Rye)
6. Mary, bpt 21 Nov 1756: m 7 Feb 1782 Levi Towle (LG p.31)
7. Joseph, bpt 18 Dec 1768: d Rye, NH 3 Mar 1841 aged 73y (VR Rye): m(1) Rye, NH 16 Nov 1794 Mary Brown (VR Rye): m(2) Rye, NH 16 Jul 1804 Olive Foss (VR Rye)
8. Benjamin, bpt 16 Dec 1770: d.y.
9. Hannah, bpt 12 Mar 1773: d Rye, NH 19 Dec 1851 aged 78y (VR Rye): m Rye, NH 2 Oct 1803 Samuel Mowe (VR Rye)
10. Benjamin, bpt 13 Jun 1776: d.y.

Locke, Richard   82c   2-0-3-0-0
    Rye Town, Rockingham Co., NH

RICHARD LOCKE, b Rye, NH 28 Jul 1720 son of John & Sarah Locke (VR Rye): d Rye, NH 22 May 1804 aged 82y (VR Rye): m abt 1745 Elizabeth Garland, b Hampton, NH 13 Mar 1724 dau of John & Elizabeth (Dearborn) Garland (HH p.722).

Children: bpt Rye, NH (VR Rye)
1. John Jr., bpt 19 Oct 1746: d Rye, NH 5 May 1801 (LG p.70): m(1) Rye, NH 29 Sep 1769 Sarah Jones (VR Rye): m(2) Rye, NH 18 Aug 1796 Thankful Blazo (VR Rye)
2. Abner, bpt 13 Mar 1748: d.y.
3. Richard, bpt 7 Jan 1750: d Rye, NH 26 Dec 1827 aged 77y (VR Rye): m Rye, NH 2 Nov 1769 Sarah Palmer (VR Rye)
4. Jacob, bpt 23 Feb 1752: d.y.
5. Abner, bpt 26 May 1754: d Rye, NH 15 Apr 1825 aged 71y (VR Rye)
6. Jacob, bpt 22 Jan 1757: d Wakefield, NH 16 Feb 1814 (LG p.70): m Rye, NH 4 Jun 1778 Mehitable Huggins (VR Rye)
7. Tryphena, bpt May 1759: d Rye, NH 3 Aug 1830 (VR Rye)
8. Job, bpt 26 Sep 1762: d Rye, NH 20 Jul 1849

1790 CENSUS OF RYE, NH

(VR Rye): m(1) 10 Nov 1785 Hannah Lang (HR p.430): m(2) Rye, NH 6 Dec 1806 Abigail Philbrick (VR Rye): m(3) Rye, NH 25 Nov 1810 Sarah Locke (VR Rye)
9. Sarah, bpt 8 Sep 1765: d 8 Feb 1813 (HR p.426)
10. Elizabeth, bpt 10 Apr 1768
11. Simon, bpt 23 Sep 1770: d Rye, NH 31 Jul 1863 (VR Rye): m(1) Greenland, NH 14 Feb 1792 Abigail Mace (LG p.71): m(2) Rye, NH 10 Nov 1803 Elizabeth Allen (VR Rye)

Locke, Richard Junr   82c   1-1-2-0-0
    Rye Town, Rockingham Co., NH

RICHARD LOCKE JR., bpt Rye, NH 7 Jan 1750 son of Richard & Elizabeth (Garland) Locke (VR Rye): d Rye, NH 26 Dec 1827 aged 77y (VR Rye): m Rye, NH 2 Nov 1769 Sarah Palmer (VR Rye), b abt 1750: d Rye, NH 8 Feb 1803 aged 53y (VR Rye). Richard served in the Rev. War under Capt. Parsons.

Children: born Rye, NH (VR Rye)
1. Richard, bpt 20 Jun 1773: d.y.
2. Joseph, bpt 4 Jun 1775: d Rye, NH 2 Nov 1853 (VR Rye): m(1) Rye, NH 13 May 1795 Lucy Marden (VR Rye): m(2) Rye, NH 11 Sep 1814 Hannah (Vittum) Berry (VR Rye)

Locke, Richard 3d   82c   1-3-3-0-0
    Rye Town, Rockingham Co., NH

RICHARD LOCKE 3d, b Rye, NH 4 Sep 1744 son of Joseph & Hannah (Jenness) Locke (VR Rye): d Northwood, NH 23 Oct 1823 aged 79y (VR Rye): m Mar 1767 Huldah Hobbs (LG p.67), b Hampton, NH 12 Jan 1746 dau of Jonathan & Mary (Berry) Hobbs (HH p.751), d 20 Dec 1828 (LG p.67).

Children: bpt Rye, NH (VR Rye)
1. Hannah, bpt Oct 1767: d.y.
2. Hannah Jenness, bpt 11 Jun 1769: d Rye, NH 6 Sep 1825 aged 55y (VR Rye): m Greenland, NH 1 Feb 1796 John Marston (LG p.140)
3. Sarah, bpt 17 Mar 1771: d Rye, NH 29 Aug 1852 (VR Rye): m Rye, NH 25 Nov 1810 Job Locke (VR Rye)

1790 CENSUS OF RYE, NH

4. James Hobbs, bpt 6 Jun 1773: d Rye, NH 8 Jan 1808 aged 34y (VR Rye): m Rye, NH 17 Apr 1801 Hannah Berry (VR Rye)
5. Asa, bpt 20 Aug 1775: d Rye, NH 23 May 1857 (VR Rye): m Rye, NH 12 Nov 1799 Elizabeth Hobbs (VR Rye)
6. Joshua, bpt 20 Aug 1775: d.y.
7. Richard, b 5 Oct 1779 (HR p.429): d Rye, NH 10 Jul 1840 aged 63y (VR Rye): m(1) Rye, NH 19 Mar 1807 Sarah Woods (VR Rye): m(2) Rye, NH 20 Feb 1817 Betsey Tucker (VR Rye)

Locke, William   82c   1-3-4-0-0
   Rye Town, Rockingham Co., NH

WILLIAM LOCKE, bpt Rye, NH Jun 1758 son of Elijah & Huldah (Perkins) Locke (VR Rye): d Alexandria, NH 9 Apr 1828 (LG p.61): m Rye, NH 28 Oct 1779 Abigail Saunders (VR Rye), bpt Rye, NH 12 Oct 1760 dau of John & Tryphena (Philbrick) Saunders (VR Rye), d Alexandria, NH 23 Oct 1828 (LG p.61).

Children: bpt Rye, NH (VR Rye)
1. John, bpt 27 May 1781: d Loudon, NH 15 Mar 1849: m(1) Sep 1797 Abigail Locke: m(2) Mehitable Bickford (LG p.131)
2. Abigail, bpt 28 Oct 1781: d Epsom, NH 5 Nov 1847: m Jeremiah Page (LG p.61)
3. Huldah, bpt 11 Oct 1783: d 28 May 1829: m Epsom, NH 1 Sep 1799 John Page (LG p.131)
4. William, bpt 9 Oct 1785: d Epsom, NH 3 Sep 1829: m 25 Dec 1808 Mercy Shaw (LG p.132)
5. Elizabeth, b 11 Jul 1788: d Chichester, NH 22 Apr 1823: m Jun 1813 John Langley (LG p.133)
6. Reuben, bpt 20 Mar 1791: d Alexandria, NH 25 May 1864: m 10 Sep 1815 Jane McMurphy (LG p.133)

Mace, Haman   82c   1-1-2-0-0
   Rye Town Rockingham Co., NH

ITHAMAR MACE, probably the Ithamar Mace bpt Gosport, NH 29 Jun 1729 son of John & Sarah (Frost) Mace (NEHGR v66 p.302): m Rye, NH 6 Dec 1764 Rachel Berry (VR Rye), bpt Rye, NH 3 Jul 1743 dau of Jotham & Mary (Bates) Berry (VR Rye). Rachel

1790 CENSUS OF RYE, NH

m(2) Joseph Hall (HR p.376). She died Rye, NH 9 Nov 1806 (VR Rye).

Children: bpt Rye, NH (VR Rye)
1. Sarah, bpt 1 Dec 1765 (VR Rye)
2. Abigail, bpt 1 Feb 1767 (VR Rye): d Rye, NH 8 Feb 1803 (VR Rye): m Greenland, NH 14 Feb 1792 Simon Locke (LG p.71)
3. John, bpt 23 Jul 1769: d Rye, NH 7 Jun 1834 (VR Rye): m Rye, NH 27 Jun 1793 Rachel Randall (VR Rye)

Mace, Levi   82c   1-3-2-0-0
    Rye Town, Rockingham Co., NH

LEVI MACE, probably the Levi Mace bpt Gosport, NH 8 Sep 1754 son of Levi & Hannah Mace (NEHGR v66 p. 219): d Rye, NH 1 Apr 1814 (VR Rye): A Levi Mace m Rye, NH Molly Seavey (HR p.536). Levi Mace was taxed in Rye for the year 1782.

Marden, Benjamin   82c   3-1-3-0-0
    Rye Town, Rockingham Co., NH

BENJAMIN MARDEN, b Rye, NH 9 Aug 1729 son of Stephen & Charity (Lang) Marden (VR Rye)): d Rye, NH 1 Jan 1805 aged 80y (VR Rye): m Rye, NH 31 Jan 1754 Rachel Dowrst (VR Rye), b Rye, NH 1 Aug 1735 dau of Solomon & Elizabeth Dowrst (VR Rye), d Rye, NH 11 Dec 1812 aged 77y (VR Rye).

Children: born Rye, NH (VR Rye)
1. Solomon Dowrst, bpt 2 Oct 1757
2. Charity, b 9 Mar 1760: m(1) Rye, NH 18 Jan 1776 Joshua Locke (VR Rye): m(2) Rye, NH 19 Oct 1797 Peter Ackerman (VR Rye)
3. Elizabeth, b 9 Feb 1762: m Simon Towle (HR p.455)
4. Stephen, bpt 4 Nov 1764: d Rye, NH 21 Sep 1844 aged 80y (VR Rye): m Rye, NH 12 Nov 1789 Molly Smith (VR Rye)
5. Rachel, b 9 Jan 1766: d Rye, NH 28 Jan 1766 (VR Rye)
6. Abiel, bpt 1 Mar 1767: d ? Rye, NH 12 Jul 1856 aged 89y (VR Rye): m Rye, NH 11 Mar 1790 William Foss (VR Rye)
7. Benjamin, bpt 18 Jun 1769: d Rye, NH 24 Jun

1790 CENSUS OF RYE, NH

    1769 (VR Rye)
8. Sarah, bpt 24 Nov 1771: d Rye, NH 27 Apr 1854 aged 83y (VR Rye): m Rye, NH 22 Oct 1795 Jonathan Philbrick (VR Rye)
9. Solomon, bpt 29 Mar 1774: d Rye, NH 10 Dec 1843 (VR Rye): m Rye, NH 15 Jul 1802 Huldah Remick (VR Rye)
10. Samuel, bpt 6 Oct 1776: d Rye, NH 11 May 1853 (VR Rye): m Rye, NH 3 Apr 1806 Sarah Philbrick (VR Rye)

Marden, Benjamin Jr.   82c   1-0-4-0-0
   Rye Town, Rockingham Co., NH

BENJAMIN MARDEN JR., b Rye, NH 4 Feb 1751 son of Benjamin & Rebecca (Whidden) Marden (VR Rye): d Rye, NH 26 Feb 1826 aged 75y (VR Rye): m(1) Rye, NH 26 Jan 1772 Hannah Moses Rand (VR Rye), bpt Rye, NH 15 Oct 1752 dau of Joshua & Mary (Moses) Rand (VR Rye), d Rye, NH 1 Sep 1812 aged 59y (VR Rye): m(2) Rye, NH 23 Jan 1817 Deliverance (Knowles) Johnson (VR Rye), bpt Rye, NH 27 Oct 1751 dau of Joseph & Love (Brackett) Knowles (VR Rye), d Rye, NH 17 Oct 1821 aged 70y (VR Rye).

Children: born Rye, NH (VR Rye)
1. Rebecca, bpt 9 Feb 1773: d Rye, NH 22 Nov 1845 (VR Rye)
2. Benjamin, bpt 23 Jul 1775
3. Nancy Tredwell, bpt 23 Mar 1777: d Rye, NH 22 Jul 1832 aged 54y (VR Rye): m Rye, NH 2 Mar 1800 Samuel Marden (VR Rye)
4. Mary, bpt 4 Apr 1779: m Rye, NH 13 May 1802 Lowell Sanborn of Gilmanton (VR Rye)

Marden, Nathaniel   82c   1-0-2-0-0
   Rye Town, Rockingham Co., NH

NATHANIEL MARDEN, bpt Rye, NH 28 Jul 1745 son of Jonathan & Hepsabeth (Hardy) Marden (VR Rye): d Rye, NH 21 Nov 1804 aged 59y (VR Rye): m(1) Rye, NH 21 Jul 1768 Hannah Berry (VR Rye), bpt 28 Jun 1747 dau of Jeremiah & Hannah (Locke) Berry (VR Rye), d Rye, NH 11 Apr 1773 aged 25y (VR Rye): m(2) Rye, NH 29 May 1777 Anna Towle (VR Rye), b Rye, NH 28 Mar 1741 dau of Jonathan & Anna (Norton) Towle (VR Rye).

1790 CENSUS OF RYE, NH

Children: born Rye, NH (VR Rye)
(by 1st wife)
1. Prudence Perry, bpt 26 Feb 1769: m abt 1791 Ebenezer Seavey
2. Keziah, bpt 10 Mar 1770
3. Betty, bpt 11 Jan 1778: d Rye, NH 17 Dec 1781 (VR Rye)

(by 2nd wife)
4. Hannah, bpt 23 Jul 1780: d Rye, NH 8 Dec 1858 aged 78y (VR Rye): m Rye, NH 21 Jul 1799 Samuel Walker (VR Rye)
5. Nathaniel, bpt 6 May 1792: d 21 Feb 1876: m Mary Ann Loutz (HR p.457)
6. Jonathan Towle, bpt Feb 1796: d Rye, NH Mar 1803 aged 8y (VR Rye)

Marden, Nathaniel Jr.   82c   1-3-6-0-0
    Rye Town, Rockingham Co., NH

NATHANIEL MARDEN JR., bpt Rye, NH 23 Mar 1746 son of Ebenezer & Esther (Berry) Marden (VR Rye): d Rye, NH 30 Mar 1823 aged 77y (VR Rye): m Elizabeth Moulton (DAR I p.437) bpt Rye, NH 8 Mar 1752 dau of Reuben & Hannah (Philbrick) Moulton (VR Rye), d Rye, NH 1 Nov 1831 aged 79y (VR Rye).

Children: born Rye, NH (VR Rye)
1. Jonathan, b 24 Apr 1770: d Rye, NH 8 Apr 1853 aged 83y (VR Rye)
2. Hannah, b 5 Jan 1772: d Portsmouth, 29 Mar 1855 aged 83y (VR Rye): m Rye, NH 9 Oct 1792 Mark Lang (VR Rye)
3. Olive, b 27 Aug 1774: d Rye, NH 15 Dec 1859 aged 85y (VR Rye): m Rye, NH 18 Oct 1795 Joseph Rand (VR Rye)
4. Lucy, b 28 Sep 1776: d Rye, NH 19 May 1813 aged 37y (VR Rye): m Rye, NH 13 May 1795 Joseph Locke 3rd (VR Rye)
5. Ebenezer, b 22 Jan 1779: d Rye, NH 5 Dec 1862 (VR Rye): m Rye, NH 26 Jun 1806 Love Berry (VR Rye)
6. James, b 6 May 1781: d Rye, NH 16 Jun 1832 aged 51y (VR Rye): m Rye, NH 4 Jan 1803 Sarah Webster (VR Rye)
7. Reuben, b 21 Apr 1783: d Rye, NH 22 Oct 1851 (VR Rye): m(1) Rye, NH 14 Apr 1810 Hannah Moulton (VR Rye): m(2) Rye, NH 1835 Charlotte (Towle) Moulton (VR Rye)

1790 CENSUS OF RYE, NH

8. Esther, b 20 Jul 1785: d Rye, NH 2 Oct 1809 aged 24y (VR Rye): m Rye, NH 4 Nov 1802 Joshua Rand (VR Rye)
9. Elizabeth, b 17 Dec 1787: d Rye, NH 12 Jul 1788 (VR Rye)
10. Elizabeth Moulton, b 6 Nov 1793: d Rye, NH 20 Sep 1877 (VR Rye): m Rye, NH 24 Apr 1834 Samuel Locke (VR Rye)

Marden, William 82c 1-2-6-0-0
   Rye Town, Rockingham Co., NH

WILLIAM MARDEN, b Rye, NH 13 May 1744 son of James & Judith (Bates) Marden (VR Rye): d Rye, NH 14 Nov 1816 aged 72y (VR Rye): m Rye, NH 29 Apr 1773 Hannah Wallis (VR Rye), b Rye, NH 2 Aug 1745 dau of Samuel & Sarah (Moses) Wallis (VR Rye), d Rye, NH 21 Sep 1830 (VR Rye). William's father James Marden died Jul 1777 (VR Rye), but his mother Judith did not die until 31 Jul 1796 (VR Rye) so perhaps she was part of his household in 1790.

Children: born Rye, NH (VR Rye)
1. Abigail, b 31 Mar 1776: d Rye, NH 25 Mar 1848 (VR Rye): m Rye, NH 4 Dec 1794 Joseph Locke (VR Rye)
2. Sarah, b 29 Oct 1778: d Rye, NH 26 May 1815 aged 36 (VR Rye): m Rye, NH 17 Dec 1801 Thomas Goss (VR Rye)
3. Hannah, b 4 Apr 1781: m Rye, NH 1 Dec 1811 William Whidden (VR Rye)
4. James, b 21 Apr 1784: d Rye, NH 5 Nov 1851 (VR Rye): m Rye, NH 11 May 1809 Polly Jenness (VR Rye)

Mason, Daniel 82c 2-3-6-0-0
   Rye Town, Rockingham Co., NH

DANIEL MASON, b abt 1742 son of Samuel & Hannah (Neal) Mason: d Rye, NH 30 Oct 1834 aged 92y (VR Rye): m Rye, NH 20 Apr 1775 Elizabeth Norton (VR Rye), b abt 1754 dau of William & Ruhamah (Neils), Norton, d Rye, NH 5 Apr 1829 aged 75y (VR Rye).

Children: 3 bpt Rye, NH (VR Rye)
1. Samuel, b abt 1775: d Portsmouth, NH 10 Sep 1837 (VR Rye): m Rye, NH 12 Nov 1801 Mercy

1790 CENSUS OF RYE, NH

    Locke (VR Rye)
2. Daniel, d Portsmouth, NH 8 Dec 1849 (VR Rye): m Rye, NH 7 Apr 1807 Mercy Rand (VR Rye)
3. Nicholas, bpt 1783: d Portsmouth, NH 28 Jul 1866 aged 83y (VR Rye): m Rye, NH 23 Aug 1807 Mary M. Rand (VR Rye)
4. Robert, d aged 6y (HR p.459)
5. Ruhamah, bpt 27 Nov 1785: m Rye, NH 10 Feb 1805 Aaron Moses (VR Rye)
6. Betsey, bpt 27 Jun 1790: d Rye, NH 20 Nov 1820 (VR Rye)

Matthes, Abraham   82c   1-1-4-0-0
    Rye Town, Rockingham Co., NH

ABRAHAM MATHES, b abt 1744 (DAR I p.443): d bef 1816: m Rye, NH 26 Jun 1774 Mary (Saunders) Thomas (VR Rye), bpt Rye, NH 20 Oct 1744 dau of John & Mary (Berry) Saunders (VR Rye), d Rye, NH 10 Apr 1816 aged 72y (VR Rye).

Children: bpt Rye, NH (VR Rye)
1. Mary, bpt 21 May 1775
2. Sally, bpt 22 Nov 1777
3. Abraham, bpt 9 Jul 1780
4. Robert, bpt 1783: m Rye, NH 12 Feb 1807 Betsey M. Randall (VR Rye)
5. Elizabeth, bpt 20 Mar 1785
6. William Thomas, bpt 16 Jan 1792: d Rye, NH 5 Jun 1873 aged 82y (VR Rye): m Rye, NH 17 Feb 1812 Elizabeth Foss (VR Rye)

Moulton, Nehemiah   82c   2-0-5-0-0
    Rye Town, Rockingham Co., NH

NEHEMIAH MOULTON, b 3 Oct 1734 son of Joseph & Bethia (Hobbs) Moulton (MHGR v6 p.263): d Rye, NH 15 Aug 1816 (VR Rye): m Sarah _____, d 18 Apr 1803 (MHGR v6 p.269).

Children: born Rye, NH (VR Rye)
1. Anna, bpt 12 Sep 1762
2. Mary, bpt 14 May 1765: d Rye, NH 31 Dec 1858 aged 94y (VR Rye)
3. Sally, bpt 28 Jan 1770: d Rye, NH 25 Jan 1850 (VR Rye): m Rye, NH 16 Jun 1796 William

1790 CENSUS OF RYE, NH

Jones (VR Rye)
4. Bethia, bpt 9 Jun 1776

Moulton, Reuben   82c   1-0-2-0-0
   Rye Town, Rockingham Co., NH

REUBEN MOULTON, b Rye, NH 4 Jan 1729 son of Jonathan & Elizabeth (Lamprey) Moulton (VR Rye): d Rye, NH 30 Mar 1803 (VR Rye): m(1) Rye, NH 24 Nov 1748 Hannah Philbrick (VR Rye), b Hampton, NH 28 Nov 1727 dau of Joses & Abigail (Locke) Philbrick (HH p.922): m (2) Portsmouth, NH 24 Oct 1775 Margaret Jones (IGI), d Rye, NH 26 Jul 1813 aged 80y (VR Rye).

Children: born Rye, NH (VR Rye)
1. Jonathan, b 27 Oct 1749: d Rye, NH 24 Mar 1767 (VR Rye)
2. Elizabeth, bpt 8 Mar 1752
3. Lucy, bpt Aug 1757: m Page Philbrick (HR p.464)

Parsons, Joseph   82c   2-1-4-0-0
   Rye Town, Rockingham Co., NH

JOSEPH PARSONS, b 14 Dec 1746 son of Samuel & Mary (Jones) Parsons (HR P.476): d Rye, NH 8 Feb 1832 aged 85y (VR Rye): m Rye, NH 31 Jan 1768 Mary Seavey (VR Rye), bpt Rye, NH 25 Jan 1746/7 dau of Amos & Mary (Langdon) Seavey (VR Rye), d Rye, NH 29 Sep 1836 (VR Rye). Joseph was a Captain in the Rev. War. His mother d Rye, NH 15 Oct 1796 (VR Rye) so may have been part of his household.

Children: born Rye, NH (VR Rye)
1. Amos Seavey, bpt 16 Oct 1768: d Rye, NH 7 Nov 1850 aged 82y (VR Rye): m(1) Rye, NH 3 Aug 1796 Patty Dow (VR Rye): m(2) Rye, NH 31 Mar 1828 Mary Langdon (VR Rye)
2. Mary, bpt 2 Sep 1770: d Rye, NH 7 Dec 1842 aged 72y (VR Rye): m Greenland, NH 19 Jan 1790 James Dow (DB p.77)
3. Samuel, bpt 12 Jul 1772: d abt 1780
4. Joseph, bpt 25 Sep 1774: m(1) Rye, NH 1798 Hannah Perkins (VR Rye): m(2) 1822 Elizabeth Monroe (HR p.477)
5. Bettey, bpt 27 Dec 1776: d Rye, NH 20 Feb

1790 CENSUS OF RYE, NH

   1843 (VR Rye): m Rye, NH 15 Aug 1799 John
   Garland (VR Rye)
6. John Wilkes, bpt 3 Oct 1779: d Rye, NH 18
   Sep 1849 (VR Rye): m Rye, NH 11 Aug 1803
   Abigail Garland (VR Rye)

Perkins, James   82c   2-1-3-0-0
   Rye Town, Rockingham Co., NH

JAMES PERKINS, bpt Hampton, NH 5 Jan 1735 son of
James & Huldah (Robie) Perkins (HH p.911): d Rye,
NH 2 Nov 1805 (VR Rye): m Rye, NH 23 Feb 1758
Abigail Locke (VR Rye), b Rye, NH 5 Sep 1736 dau
of Jonathan & Sarah (Haines) Locke (VR Rye), d
Rye, NH Feb 1803 (VR Rye).

Children: bpt Rye, NH (VR Rye)
1. Mary, bpt 24 Jun 1759: m Rye, NH 1 Apr 1777
   Nathaniel Emery (VR Rye)
2. Abigail, bpt 12 Oct 1760: d Rye, NH 23 Jun
   1844 aged 83y (VR Rye): m Rye, NH 18 Oct
   1778 John Garland (VR Rye)
3. Sarah, bpt 12 Sep 1762: d Hampton, NH 18 Dec
   1835 (HH p.911): m Greenland, NH 10 Oct 1782
   William Emery (VR Green p.7)
4. John, bpt 18 Nov 1764: m Rye, NH 26 Feb 1789
   Ruth Nudd (VR Rye)
5. Nancy (Anna), bpt 24 May 1767: d Rye, NH 4
   Apr 1811 aged 44y (VR Rye): m Rye, NH 4 Mar
   1787 Jonathan Sherburne (VR Rye)
6. James, bpt Apr 1769: d Rye, NH 2 May 1852
   (VR Rye): m(1) 6 Feb 1791 Mary Perkins (LG
   p.118): m(2) Rye, NH 14 Jun 1812 Widow
   Mehitable Garland (VR Rye)
7. Jonathan, bpt 16 Feb 1772: d Rye, NH 13 Aug
   1809 aged 37y (VR Rye): m Rye, NH 1801 Mary
   Locke (VR Rye)
8. Josiah, bpt 30 Jun 1774: d Rye, NH 5 Dec
   1848 aged 74y (VR Rye): m Rye, NH Spring
   1807 Betsey Batchelder (VR Rye)
9. Huldah, bpt 25 May 1777: d 8 Sep 1801 (LG
   p.52): m Rye, NH 8 Sep 1799 Nathaniel Thurston (VR Rye)
10. Hannah, bpt 16 Jul 1780: d Rye, NH 17 Mar
    1801 aged 20y (VR Rye): m Rye, NH 1798
    Joseph Parsons (VR Rye)

1790 CENSUS OF RYE, NH

Perkins, John 82c 1-1-1-0-0
    Rye Town, Rockingham Co., NH

JOHN PERKINS, bpt Rye, NH 18 Nov 1764 son of James & Abigail (Locke) Perkins (VR Rye): m Rye, NH 26 Feb 1789 Ruth Nudd (VR Rye).

Children: (HR p.485)
 1. James, b 1790: m Huldah Seavey
 2. Jonathan, b 1792: m Phebe Robinson
 3. Nancy, b 1795: m Samuel Nudd
 4. Elias, b 13 Mar 1797: m Rye, NH 7 Jul 1822 Mary Lang (VR Rye)

Philbrook, Anna 82c 1-4-4-0-0
    Rye Town, Rockingham Co., NH

ANNA PHILBRICK (widow of Joseph), b Hampton, NH 28 Mar 1741 dau of Jonathan & Anna (Norton) Towle (HH p.1002): d Rye, NH 5 Jan 1824 aged 83y (CG p.122): m Rye, NH 2 Dec 1760 Joseph Philbrick (VR Rye), b Hampton, NH 10 Aug 1735 son of Joses & Abigail (Locke) Philbrick (HH p.922), d Rye, NH 11 Sep 1788 aged 53y (CG p.122).

Children: born Rye, NH (VR Rye)
 1. Joses, bpt 8 Nov 1761: d Rye, NH 27 Sep 1811 aged 50y (VR Rye): m Rye, NH 7 Jul 1782 Susannah Pitman (VR Rye)
 2. Anna (Nancy), bpt 15 Apr 1764: m Rye, NH 13 Mar 1796 Josiah Weeks (VR Rye)
 3. Abigail, bpt 9 Oct 1768: d Rye, NH 11 Mar 1810 aged 41y (VR Rye): m Rye, NH 9 Dec 1806 Job Locke (VR Rye)
 4. Hannah, b 12 Dec 1770: d Rye, NH 10 Sep 1831 aged 60y (VR Rye)
 5. Jonathan, b 17 Sep 1773: d Rye, NH 26 Apr 1843 aged 70y (VR Rye): m Rye, NH 22 Oct 1795 Sarah Marden (VR Rye)
 6. Daniel, bpt 10 Mar 1776: m 1800 Dolly Grove (HR p.490)
 7. Levi, bpt 28 Jun 1778: m Mary Nudd (HR p.490)
 8. James, b 8 Jul 1780: d Rye, NH 25 Oct 1855 (VR Rye): m Rye, NH 21 May 1801 Abigail Perviere (VR Rye)
 9. Joseph, b 14 Jun 1783: d Demerara, West Indies 5 May 1826 (VR Rye)

1790 CENSUS OF RYE, NH

10. Sally, bpt 1 Sep 1788: d Rye, NH 23 Mar 1860
    aged 71y (VR Rye): m Rye, NH 3 Apr 1806
    Samuel Marden Jr (VR Rye)

Philbrook, Jonathan   82c   2-2-3-0-0
    Rye Town, Rockingham Co., NH

JONATHAN PHILBRICK, bpt Rye, NH 1 Dec 1745 son of
Joses & Abigail (Locke) Philbrick (VR Rye): d Rye,
NH 1 Apr 1822 aged 76y (VR Rye): m Rye, NH 8 Dec
1768 Mary Marden (VR Rye), bpt Rye, NH 4 Feb 1750
dau of Ebenezer & Esther (Berry) Marden (VR Rye),
d 15 Nov 1834 (CG p.122).

Children: born Rye, NH
1. Daniel, b 12 Jul 1769: d York, Me. 14 May
   1840: m(1) Rye, NH 25 Dec 1794 Betsey Wells
   (VR Rye): m(2) 25 Dec 1795 Mary Todd of
   Kittery (Hist & Gen of Me by Little v.3
   p.1603)
2. Jonathan, bpt 11 Oct 1772 (VR Rye): m Rye,
   NH 1 Jun 1797 Sarah Wells (VR Rye)
3. Abigail, bpt 10 Nov 1776 (VR Rye): m Rye, NH
   10 Dec 1801 James Chapman (VR Rye)
4. Ephraim, b 9 Sep 1779-80: d Rye, NH 25 Jan
   1860 aged 79y (VR Rye): m Sarah Webster (HR
   p.492)
5. Elizabeth, b 2 Nov 1783: d Rye, NH 29 Jan
   1816 aged 32y (VR Rye): m Rye, NH 8 Dec 1809
   Joseph Jenness (VR Rye)
6. Joseph, bpt 31 Aug 1788 (VR Rye): d Rye, NH
   12 Apr 1879 aged 90y 11mo (VR Rye): m Rye,
   NH 10 May 1810 Betsey Page (HR p.492)

Philbrook, Joses   82c   1-2-2-0-0
    Rye Town, Rockingham Co., NH

JOSES PHILBRICK, bpt 8 Nov 1761 son of Joseph &
Anna (Towle) Philbrick (VR Rye): d Rye, NH 27 Sep
1811 aged 50y (VR Rye): m Rye, NH 7 Jul 1782
Susannah Pitman (VR Rye), b abt 1765, d Rye, NH 15
Apr 1843 aged 78y (VR Rye).

Children: born Rye, NH (VR Rye)
1. Polly, b 5 Dec 1782: d Rye, NH 11 Jul 1854
   aged 71y (VR Rye): m Rye, NH 12 May 1808
   Samuel Rand (VR Rye)

1790 CENSUS OF RYE, NH

2. Benjamin, b 27 Sep 1785: d Rye, NH 11 Mar 1820 aged 34y (VR Rye): m(1) Rye, NH 8 Feb 1807 Widow Mary Varrel (VR Rye): m(2) Polly Randall dau of Hannah Randall (HR p.518)
3. Joseph, b 19 Sep 1788: m Rye, NH 9 Mar 1813 Sally Emery (VR Rye)
4. Nancy, b 8 Apr 1792: m Kittery, ME 1813-14 George Ormsby (VR Kit p.205)
5. Hannah, b 7 Apr 1795: m Greenland, NH 2 Mar 1814 Hezekiah Kimball (IGI)
6. Reuben, b 1 Sep 1798
7. Charles Pinckney, b 7 Oct 1799
8. Lyman, b 3 Oct 1802: m Lydia Watkins (HR p.491)
9. George Clinton, b 29 May 1805: m Mary Nutting (HR p.493)
10. John Walbach, b 22 Aug 1808: d 2 Feb 1861 (HR p.491)

Philbrook, Joses Junr   82c   1-1-1-0-0
    Rye Town, Rockingham Co., NH

JOSES PHILBRICK JR., b Rye, NH 22 Jul 1766 son of Daniel & Abigail (Marden) Philbrick (VR Rye): d Rye, NH 21 Jul 1835 aged 68y (VR Rye): m Rye, NH 12 Jan 1790 Sarah Smith (VR Rye), bpt Rye, NH 11 Oct 1772 dau of David & Mary (Marden) Smith (VR Rye), d Rye, NH 22 Dec 1842 aged 71y (VR Rye).

Children: born Rye, NH (VR Rye)
1. Daniel, bpt 17 Jul 1791: d Portsmouth, NH 20 Jul 1868 (VR Rye): m Kittery, ME 7 Aug 1817 Pamelia Gunnison (VR Kit p.206)
2. Mary, bpt 15 Jul 1792: d Portsmouth NH 14 Apr 1867 aged 75y (VR Rye): m 1818 Richard Webster
3. Sally, bpt 5 Jul 1795: d Rye, NH 2 Apr 1829 aged 34y (VR Rye): m Benjamin Garland
4. David, bpt 11 Jun 1797: m Sarah Lamos
5. Thomas, bpt 15 Aug 1799: d Rye, NH 15 Mar 1858 aged 58y (VR Rye): m Clarissa Shaw
6. John, bpt 11 Nov 1804: d Rye, NH 12 Sep 1877 (VR Rye): m Rye, NH 25 Dec 1831 Sarah Brown (VR Rye)
7. Abigail, b 1 Sep 1805 (HR p.492): d Portsmouth, NH 27 Jan 1848 aged 42y (VR Rye): m 8 Sep 1824 Samuel Parsons
8. William, b 20 Jun 1812 (HR p.492): d Rye, NH

1790 CENSUS OF RYE, NH

1 Nov 1839 aged 27y (VR Rye): m Abigail Williams

Philbrook, Reuben 82c 4-1-3-0-0
    Rye Town, Rockingham Co., NH

REUBEN PHILBRICK, b Hampton, NH 27 Sep 1737 son of Joses & Abigail (Locke) Philbrick (HH p.922): d Rye, NH 26 Jun 1819 aged 83y (VR Rye): m(1) abt 1772 Hannah Locke (LG p.53), b Rye, NH 18 Feb 1737/8 dau of William & Elizabeth (Rand) Locke (VR Rye): m(2) abt 1775 Widow Mary Wedgewood: m(3) Rye, NH 4 Feb 1805 Mary (Dalton) Jenness (VR Rye), d Rye, NH 25 Dec 1805 (VR Rye): m(4) Rye, NH 9 Sep 1806 Mary Beck (VR Rye), d Rye, NH 30 Jun 1826 (VR Rye).

Children: born Rye, NH (VR Rye)
(by 1st wife)
1. Reuben, b 9 Sep 1773: d Rye, NH 12 Jun 1831 aged 59y (VR Rye): m Rye, NH 4 Sep 1794 Betsey Jenness (VR Rye)
(by 2nd wife)
2. Hannah, b 7 Jan 1776: m Rye, NH 1 Aug 1792 Amos Towle (VR Rye)
3. Sally, b 13 Apr 1778: d Rye, NH 1 Nov 1808 (VR Rye): m Rye, NH 8 Dec 1801 Joseph Jenness (VR Rye)
4. Joses, b 19 May 1781: d Rye, NH 18 Jun 1838 aged 57y (VR Rye): m(1) Rye, NH 3 Nov 1803 Mary Page (VR Rye): m(2) Nancy (Jenness) Woodman

Poor, Robert 82c 1-1-2-0-0
    Rye Town, Rockingham Co., NH

ROBERT POWERS, came from England and served in the Rev. War. He died in Rye, NH 29 Apr 1807 (VR Rye): m Rye, NH 4 Jul 1788 Betsey Shapley (VR Rye), bpt Gosport, NH 6 Mar 1768 dau of Henry Carter & Judith (Randall) Shapley (NEHGR v66 p.295), d Rye, NH 10 Jun 1850 aged 84y (VR Rye).

Children: born Rye, NH (VR Rye)
1. Robert, b 1787: d at sea, 25 Dec 1810 (VR Rye)
2. Judith, bpt 22 Nov 1789: m Abner Blaisdell

1790 CENSUS OF RYE, NH

3. Sally, bpt 27 Nov 1791: d Rye, NH 21 May 1867 aged 75y (VR Rye)
4. Eliza, bpt 9 Nov 1794: d Rye, NH 26 Dec 1871 (VR Rye)
5. Mary, bpt Apr 1796 (HR p.498): d Rye, NH 18 Jan 1869 (VR Rye): m Rye, NH 27 Oct 1816 John Locke (VR Rye)
6. George, bpt 22 Apr 1798
7. Abigail Daniels, bpt 3 May 1801: m Calvin Knowlton
8. Daniel Sheafe, bpt 4 Nov 1804
9. Nancy, bpt 1806 (HR p.498)

Porter, Huntington 82c 2-2-2-0-0
    Rye Town, Rockingham Co., NH

HUNTINGTON PORTER, b Bridgewater, MA 27 Mar 1755 son of John & Mary (Huntington) Porter (VR Brid P.265): d Lynn, MA 7 Mar 1844 (VR Rye): m(1) Haverhill, MA 28 Jun 1786 Susannah Sargent (VR Hav p.261), b Haverhill, MA 1 Feb 1765 dau of Nathaniel & Rhoda (Barnard) Sargent (VR Hav p.267), d Rye, NH 24 Feb 1794 (VR Rye): m (2) 30 Mar 1797 Sarah Moulton (HH p. 870), b Hampton, NH 13 Jun 1779 dau of Jonathan & Sarah (Emery) Moulton (HH p.870), d Rye, NH 2 Jan 1835 aged 56y (VR Rye).

Children: born Rye, NH (VR Rye)
(by 1st wife)
1. Samuel H., bpt 15 Jul 1787
2. Nathaniel Sargent, bpt 7 Jun 1789: d Rye, NH 20 Sep 1827 (VR Rye): m Elizabeth Comstock
3. John, b 29 Sep 1791: d Rye, NH 29 Mar 1825 aged 34y (VR Rye)
4. Caroline, bpt 15 Dec 1793: d 8 Dec 1869 (HR p.499)
(by 2nd wife)
5. Maria, b 12 Feb 1798: m Rye, NH 18 Dec 1821 Asa Robinson (VR Rye)
6. Eliphalet, bpt 4 May 1800: d at sea, 31 Jan 1824 aged 25y (VR Rye)
7. Oliver, bpt 14 Mar 1802
8. Louisa, bpt 29 May 1803: m Rye, NH 26 May 1835 William Weeks (VR Rye)
9. Martha R., bpt 23 Jun 1805: m C.K. Dilloway
10. Sarah E., bpt 25 Jun 1809: m Rye, NH 31 Jul 1833 Rev. Charles Adams (VR Rye)

11. Olivia, bpt 17 Mar 1811: m Rye, NH 16 Aug 1837 Luther Hall (VR Rye)
12. Huntington, bpt 7 Feb 1813: d Rye, NH 7 Jun 1836 aged 23y 6mo (VR Rye)
13. Emery Moulton, bpt 24 Sep 1815: m _____ Wentworth
14. Charles H., bpt 18 Aug 1816: d Rye, NH 1 Sep 1816 (VR Rye)
15. Charles H. (twin), bpt 21 Sep 1817
16. William H. (twin), bpt 21 Sep 1817

Rand, George   83a   2-2-7-0-0
    Rye Town, Rockingham Co., NH

GEORGE RAND, b Rye, NH 4 Apr 1744 son of Joshua & Ruth Rand (VR Rye): d Rye, NH Mar 1803 aged 59y (VR Rye): m Rye, NH 19 May 1768 Naomie Sherburne (VR Rye).

Children: born Rye, NH (VR Rye)
1. Margaret (Martha), bpt 12 Feb 1769
2. John, b 5 Mar 1772; bpt 3 May 1772
3. Betsey, b 14 Feb 1774; bpt 19 May 1776: m? Benjamin Sanborn
4. George, bpt 19 May 1776
5. Richard, b 29 Oct 1778
6. Enoch, b 20 Sep 1780
7. Ebenezer, b 15 Feb 1784

Rand, John   83a   1-2-6-0-0
    Rye Town, Rockingham Co., NH

JOHN RAND, bpt Rye, NH 14 Feb 1742 son of Joshua & Mary (Moses) Rand (VR Rye): d Rye, NH 17 Sep 1808 aged 67y (VR Rye): m Rye, NH 4 Jun 1772 Hannah Seavey (VR Rye), bpt Rye, NH 20 May 1750 dau of Henry & _____ (Smith) Seavey (VR Rye), d Rye, NH 13 May 1812 aged 62y (VR Rye).

Children: bpt Rye, NH (VR Rye)
1. Elizabeth, bpt 13 Jun 1773: d Rye, NH 15 Aug 1857 aged 84y (VR Rye): m Rye, NH 29 Mar 1810 Joshua Rand (VR Rye)
2. Mary, bpt Feb 1776: d Rye, NH 26 Jan 1825 aged 50y (VR Rye)
3. John, bpt 24 May 1778: d Rye, NH 5 Aug 1861 (VR Rye): m(1) 1808 Sidney Lang (Straff

1790 CENSUS OF RYE, NH

      p.429): m(2) Rye, NH 1 Jun 1851 Mrs. Nancy
Haley (VR Rye): m(3) Deborah Burleigh
4. Hannah, bpt Aug 1781: d Rye, NH 14 Apr 1850 aged 68y (VR Rye): m(1) Rye, NH 15 Nov 1804 William Foye (VR Rye): m(2) Rye, NH 19 Oct 1828 John Y. Randall (VR Rye)
5. Joshua, bpt 1784: d Rye, NH 22 Jan 1867 aged 82y (VR Rye)
6. Sally, bpt 2 Sep 1787: d Rye, NH 15 Mar 1860 aged 74y (VR Rye): m Rye, NH 12 Apr 1812 Jonathan Woodman (VR Rye)
7. Olive, bpt 11 Jul 1789: d Rye, NH 24 Feb 1836 aged 47y (VR Rye)
8. Nancy, bpt 14 Sep 1794: d Rye, NH 7 Dec 1842 aged 48y (VR Rye): m Rye, NH 20 Mar 1817 Ephraim Rand Hall (VR Rye)

Rand, Joseph   82c   2-3-3-0-0
    Rye Town, Rockingham Co., NH

JOSEPH RAND, bpt Rye, NH 15 Sep 1739 son of Joshua & Mary (Moses) Rand (VR Rye): m Rye, NH 24 May 1764 Susannah Goss (VR Rye), bpt Rye, NH 23 Sep 1744 dau of Jethro & Esther (Rand) Goss (VR Rye).

Children: born Rye, NH (VR Rye)
1. Zeb, bpt 12 May 1765
2. Joshua, bpt Mar 1768
3. Joseph, b 1769: d Rye, NH 18 Aug 1855 aged 86y (VR Rye): m Rye, NH 18 Oct 1795 Olive Marden (VR Rye)
4. Molly, bpt 31 Mar 1771
5. Zebedee, bpt 2 May 1773
6. Olly, bpt 21 May 1775
7. Samuel Hunt, bpt 25 May 1777: d Rye, NH 25 Jun 1846 aged 69y (VR Rye): m Rye, NH 12 May 1808 Polly Philbrick (VR Rye)
8. Joshua, b 23 Aug 1779 (HR p.501): d Rye, NH 20 Sep 1852 (VR Rye): m(1) Rye, NH 4 Nov 1802 Esther Marden (VR Rye): m(2) Rye, NH 29 Mar 1810 Elizabeth Rand (VR Rye)
9. Levi, bpt 21 Jun 1782
10. Sally, bpt 2 Oct 1785: d Rye, NH 9 Aug 1825 aged 40y (VR Rye)

Rand, Joseph Junr   82c   1-1-2-0-0
    Rye Town, Rockingham Co., NH

1790 CENSUS OF RYE, NH

JOSEPH RAND JR., possibly the Joseph b Rye, NH 11 Jan 1763 son of Joseph & Deborah (Seavey) Rand (VR Rye).

Rand, Nathaniel   82c   2-2-7-0-0
    Rye Town, Rockingham Co., NH

NATHANIEL RAND, b Rye, NH 12 Mar 1737 son of Richard & Abiel Rand (VR Rye): d Rye, NH Jun 1803 (VR Rye): m Rye, NH 8 Dec 1757 Mary Leavitt (VR Rye), b ? 17 Jan 1736 dau of Samuel & Ruth (Johnson) Leavitt (HH p.813).

Children: born Rye, NH (VR Rye)
1. Richard, b 18 Mar 1758: d in Rev. War
2. Samuel, b 28 Jan 1760: d in Rev. War
3. Olly, b 5 Apr 1762: m Rye, NH 23 Nov 1785 Jonathan Locke (VR Rye)
4. Mary, b 21 Mar 1764: m Rye, NH 16 Nov 1790 Richard Cate (VR Rye)
5. Nathaniel, b 8 Sep 1766: m Rye, NH 5 Nov 1791 Abigail Trefethern (VR Rye)
6. Susannah, b 31 Aug 1768: d Rye, NH 24 Jun 1841 aged 73y (VR Rye): m(1) Rye, NH 21 Nov 1793 Jeremiah Locke (VR Rye): m(2) Rye, NH 22 Apr 1810 Thomas Babb (VR Rye)
7. Mehitable, b 10 Dec 1770: d Nov 1852 (LG p.144): m Rye, NH 14 Jan 1800 Jeremiah Locke (VR Rye)
8. Sally, b 25 Dec 1772; bpt 17 Jan 1773: d.y.
9. Sarah, bpt 5 Aug 1774: m Rye, NH 2 Mar 1797 Benjamin Mason (VR Rye)
10. Ruth, bpt 15 Sep 1776: m Rye, NH 28 Sep 1801 Samuel Cate (VR Rye)
11. Tabitha, bpt Aug 1777
12. Samuel, b 11 Jan 1780: m Mary Hanson
13. Molly, bpt 4 Jul 1782
14. Aphia, b 5 Feb 1784

Rand, Nathaniel Jr   83a   1-0-2-0-0
    Rye Town, Rockingham Co., NH

NATHANIEL RAND JR., m Rye, NH 28 May 1778 Mary Ordiorne (VR Rye).

Children: bpt Rye, NH (VR Rye)

1790 CENSUS OF RYE, NH

1. Sally, bpt 25 Jul 1779

Rand, Ruth   83a   0-4-3-0-0
    Rye Town, Rockingham Co., NH

RUTH RAND, (widow of Joshua), bpt Rye, NH 30 May 1756 dau of William & Ruth (Moses) Seavey (VR Rye): d Rye, NH 2 Jul 1829 aged 74y (VR Rye): m Rye, NH 2 Oct 1777 Joshua Rand Jr. (VR Rye), bpt Rye, NH Jan 1758 son of Joshua & Mary (Moses) Rand (VR Rye), d Rye, NH 13 Mar 1791 (VR Rye).

Children: born Rye, NH (VR Rye)
1. Daniel, bpt 9 Aug 1778: d Rye, NH 10 Oct 1851 (VR Rye): m Rye, NH 24 Feb 1801 Dolly Seavey (VR Rye)
2. Joshua, bpt 9 Jul 1780: m Betsey Houston
3. William Seavey, bpt Aug 1781: d Rye, NH 22 Jun 1854 aged 73y (VR Rye): m Rye, NH 12 Aug 1804 Dolly Rollins (VR Rye)
4. Samuel, bpt 22 Jun 1783: d Portsmouth, NH 17 Mar 1822: m(1) Portsmouth, NH 11 Mar 1809 Martha Locke: m(2) Portsmouth, NH 29 Oct 1811 Hannah Locke (LG p.302)
5. Theodore, bpt 15 Apr 1787: d at sea
6. Mehitable, bpt 15 Jun 1788: m Rye, NH 7 Mar 1809 James Elkins (VR Rye)
7. Moses, bpt 30 Aug 1789: d Portsmouth, NH 10 Jun 1811 aged 23y (VR Rye)
8. James, d at sea, 23 Nov 1807 (VR Rye)
9. Mary, b (HR p.501) m Rye, NH 23 Aug 1807 Nicholas Mason (VR Rye)

Rand, Samuel   83a   2-1-3-0-0
    Rye Town, Rockingham Co., NH

SAMUEL RAND, b Rye, NH 6 Aug 1724 son of Samuel & Abigail Rand (VR Rye): m Rye, NH 10 May 1748 Sarah Dowrst (VR Rye), b Rye, NH 19 Jan 1729 dau of Solomon & Elizabeth (Brown) Dowrst (VR Rye).

Children: born Rye, NH (VR Rye)
1. Thomas, b 27 Mar 1749
2. Sarah, bpt 17 Nov 1751
3. Samuel, bpt 23 Dec 1753: d Rye, NH Mar 1803 aged abt 50y (VR Rye)
4. Elizabeth, b 8 Jan 1757

1790 CENSUS OF RYE, NH

5. Abigail, b 6 Oct 1759
6. Thomas, b 6 Jun 1760 : d Rye, NH 27 Feb 1839 aged 79y (VR Rye): m Rye, NH 4 Apr 1790 Mary Tuck (VR Rye)
7. Rachel, b 20 Apr 1762: m Rye, NH 5 Dec 1783 Daniel Seavey (VR Rye)
8. Dowrst, b 24 Jun 1764: d Rye, NH 12 Jan 1847 aged 82y (VR Rye): m Hannah Lang (LF p.56)
9. Billey, b 30 Oct 1766: d Rye, NH 2 Apr 1819 aged 52y (VR Rye): m Rye, NH 29 May 1800 Patty Moses (VR Rye)

Rand, Stephen   83a 1-1-4-0-0
    Rye Town, Rockingham Co., NH

STEPHEN RAND, b 12 Sep 1759 son of Stephen & Mercy (Palmer) Rand (HR p.513): d Rye, NH 31 Mar 1826 aged 66y (VR Rye): m(1) Rye, NH 17 May 1781 Sarah Fogg (VR Rye), b 10 Sep 1764 (HR p.513), d Rye, NH 19 Jun 1803 (VR Rye): m(2) Rye, NH 17 Sep 1807 Ruth Tarlton (VR Rye), b abt 1762 dau of ? Joseph & Mary (Goss) Tarlton, d Rye, NH 1 Nov 1837 aged 75y (VR Rye).

Children: (HR p.513)
1. Stephen, b 12 May 1782: d Boston, MA 4 Jan 1871 (VR Rye): m Rye, NH 8 Jun 1806 Betsey Tarlton (VR Rye)
2. Polly, b 15 Aug 1785: d Rye, NH 20 Jul 1868 aged 82y (VR Rye): m Rye, NH 9 Dec 1839 John Brown (VR Rye)
3. Mercy, b 26 Mar 1788/9: m Rye, NH 7 Apr 1807 Daniel Mason (VR Rye)
4. Daniel Fogg, b 7 Jan 1792: d 1 Oct 1859 (HR p.513): m Mary Richardson
5. Caroline, b 6 Nov 1796: d Rye, NH 5 Mar 1886 aged 89y (VR Rye): m Rye, NH 2 Aug 1819 Richard Jenness (VR Rye)
6. Sarah, b 25 Jul 1799: d Rye, NH 9 Sep 1802 aged 3y (VR Rye)

Rand, Thomas   83a   1-0-1-0-0
    Rye Town, Rockingham Co., NH

THOMAS RAND, b Rye, NH 6 Jun 1760 son of Samuel & Sarah (Dowrst) Rand (VR Rye): d Rye, NH 27 Feb 1839 (VR Rye): m Rye, NH 4 Apr 1790 Mary Tuck (VR

1790 CENSUS OF RYE, NH

Rye), b 24 Mar 1763 dau of John & Mary (Parsons) Tuck (HR p.552), d Rye, NH 19 Mar 1835 aged 72y (VR Rye).

Children: born Rye, NH (VR Rye)
1. John Tuck, bpt 6 May 1792: d Rye, NH 29 May 1867 aged 75y (VR Rye): m Rye, NH 4 May 1820 Betsey Dow (VR Rye)
2. Mary Jones Wallis, b 12 Mar 1793
3. Samuel, b 16 Feb 1796: d Newcastle, NH 10 Mar 1875 aged 80y (VR Rye): m Kittery, ME 5 Mar 1827 widow Sarah Currier (VR Kit p.277)
4. Thomas, bpt 23 Jun 1799
5. Florinda, bpt 12 Mar 1801: d Rye, NH 25 Aug 1866 aged 65y (VR Rye)
6. Thomas, bpt 7 Aug 1803: d 22 Jan 1866 (HR p.505): m Rye, NH 24 Nov 1831 Sarah Ann Brown (VR Rye)
7. Edward, bpt 12 Jan 1806: d Portsmouth, NH 18 Nov 1868 (VR Rye): m Caroline Paul
8. Jedediah, b 2 Dec 1808: d 23 Jan 1892 (HR p.505): m Eliza J. Yeaton

Rand, William   83a   2-0-1-0-0
    Rye Town, Rockingham Co., NH

WILLIAM RAND, b 1736: d 1811 (DAR I p.555): m Rye, NH 8 Feb 1753 Sarah Tucker (VR Rye).

Children: born Rye, NH (VR Rye)
1. John, b 20 Jan 1756

Rendall, George   83a   2-0-3-0-0
    Rye Town, Rockingham Co., NH

GEORGE RANDALL, probably the George b Rye, NH 15 Sep 1733 son of Edward & Hannah (Wallis) Randall (VR Rye): d bef 1812: m Rye, NH 18 Jul 1751 Sarah Berry (VR Rye), b abt 1732 dau of Jotham & Mary (Bates) Berry, d Rye, NH 27 Feb 1812 aged 80y (VR Rye).

Children: born Rye, NH (VR Rye)
1. Sarah, bpt 13 Sep 1752
2. Sarah, bpt 7 Apr 1754: d Rye, NH Mar 1803 (VR Rye): m Rye, NH 3 Jan 1788 John Nelson (VR Rye)

1790 CENSUS OF RYE, NH

3. Edward, bpt Aug 1758
4. Amelia Berry, bpt 28 Sep 1760: m(1) Rye, NH 29 Nov 1792 Samuel Saunders (VR Rye): m(2) Rye, NH 7 Jun 1796 John Bragg (VR Rye)
5. George, bpt Mar 1762: d Rye, NH 24 Dec 1820 (VR Rye): m Rye, NH 14 Nov 1782 Elizabeth Berry (VR Rye)
6. Rachel, bpt 16 Jan 1765: d Rye, NH 17 Feb 1830 aged 66y (VR Rye): m Rye, NH 27 Jun 1793 John Mace (VR Rye)
7. Abigail, bpt 9 Jul 1769: m Rye, NH 14 Jun 1790 John son of Levi Goss (VR Rye)
8. William Bates, bpt 27 Jun 1771: d at sea, 10 Jun 1811 aged 50y (VR Rye): m Rye, NH 29 Feb 1793 Deborah Yeaton (VR Rye)

Rendall, George Junr   83a   1-2-2-0-0
    Rye Town, Rockingham Co., NH

GEORGE RANDALL JR., bpt Rye, NH Mar 1762 son of George & Sarah (Berry) Randall (VR Rye): d Rye, NH 24 Dec 1820 (VR Rye): m Rye, NH 14 Nov 1782 Elizabeth Berry (VR Rye), bpt Rye, NH 4 Mar 1764 dau of Samuel & Mary (Foss) Berry (VR Rye), d Rye, NH 28 Jun 1842 aged 77y (VR Rye).

Children: born Rye, NH (VR Rye)
1. Mary, bpt 3 Apr 1785: d Rye, NH 19 Mar 1808 (VR Rye): m Rye, NH 28 Nov 1805 Joseph Hall (VR Rye)
2. Edward, bpt 3 Apr 1785: d at sea, 18 Apr 1806 (VR Rye)
3. Betsey, b 1787: d Rye, NH 27 Apr 1863 aged 75y (VR Rye): m(1) Rye, NH 12 Feb 1807 Robert Mathes (VR Rye): m(2) Rye, NH 21 Jun 1815 John Downs (VR Rye)
4. Samuel B., b 11 Jan 1789 (HR p. 516): d Rye, NH 9 Jan 1861 aged 72y (VR Rye): m Rye, NH 26 Jan 1817 Betsey Smith (VR Rye)
5. William B., b Nov 1791 (HR p.516): d Rye, NH 17 Sep 1827 (VR Rye): m Rye, NH 8 Apr 1821 Sally Johnson Goss (VR Rye)
6. Lovey Brackett, bpt 2 Nov 1794: m(1) Rye, NH 14 Dec 1815 Samuel Haley (VR Rye): m(2) Rye, NH 1829 Samuel Robinson (VR Rye)
7. Abigail, bpt 11 Dec 1796
8. George, b abt 1797: d Portsmouth, NH Jul 1852 aged 55y (VR Rye): m aft 1827 Sally

1790 CENSUS OF RYE, NH

Johnson Goss

Remick, Mary   83a   0-1-2-0-0
    Rye town, Rockingham Co., NH

MARY (Meribah) REMICK (widow of Isaac), b Rye, NH 13 Jul 1734 dau of David & Sarah Smith (VR Rye): d aft 1790: m Rye, NH 23 Jan 1755 Isaac Remick (VR Rye), d bef Oct 1781.

Children: born Rye, NH (VR Rye)
1. Sarah, bpt 7 Nov 1756
2. David, bpt Mar 1759
3. Meribah, bpt Nov 1760: m Cotton Palmer
4. Thomas, bpt Sep 1762
5. Mary bpt 1 Dec 1765: d Rye, NH 23 Feb 1829 (VR Rye)
6. Joseph, bpt Oct 1769: d Rye, NH 14 Jul 1827 aged 63y (VR Rye): m Rye, NH 5 Mar 1801 Sally Paul (VR Rye)
7. Isaac, bpt Oct 1769: d Rye, NH 3 Feb 1834 aged 66y (VR Rye): m(1) Rye, NH 19 Nov 1790 Jane Foss (VR Rye): m(2) Rye, NH 7 Nov 1793 Esther Yeaton (VR Rye): m(3) Rye, NH 24 Nov 1808 Lydia Varrell (VR Rye): m(4) Rye, NH 28 Jan 1827 Hannah Varrell (VR Rye)
8. Betsey, bpt Jun 1771: m Hampton, NH 18 Jul 1791 Jonathan Hobbs (HH p.751)
9. Hannah, bpt 3 May 1774: d Rye, NH 8 Apr 1844 aged 70y (VR Rye): m Rye, NH 23 Nov 1797 Andrew Clark (VR Rye)
10. Huldah, bpt 6 Oct 1776: d Rye, NH 30 Jan 1841 (VR Rye): m Rye, NH 15 Jul 1802 Solomon Marden (VR Rye)
11. Jane Kitson, bpt 19 Jul 1778: d Rye, NH 27 May 1847 (VR Rye): m Solomon Foss
12. Moses, bpt 7 Oct 1781: d Kittery, Me. 22 May 1837 (VR Rye): m Rye, NH 3 Mar 1805 Anna Lang (VR Rye)

Salter, Alexander   83a   2-2-2-0-0
    Rye Town, Rockingham Co., NH

ALEXANDER SALTER, b Rye, NH 3 Oct 1744 son of Alexander & Elizabeth (Sanborn) Salter (VR Rye): d Rye, NH Mar 1801 aged 58y (VR Rye): m Abiah Webster, b Rye, NH 3 Sep 1742 dau of Josiah &

1790 CENSUS OF RYE, NH

Patty (Goss) Webster (VR Rye): d Rye, NH 10 May 1811 aged 69y (VR Rye). Alexander was a Sargeant in Capt. Joseph Parsons' Co. in the Rev. War. He enlisted in Oct 1775 and was mustered at Great Island (Newcastle).

Children: born Rye, NH (VR Rye)
1. Lucy, bpt 5 Nov 1769
2. Sarah, bpt 1 Sep 1771
3. Alexander, bpt 7 Jun 1778: m Rye, NH 18 Mar 1803 Molly Berry (VR Rye)
4. Webster, bpt 27 Jan 1783: m Rye, NH 14 Dec 1806 Sally Libby (VR Rye)

Sanders, Robert   83a   2-1-1-0-0
    Rye Town, Rockingham Co., NH

ROBERT SAUNDERS, b abt 1715 probably the son of Robert & Mary Saunders of Gosport, NH who came from Torbay, Eng.: d Rye, NH 7 Mar 1807 aged 92y (VR Rye): m Elizabeth Berry. Elizabeth was probably dead bef 1790. Jonathan B. Waldron came from Portsmouth to live with Robert Saunders. Jonathan was born abt 1761 son of George & Esther (Harvey) Waldron of Portsmouth: d Rye, NH 25 Oct 1813 aged 52y (VR Rye): m Rye, NH 24 Sep 1789 Elizabeth Foss (VR Rye), b abt 1763 dau of Joshua & Rachel (Marden) Foss, d Rye, NH 5 Jan 1835 aged 72y (VR Rye).

Children (of Robert SAUNDERS):
1. Robert, bpt Rye, NH 30 Mar 1742 (VR Rye)

Children (of Jonathan B. WALDRON): born Rye, NH (VR Rye)
1. Elizabeth Saunders, b 16 Dec 1790: d Rye, NH 1 Nov 1857 aged 67y (VR Rye): m Rye, NH 26 Nov 1812 Samuel Varrell (VR Rye)
2. Polly Westbrook, b 17 Aug 1792: d Rye, NH 22 Aug 1831 aged 39y (VR Rye): m Rye, NH 21 Dec 1817 Samuel J. Locke (VR Rye)
3. Robert Saunders, b 9 Jun 1794: d Rye, NH 25 Jul 1835 aged 42y (VR Rye): m(1) 10 Jul 1814 Martha Lang (Straff p.551): m(2) abt 1831 Hannah Drown
4. Joshua Foss, b 11 Dec 1796: d Portsmouth, NH 15 Jun 1855 (VR Rye): m Sophia Towle
5. Richard Harvey, b 30 Sep 1798: d Portsmouth, NH May 1864 (VR Rye): m(1) Sarah Randall:

1790 CENSUS OF RYE, NH

  m(2) abt 1846 Lydia Todd
6. George, bpt 25 Apr 1802: m Huldah Ladd

Sanders, Robert Junr 83a 1-3-2-0-0
  Rye Town, Rockingham Co., NH

ROBERT SAUNDERS JR., bpt Rye, NH 3 Jul 1743 son of
John & Mary (Berry) Saunders (VR Rye): d (bur)
Effingham, NH (LG p.60): m Rye, NH 7 Jul 1765 Mary
Locke (VR Rye), bpt Rye, NH 23 Nov 1744 dau of
Elijah & Huldah (Perkins) Locke (VR Rye), d (bur)
Effingham, NH 1840 aged 96y (LG p.60).

Children: born Rye, NH (VR Rye)
1. Robert, bpt 12 Oct 1766: d 10 Aug 1829
  (Family Record): m Rye, NH 12 Apr 1787 Mary
  Foss (VR Rye)
2. Mary, bpt 16 Aug 1767: m Joseph Chapman
3. Elijah, bpt 20 Aug 1769: m Rye, NH 29 Nov
  1792 Mercy Rand (VR Rye)
4. John, bpt 10 Apr 1774: m _____ Chapman
5. Nathaniel, bpt 29 Nov 1778: m _____ Goss
6. William, m _____ Hall

Sanders, Robert 3d 83a 1-2-1-0-0
  Rye Town, Rockingham Co., NH

ROBERT SAUNDERS 3d, bpt 12 Oct 1766 son of Robert
& Mary (Locke) Saunders (VR Rye): d 10 Aug 1829
(Family Record): m Rye, NH 12 Apr 1787 Mary Foss
(VR Rye), bpt Rye, NH 11 Feb 1764 dau of Job &
Sarah (Lang) Foss (VR Rye), d 12 Jul 1833 (Family
Record).

Children: (Family Record & VR Rye)
1. John, b 25 May 1787/8: d Jan 1874: m 21 Apr
  1813 Betsey Buzzell
2. Sally, bpt 23 Nov 1788 (VR Rye)
3. Robert, bpt 31 Oct 1790 (VR Rye): d 31 May
  1869: m Comfort Philbrick
4. Job, bpt 26 May 1793 (VR Rye): d 30 Aug
  1880: m 29 Apr 1816 Mary (Polly) McFarland
5. Dorothy Wallis, bpt 8 Mar 1795 (VR Rye): d
  19 May 1870
6. Huldah, b 17 Jul 1797: d 20 Sep 1888: m
  Silas F. Morse
7. Elijah, b Chichester, NH 5 Dec 1799: d 18

1790 CENSUS OF RYE, NH

    Feb 1885: m Molly Philbrick
8. Edward Treadwick, b 29 Jul 1803: d 25 Feb 1881: m Caroline Manson
9. William, b 28 May 1806: d 25 Sep 1865: m _____ Wallace

Sanders, Sarah   83a   0-1-2-0-0
    Rye Town, Rockingham Co., NH

SARAH SAUNDERS (widow of William), b Rye, NH 28 Jul 1763 dau of John & Tryphena (Philbrick) Saunders (VR Rye): d 7 Apr 1845 (bur) Alexandria, NH (VG p.21): m(1) Rye, NH 6 Mar 1783 William Saunders (VR Rye), b Rye, NH 19 Oct 1759 son of George & Sarah (Currier) Saunders (VR Rye), d bef 1790: m(2) Rye, NH 25 Aug 1794 Joseph Varrell (VR Rye), b 29 Oct 1771 son of Joseph & Abigail (Varrell) Varrell, d 23 Mar 1854 (bur) Alexandria, NH (VG p.21).

Children: born Rye, NH (VR Rye)
1. William, bpt 20 Mar 1785 (VR Rye)
2. Betsey, bpt 20 Nov 1785 (VR Rye): m Rye, NH 6 Feb 1810 Daniel Page (VR Rye)
3. John, b 2 Mar 1789: d Rye, NH 26 Feb 1868 (VR Rye)

Sanders, Sarah   83a   1-0-4-0-0
    Rye Town, Rockingham Co., NH

SARAH SAUNDERS (widow of George), probably the Sarah bpt Gosport, NH 7 Mar 1735/6 dau of Thomas & Sarah Currier (NEHGR v66 p.152): d Rye, NH 5 May 1813 aged 78y (VR Rye): m Gosport, NH 20 May 1754 George Saunders (NEHGR v66 p.146), bpt Gosport, NH 13 Aug 1732 son of Robert & Mary Saunders (NEHGR v66 p.148), d Rye, NH 1786 (VR Rye). George served in Capt. Parsons's Co. in the Rev. War.

Children: born Rye, NH (VR Rye)
1. Elizabeth, b 29 Jun 1755; bpt Gosport, NH 13 Jul 1755 (NEHGR v66 p.219)
2. Sarah, bpt 18 Sep 1757
3. William, b 19 Oct 1759: d bef 1790: m Rye, NH 6 Mar 1783 Sarah Saunders (VR Rye)
4. George, bpt 2 Sep 1764
5. Martha, b 29 May 1766: m Elijah Wadleigh

1790 CENSUS OF RYE, NH

6. Mercy Haines, b 24 Aug 1767: d Rye, NH 18 Nov 1847 aged 80y (VR Rye): m Rye, NH 13 Sep 1787 James Shapley (VR Rye)
7. George, b 3 Jun 1769: m Mary Saunders
8. Samuel, b 21 Nov 1771: m Rye, NH 29 Nov 1792 Amelia Randall (VR Rye)
9. Sarah, b 20 Aug 1773: d Rye, NH 17 Apr 1846 aged 75y (VR Rye): m Rye, NH 27 Aug 1793 Benjamin Randall (VR Rye)
10. Mary, bpt 3 Nov 1776: m Rye, NH 19 Feb 1796 Reuben Shapley (VR Rye)
11. Hannah, b 4 Jun 1779: d Alexander, NH 12 Aug 1865 (LG p.60): m Rye, NH 21 Jan 1802 Elijah Locke Jr. (VR Rye)

Seavey, Amos 83a 1-0-4-0-0
   Rye Town, Rockingham Co., NH

AMOS SEAVEY, b abt 1718 son of William & Mary (Hincks) Seavey: d Rye, NH 19 Feb 1807 aged 89y (VR Rye): m Rye, NH 25 Oct 1744 Mary Langdon (VR Rye), b 1725 dau of Joseph & Mary (Banfield) Langdon (HR p.410), d Rye, NH 23 Feb 1807 aged 83y (VR Rye).

Children: born Rye, NH (VR Rye)
1. William, bpt 11 Aug 1745: d Rye, NH 15 Mar 1829 aged 84y (VR Rye): m Portsmouth, NH 19 May 1766 Anna Trefethern (Straff p.468)
2. Mary, bpt 25 Jan 1746/7: d Rye, NH 29 Sep 1836 (VR Rye): m Rye, NH 31 Jan 1768 Dr. Joseph Parsons (VR Rye)
3. Hannah, bpt 9 Apr 1749: m Rye, NH 22 Feb 1774 Richard Jenness (VR Rye)
4. Joseph Langdon, bpt 9 Jun 1751: d Rye, NH 4 Mar 1803 aged 52y (VR Rye): m(1) Rye, NH 17 Jul 1777 Elizabeth Garland (VR Rye): m(2) Exeter, NH 13 Jun 1790 Martha Patten (HE p.60)
5. Elizabeth, b 19 Jun 1753 (CG p.121): d Rye, NH 17 Dec 1823 aged 67y (VR Rye): m Rye, NH 21 Aug 1777 Isaac Dow (VR Rye)
6. Anne, bpt 16 Nov 1755: d Rye, NH 26 Jan 1827 aged 72y (VR Rye): m Rye, NH 20 Nov 1791 John Seavey (VR Rye)
7. Martha, bpt Jun 1758: d Rye, NH 27 May 1830 aged 72y (VR Rye): m Rye, NH 11 Mar 1787 Benjamin Jenness (VR Rye)

1790 CENSUS OF RYE, NH

8. Dorothy, bpt 27 Sep 1761: d Rye, NH 7 Jan 1827 aged 66y (VR Rye)
9. Abigail, bpt 10 Jun 1764: d Rye, NH 13 Mar 1851 aged 88y (VR Rye): m Rye, NH 28 Jan 1790 John Garland Jr. (HR p.527 & IGI))

Seavey, Daniel   83a   1-2-2-0-0
   Rye Town, Rockingham Co., NH

DANIEL SEAVEY, bpt Rye, NH 1 May 1763 son of William & Ruth (Moses) Seavey (VR Rye): m Rye, NH 5 Dec 1783 Rachel Rand (VR Rye), b Rye, NH 20 Apr 1762 dau of Samuel & Sarah (Dowrst) Rand (VR Rye).

Children: born Rye, NH (VR Rye)
1. Aaron, bpt 22 May 1785
2. Sally, bpt 8 Jul 1787
3. William, bpt 10 Oct 1790
4. Lucy Wainwright, bpt 4 Jun 1797
5. Mehitable, bpt 14 Feb 1802

Seavey, Ebenezer   83a   1-0-2-0-0
   Rye Town, Rockingham Co., NH

EBENEZER SEAVEY, bpt Rye, NH 9 Jun 1765 son of Paul & Sarah (Wallis) Seavey (VR Rye): m(1) Prudence Perry Marden, bpt Rye, NH 26 Feb 1769 dau of Nathaniel & Hannah (Berry) Marden (VR Rye): m(2) ? ____ dau of Nathaniel & Hannah Berry.

Children: born Rye, NH (VR Rye)
1. Hannah, bpt 13 May 1792: d 15 May 1847: m 6 Oct 1806 William Jenness of Rochester (Straff p.298)
2. Sarah, bpt 13 May 1792: m 3 Nov 1811 James Leighton (Straff p.329)
3. Betsey, bpt 28 Dec 1794: d 30 Apr 1823: m Solomon Jenness (Straff p.298)
4. Ebenezer Wallis, bpt 30 Jun 1796
5. Anne Towle, bpt 1 Jul 1798: m (prob) 22 Oct 1821 Stephen Jenness (Straff p.299)
6. William, bpt Dec 1800: m ____ Jenness
7. Mary Meder, bpt 9 Feb 1805
8. Gideon, d.y. (HR p.529)

Seavey, James   83a   4-0-1-0-1

1790 CENSUS OF RYE, NH

Rye Town, Rockingham Co., NH

JAMES SEAVEY, b abt 1721 son of James & Abigail (Pickering) Seavey (LND p.619): d Rye, NH 19 Oct 1801 (VR Rye): m Elizabeth Langdon (HR p.527), b abt 1733 dau of Joseph & Mary (Banfield) Langdon (LND p.414), d Rye, NH 14 Jul 1804 aged 71y (VR Rye).

Children: born Rye, NH (VR Rye)
1. James, bpt 14 Nov 1756: d Rye, NH 15 Jul 1811 aged 54y (VR Rye)
2. John, bpt 4 Mar 1760: d Rye, NH 9 Feb 1821 aged 61y (VR Rye): m Rye, NH 20 Nov 1791 Anna Seavey (VR Rye)
3. Joseph, bpt Dec 1767: d Rye, NH 8 Nov 1849 (VR Rye): m Mary Whidden

Seavey, James Junr   83a   3-0-1-0-0
     Rye Town, Rockingham Co., NH

JAMES SEAVEY JR., probably the James Seavey Jr. b abt 1754 son of Henry & _____ (Smith) Seavey: d Rye, NH 1 Apr 1829 aged 75y (VR Rye): m Rye, NH 23 May 1780 Patience Berry (VR Rye), b Rye, NH 13 Feb 1762 dau of Jeremiah & Hannah (Locke) Berry (VR Rye), d Rye, NH 13 Aug 1826 (VR Rye).

Seavey, Joseph   83a   1-2-3-0-0
     Rye Town, Rockingham Co., NH

JOSEPH SEAVEY, bpt Rye, NH 30 Mar 1746 son of Henry Jr. & Elizabeth (Fuller) Seavey (VR Rye): d aft 1808: m(1) Rye, NH 24 Dec 1769 Sarah Locke (VR Rye), bpt Rye, NH 13 Oct 1751 dau of Francis & Sarah (Page) Locke (VR Rye): m(2) Rye, NH 2 Oct 1771 Susannah Kenison (VR Rye), d Rye, NH 12 Sep 1808 (VR Rye).

Children: born Rye, NH (VR Rye)
(by 1st wife)
 1. Joseph, bpt 25 Nov 1770
(by 2nd wife)
 2. Hannah, bpt 29 Mar 1774
 3. Mary, bpt 12 Jan 1777
 4. Samuel, bpt 11 Jun 1780
 5. Abigail, bpt 22 Sep 1782

1790 CENSUS OF RYE, NH

6. Sally, bpt 13 Aug 1786
7. Joseph, bpt 6 Jul 1788
8. William, bpt 9 Oct 1791

Seavey, Joseph Langdon   83a   2-1-4-0-1
   Rye Town, Rockingham Co., NH

JOSEPH LANGDON SEAVEY, bpt Rye, NH 9 Jun 1751 son of Amos & Mary (Langdon) Seavey (VR Rye): d Rye, NH 4 Mar 1803 aged 52y (VR Rye): m(1) Rye, NH 17 Jul 1777 Elizabeth Garland (VR Rye), bpt Rye, NH 12 Oct 1760 dau of Benjamin & Sarah (Jenness) Garland (VR Rye), d Rye, NH 19 Nov 1786 aged 26y (VR Rye): m(2) Exeter, NH 13 Jun 1790 Martha Patten of Candia, NH (HE p.60), d Rye, NH 20 Oct 1850 aged aged 88y (VR Rye).

Children: born Rye, NH (VR Rye)
(by 1st wife)
1. Sarah, bpt 17 May 1778: d Rye, NH 1797 aged 20y (VR Rye)
2. Polly, bpt 11 Jun 1780: d Rye, NH 1 Mar 1832 aged 52y (VR Rye): m Rye, NH 16 Mar 1806 Simon Brown (VR Rye)
3. Elizabeth, bpt 15 Sep 1782: d Rye, NH 11 Jun 1835 aged 53y (VR Rye): m(1) Rye, NH 26 Apr 1804 Joseph Brown Jr. (VR Rye): m(2) Rye, NH 18 Dec 1809 Richard Jenness Jr. (VR Rye)
4. Theodore Jackson, bpt 3 Jul 1785: d Rye, NH 15 Jul 1857 aged 71y (VR Rye): m Rye, NH 21 Dec 1820 Betsey Stevenson (VR Rye)

(by 2nd wife)
5. Ephraim, bpt 19 Feb 1792: d Rye, NH 15 Sep 1870 aged 78y (VR Rye): m Rye, NH 1823 Betsey Garland (VR Rye)
6. Mary (Martha), bpt 21 Jul 1793: d Portsmouth, NH 23 Jun 1866 aged 72y (VR Rye): m Rye, NH 28 Nov 1816 Amos Garland (VR Rye)
7. Sidney Sargent, bpt 7 May 1797: d Rye, NH 8 Mar 1858 aged 62y (VR Rye): m 22 Dec 1813 John L. Seavey (HR p.528)
8. Joseph Langdon, bpt 30 Dec 1798: d Rye, NH 2 Mar 1860 aged 61y (VR Rye): m Rye, NH 15 Nov 1832 Temperance Langdon (VR Rye)

Seavey, Paul   83a   1-4-4-0-0
   Rye Town, Rockingham Co., NH

1790 CENSUS OF RYE, NH

PAUL SEAVEY, b abt 1740 son of James & Abigail (Pickering) Seavey (LND p.619): d abt 1800 (DAR I p.602): m Rye, NH 10 May 1764 Sarah Wallis (VR Rye), b abt 1743 dau of Samuel & Sarah (Moses) Wallis.

Children: born Rye, NH (VR Rye)
1. Ebenezer, bpt 9 Jun 1765: d (Lived at Rochester, NH): m(1) Prudence Perry Marden: m(2) ? _____ Berry
2. Deborah, bpt 22 Feb 1767
3. Hannah, bpt 7 May 1769: d Rye, NH 2 Nov 1848 aged 80y (VR Rye): m Rye, NH 23 Mar 1790 Jonathan Wedgewood (VR Rye)
4. Sarah, bpt 14 Jun 1772: m Rye, NH 6 Mar 1791 Joseph Goss (VR Rye)
5. Mehitable, bpt 5 Mar 1775: d Rye, NH 2 May 1850 (VR Rye): m(1) Rye, NH 30 Sep 1792 Peter Garland Jr. (VR Rye): m(2) Rye, NH 14 Jun 1812 James Perkins (VR Rye)
6. Samuel Wallis, bpt Oct 1779: m Kittery, ME Feb 1803 Dorothy (Parsons) Follet (VR Kit p.174)
7. Joshua, b 1777 (HR p.529): m Rye, NH 16 Apr 1797 Betsey Webster (VR Rye)
8. William, bpt 26 Mar 1782: d Demerara, West Indies
9. Fanny, b Oct 1787 (HR p.528): d Rye, NH 15 Jun 1857 aged 69y (VR Rye): m Rye, NH 15 May 1803 Benjamin Garland (VR Rye)
10. Gideon (HR p.528)

Seavey, William   83a   1-2-7-0-0
    Rye Town, Rockingham Co., NH

WILLIAM SEAVEY, bpt Rye, NH 11 Aug 1745 son of Amos & Mary (Langdon) Seavey (VR Rye): d Rye, NH 15 Mar 1829 aged 84y (VR Rye): m Portsmouth, NH 19 May 1766 Anna Trefethern (Straff p.468), b abt 1748, d Rye, NH 17 Nov 1826 aged 78y (VR Rye).

Children: born Rye, NH (VR Rye)
1. Elizabeth, b abt 1767: d Rye, NH 10 Feb 1805 (VR Rye): m John Foye
2. Mary, bpt 24 Nov 1769: d Rye, NH 19 Oct 1820 aged 49y (VR Rye): m Ebenezer Odiorne
3. Anna, bpt 19 Apr 1772: m Levi Dearborn
4. William, bpt 29 May 1774: d Rye, NH 19 Sep

1790 CENSUS OF RYE, NH

   1854 aged 80y (VR Rye): m Elizabeth Ayers
5. Hannah, bpt 10 Nov 1776: d Rye, NH 14 Nov 1803 aged 27y (VR Rye): m Rye, NH 23 Feb 1795 William Foye (VR Rye)
6. Martha, b 1780: d Rye, NH 7 Jun 1855 (VR Rye): m Rye, NH 5 Apr 1798 Samuel Willey (VR Rye)
7. Dorothy, bpt Aug 1781: d Rye, NH 16 Oct 1865 aged 84y (VR Rye): m Rye, NH 24 Feb 1801 Daniel Rand (VR Rye)
8. Amos, bpt 20 May 1787: d Greenland, NH 5 Sep 1852 (VR Rye): m Rye, NH 16 Jun 1807 Sarah Drake (VR Rye)
9. Abigail, bpt 3 Jul 1791: m Joseph Widden
10. John Langdon, bpt 8 Sep 1793: d Rye, NH 26 Aug 1845 aged 52y (VR Rye): m 22 Dec 1813 Sidney Seavey (HR p.530)

Shapley, Betsey   83a   0-0-2-0-0
   Rye Town, Rockingham Co., NH

BETSEY SHAPLEY (widow of Henry), bpt Gosport, NH 28 May 1727 dau of Robert & Mary Saunders (NEHGR v66 p.301): d Rye, NH 3 Feb 1808 (VR Rye): m Gosport, NH 17 Jul 1747 Henry Shapley (NEHGR v66 p.145), bpt Gosport, NH 28 May 1727 son of Reuben & Eleanor Shapley (NEHGR v66 p.302).

Children: born Gosport, NH (NEHGR v67 p.244)
1. Henry Carter, b 19 Apr 1748; bpt 24 Apr 1748: d Rye, NH 17 Mar 1830 aged 87y (VR Rye): m(1) Gosport, NH 26 Oct 1767 Judith Randall (NEHGR v66 p.147): m(2) Rye, NH 18 Nov 1772 Ruth Pitman (VR Rye): m(3) Rye, NH 22 Sep 1811 Sally Caswell (VR Rye)
2. Reuben, b 12 Apr 1750: m (1) _____ Blaisdell: m(2) Concord, NH 14 Mar 1802 Nancy Clark (NHGR v6 p. 107)
3. Elizabeth, b 19 Oct 1751: m(1) Gosport, NH 26 Oct 1768 Benjamin Randall (NEHGR v.66 p.147): m(2) Rye, NH 11 Nov 1780 William Pierce (VR Rye)
4. Edward, b 5 Jun 1753: m Greenland, NH 20 Dec 1779 Hepzibah Rand (VR Green p.8)
5. James, bpt 23 Feb 1755
6. Sarah, b 12 Feb 1757: d Rye, NH 27 Nov 1819 (VR Rye): m(1) 22 Sep 1776 John Mace: m(2) Rye, NH 25 Jun 1801 Daniel Goss (VR Rye)

1790 CENSUS OF RYE, NH

7. John, b 8 Feb 1759: m _____ Leighton
8. Mary, bpt 26 Apr 1761
9. James, b 29 Mar 1763: d Rye, NH 4 Aug 1821 (VR Rye): m Rye, NH 13 Sep 1787 Mercy Saunders (VR Rye)
10. Robert, b 20 Jan 1765
11. Benjamin Carter, b 23 May 1767: m Nancy Blaisdell
12. Mary Saunders, bpt 25 Feb 1769: m Rye, NH 27 Apr 1789 John Robinson (VR Rye)

Shapley, Henry   83a   4-1-2-0-0
    Rye Town, Rockingham Co., NH

HENRY CARTER SHAPLEY, bpt Gosport, NH 24 Apr 1748 son of Henry & Elizabeth (Saunders) Shapley (NEHGR v66 p.215): d Rye, NH 17 Mar 1830 aged 87y (VR Rye): m(1) Gosport, NH 26 Oct 1767 Judith Randall (NEHGR v66 p.147), bpt Gosport, NH 27 Sep 1741 dau of Daniel & Elizabeth Randall (NEHGR v66 p.210), d bef 1772: m(2) Rye, NH 18 Nov 1772 Ruth Pitman (VR Rye): m(3) Rye, NH 22 Sep 1811 Sally Caswell (VR Rye), b abt 1779, d Rye, NH 2 Oct 1853 aged 74y (VR Rye). Henry served as a Corporal under Capt. Parsons in the Rev. War.

Children:
(by 1st wife)
1. Betsey (b bef m), bpt Gosport, NH 6 Mar 1768 (NEHGR v66 p.295: d Rye, NH 10 Jun 1850 (VR Rye): m Rye, NH 4 Jul 1788 Robert Powers (VR Rye)
2. Henry J., bpt Gosport, NH 6 Mar 1768 (NEHGR v66 p.295): d Rye, NH 13 Jul 1845 (VR Rye): m Rye, NH 16 Sep 1790 Mary Berry (VR Rye)
(by 2nd wife)
3. Reuben, bpt Rye, NH 30 Jun 1774 (VR Rye): m Rye, NH 19 Feb 1796 Mary Saunders (VR Rye)
4. Judith, bpt Rye, NH 30 Jun 1774 (VR Rye)
5. Sally, bpt Rye, NH 30 Jun 1774 (VR Rye)
(by 3rd wife)
6. George W. (b bef m): m Ann Gray
7. Robert, bpt Rye, NH 11 Jun 1809 (VR Rye): m Rye, NH 1854 Ann Knowland (VR Rye)

Sleeper, Tristram Coffin   83a   2-1-3-0-0
    Rye Town, Rockingham Co., NH

1790 CENSUS OF RYE, NH

TRISTRAM COFFIN SLEEPER, bpt Kingston, NH 10 Jul 1744 son of Benjamin & Abigail (Coffin) Sleeper (NHGR v.5 p.111): d Rye, NH 26 Jan 1811 aged 67y (VR Rye): m Rye, NH 18 Dec 1766 Ruth Tarlton (VR Rye), b abt 1747, d Rye, NH 23 Feb 1832 aged 85y (VR Rye).

Children: born Rye, NH (VR Rye)
1. Thomas, bpt 20 Sep 1767: m Rye, NH 1798 Sally Berry (VR Rye)
2. Eliphalet, bpt 25 Nov 1770: d Rye, NH 17 Mar 1843 aged 73y (VR Rye): m Rye, NH 31 Mar 1800 Polly Jenness (VR Rye)
3. Molly, bpt 20 Dec 1772: d Rye, NH 19 Jun 1841 aged 68y (VR Rye): m Rye, NH 2 Mar 1794 David Wedgewood (VR Rye)
4. William, bpt 12 May 1776: d Rye, NH 2 Jan 1861 aged 85y (VR Rye): m Rye, NH 1803 Sally Smith of Exeter (VR Rye)
5. Benjamin, bpt 9 May 1779

Smith, David   83a   2-2-3-0-0
   Rye Town, Rockingham Co., NH

DAVID SMITH, b Rye, NH 18 Jan 1741 son of David & Sarah Smith (VR Rye): d Rye, NH 1 Jun 1804 aged 70y (VR Rye): m Rye, NH 31 Oct 1765 Mary Marden (VR Rye), b abt 1735 dau of Thomas & Mary (Smith) Marden, d Rye, NH 22 Nov 1810 aged 75y (VR Rye).

Children: born Rye, NH (VR Rye)
1. Mary, bpt 13 Aug 1769: d Rye, NH 4 Dec 1849 aged 80y (VR Rye): m Rye, NH 12 Nov 1789 Stephen Marden (VR Rye)
2. Salley, bpt 11 Oct 1772: d Rye, NH 22 Dec 1842 aged 71y (VR Rye): m Rye, NH 12 Jan 1790 Joses Philbrick (VR Rye)

Smith, Samuel   83a   1-1-2-0-0
   Rye Town, Rockingham Co., NH

SAMUEL SMITH, b abt 1753: d Rye, NH 4 Jan 1824 aged 71y (VR Rye): m Mar 1786 Elizabeth Hall (HR p.543), bpt Rye, NH 9 Aug 1761 dau of Joseph & Esther (Tucker) Hall (VR Rye), d Rye, NH 11 Sep 1847 aged 87y (VR Rye).

1790 CENSUS OF RYE, NH

Children: born Rye, NH (VR Rye)
1. William, bpt 4 Sep 1790
2. Esther, bpt 4 Sep 1790: m Jeremiah Sanborn
3. John, bpt 9 Oct 1791: m Nancy Sanborn
4. Betsey, bpt 18 Oct 1795: d Portsmouth, NH 14 Sep 1873 aged 78y (VR Rye): m Rye, NH 26 Jan 1817 Samuel B. Randall (VR Rye)
5. Joseph Hall, bpt 19 Nov 1797: d Rye, NH 20 Jan 1816 aged 19y (VR Rye)

Trefethern, William   83a   1-3-3-0-0
   Rye Town, Rockingham Co., NH

WILLIAM TREFETHERN, b Rye, NH 5 Jun 1751 son of Robinson & Abigail (Locke) Trefethern (VR Rye): d Rye, NH 17 Jun 1825 aged 74y (VR Rye): m Rye, NH 27 Jan 1774 Elizabeth Tucker (VR Rye), bpt Rye, NH 17 Feb 1754 dau of Nathaniel & Elizabeth (Hall) Tucker (VR Rye), d Rye, NH 12 Feb 1837 aged 83y (VR Rye). William served in Capt. Parsons Co., in the Rev. War.

Children: born Rye, NH (VR Rye)
1. William, bpt 18 Jun 1775: d Rye, NH 5 Oct 1853 (VR Rye): m(1) Rye, NH 20 Jan 1801 Lydia Berry (VR Rye): m(2) Rye, NH 1 Feb 1821 Susannah Piper (VR Rye)
2. Nathaniel, bpt 2 Oct 1777: d 11 Jun 1784 (LG p.69)
3. Nabby, bpt 7 Oct 1780: d 20 Jun 1784 (LG p.69)
4. Betsey, bpt 1783: d Barnstead, NH unmd
5. Nathaniel Tucker, bpt 15 May 1785: d Rye, NH 18 Mar 1856 (VR Rye): m Rye, NH 1 Jul 1807 Charlotte Jewell (VR Rye)
6. Joseph, bpt 29 Mar 1788: d Rye, NH 10 Feb 1859 (VR Rye): m Rye, NH 29 Jan 1810 Hannah Berry (VR Rye)
7. Nancy, bpt 14 Nov 1790: m Rye, NH 28 Mar 1819 Samuel Ayers (VR Rye)
8. Polly, bpt 18 Nov 1792: m George Ramstead
9. Henry, bpt 8 Mar 1795 : d 8 Sep 1828 (LG p.69): m Mary Brown
10. John Adams, bpt 11 Aug 1799: d Rye, NH 4 Oct 1870 (VR Rye): m Rye, NH 20 Nov 1834 Mary Locke (VR Rye)
11. Sebastian, b 27 Jan 1801 (HR p.549): d 18 Aug 1875 (LG p.69): m Nov 1835 Elizabeth

1790 CENSUS OF RYE, NH

Locke
12. Thomas, bpt 13 Jun 1802

Tucker, Nathaniel   83a   2-0-4-0-0
    Rye Town, Rockingham Co., NH

NATHANIEL TUCKER, b Rye, NH 18 Sep 1732 son of
William & Mary (Archer) Tucker (VR Rye): d bef
1807: m Rye, NH 8 Feb 1753 Elizabeth Hall (VR
Rye), b Gosport, NH 12 Apr 1732 dau of Joseph &
Mary (Merrifield) Hall (NEHGR v.66 p.303), d Rye,
NH 18 Jul 1807 aged 75y (VR Rye). Nathaniel was
in the French & Indian War.

Children: born Rye, NH (VR Rye)
  1. Elizabeth, b 19 Nov 1753: d Rye, NH 12 Feb
     1837 aged 83y (VR Rye): m Rye, NH 27 Jan
     1774 William Trefethern (VR Rye)
  2. Sarah, b 31 May 1756: d Rye, NH 15 Jun 1833
     aged 77y (VR Rye): m Rye, NH 6 Mar 1783 John
     Foss (VR Rye)
  3. Nathaniel, bpt 8 Oct 1758: d at sea, 1807
     (HR p.553)
  4. William, b 31 Jan 1763: d Rye, NH 9 Aug 1820
     (VR Rye): m Rye, NH 13 Mar 1787 Olive Saunders (VR Rye)
  5. Richard, b 27 Nov 1764
  6. Joseph, b 19 Sep 1773: d 14 Mar 1811 aged
     38y (VR Rye): m(1) Rye, NH 23 Jul 1795
     Elizabeth Lear (VR Rye): m(2) Rye, NH 29 Jan
     1806 Betsey Reid (VR Rye)
  7. Molly, bpt 5 Jun 1774 (VR Rye) - Nathaniel
     Tucker took to bring up

Tucker, William   83a   1-1-2-0-0
    Rye Town, Rockingham Co., NH

WILLIAM TUCKER, b Rye, NH 31 Jan 1763 son of
Nathaniel & Elizabeth (Hall) Tucker (VR Rye): d
Rye, NH 9 Aug 1820 (VR Rye): m Rye, NH 13 Mar 1787
Olive Saunders (VR Rye), b 1766 dau of John &
Tryphena (Philbrick) Saunders (HR p.553): d Rye,
NH 4 Nov 1816 aged 50y (VR Rye).

Children: born Rye, NH (VR Rye)
  1. John, bpt 23 Nov 1788
  2. Sally, b (HR p.553): m Levi Jenness

1790 CENSUS OF RYE, NH

3. Richard, bpt 21 Mar 1790
4. William, bpt 4 Dec 1791: m Betsey Saunders
5. Tryphena, b (HR p.553)
6. Betsey, b 6 May 1798: d Concord, NH 26 Feb 1847 (LG p.141): m Rye, NH 20 Feb 1817 Richard Locke (VR Rye)
7. Olive, bpt 2 Nov 1794: m New Castle, NH 12 Mar 1817 Daniel Weeks (NHGR v2 p.38)

Verriel, Edward   83a   1-3-2-0-0
  Rye Town, Rockingham Co., NH

EDWARD VARRELL, bpt Gosport, NH 21 Jun 1752 son of John & Rachel (Sadler) Varrell (NEHGR v66 p.218): d Rye, NH 13 Oct 1818 (VR Rye): m(1) Rye, NH 4 Nov 1773 Elizabeth Saunders (VR Rye): m(2) Rye, NH 19 Nov 1784 Mary Berry (VR Rye), bpt Rye, NH 12 May 1765 dau of Timothy & Mary (Tucker) Berry (VR Rye), d Rye, NH 23 Feb 1849 (VR Rye). Edward served in Capt. Joseph Parsons' Co. in the Rev. War.

Children: born Rye, NH (VR Rye)
(by 1st wife)
1. Rachel, bpt 13 Nov 1774: m _____ Perkins
2. Betty, bpt 9 Jun 1776: d Portsmouth, NH 15 Feb 1869 (HR p.557): had a child by Andrew Clark
3. William, bpt 12 Jul 1778: d 23 Nov 1820 (bur Portsmouth, NH): m Portsmouth, NH 12 Aug 1800 widow Lydia Currier (VG p.336 & IGI)
4. Betsey, 1781: d.y.
5. Richard Tucker, bpt 3 Apr 1785: d bef 1805: m Rye, NH 31 Oct 1803 Mary Randall (VR Rye)
6. Edward, bpt 3 Apr 1785: d 10 Mar 1869 (VG p.336): m Rye,NH 3 Aug 1809 Mary Dearborn (VR Rye)
(by second wife)
7. Samuel, bpt 10 Jun 1787: d Rye, NH 29 Oct 1857 aged 70y (VR Rye): m Rye, NH 26 Nov 1812 Elizabeth Waldron (VR Rye)
8. Mary, bpt 10 Apr 1791: m Rye, NH 5 Apr 1812 Eben Gove (VR Rye)
9. John, bpt 9 Mar 1794: m Salisbury, MA Aug 1810 Betsey Brown (IGI)
10. Sarah, bpt 11 Aug 1799: m(1) Rye, NH 14 Jun 1829 Hiram Jenkins (VR Rye): m (2) __ Grove
11. Abigail, b Jan 1799 (HR p.557): d Ports-

1790 CENSUS OF RYE, NH

mouth, NH 11 Feb 1867 aged 55y (VR Rye): m Rye, NH 1 Mar 1827 Jonathan Batchelder (VR Rye)
12. Joseph, bpt 19 Apr 1801: m Eunice Brown
13. Nancy, d.y. (HR p.557)
14. Richard, b abt 1805: d Rye, NH 21 Mar 1861 aged 55y (VR Rye): m Rye, NH 4 Mar 1824 Molly (Berry) Mace (VR Rye)

Verriel, Hannah   83a   0-0-6-0-0
   Rye Town, Rockingham Co., NH

HANNAH VERRILL, probably the Widow Hannah Varrell listed in the inventory for the town of Rye for the years 1789 & 1790. A Hannah Varrell (widow of John) died Rye, NH 1 Feb 1839 aged 66y (VR Rye). No guess as to the other members of the household.

Verriel, John   83a   1-1-2-0-0
   Rye Town, Rockingham Co., NH

JOHN VERRILL, bpt Rye, NH 20 May 1759 son of Solomon & Deborah (Bartlett) Verrill (VR Rye): d Rye, NH 10 Sep 1811 aged 52y (VR Rye): m(1) Rye, NH 22 Apr 1784 Anna Lang (VR Rye), bpt Rye, NH 3 Apr 1763 dau of Mark & Salome (Goss) Lang (VR Rye), d Rye, NH 26 Jul 1807 aged 44y (VR Rye): m(2) Rye, NH 8 May 1808 Eleanor Norton (VR Rye), b abt 1760 dau of John & Hannah (Burleigh) Norton (HR p.466), d Rye, NH 6 Mar 1847 aged 87y (VR Rye).

Children: born Rye, NH (VR Rye)
1. Nathaniel, bpt 30 Apr 1786: d Rye, NH 18 Jan 1856 aged 70y (VR Rye): m 1811 Hannah Lewis
2. Sally, bpt 21 Jun 1789
3. Betsey, b abt 1792: d Rye, NH 26 Jan 1811 aged 19y (VR Rye)
4. John, bpt 1 Aug 1795
5. Washington, bpt 21 Dec 1800: d Rye, NH 28 Dec 1857 (VR Rye): m Candia, NH 1820 Mary Lang (LF p.81)

Wallis, Ebenezer   83a   2-0-2-0-0
   Rye Town, Rockingham Co., NH

1790 CENSUS OF RYE, NH

EBENEZER WALLIS, b abt 1722 son of Samuel & Hannah (Seavey) Wallis (see NH Probate v.3 p.55): d Rye, NH 30 Mar 1812 aged 90y (VR Rye): m Dorothy Lang, bpt 25 Apr 1725 dau of John & Sarah (Bickford) Lang (LF p.54), d Rye, NH 20 Oct 1813 aged 89y (VR Rye). They had no children, but Ebenezer's nephew Gideon Seavey son of Paul & Sarah (Wallis) Seavey supposedly lived with them.

Wallis, Samuel   83a   3-0-2-1-0
    Rye Town, Rockingham Co., NH

SAMUEL WALLIS, b abt 1720 (DAR I p.713) son of Samuel & brother of Ebenezer Wallis: d 1793 : m(1) Sarah Moses, bpt Portsmouth NH 10 Sep 1721 dau of James & Martha (Jackson) Moses (LND p.496): m(2) Widow Deborah Reeder (HR p.563).

Children: bpt Rye, NH (VR Rye)
  1. Sarah, b abt 1743: m Rye, NH 10 May 1764 Paul Seavey (VR Rye)
  2. Hannah, bpt 11 Aug 1745: d Rye, NH 21 Sep 1830 (VR Rye): m Rye, NH 29 Apr 1773 William Marden (VR Rye)
  3. Samuel, bpt 16 Aug 1746/7: d Rye, NH 25 Feb 1832 aged 85y (VR Rye): m Rye, NH 16 Nov 1773 Elizabeth Parsons (VR Rye)
  4. Abigail, d abt 1833 (HR p.563): m Rye, NH 13 Jun 1776 Nadab Moses (VR Rye)
  5. Mary, bpt 7 Jan 1750: m Rye, NH 25 Dec 1781 Joseph Tucker (VR Rye)
  6. Martha, bpt 29 Mar 1752: m Rye, NH 1 Mar 1796 John Langmaid (VR Rye)
  7. James, bpt 15 Aug 1756
  8. Deborah, bpt 28 Oct 1759
  9. Betsey, bpt Mar 1762: d Rye, NH 9 Feb 1821 aged 59y (VR Rye): m Rye, NH 17 Nov 1785 Levi Jenness (VR Rye)

Wallis, Samuel Junr   83a   1-1-2-0-0
    Rye Town, Rockingham Co., NH

SAMUEL WALLIS JR., bpt Rye, NH 16 Aug 1746/7 son of Samuel & Sarah (Moses) Wallis (VR Rye): d Rye, NH 25 Feb 1832 aged 85y (VR Rye): m Rye, NH 16 Nov 1773 Elizabeth Parsons (VR Rye), bpt 14 Jul 1754 dau of Samuel & Mary (Jones) Parsons (HR p.476),

1790 CENSUS OF RYE, NH

d Rye, NH 9 Jun 1827 aged 73y (VR Rye). Samuel was an ensign in Capt. Parsons Co. in the Rev. War.

Children: born Rye, NH (VR Rye)
1. Sarah, bpt 20 Mar 1777
2. Mary Jones, bpt 1 Jun 1777: d 1 Dec 1839: m Rye, NH 8 May 1796 Isaac Waldron (VR Rye)

Webster, John   83a   1-2-7-0-0
    Rye Town, Rockingham Co., NH

JOHN WEBSTER, b Rye, NH 18 Jan 1751 son of Josiah & Patty (Goss) Webster (VR Rye): d Rye, NH 22 Sep 1823 aged 72y (VR Rye): m Dolly Chapman (DAR I p.725), b abt 1753, d Rye, NH 9 Aug 1837 aged 84y (VR Rye).

Children: bpt Rye, NH (VR Rye)
1. Abigail, bpt Aug 1777: d Rye, NH 4 Sep 1860 (VR Rye): m Rye, NH Feb 1798 Samuel B. Berry (VR Rye)
2. Mary, bpt 25 Apr 1779
3. Martha, bpt Aug 1781: d Rye, NH 2 May 1856 aged 75y (VR Rye): m Rye, NH 26 Apr 1801 Jethro Locke (VR Rye)
4. Dolly, bpt 1784: m Rye, NH 20 Jul 1806 Stephen Green (VR Rye)
5. Anne, bpt 2 Sep 1787: m Rye, NH 22 Nov 1810 Alexander Salter (VR Rye)
6. Jeremy, bpt 27 Jun 1790
7. Jeremy, bpt 15 Jul 1792: d Rye, NH 4 Mar 1842 aged 50y (VR Rye): m Rye, NH 24 May 1837 Eliza Rand (VR Rye)
8. John Hobbs, bpt Sep 1795: d Rye, NH 2 Aug 1866 aged 71y (VR Rye): m Rye, NH 20 Sep 1827 Elizabeth Clark (VR Rye)
9. Mary, bpt 8 Jul 1798: m Rye, NH 14 Feb 1816 Noah Wiggin (VR Rye)

Webster, Josiah   83a   1-3-3-0-0
    Rye Town, Rockingham Co., NH

JOSIAH WEBSTER, bpt Rye, NH 22 May 1757 son of Josiah & Patty (Goss) Webster (VR Rye): d Rye, NH 16 May 1805 aged 48y (VR Rye): m Portsmouth, NH 15 Nov 1780 Sarah Locke (LG p.111), bpt Rye, NH 29 Nov 1761 dau of David & Hannah (Lovering) Locke

1790 CENSUS OF RYE, NH

(VR Rye).

Children: born Rye, NH (VR Rye)
1. Mary, b 17 Apr 1781: m Rye, NH 1806 Henry Elkins (VR Rye)
2. Josiah, b 6 Jan 1783: d Portsmouth, NH 9 Dec 1833: m Portsmouth, NH 20 May 1806 Hannah Grant (LG p.249)
3. David, b 23 Sep 1785: m Rye, NH 1 Feb 1809 Eunice Nowell (VR Rye)
4. Sarah, bpt 25 Jun 1786: m 1807 Ephraim Philbrick (LG p.250)
5. John, b 23 Jun 1788
6. Fanny, b 26 Mar 1790: d Boston, MA 25 Dec 1808 aged 15y (VR Rye)
7. Nathaniel, b 4 Mar 1793: d New Orleans
8. Martha, b 10 Apr 1795: d Rye, NH 25 Oct 1846 aged 51y (VR Rye): m Rye, NH 9 Dec 1819 James Brown (VR Rye)
9. Levi Lock, bpt 23 May 1797: m Elizabeth Macy

Webster, Richard   83a   1-1-7-0-0
    Rye Town, Rockingham Co., NH

RICHARD WEBSTER, b Rye, NH 1 Jan 1754 son of Josiah & Patty (Goss) Webster (VR Rye): d Rye, NH 16 Jan 1836 aged 83y (VR Rye): m Rye, NH 29 Oct 1778 Elizabeth Randall (VR Rye), b Rye, NH 10 Apr 1755 dau of Mark & Abigail (Philbrick) Randall (VR Rye), d Rye, NH 14 Mar 1826 aged 70y (VR Rye). Richard was in the Rev. War serving under Capt. Parker at Fort Sullivan & with Capt. Parsons in Rhode Island.

Children: born Rye, NH (VR Rye)
1. Betsey, b 3 Mar 1779: m Rye, NH 16 Apr 1797 Joshua Seavey (VR Rye)
2. Abigail, bpt 7 Oct 1780: m Rye, NH Apr 1809 Levi Randall (VR Rye)
3. Martha, bpt Aug 1781: d Portsmouth, NH 13 Oct 1865 aged 84y (VR Rye): m(1) Rye, NH 3 Feb 1822 Ebenezer Odiorne (VR Rye): m(2) Rye, NH 5 Nov 1829 John Foye (VR Rye)
4. Sarah, b 12 Jul 1783: m Rye, NH 4 Jan 1803 James Marden (VR Rye)
5. Hannah, bpt 20 Feb 1785: m Rye, NH 16 Sep 1813 John Jenness (VR Rye)
6. Olive, bpt 7 Jan 1787: d Rye, NH 15 Aug 1802

1790 CENSUS OF RYE, NH

      aged 5y 9mo (VR Rye)
7. Richard, b 6 Oct 1788: d Portsmouth, NH 1 Nov 1856 (VR Rye): m 1813 Mary Philbrick
9. Mark, bpt 26 Jun 1791: d Rye, NH 17 Jul 1865 aged 71y (VR Rye): m Rye, NH 26 Nov 1829 Mary Ann Lang (VR Rye)

Wells, Samuel   83a   3-1-7-0-0
    Rye Town, Rockingham Co., NH

SAMUEL WELLS, b Portsmouth, NH 2 Dec 1735 son of Samuel & Priscilla (Dowse) Wells (NEHGR v27 p.11): d aft 1790 DAR II p.222): m Rye, NH 28 Apr 1763 Elizabeth Thompson (VR Rye).

Children: born Rye, NH (VR Rye)
1. Sarah, bpt 24 Nov 1765
2. Simeon, bpt 17 Jun 1768: m(1) Sally Batchelder: m(2) _____ Shaw
3. Olly, bpt 29 Jul 1770: m ? Rye, NH Feb 1799 Joseph Batchelder (VR Rye)
4. Elizabeth, bpt Dec 1773: m ? Rye, NH 25 Dec 1794 Daniel Philbrick (VR Rye)
5. Samuel, bpt 2 Jun 1776: m Hannah Brown
6. Molly, bpt 2 Aug 1778: m Rye, NH 16 Nov 1796 Jethro Goss (VR Rye)
7. Deborah, bpt 29 Jul 1781

Williams, John Floyd   83a   2-1-2-0-0
    Rye Town, Rockingham Co., NH

JOHN FLOYD WILLIAMS, probably the John F. Williams who married in Rye, NH 4 Jul 1790 Peggy Appleton (VR Rye). Perhaps this was a second marriage. The Inventory for 1790 Town of Rye, NH has on its list "Doc John Williams" as well as Margaret Appleton. Neither appear on the lists for the following years.

Yeaton, Joseph   83a   2-0-2-0-0
    Rye Town, Rockingham Co., NH

JOSEPH YEATON, possibly son of John & Elizabeth (Randall) Yeaton: m(1) _____ : m(2) Rye, NH 17 Jul 1751 Susannah Lang (VR Rye), dau of William & Susannah (Savage) Lang (NH Probate v6 p.396).

1790 CENSUS OF RYE, NH

Children: born Rye, NH (VR Rye)
(by 1st wife)
1. Mary, b abt 1747: d Rye, NH 20 Aug 1831 aged 84y (VR Rye): m Rye, NH 18 Sep 1767 Peter Johnson (VR Rye)
2. Sarah, bpt 27 Nov 1748
3. Sarah, bpt 30 Sep 1750

(by 2nd wife)
4. Joseph Jr., bpt 12 Jul 1752: d Pittsfield, NH 1806 (NH Gran Mo v42 p.57): m Rye, NH 5 Feb 1776 Elizabeth Rand (VR Rye)
5. Anna, bpt 23 Dec 1753
6. William, bpt Jul 1756: d Epsom, NH 1831 (NH Gran Mo v42 p.56): m Rye NH 17 Sep 1780 Hannah Towle (VR Rye)
7. Elizabeth, bpt Sep 1758: d Eliot, ME 27 Jun 1833 (NEHGR v95 p.270): m Rye, NH 18 Apr 1779 Samuel Shapley (VR Rye)
8. John, bpt 29 Mar 1761
9. Hannah, bpt 19 Jun 1763: m Rye, NH 26 Nov 1787 Stephen Tucker of Kittery (VR Rye)
10. Susannah, bpt May 1765
11. Philip, bpt 17 Jun 1768: m Rye, NH 1797 Huldah Saunders (VR Rye)
12. Susan, d (Lived in Eliot, ME): m Kittery, ME 26 Sep 1789 Jacob Remick (VR Kit p.245)
13. Deborah, b abt 1769: d Rye, NH 21 Dec 1807 aged 38y (VR Rye): m Rye, NH 29 Feb 1793 William Bates Randall (VR Rye)

1790 CENSUS REFERENCES

CG	--------	Colonial Gravestone Inscriptions by Mrs. C. Goss (Clearfield Co. 1989)
DAR	--------	DAR Patriot Index vol I & vol II (DAR Lib. 1966 & 1980)
DB	--------	The Book of Dow by Robert P. Dow (Claremont, NH 1929)
DG	--------	Drake Family of NH by Alice Thompson (N.H. Hist. Society 1962)
HE	--------	History of Exeter, NH by Charles Bell (Heritage Books, Inc. 1979)
HH	--------	History of Hampton, NH, by Joseph Dow (N.H. Pub. Co. 1970)
HR	--------	History of Rye, NH by Langdon B. Parsons (Rumford Print. Co. 1905)
IGI	--------	International Genealogical Index
JG	--------	Jenness Genealogy by Eloise Leonard (DAR Lib. 1955)
LF	--------	Lang Family by Howard P. Moore (Tuttle Co. 1935)
LG	--------	Hist. & Gen. of Capt. John Locke by Arthur Locke (Locke Fam. Assoc. 1985)
LIB	--------	Libby Family in America by Charles Libby (Portland, ME 1882)
LND	--------	Gen. Dict. of ME & NH by Libby, Noyes & Davis (Gen. Pub. Inc. 1988)
MHGR	--------	Maine Hist. & Gen. Recorder (Gen. Pub. Inc. 1973)
NEHGR	--------	New England Hist. & Gen. Register
NHGR	--------	New Hampshire Gen. Record vols 1-7 (Dover, NH 1904-1910)
Old Kit	---	Old Kittery & Her Families by Everett Stackpole (New Eng. Hist. Press 1981)
Straff	----	Early Marriages of Straff. Co., NH by R. Canney (Heritage Books, Inc. 1991)
VG	--------	Hist. & Gen. of Varrell-Verrill Family by H. Round (privately printed 1968)
VR Brid	---	Vital Records of Bridgewater, MA (New Eng. Hist. & Gen. Society 1916)
VR Green	--	Vital Records of Greenland, NH by Priscilla Hamond (DAR Lib. 1938)
VR Hav	----	Vital Records of Haverhill, MA (Topsfield Hist. Soc. 1911)
VR Kit	----	Vital Records of Kittery, ME by Maine Hist. Society (Picton Press 1991)
VR Rye	----	Vital Records of Rye, NH (original church, town & genealogical records)

INDEX TO 1790 RYE CENSUS

ACKERMAN
  Peter..........246,278
ADAMS
  Charles............289
ALLEN
  Elizabeth..........276
  Jude...............239
  Salome........239,240
AMAZEEN
  Abigail............274
APPLETON
  Peggy..............316
ARCHER
  Mary...237,246,255,310
AYERS
  Elizabeth..........306
  Samuel.............309
BABB
  Thomas.............292
BALL
  Mary...............239
BANFIELD
  Mary..........301,303
BARNARD
  Rhoda..............289
BARTLETT
  Deborah............312
BATCHELDER
  _____...............257
  Abigail D..........264
  Betsey.............284
  John...............266
  Jonathan...........312
  Joseph.............316
  Sally..............316
BATES
  Judith.....243,269,281
  Mary....234,236-37,255
                277,295
  William............234
BEALS
  Hannah (Tarlton)...269
BECK
  Mary...............288
BERRY
  Abigail.......236,264
  Betsey.............235

BERRY
  Betsey Garland.....233
  Charity........234,259
  Charles............233
  Dolly..............238
  Ebenezer...233,236,249
  Eleanor............238
  Eliza..............238
  Elizabeth..236,296,298
  Esther.........280,286
  Hannah....234,238,277
                279,302,309
  Hannah Locke.......235
  Hannah (Vittum)....276
  Huldah.............236
  Isaac..............233
  Jacob..............233
  James Towle........236
  Jeremiah....233-35,237
                238,245,247
                279,303
  Joses..............234
  Joseph.........236,237
  Joseph Jenness.....235
  Jotham......234,236-37
                255,277,295
  Judith.............235
  Levi........234-36,259
  Love...........238,280
  Lydia......234,238,309
  Mary....234-35,237,246
                247,255-56,265
                271,276,282,299
                307,311
  Mehitable..........237
  Merrifield.233,236,258
  Molly...236-37,298,312
  Nancy Jenness......236
  Nathaniel......237,255
                267,302
  Nehemiah...........233
  Olive..........235,258
  Olly...............236
  Patience.......234,303
  Patty..........238,245
  Rachel.....235,255,277
  Richard............233

319

INDEX TO 1790 RYE CENSUS

BERRY
  Sally..........235,308
  Samuel..234-37,246,296
  Samuel B.......238,314
  Sarah...233-35,237,253
                    295-96
  Sarah Sargent......238
  Sarah Wentworth....238
  Solomon............234
  Susannah...........237
  Thomas Garland.....233
  Timothy....235,237,311
  William.....233-34,237
                       238
BICKFORD
  Mehitable..........277
  Sarah......244,266,313
BLAISDELL
  _____............306
  Abner..............288
  Nancy..............307
BLAKE
  Abigail............269
  Sarah..............241
BLAZO
  Thankful.......273,275
BOWLEY
  James..............272
BRACKETT
  Eleanor............234
  Love...234,237,265,279
  Phebe..............238
  Samuel.............238
BRAGG
  John...............296
BRIGGS
  Elizabeth..........242
BROWN
  Abigail........239,240
  Alexander..........241
  Benjamin...........239
  Betsey.............311
  Elizabeth...239-40,249
              251,271,293
  Elizabeth (Seavey).258
  Eunice.............312
  Hannah.............316
  James.........239,315
  Jeremiah...........239

BROWN
  Job Jenness........240
  John....239-40,253,257
                   263,294
  John Sam Jenness...240
  Jonathan...239,240,268
                     271
  Joseph..239-40,251,304
  Josiah.............239
  Mary....239-40,275,309
  Patty..............241
  Samuel.............240
  Sarah.........239,287
  Sarah Ann..........295
  Sarah Hook.........265
  Simon..........244,304
  William............239
BUNKER
  James..............256
BURLEIGH
  Deborah............291
  Hannah.............312
BURNHAM
  _____...........239
BUTLER
  Joseph.............247
BUZZELL
  Betsey.............299
CARLETON
  Polly..............270
CARYL
  John...............253
CASWELL
  John...............272
  Michael............254
  Sally..........306,307
  Samuel.............254
  William............254
CATE
  Martha.............234
  Richard............292
  Samuel.............292
CHAPMAN
  _____...........299
  Dolly..............314
  James..............286
  Joseph.............299
  Phebe..............269
  Samuel.............260

INDEX TO 1790 RYE CENSUS

CHAPMAN
  Simon..............244
CHESLEY
  Simon..............243
CLARK
  Andrew 297,311
  Elizabeth 314
  Nancy 306
CLEMENS
  Abraham...........258
CLIFFORD
  Hannah............265
COFFIN
  Abigail....256,258,308
  Amos..............262
  Martha............240
  Mary..........259,262
  Theodore......240,265
COLLINS
  Ebenezer..........267
COMSTOCK
  Elizabeth.........289
CONNER
  Pamelia...........270
CRICKETT
  Mary..............267
CROCKETT
  Jonathan..........266
CURRIER
  Lydia.............311
  Sarah.........295,300
  Thomas............300
DALTON
  Abigail...........241
  Benjamin...239,241,251
  Daniel Philbrick...241
  Mary..........241,288
  Michael...........241
  Sarah.............239
DAVIDSON
  John..............241
  Josiah............241
  William...........241
DAVIS
  Amos..............268
  Clarissa F........268
DEARBORN
  Abigail...........269
  Elizabeth.....240,248

  250-51,262,275
DEARBORN
  Gilman............238
  Levi..............305
  Mary..............311
  Sarah.........259,263
DILLOWAY
  C.K...............289
DOLBER (DOLBEE)
  Aster.............242
  Billy.............242
  John..............242
  Jonathan...... 241,242
  Molly.............242
  Nicholas......241,242
  Patty (Martha) ...242
  Stephen...........242
DOW
  Amos..............242
  Betsey........242,295
  Eleanor...........238
  Hannah.........258-62
  Henry.........242,243
  Isaac..234,242,259,301
  James.......242-43,283
  Joseph............237
  Martha............272
  Martha Locke......243
  Mary...235,259,262,274
  Patty.........242,283
  Sarah.........253,264
  Simon.........260,264
DOWNS
  John..............296
DOWRST
  Mary..........245,247
  Rachel............278
  Samuel............245
  Sarah......293,294,302
  Solomon.......278,293
DOWSE
  Priscilla.........316
DRAKE
  Abigail...........263
  Data..............242
  Mary (Jenness).....261
  Mercy.............266
  Nathaniel.........263
  Samuel............263

INDEX TO 1790 RYE CENSUS

DRAKE
  Sarah..............306
DREW
  Betsey.............266
DROWN
  Hannah.............298
EDMONDS
  Polly..............260
ELKINS
  Abigail............244
  Henry......243,271,315
  James..........243,293
  Mary...........243,271
  Olive..............243
  Olive (Marden).....269
  Samuel.............243
  William............244
EMERY
  Nathaniel..........284
  Sally..............287
  Sarah..............289
  William............284
FABENS
  Elizabeth..........242
  Lydia..............242
FARRINGTON
  Sarah..............268
FERNALD
  Hannah.............248
FISHER
  Nancy (Watts)......271
FITZGERALD
  Daniel.............244
  Molly..............244
  Nancy..............244
  Richard............237
FOGG
  Jeremiah...........266
  Sarah..............294
FOLLET
  Dorothy (Parsons)..305
FOLSOM
  Abraham............267
  Ann................257
FOSS
  Abigail............246
  Anna Partridge.....245
  Betsey.............245
  Comfort........245,267

FOSS
  Dorothy............244
  Ebenezer.......244,247
  Elizabeth...246-47,282
                    298
  Hannah.....244,247,257
  James Seavey.......247
  Jane...........246,297
  Jeremiah Berry.....247
  Job.....238,244-46,299
  John........244-46,310
  Joshua......244-47,298
  Mark...............244
  Mary....244-47,296,299
  Molly..........235,236
  Nathaniel...236,246-47
  Olive..........245,275
  Olive Rand.........246
  Patience...........247
  Patty W............245
  Phineas............246
  Polly..........247,253
  Rachel.............246
  Richard............245
  Robinson...........245
  Sally..........238,239
  Samuel..........245-47
  Samuel Dowrst......234
                 246-47
  Sarah...........244-47
  Solomon........246,297
  Wallis.........245,247
  William.....246-47,278
FOYE
  Charles............247
  Eunice.............248
  John....247-48,305,315
  Nathaniel G........243
  Stephen............248
  William....248,291,306
FROST
  Sarah..............277
FULLER
  Elizabeth..........303
  Theodore...........261
GALLOWAY
  Elizabeth......260,262
GARLAND
  Abigail..248-50,258-59

INDEX TO 1790 RYE CENSUS

GARLAND
- Amos.......248,263,304
- Anna................251
- Benjamin...233,248,249
  251,258,287
  304,305
- Betsey.............304
- Betsey Godfrey.....250
- Elizabeth..248,251,272
  273,275-76,301,304
- Elizabeth H........250
- James..............249
- John...240,248-51,262
  275,284,302
- John Sanborn.......250
- Jonathan...........251
- Joseph.........249-51
- Levi............250-51
- Mary....239-40,249-51
  271
- Mehitable......250,284
- Mehitable Godfrey..250
- Nancy..............251
- Peter.......250-51,305
- Polly.........233,236
  262,284
- Reul...............249
- Sally..............248
- Sarah......241,249,251
  257,261
- Simon..........249,251
- Thomas.............249
- William............249

GILMAN
- Bradstreet.........267

GOODWIN
- Elizabeth.......262-63
- Thomas.............262

GOSS
- _____............299
- Betsey.............252
- Daniel.........252,306
- Elizabeth 252
- James 252
- Jethro 252,266,291
  316
- John 252,296
- Joseph.............305
- Joshua.............252

GOSS
- Levi...........252,296
- Mary...........260,294
- Michael D..........252
- Molly..............253
- Nathan.........252,264
- Patty.......298,314-15
- Richard............253
- Sally..............253
- Sally Johnson...296-97
- Salome.........272,312
- Sarah..............268
- Simon..........235,253
- Susanna............291
- Thomas......252-53,260
  262,281

GOULD
- Christopher........253
- Ephraim............253
- Hannah.............253
- Mary...............253
- Ruth...............253

GOVE
- Eben...............311
- Ebenezer...........270
- Hannah.............239

GRACE
- Benjamin...........248

GRANT
- Hannah.............315
- John...............244

GRAY
- Ann................307
- Lucretta...........239

GREEN
- Charles............254
- Dorcas Marden......254
- Ephraim............254
- John...............254
- Jonathan...........270
- Joseph.............254
- Mary...............254
- Richard.........253-54
- Samuel Marden......254
- Stephen............314
- Thomas.............254

GROVE
- _____............311
- Dolly..............285

323

INDEX TO 1790 RYE CENSUS

GUNNISON
  Pamelia............287
HAINES
  Mary (Berry).......271
  Olive..............268
  Sarah.....269,273,284
HALEY
  Nancy..............291
  Samuel.............296
HALL
  _____............299
  Edward.........254-55
  Elizabeth..245,255,308
              309-10
  Ephraim R......254,291
  Esther........237,255
  Hannah.............255
  Hartwell...........244
  Joseph....235,254-55
       278,296,308,310
  Luther.............290
  Lydia..............269
  Mary..........252,260
  Mary Tucker........255
  Sarah..............255
  William............254
  William Tucker.....255
HAM
  John...............247
HANSON
  Mary...............292
HARDY
  Hepsabeth..........279
HARVEY
  Esther.............298
HAYES
  _____............265
  Tamsin.............234
HIBBARD
  Dorcas.............268
HINCKS
  Mary...............301
HOBBS
  Bethia.............282
  Elizabeth..........277
  Elizabeth Jenness..256
  Esther.............264
  Huldah......272,275-76
  James..............255

HOBBS
  Jonathan....255-56,276
                    297
  Lucy...............255
  Molly..............256
  Nancy..............256
  Nathaniel..........256
  Perna Judkins......256
  Sally..............256
HODGDON
  Sally..............247
HOLMES
  Charlotte..........245
  Olive..............233
HOOK
  Sarah..............262
HOUSTON
  Betsey.............293
HOWE
  Elizabeth..........249
HOYT
  Betsey G...........268
HUGGINS
  Mehitable..........275
HUNT
  Elizabeth..........244
HUNTINGTON
  Mary...............289
JACKSON
  Martha.............313
  Mehitable..........246
JENKINS
  Hiram..............311
JENNESS
  _____............302
  Aaron..............234
  Abigail....258,263,273
  Abigail Coffin.....256
  Alexander Shapley..263
  Amos Coffin........262
  Amos Seavey........256
  Anna...........257,263
  Benjamin...256,260,301
  Benjamin Garland...259
  Betsey......261-63,288
  Clarissa...........261
  Comfort........240,257
  Data...............257
  David Wedgewood....261

324

INDEX TO 1790 RYE CENSUS

JENNESS
  Elizabeth..255,259,263
  Francis.........257-58
  Hall Jackson......257
  Hannah......257-58,260
           261,274,276
  Hezekiah...........257
  Isaac..............259
  James..............261
  Job............240,257
  John....248,257-58,260
           263,315
  John Bean......236,258
  Jonathan....248,258-61
           273
  Joseph.....235,259,262
           286,288
  Joseph Tarlton.....261
  Joses..............262
  Josiah.............260
  Levi....259-60,263,310
           313
  Martha Wallis......260
  Mary....240,257,259-61
           263
  Mary (Dalton)......288
  Molly..............261
  Nancy......239,257,261
           263,288
  Nathaniel...258,260-62
  Noah...........260,262
  Olive......248,258,263
  Patty..............260
  Peter..............263
  Peter Mitchell.....258
  Polly...256-57,259,261
           262,281,308
  Polly Seavey.......256
  Richard..256-59,261-63
           274,294,301,304
  Sally..............257
  Samuel.....257,259,261
           262-63,272
  Samuel Wallis......260
  Sarah....233-35,248-49
           258-59,262,304
  Sarah Dearborn.....260
  Sarah T............261
  Simon..........260-63

JENNESS
  Solomon............302
  Stephen............302
  Thomas.............261
  William........259,302
JEWELL
  Charlotte..........309
JOHNSON
  Edmond.........236,264
  Esther.............264
  Deliverance (Knowles)
           279
  Mary...............264
  Peter......253,264,317
  Ruth...........264,292
  Sally..............264
  Sarah..........252,264
  Simon..............264
JONES
  Margaret...........283
  Mary...........283,313
  Sarah..........273,275
  William............283
KATE (see CATE)
KENISON
  Susannah...........303
KIMBALL
  Hannah.............242
  Hezekiah...........287
KINGMAN
  Mary...............236
KNOWLAND
  Ann................307
KNOWLES
  Anna Brackett......265
  Amos...............265
  Deliverance.....264-65
           279
  Esther.............269
  Ezekiel............265
  Hannah.....234,265,270
  John Clifford......265
  Joseph.........265,279
  Nathan.............265
  Samuel.............265
  Sarah..............265
  Simon..............265
  Susannah...........240

INDEX TO 1790 RYE CENSUS

KNOWLTON
  Calvin...............289
KNOX
  Anna................259
LADD
  Huldah..............299
LAKE
  _____...............237
  James...............237
LAMOS
  Sarah...............287
LAMPREY
  Elizabeth...........283
  Mary Smith..........254
  Morris..............270
LANCASTER
  Mary...........260,264
LANE
  Isaac...............250
  Sarah...............233
LANG
  Anna.......267,297,312
  Betsey.........237,267
  Bickford....266,269-70
  Charity........241,278
  Dorothy.............313
  Hannah.....266,272,276
                    294
  John......244,266,313
  Levi................267
  Mark.......272,280,312
  Martha.........266,298
  Mary.......266,285,312
  Mary Ann............316
  Richard........245,267
  Samuel..............267
  Sarah....244-45,266-67
                    299
  Sidney..............290
  Susanna........266,316
  Thomas..............266
  William........266,316
LANGDON
  Elizabeth...........303
  Joseph.........301,303
  Mary...242,256,283,301
                 304-05
  Temperance..........304

LANGLEY
  John................277
LANGMAID
  John................313
LEAR
  Alexander...........267
  Almira (Shaw)......274
  Benjamin............267
  Elizabeth......267,310
  Mehitable O.........267
  Molly...............267
  Samuel..............267
LEAVITT
  Benning.............258
  Jonathan............250
  Mary.......250,274,292
  Nancy............250-51
  Samuel..............292
LEIGHTON
  _____...............307
  James...............302
LEWIS
  Hannah..............312
LIBBY
  Aaron Seavey........268
  Abram...............268
  Abraham.............267
  Benjamin............268
  Daniel Rand.........268
  David...............242
  Elias...............268
  Elizabeth...........265
  Hitty...............268
  Joseph..........267-68
  Maria...............268
  Mary...........247,267
  Mehitable...........268
  Nancy Griffith......268
  Reuben..........246,268
  Richard.............268
  Ruth Moses..........268
  Sally..........268,298
  Samuel..............268
  Sarah...............268
  William Seavey......268
LOCKE (LOCK)
  Abigail ...235,249,253
    259,266,270,273,277
        283-86,288,309

326

INDEX TO 1790 RYE CENSUS

LOCKE
Abigail D..........269
Abner..........273,275
Anna..............272
Annah..............269
Asa...........256,277
Benjamin......269,275
Daniel.........272-73
David...243,269-70,314
Elijah.....240,266,270
  271,277,299,301
Elvin..............274
Elizabeth..239,261,270
  276-77,310
Elizabeth Garland..272
Francis............303
George Washington..273
Hall Jackson.......273
Hannah.....233,235,237
  247,271-72,275-76
  279,288,293,303
Hannah Jenness.....276
Hannah W...........235
Huldah........270,277
Jacob..............275
Jane...............239
James.........234,238
James Hobbs........277
Jeremiah...271,273,292
Jethro........273,314
Job.....272,275-76,285
John....263,269-70,273
  274-75,277,289
John W. P..........272
Jonathan....269,273-74
  284,292
Joseph..235,240,271-76
  280-81
Joseph L...........274
Joshua......275,277-78
Levi..........269,271
Martha.....266,270,293
Mary....239,263,269-73
  275,284,299,309
Mary B.............272
Mary Olive........274
Mercy..............282
Michael............274
Molly..............273

LOCKE
Nabby..............274
Nancy..............270
Patty..............249
Polly W............272
Rachel.............239
Reuben........269,277
Richard..272-73,275-77
  311
Sally..............272
Sally Wood.........272
Samuel.............281
Samuel J. 298
Sarah......258,265,269
  272,276,303,314
Sarah Ann......257,274
Simeon.............269
Simon.........276,278
Tryphena...........275
William.....234,269-71
  274,277,288
LOUTZ
Mary Ann...........280
LOVERING
Hannah......269-70,314
John...............269
MACE
Abigail.......276,278
Ithamar.......235,277
John....277-78,296,306
Levi...............278
Molly (Berry)......312
Rachel (Berry).....255
Sarah.........252,278
MACY
Elizabeth..........315
MANSON
Caroline...........300
Margery............274
MARDEN
Abiel.........247,278
Abigail....241,273,281
  287
Benjamin.......278-79
Betty..............280
Charity.......275,278
Dorcas.............253
Ebenezer...238,280,286
Eliza..........235-36

INDEX TO 1790 RYE CENSUS

MARDEN
  Elizabeth......278,281
  Elizabeth Moulton..281
  Esther.........281,291
  Hannah......241,280-81
  James...243,269,280-81
                      315
  John...............265
  Jonathan........279-80
  Jonathan Towle.....280
  Josiah.............238
  Keziah.............280
  Lucy...........276,280
  Mary....279,286-87,308
  Nancy Tredwell.....279
  Nathaniel...234,279-80
                      302
  Olive..243,269,280,291
  Prudence Perry.....280
                  302,305
  Rachel.....246,278,298
  Rebecca............279
  Reuben.............280
  Samuel.........279,286
  Sarah......253,265,279
                  281,285
  Solomon........279,297
  Solomon Dowrst.....278
  Stephen....241,278,308
  Thomas.............308
  William....246,281,313
MARSTON
  Catherine......243,271
  John...............276
  Lydia..............238
  Mary...............261
  Patience.......249,251
MASON
  Benjamin...........292
  Betsey.............282
  Daniel.......281-82,294
  Hannah Neal........248
  Mary...............260
  Nicholas.......282,293
  Patty (Foss).......245
  Robert.............282
  Ruhamah............282
  Samuel.............281

MATHES (MATTHEWS)
  Abraham............282
  Elizabeth..........282
  Mary...............282
  Robert.........282,296
  Sally..............282
  William............245
  William Thomas.....282
MAY
  Mary...........239,241
MCFARLAND
  Mary...............299
MCMURPHY
  Jane...............277
MERRIFIELD
  Mary...........255,310
MILLS
  Charles............239
MONROE
  Elizabeth..........283
MORRISON
  Mary...............267
  Rachel.............251
MORSE
  Silas F............299
MOSES
  Aaron..............282
  James..............313
  Mary....252,279,290-91
                      293
  Nadab..............313
  Patty..............294
  Ruth.......268,293,302
  Sarah......281,305,313
MOULTON
  Abigail............270
  Anna...............282
  Bethia.............283
  Charlotte (Towle)..280
  Elizabeth......240,251
                  280,283
  Hannah.............280
  Jonathan.......283,289
  Joseph.............282
  Lucy...............283
  Mary...............282
  Nehemiah...........282
  Reuben........ 280,283
  Sally..............282

INDEX TO 1790 RYE CENSUS

MOULTON
  Sarah..............289
MOW (MOWE)
  Ephraim...........253
  Mary..............253
  Samuel............275
NEAL
  Hannah............281
  William...........274
NEILS
  Ruhamah...........281
NELSON
  John..............295
NEWTON
  James.............247
NORTON
  Abigail...........251
  Anna..........279,285
  Eleanor...........312
  Elizabeth.........281
  John..............312
  William...........281
NOWELL
  Eunice............315
NUDD
  Mary..............285
  Ruth...........284-85
  Samuel............285
NUTTER
  Abigail...........254
NUTTING
  Mary..............287
ODIORNE
  Ebenezer......305,315
  Martha............248
  Mary..............292
  Mary (Yeaton).....274
ORMSBY
  George............287
PAGE
  Betsey............286
  Daniel............300
  Jeremiah..........277
  John..............277
  Mary..........257,288
  Sarah.........261,303
PALMER
  Cotton............297
  Mercy.............294

PALMER
  Sarah..........275-76
PARKER
  Anna..............259
PARSONS
  Amos..............242
  Amos Seavey.......283
  Bettey............283
  Dorothy...........305
  Elizabeth.....249,313
  John W........249,284
  Joseph..243,283-84,301
  Mary......243,283,295
  Samuel.....283,287,313
PATTEN
  Martha........301,304
PAUL
  Caroline..........295
  Sally.............297
PEARSON
  Caleb.............268
PERKINS
  _____..............311
  Abigail.....248-49,260
                     284
  Elias.............285
  Hannah......252,283-84
  Hannah Parish.....239
  Huldah..260,266,270-71
                277,284,299
  James...249,270,284-85
                        305
  John...........284-85
  Jonathan.......284-85
  Josiah............284
  Kezia.............236
  Martha.........242-43
  Mary..............284
  Nancy..........284-85
  Polly.............250
  Sarah.............284
PERVIERE
  Abigail...........285
PHILBRICK
  Abigail....258,272,276
                  285-87,315
  Anna..............285
  Benjamin..........287
  Charles Pinckney..287

INDEX TO 1790 RYE CENSUS

PHILBRICK
- Comfort............299
- Daniel..241,285-87,316
- David..............287
- Elizabeth......259,286
- Ephraim.......286,315
- George Clinton.....287
- Hannah.....280,283,285 287-88
- James..............285
- John...............287
- John Walbach.......287
- Jonathan...239.279,285 286
- Joseph......272,285-87
- Joses...235,283,285-88 308
- Josiah.............243
- Levi...............285
- Lyman..............287
- Mary...........287,316
- Mercy..............241
- Molly..............300
- Nancy..........285,287
- Page...............283
- Polly..........286,291
- Reuben......261,287-88
- Sally....... 286-88
- Sarah......249,259,279
- Thomas.............287
- Tryphene...277,300,310
- William............287

PICKERING
- Abigail........303,305
- Lydia..............242

PIERCE
- William............306

PIPER
- Susannah...........309

PITMAN
- Ruth............306-07
- Susannah.......285-86

PLAISTED
- Elizabeth..........262

POORE (see POWERS)

PORTER
- Caroline...........289
- Charles H..........290
- Eliphalet..........289

PORTER
- Emery Moulton......290
- Huntington.....289,290
- John...............289
- Louisa.............289
- Maria..............289
- Martha R...........289
- Nathaniel Sargent..289
- Oliver.............289
- Olivia.............290
- Samuel H...........289
- Sarah E............289
- William H..........290

POWERS (POORE)
- Abigail Daniels....289
- Daniel Sheafe......289
- Eliza..............289
- George.............289
- Judith.............288
- Mary...............289
- Nancy..............289
- Robert.........288,307
- Sally..............289

PRESCOTT
- Hannah..............269
- Timothy............269

QUINCY
- Eunice.............274

RAMSTEAD
- George.............309

RAND
- Abigail............294
- Aphia..............292
- Betsey.............290
- Billey.............294
- Caroline.......261,294
- Daniel.........293,306
- Daniel Fogg........294
- Deborah............267
- Dowrst.........266,294
- Ebenezer...........290
- Edward.............295
- Eliza..............314
- Elizabeth...288,290-91 293,317
- Enoch..............290
- Ephraim............254
- Esther......252,266,291
- Florinda...........295

INDEX TO 1790 RYE CENSUS

RAND
- George............290
- Hannah.........248,291
- Hannah Moses.......279
- Hepzibah...........306
- James..............293
- Jedediah...........295
- Jemima.............268
- John.......233,290,295
- John T.........242,295
- Joseph..267,280,291-92
- Joshua.....252,279,281
  290-91,293
- Levi...............291
- Margaret...........290
- Martha.........274,290
- Mary....250,290,292-93
- Mary Jones Wallis..295
- Mary M.............282
- Mary (Smith).......255
- Mehitable...243,292-93
- Mehitable C........268
- Mercy......282,294,299
- Molly...........291-92
- Moses..............293
- Nancy..........254,291
- Nathaniel......274,292
- Olive.......273-74,291
- Olly............291-92
- Polly..............294
- Rachel.....233,294,302
- Richard........290,292
- Ruth............292-93
- Sally...........291-93
- Samuel.....247,286,292
  293-95,302
- Samuel Hunt........291
- Sarah.......252,254-55
  292-94
- Stephen............294
- Susan..............273
- Susannah...........292
- Tabitha............292
- Theodore...........293
- Thomas......257,293-95
- William............295
- William Seavey.....293
- Zeb................291
- Zebedee............291

RANDALL
- Abigail........252,296
- Amelia.............301
- Amelia Berry.......296
- Benjamin.......301,306
- Betsey.............296
- Betsey M...........282
- Daniel.............307
- Edward..........295-96
- Elizabeth......315-16
- Elizabeth (Galloway)..
  260,262
- George...235-36,295-96
- Hannah.....236,272,287
- Jesse..............262
- John Y.............291
- Judith......288,306-07
- Levi...............315
- Lovey Brackett.....296
- Mark...........258,315
- Mary...241,254,296,311
- Polly..............287
- Rachel.........278,296
- Samuel B.......296,309
- Sarah..258,260,295,298
- Sarah S............260
- William............272
- William Bates..296,317
- William S..........272

REEDER
- Deborah............313

REID
- Abigail............247
- Betsey.............310

REMICK
- Betsey.............297
- David..............297
- Hannah.............297
- Huldah.........279,297
- Isaac......246,266,297
- Jacob..............317
- Jane...............246
- Jane Kitson........297
- Joseph.............297
- Mary...............297
- Meribah............297
- Moses..............297
- Sarah..............297
- Thomas.............297

331

INDEX TO 1790 RYE CENSUS

RHIMES
Margaret...........267
RICHARDSON
Mary...............294
ROBERTS
____...............241
ROBIE
Huldah........270,284
John...............251
ROBINSON
Asa................289
John...............307
Phebe..............285
Ruenna.............268
Samuel.............296
ROLLINS
Dolly..............293
RUNDLET
____...............253
SADLER
Rachel.............311
SALTER
Alexander...235,297-98
            314
John...............250
Lucy........250-51,298
Sally..............267
Sarah..............298
Webster........268,298
SANBORN
Benjamin...........290
Elizabeth..........297
Jeremiah...........309
Josiah.............269
Lowell.............279
Nancy..............309
Sarah..............268
SARGENT
Nathaniel..........289
Susannah...........289
SAUNDERS (SANDERS)
Abigail........271,277
Betsey.....300,306,311
Dorothy Wallis.....299
Edward Treadwick...300
Elijah.............299
Elizabeth..300,307,311
Esther.............265
George.........300-01

SAUNDERS
Hannah.........271,301
Huldah.........299,317
Job................299
John...265,277,282,299
            300,310
Martha.............300
Mary.......252,282,299
            301,307
Mary J.............259
Mercy..............307
Mercy Haines.......301
Nathaniel..........299
Olive..............310
Robert.....244,270,298
            299,300,306
Sally..............299
Samuel.........296,301
Sarah...........300-01
Tryphene...........234
William........299,300
SAVAGE
Susanna........266,316
SEAVEY
Aaron..............302
Abigail.251,302-03,306
Amasa..............268
Amos...242,256,283,301
            304-06
Anna...........303,305
Anne...............301
Anne Towle.........302
Betsey.............302
Daniel.........294,302
Deborah....267,292,305
Dolly..............293
Dorothy........302,306
Ebenezer...280,302,305
Ebenezer Wallis....302
Elizabeth..242,248,258
            301,304-05
Ephraim............304
Fanny..........251,305
Gideon.....302,305,313
Hannah..248,290,301-03
            305-06,313
Henry..........290,303
Hepsibah...........247
Huldah.............285

332

INDEX TO 1790 RYE CENSUS

SEAVEY
- James......234,303,305
- John...........301,303
- John Langdon...304,306
- Joseph.........303-04
- Joseph Langdon.....248, 301,304
- Joshua........305,315
- Lucy Wainwright....302
- Martha.....256,301,304, 306
- Mary......243,283,301, 303-05
- Mary Meder........302
- Mehitable.....251,268, 302,305
- Molly.............278
- Moses.............270
- Paul......302,305,313
- Ruth..............293
- Polly.............304
- Sally.........302,304
- Samuel............303
- Samuel Wallis.....305
- Sarah......302,304-05
- Sidney............306
- Sidney Sargent....304
- Theodore Jackson...304
- William....268,293,301, 302,304-05

SHAPLEY
- Alexander.........263
- Benjamin Carter....307
- Betsey.....288,306-07
- Edward............306
- Eliza.............245
- Elizabeth.........306
- Elizabeth (Goodwin)262
- George W..........307
- Henry......237,306-07
- Henry Carter...288,306, 307
- Henry J...........307
- James......301,306-07
- John..............307
- Judith............307
- Mary..............307
- Mary Saunders.....307
- Olive.............263

SHAPLEY
- Reuben......301,306-07
- Robert............307
- Sally.............307
- Samuel............317
- Sarah.............306

SHAW
- _............316
- Abigail...........241
- Almira............274
- Clarissa..........287
- Mercy.............277
- Moses.............241

SHEPHARD
- Joseph............245

SHERBURNE
- Jonathan..........284
- Naomie............290
- Sally.............242

SLEEPER
- Benjamin..........308
- Eliphalet.....261,308
- Molly.............308
- Nancy.............262
- Thomas........233,308
- Tristram Coffin....308
- William...........308

SMITH
- _........290,303
- Betsey........296,309
- David..255,287,297,308
- Elizabeth.........267
- Esther............309
- John..........247,309
- Joseph............251
- Joseph Hall.......309
- Mary....254-55,297,308
- Meribah...........297
- Molly.............278
- Salley............308
- Samuel........255,308
- Sarah.............287
- William...........309

STANTON
- John..............266

STEVENS
- Lydia.............248

STEVENSON
- Betsey............304

333

INDEX TO 1790 RYE CENSUS

SUFFERANCE
Ephraim............253
TARLTON
Betsey.............294
Hannah.............269
Joseph.............294
Mary...............267
Mary (Goss)........260
Mercy..............257
Ruth...........294,308
THOMAS
Mary (Saunders)....282
THOMPSON
Elizabeth..........316
THURSTON
Nathaniel..........284
TIBBETS
Jacob..............235
TODD
Lydia..............299
Mary...............286
TOWLE
Abigail.........273-74
Abraham............270
Amos...............288
Ann................272
Anna....269-70,279,285
                   286
Charlotte..........280
Hannah.............317
Huldah.....233,236,258
James..............236
Jonathan...255,279,285
Levi...............275
Mary...........253,255
Rachel.............271
Samuel.............264
Simon..............278
Sophia.............298
TREFETHERN
Abigail............292
Anna...........301,305
Betsey.............309
Henry..............309
John Adams.........309
Joseph.........235,309
Nabby..............309
Nancy..............309
Nathaniel..........309

TREFETHERN
Nathaniel Tucker...309
Polly..............309
Robinson...........309
Salome.............246
Sebastian..........309
Temperance.........233
Thomas.............310
William....234,238,309
                   310
TRUNDY
Sally..............252
TUCK
John...............295
Josiah.............266
Mary...............294
TUCKER
Betsey.........277,311
Elizabeth.......309-10
Esther......254-55,308
John...............310
Joseph.........310,313
Mary.....235-37,246-47
                   311
Molly..............310
Nathaniel...245,309-10
Olive..............311
Richard.........310-11
Sally..............310
Sarah...244-45,295,310
Stephen............317
Tryphena...........311
William....237,246,255
                310-11
UNDERWOOD
Abigail............274
VARRELL
Abigail........300,311
Betsey..........311-12
Betty..............311
Edward.........237,311
Hannah.........297,312
John............311-12
Joseph.........300,312
Lydia..............297
Mary...........287,311
Nancy..............312
Nathaniel..........312
Rachel.............311

INDEX TO 1790 RYE CENSUS

VARRELL
  Richard............312
  Richard Tucker.....311
  Sally..............312
  Samuel........298,311
  Sarah..............311
  Solomon............312
  Washington.........312
  William.......236,311
VENNARD
  Mary...............274
VITTUM
  Hannah.............276
WADLEIGH
  Elijah.............300
WALDRON
  Elizabeth..........311
  Elizabeth S........298
  George.........298-99
  Isaac..............314
  Jonathan B.....247,298
  Joshua Foss........298
  Polly Westbrook....298
  Richard Harvey.....298
  Robert Saunders....298
WALKER
  Samuel.............280
WALLACE
  ___...............300
WALLIS
  Abigail............313
  Betsey.............313
  Deborah............313
  Ebenezer...........313
  Elizabeth......260,263
  Hannah.....281,295,313
  James..............313
  John...............271
  Martha.............313
  Mary...............313
  Mary Jones.........314
  Samuel.....260,281,305
                      313
  Sarah...244-46,302,305
                   313-14
WARREN
  A. K...............238
WATERHOUSE
  Solomon............269

WATERS
  Elizabeth..........253
WATKINS
  Lydia..............287
WATSON
  Asa................274
WATTS
  Nancy..............271
WEBSTER
  Abiah.........250,297
  Abigail.234,238,314-15
  Anne...............314
  Betsey........305,315
  David..............315
  Dolly..............314
  Fanny..............315
  Hannah........258,315
  Jeremy.............314
  John...........314-15
  John Hobbs.........314
  Joshua.............269
  Josiah......298,314-15
  Levi Lock..........315
  Mark...............316
  Martha..239,273,314-15
  Mary.......243,314-15
  Nathaniel..........315
  Olive..............315
  Richard.....287,315-16
  Sarah......280,286,315
WEDGEWOOD
  Betsey.............235
  David......259,261,308
  Hannah.............258
  Jonathan...........305
  Mary.......260-61,288
  Sallie.............274
WEEKS
  Daniel.............311
  Josiah.............285
  William............289
WELLS
  Betsey.............286
  Deborah............316
  Elizabeth 316
  Molly..............316
  Olly...............316
  Polly..............252
  Samuel.............316

INDEX TO 1790 RYE CENSUS

WELLS
  Sarah..........286,316
  Simeon.............316
WENDALL
  Elizabeth......234,238
WENTWORTH
  _____............290
WHIDDEN
  Joseph.............306
  Mary...............303
  Rebecca............279
  Thomas.............245
  William............281
WHITE
  Nathaniel..........259
  Salome........271,274

WIGGIN
  Noah...............314
Willey
  Samuel.............306
WILLIAMS
  Abigail............288
  John Floyd.........316
WINFIELD
  Elizabeth..........268
WOODMAN
  Betsey.............251
  Jonathan.......257,291
  Nancy (Jenness)....288
WOODS
  Sarah..............277
YEATON
  Anna..........259,317
  Deborah.......296,317
  Eliza J............295
  Elizabeth.....266,317
  Esther........266,297
  Esther (Saunders)..265
  Hannah.............317
  John........265,316-17
  Joseph..239,264,316-17
  Mary....264-66,274,317
  Philip.............317
  Sarah..............317
  Susan..............317
  Susannah...........317
  William............317